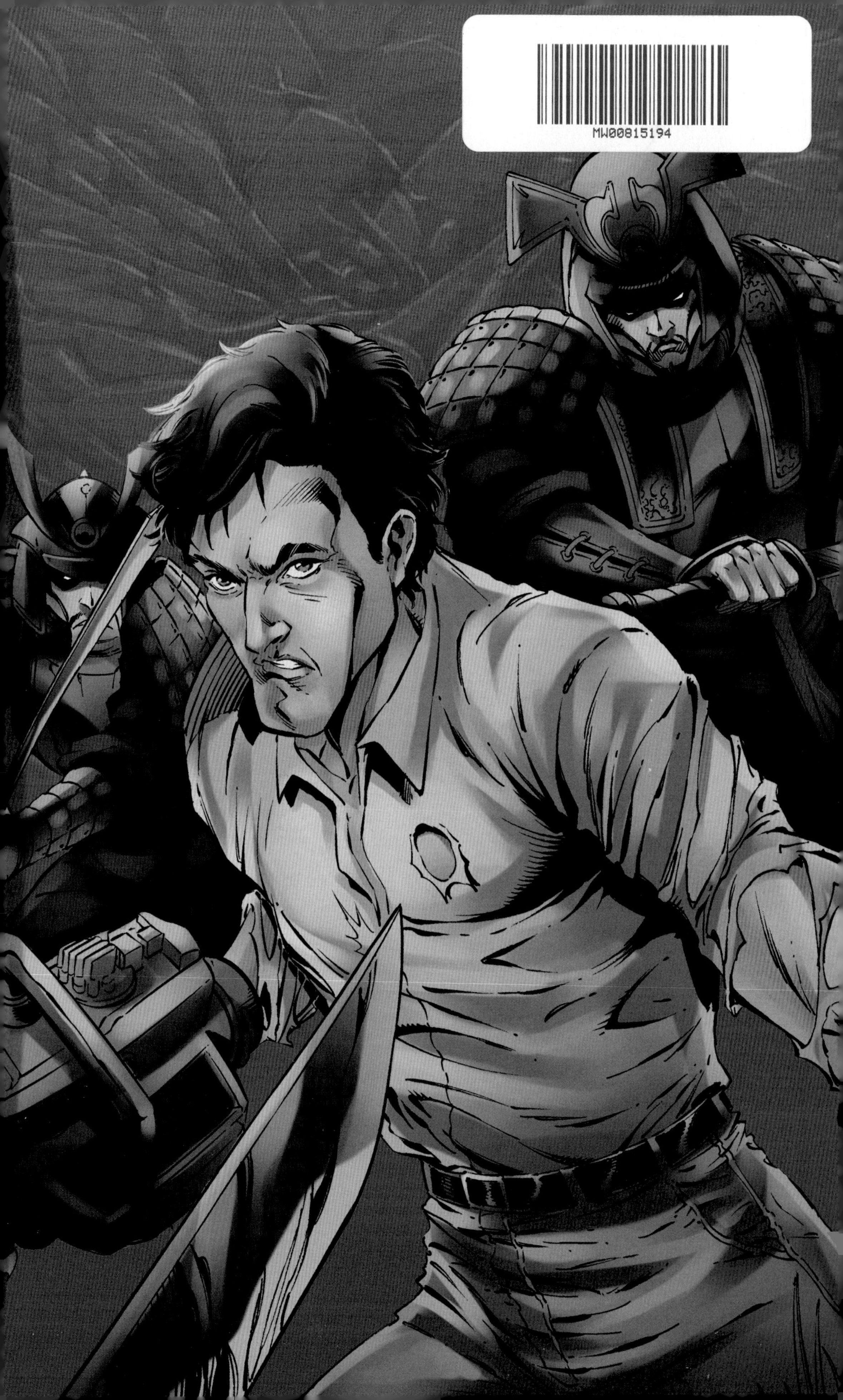

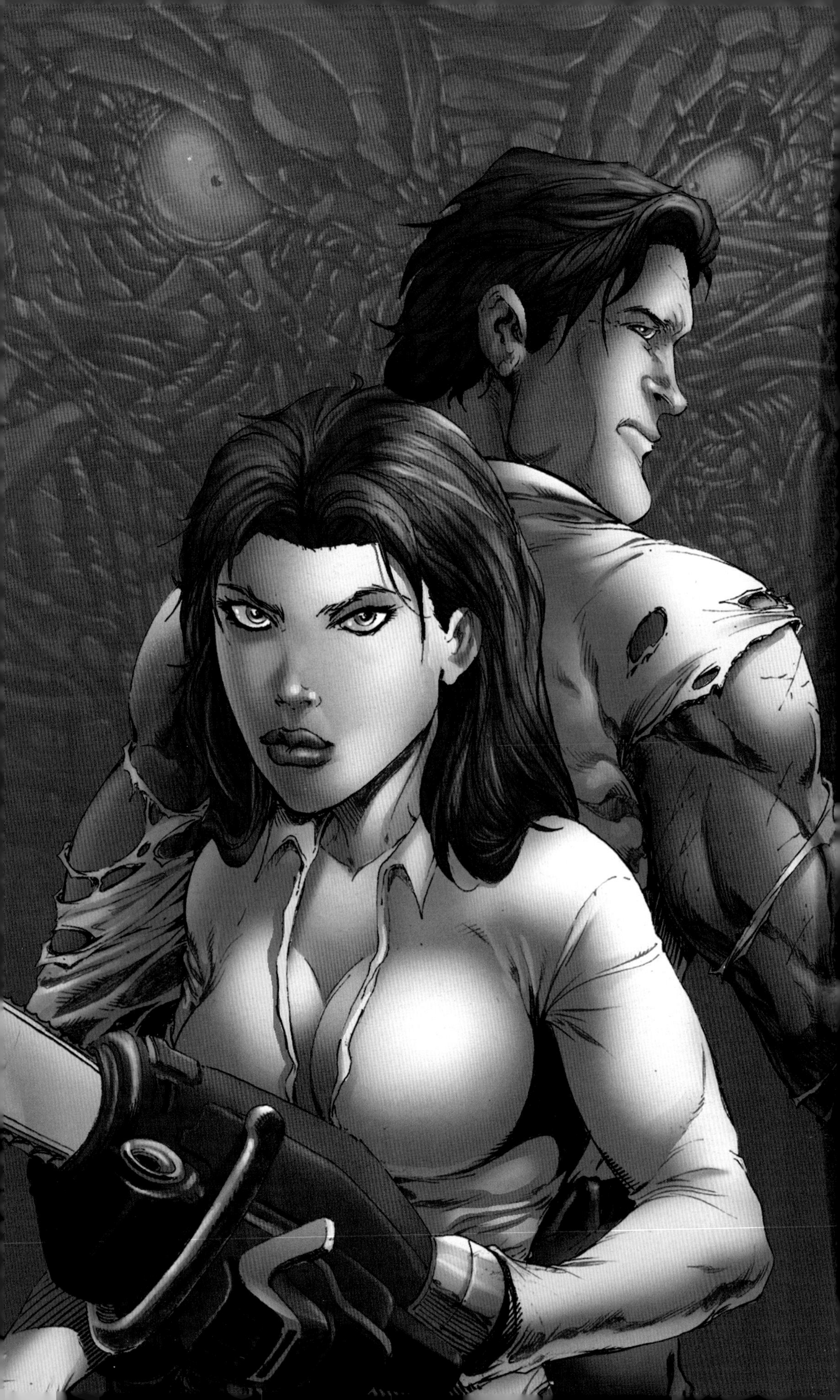

ARMY OF DARKNESS™

HAIL TO THE QUEEN, BABY!

written by
ELLIOTT R. SERRANO

pencils by
MARAT MYCHAELS (issues 1-4)
DIETRICH SMITH (issues 5-7)

inks by
CHRIS IVY (issues 1-4)

colors by
GABRIEL BELLUCO (issues 1-4)
THIAGO DAL BELLO (issues 5-7)

letters by
BILL TORTOLINI

collection cover by
TIM SEELEY

DYNAMITE®

Visit us online at www.DYNAMITE.com
Follow us on Twitter @dynamitecomics
Like us on Facebook /Dynamitecomics
Watch us on YouTube /Dynamitecomics

Nick Barrucci, CEO / Publisher
Juan Collado, President / COO
Joe Rybandt, Senior Editor
Josh Johnson, Art Director
Rich Young, Director Business Development
Jason Ullmeyer, Senior Graphic Designer
Josh Green, Traffic Coordinator
Chris Caniano, Production Assistant

www.MGM.com

First Printing   ISBN-10: 1-60690-387-X   ISBN-13: 978-1-60690-387-2   10 9 8 7 6 5 4 3 2 1

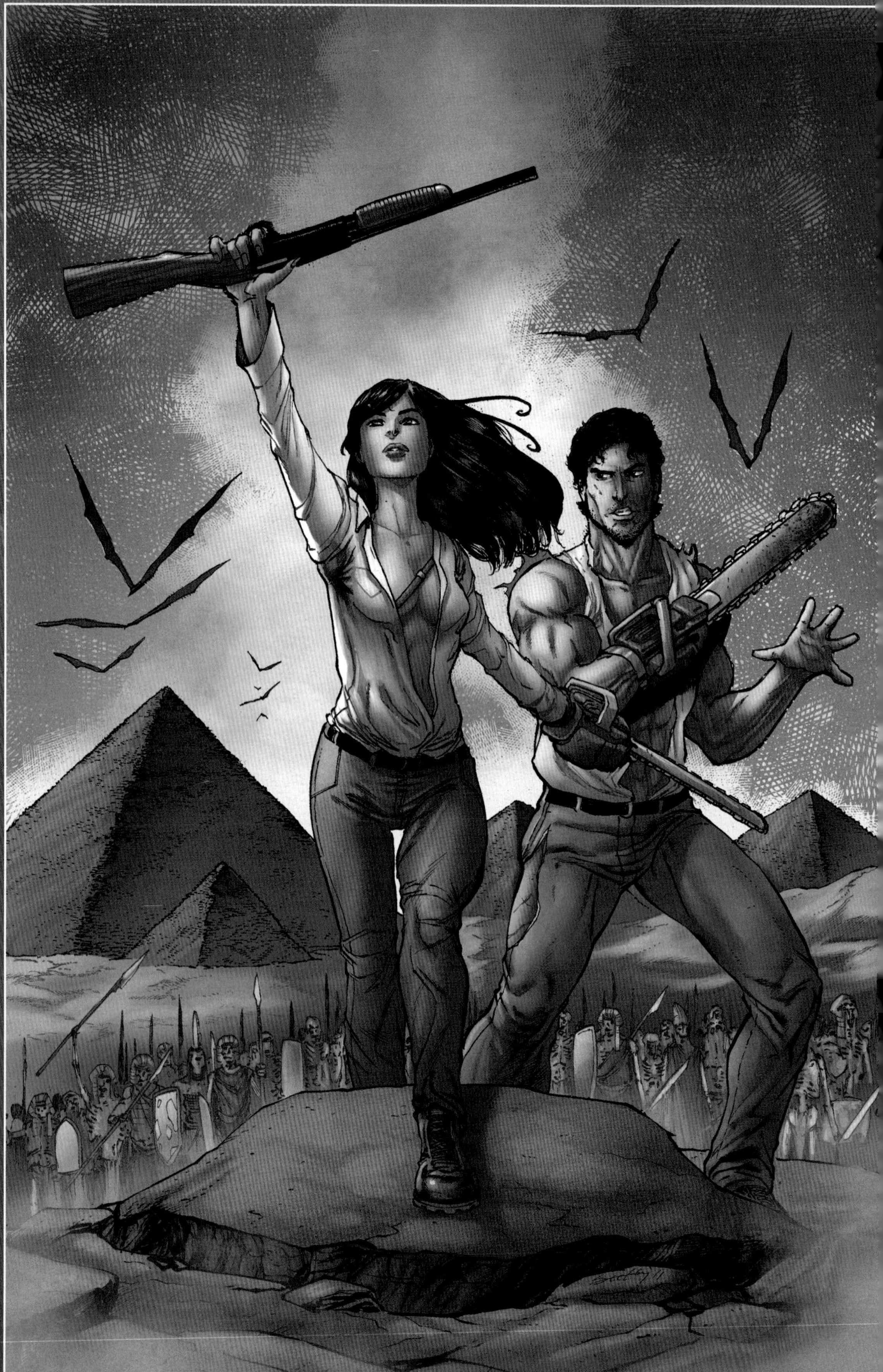

cover to issue #1 by TIM SEELEY, colors by ADRIANO LUCAS

The place: somewhere in time.
That's kind of vague, don't you think?
Who's telling the story, here?
Sigh. Go ahead. But you really need to work on your set up.
Look, when you come into the story you can tell it your way.
Deal. Proceed.
My name is **Ash** and I am a **slave**--
Wow, why not just start with 'a long time ago in a galaxy far, far aw--
WOULD YOU PLEASE **SHUT UP** ALREADY?!
Just making an observation. That's been done before--
SMART-STOP
Could you just let me get through this? I'm not having the best day right now--
Oopsie.
SMART-STOP
ASHLEY
--yeah sure, they may have heard this set up before. But trust me--

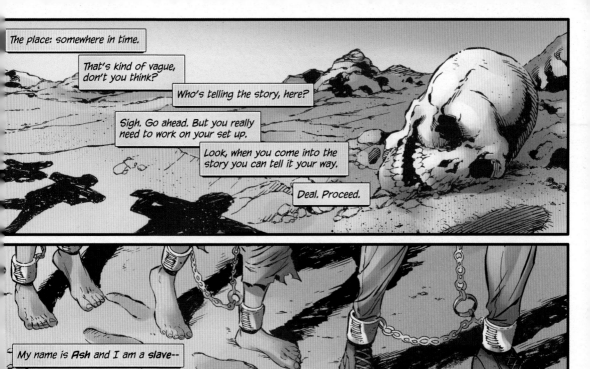

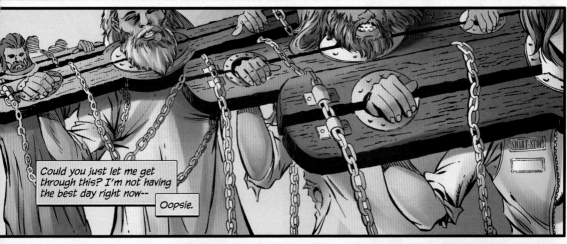

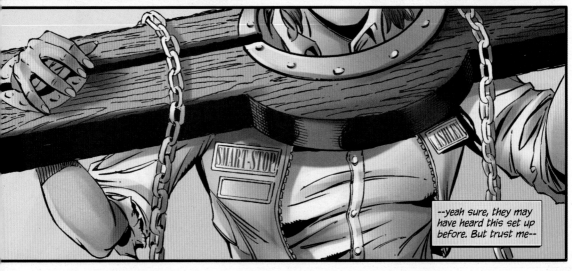

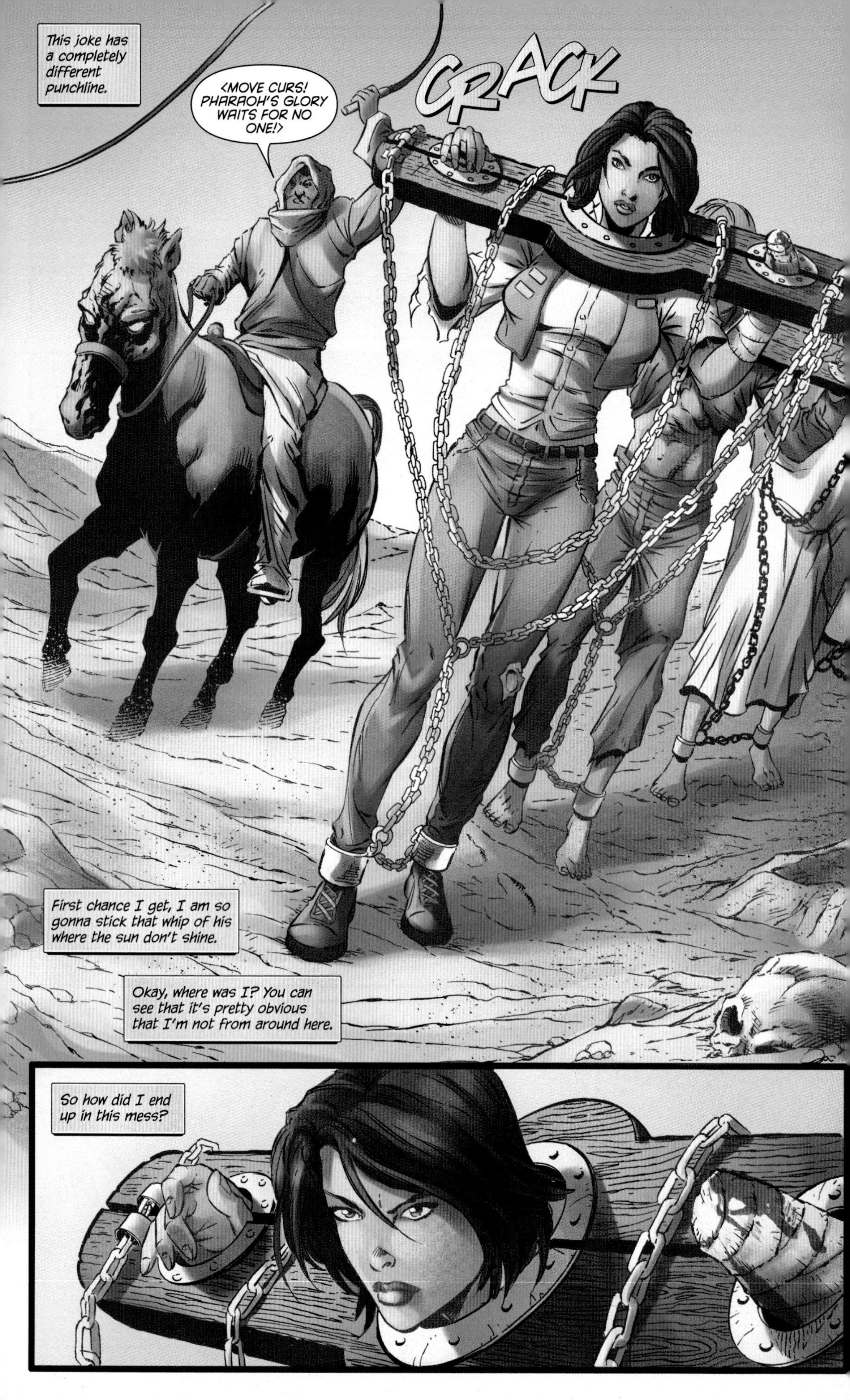
This joke has a completely different punchline.
<MOVE CURS! PHARAOH'S GLORY WAITS FOR NO ONE!>
CRACK
First chance I get, I am so gonna stick that whip of his where the sun don't shine.
Okay, where was I? You can see that it's pretty obvious that I'm not from around here.
So how did I end up in this mess?

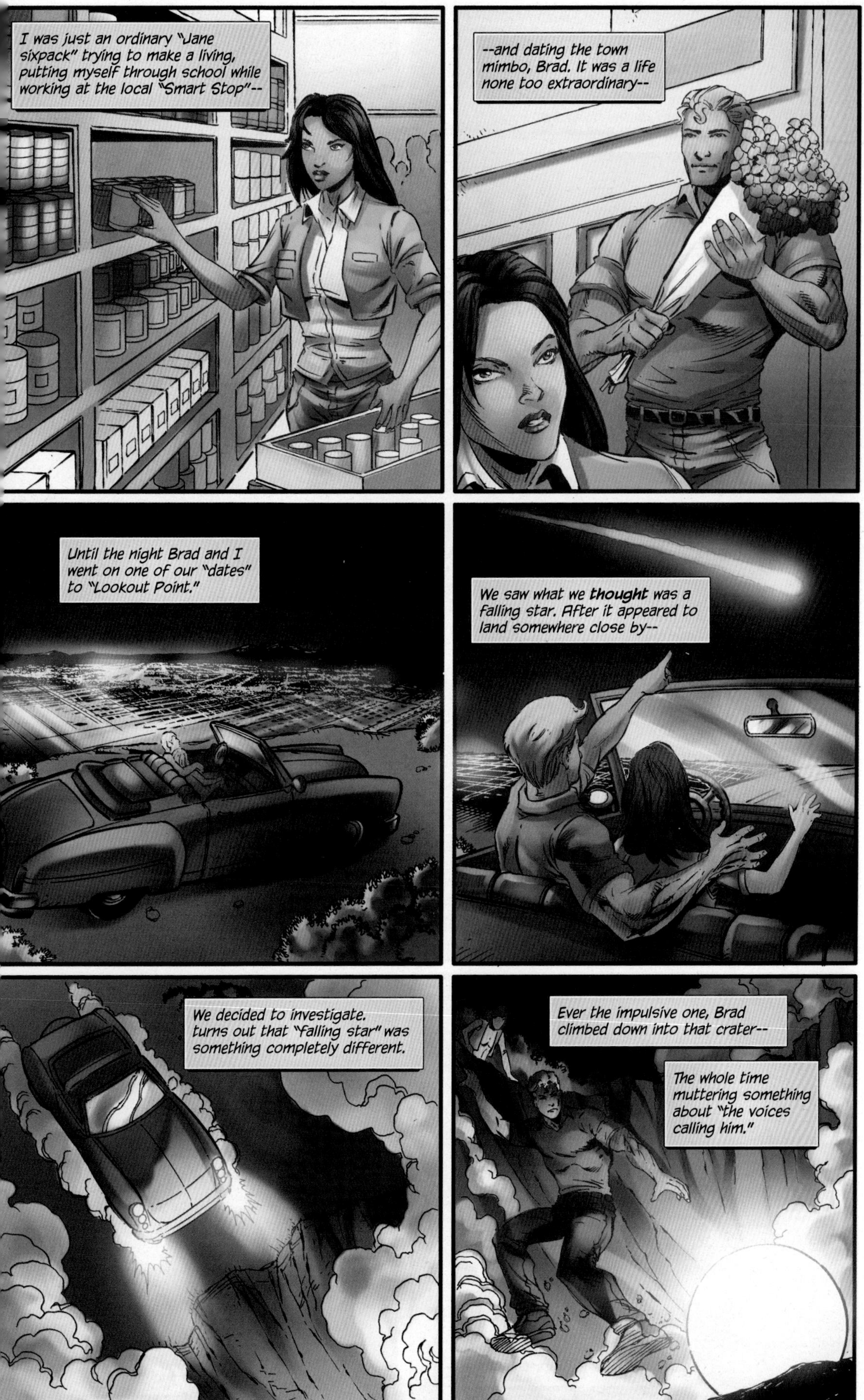
I was just an ordinary "Jane sixpack" trying to make a living, putting myself through school while working at the local "Smart Stop"--
--and dating the town mimbo, Brad. It was a life none too extraordinary--
Until the night Brad and I went on one of our "dates" to "Lookout Point."
We saw what we **thought** was a falling star. After it appeared to land somewhere close by--
We decided to investigate. turns out that "falling star" was something completely different.
Ever the impulsive one, Brad climbed down into that crater--
The whole time muttering something about "the voices calling him."

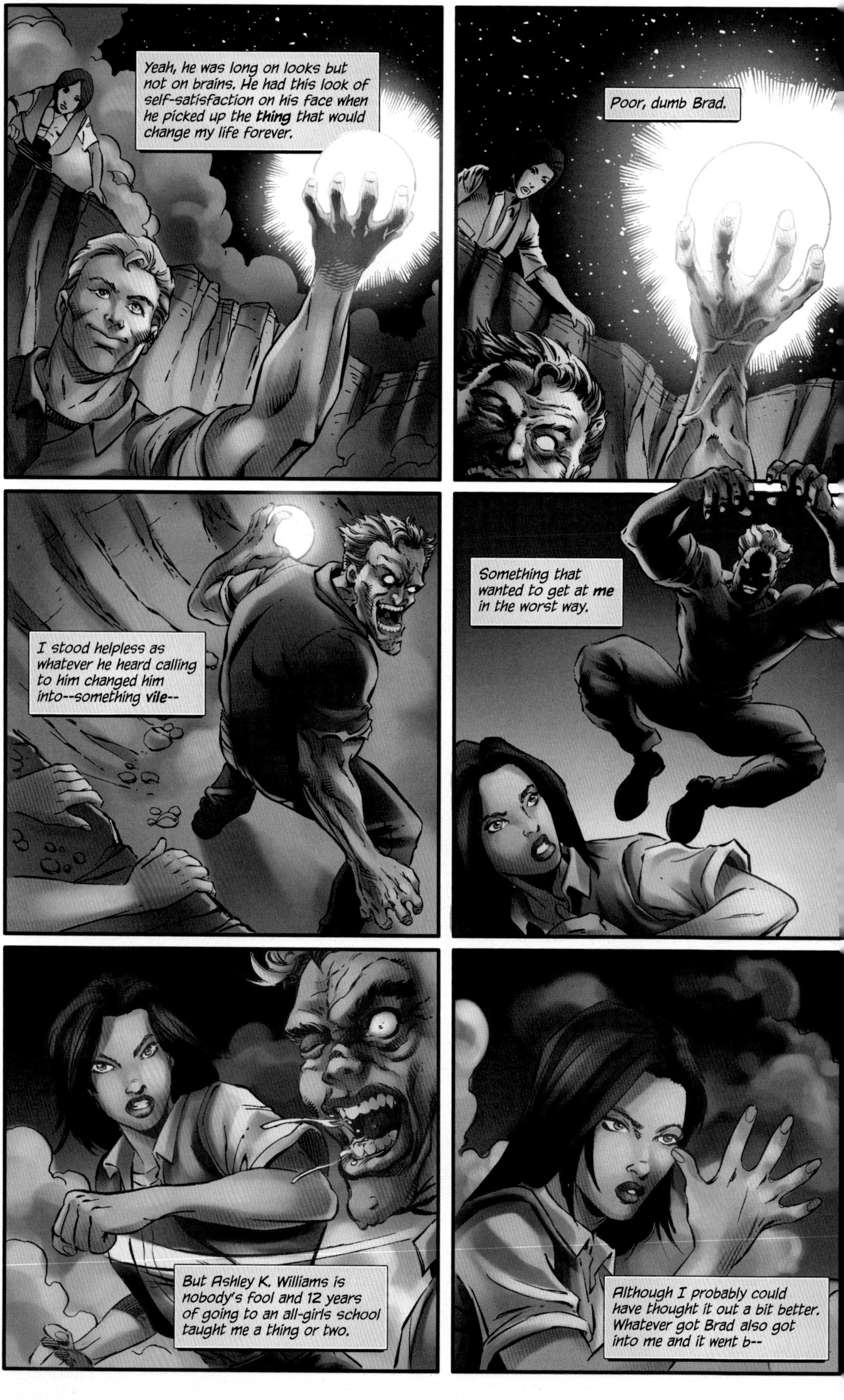
Yeah, he was long on looks but not on brains. He had this look of self-satisfaction on his face when he picked up the **thing** that would change my life forever.
Poor, dumb Brad.
I stood helpless as whatever he heard calling to him changed him into--something **vile**--
Something that wanted to get at **me** in the worst way.
But Ashley K. Williams is nobody's fool and 12 years of going to an all-girls school taught me a thing or two.
Although I probably could have thought it out a bit better. Whatever got Brad also got into me and it went b--

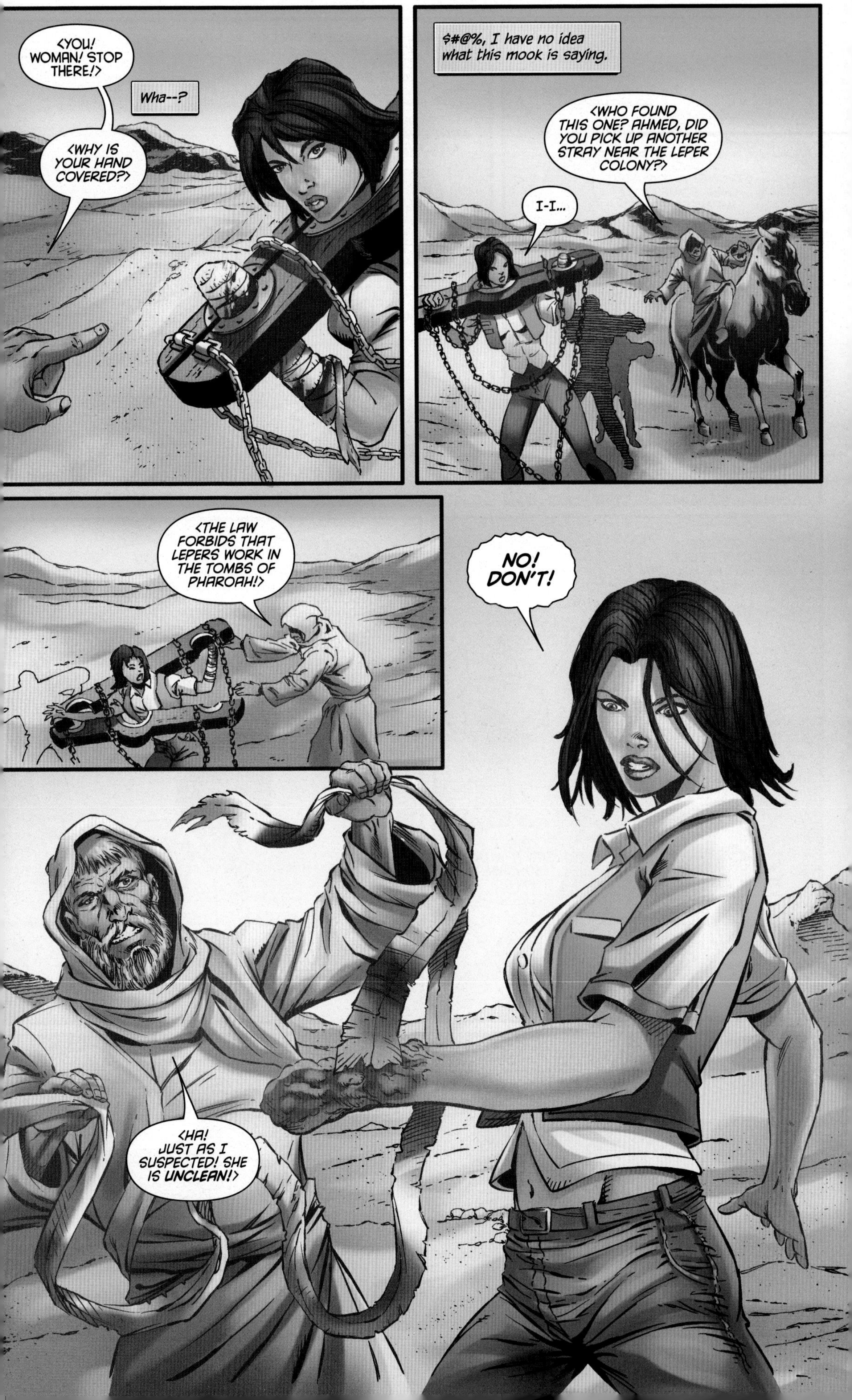

<YOU! WOMAN! STOP THERE!>
Wha--?
<WHY IS YOUR HAND COVERED?>
$#@%, I have no idea what this mook is saying.
<WHO FOUND THIS ONE? AHMED, DID YOU PICK UP ANOTHER STRAY NEAR THE LEPER COLONY?>
I-I...
<THE LAW FORBIDS THAT LEPERS WORK IN THE TOMBS OF PHAROAH!>
NO! DON'T!
<HA! JUST AS I SUSPECTED! SHE IS UNCLEAN!>

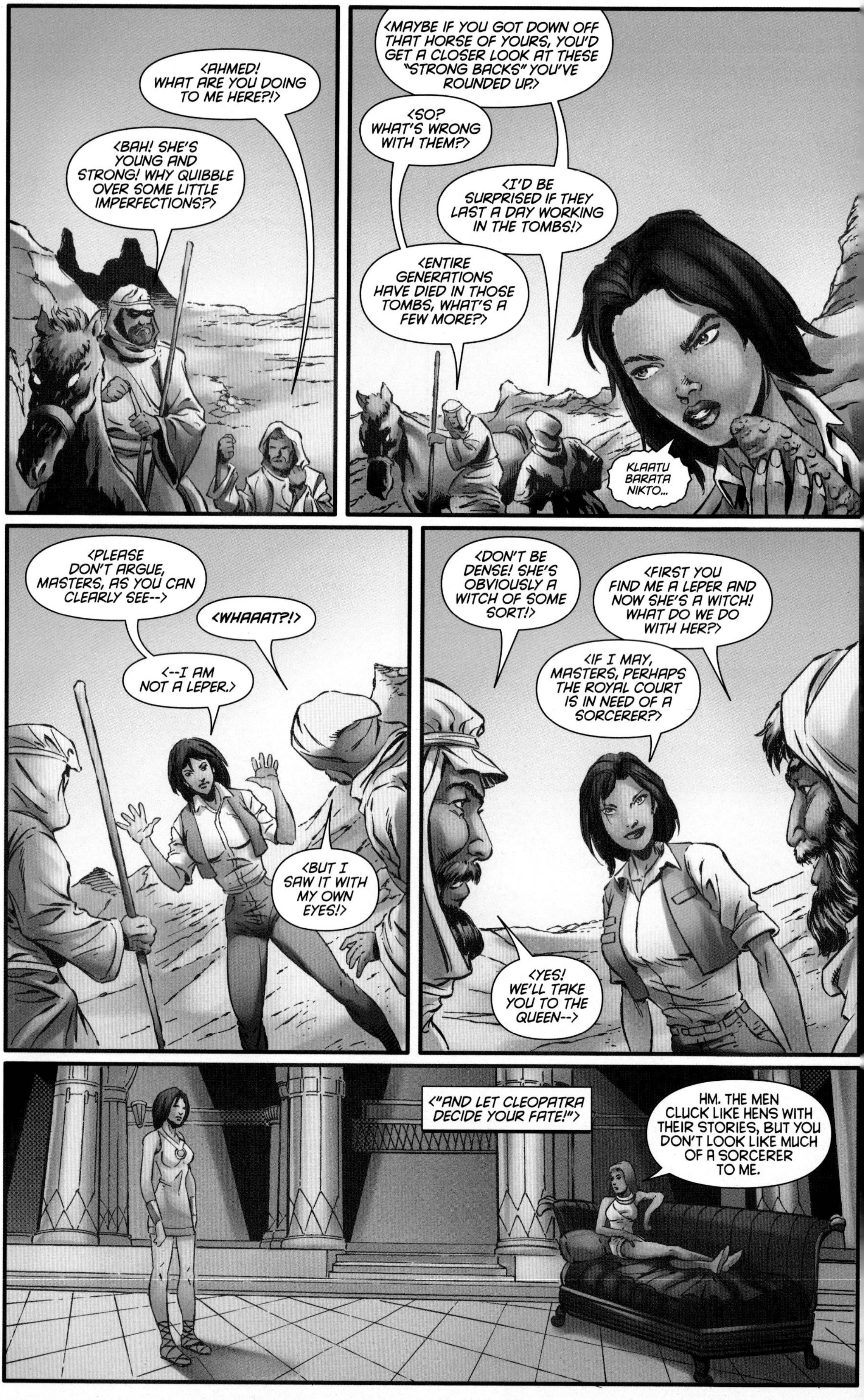

<AHMED! WHAT ARE YOU DOING TO ME HERE?!>
<BAH! SHE'S YOUNG AND STRONG! WHY QUIBBLE OVER SOME LITTLE IMPERFECTIONS?>
<MAYBE IF YOU GOT DOWN OFF THAT HORSE OF YOURS, YOU'D GET A CLOSER LOOK AT THESE "STRONG BACKS" YOU'VE ROUNDED UP.>
<SO? WHAT'S WRONG WITH THEM?>
<I'D BE SURPRISED IF THEY LAST A DAY WORKING IN THE TOMBS!>
<ENTIRE GENERATIONS HAVE DIED IN THOSE TOMBS, WHAT'S A FEW MORE?>
KLAATU BARATA NIKTO...
<PLEASE DON'T ARGUE, MASTERS, AS YOU CAN CLEARLY SEE-->
<WHAAAT?!>
<--I AM NOT A LEPER.>
<BUT I SAW IT WITH MY OWN EYES!>
<DON'T BE DENSE! SHE'S OBVIOUSLY A WITCH OF SOME SORT!>
<FIRST YOU FIND ME A LEPER AND NOW SHE'S A WITCH! WHAT DO WE DO WITH HER?>
<IF I MAY, MASTERS, PERHAPS THE ROYAL COURT IS IN NEED OF A SORCERER?>
<YES! WE'LL TAKE YOU TO THE QUEEN-->
<"AND LET CLEOPATRA DECIDE YOUR FATE!">
HM. THE MEN CLUCK LIKE HENS WITH THEIR STORIES, BUT YOU DON'T LOOK LIKE MUCH OF A SORCERER TO ME.

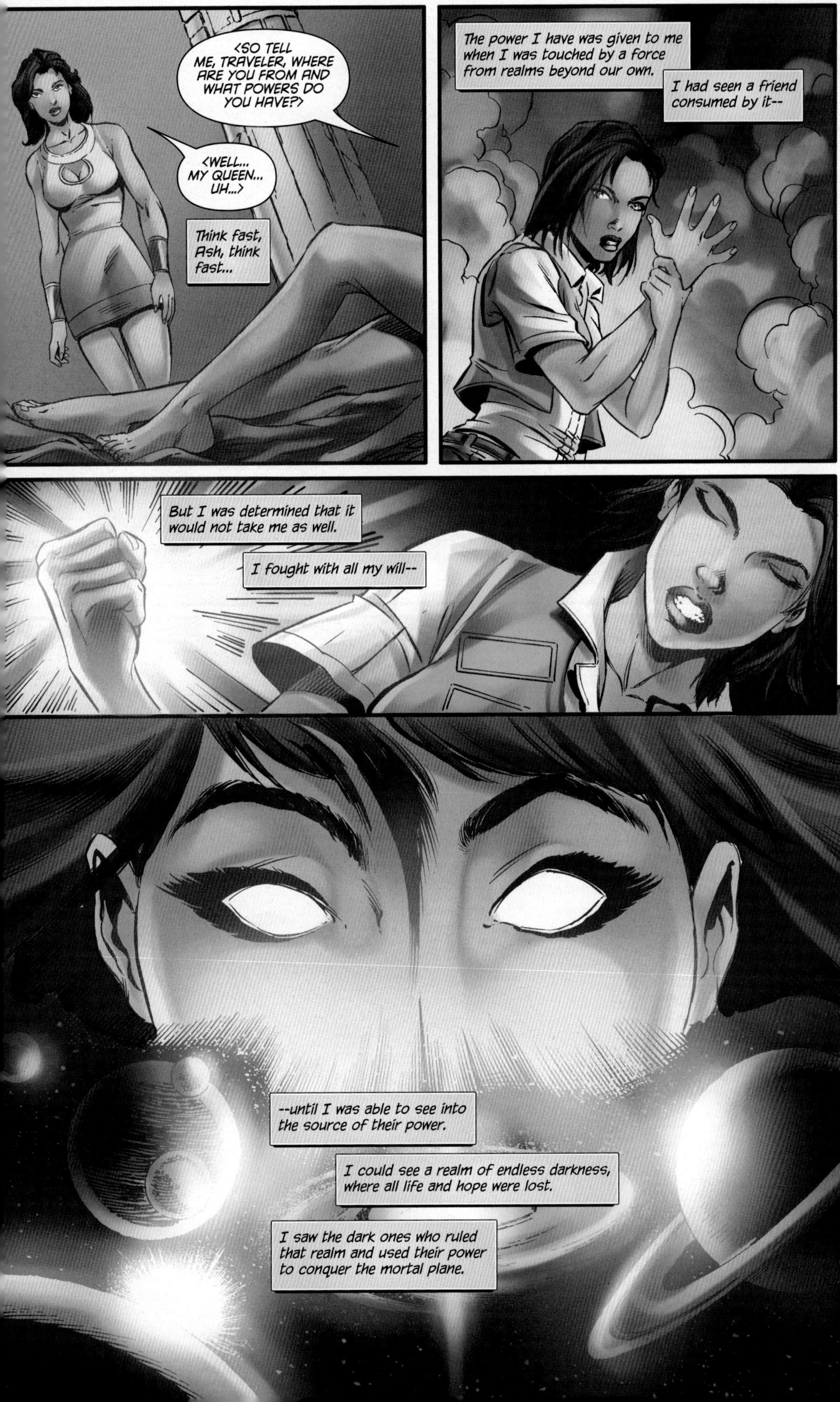
<SO TELL ME, TRAVELER, WHERE ARE YOU FROM AND WHAT POWERS DO YOU HAVE?>
<WELL... MY QUEEN... UH...>
Think fast, Ash, think fast...
The power I have was given to me when I was touched by a force from realms beyond our own.
I had seen a friend consumed by it--
But I was determined that it would not take me as well.
I fought with all my will--
--until I was able to see into the source of their power.
I could see a realm of endless darkness, where all life and hope were lost.
I saw the dark ones who ruled that realm and used their power to conquer the mortal plane.

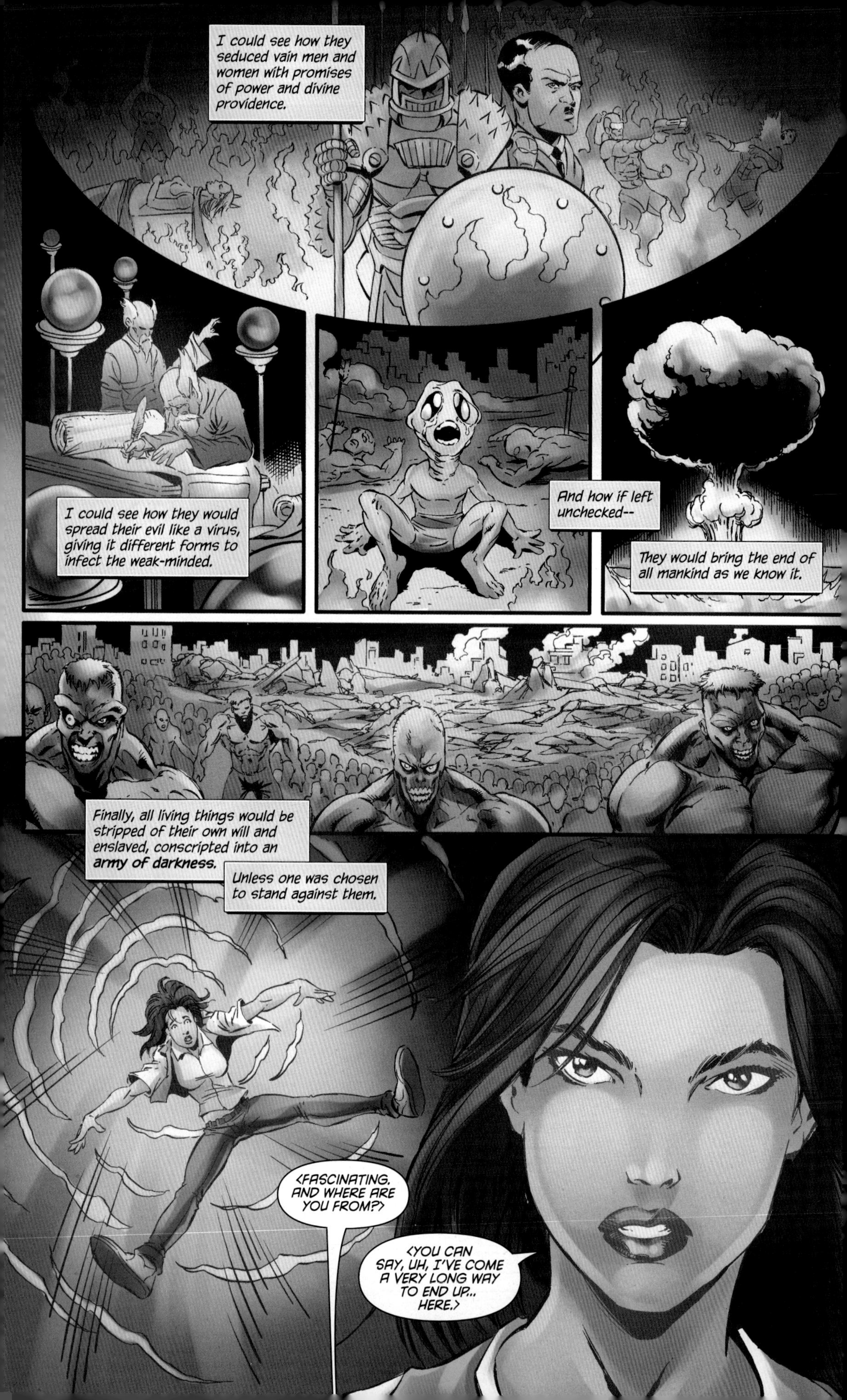
I could see how they seduced vain men and women with promises of power and divine providence.
I could see how they would spread their evil like a virus, giving it different forms to infect the weak-minded.
And how if left unchecked--
They would bring the end of all mankind as we know it.
Finally, all living things would be stripped of their own will and enslaved, conscripted into an **army of darkness.**
Unless one was chosen to stand against them.
<FASCINATING. AND WHERE ARE YOU FROM?>
<YOU CAN SAY, UH, I'VE COME A VERY LONG WAY TO END UP... HERE.>

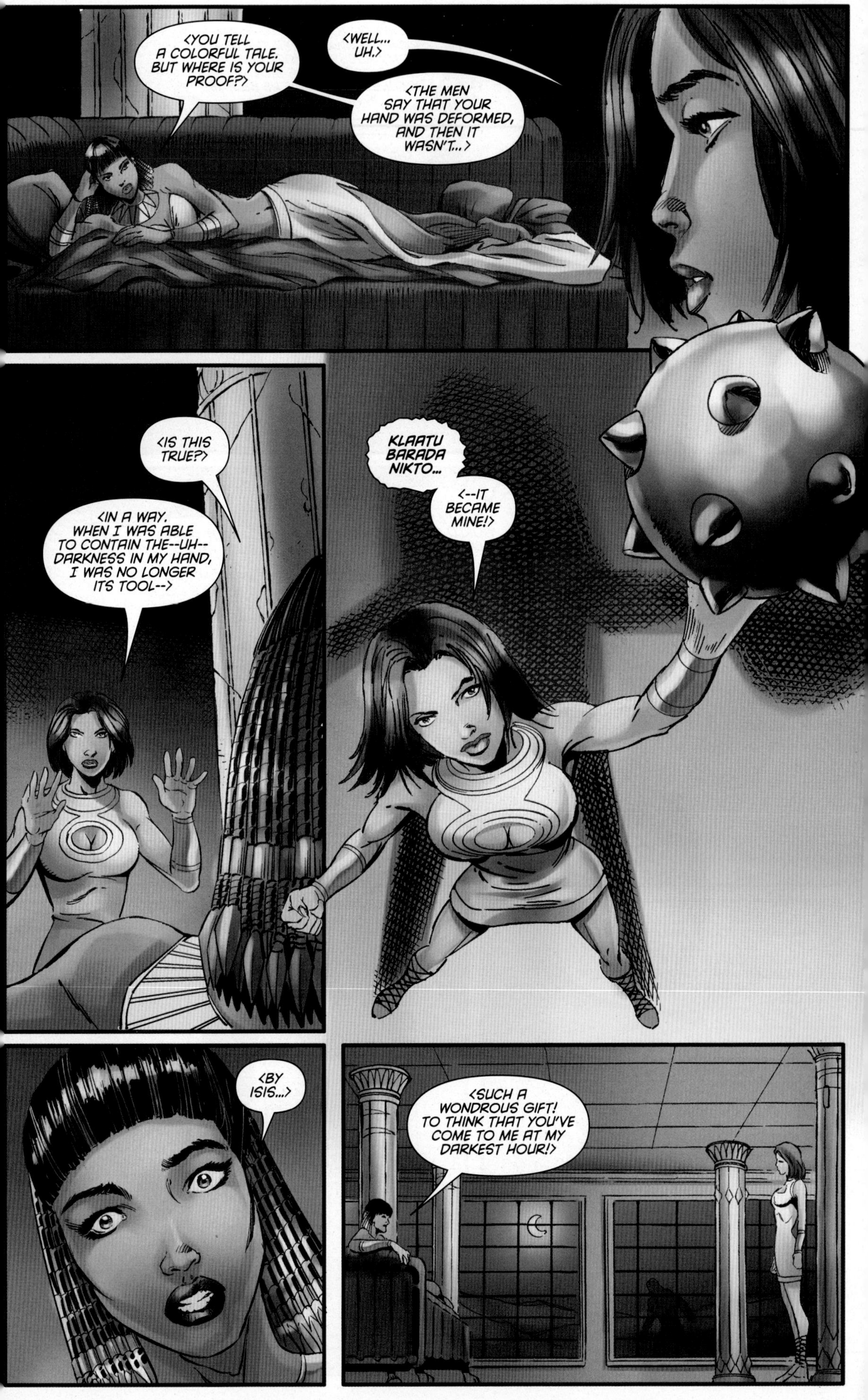

<YOU TELL A COLORFUL TALE. BUT WHERE IS YOUR PROOF?>
<WELL... UH.>
<THE MEN SAY THAT YOUR HAND WAS DEFORMED, AND THEN IT WASN'T...>
<IS THIS TRUE?>
<IN A WAY. WHEN I WAS ABLE TO CONTAIN THE--UH--DARKNESS IN MY HAND, I WAS NO LONGER ITS TOOL-->
KLAATU BARADA NIKTO...
<--IT BECAME MINE!>
<BY ISIS...>
<SUCH A WONDROUS GIFT! TO THINK THAT YOU'VE COME TO ME AT MY DARKEST HOUR!>

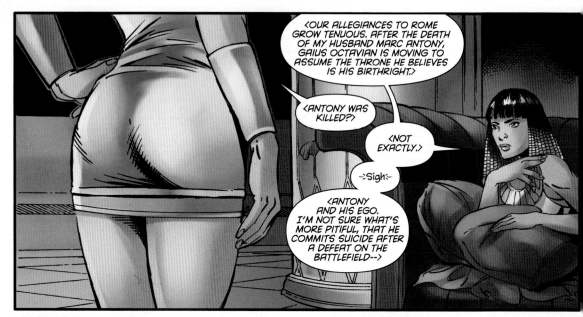

<OUR ALLEGIANCES TO ROME GROW TENUOUS. AFTER THE DEATH OF MY HUSBAND MARC ANTONY, GAIUS OCTAVIAN IS MOVING TO ASSUME THE THRONE HE BELIEVES IS HIS BIRTHRIGHT.>

<ANTONY WAS KILLED?>

<NOT EXACTLY.>

~Sigh~

<ANTONY AND HIS EGO. I'M NOT SURE WHAT'S MORE PITIFUL, THAT HE COMMITS SUICIDE AFTER A DEFEAT ON THE BATTLEFIELD-->

<OR THAT HE EXPECTS ME TO FOLLOW SUIT.>

<MEN, THEY REALLY BELIEVE THE WORLD COMES TO AN END WHEN THEY'RE NOT AROUND.>

<BUT AN ALLY SUCH AS YOU, WITH SUCH A POWERFUL WEAPON, CAN KEEP CAESAR'S DOGS IN LINE AND MY HOUSE AS KEEPERS OF THE THRONE.>

~Snort~
<TELL ME ABOUT IT.>

<YOU KNOW, I REALLY COULD USE A WOMAN'S TOUCH IN THE COURT OF SORCERY. THOSE OLD MEN AND THEIR RITUALS. I'M STARTING TO WONDER WHAT THEY REALLY KEEP THEIR GOATS FOR-->

KNOCK KNOCK

<STRANGE, I WASN'T EXPECTING ANYONE.>

<YES?>

<C-C-CANDY GRAM.>

<WHAT IS A "CANDY GRAM"?>

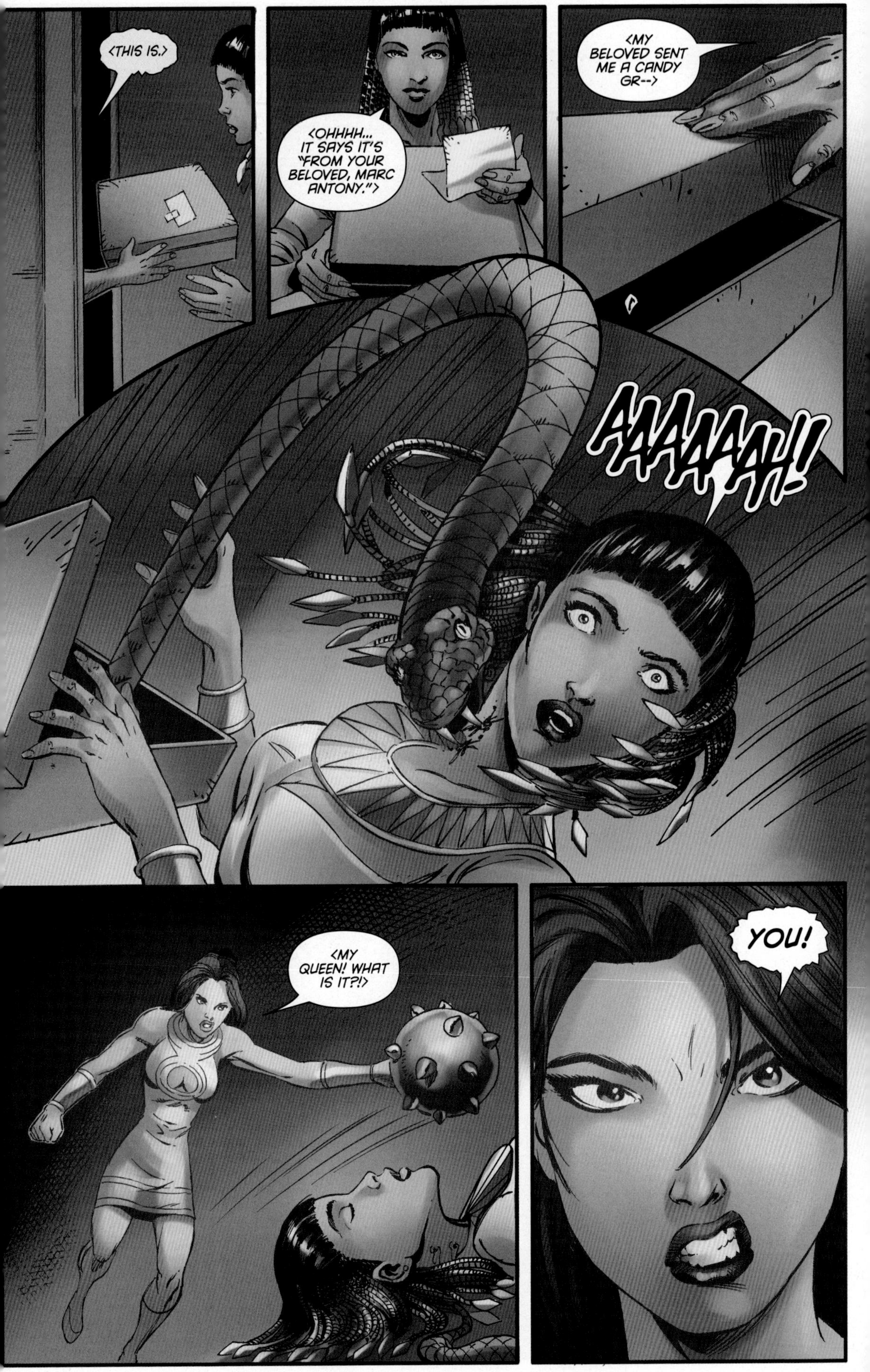
<THIS IS.>
<OHHHH... IT SAYS IT'S "FROM YOUR BELOVED, MARC ANTONY.">
<MY BELOVED SENT ME A CANDY GR-->
AAAAAAH!
<MY QUEEN! WHAT IS IT?!>
YOU!

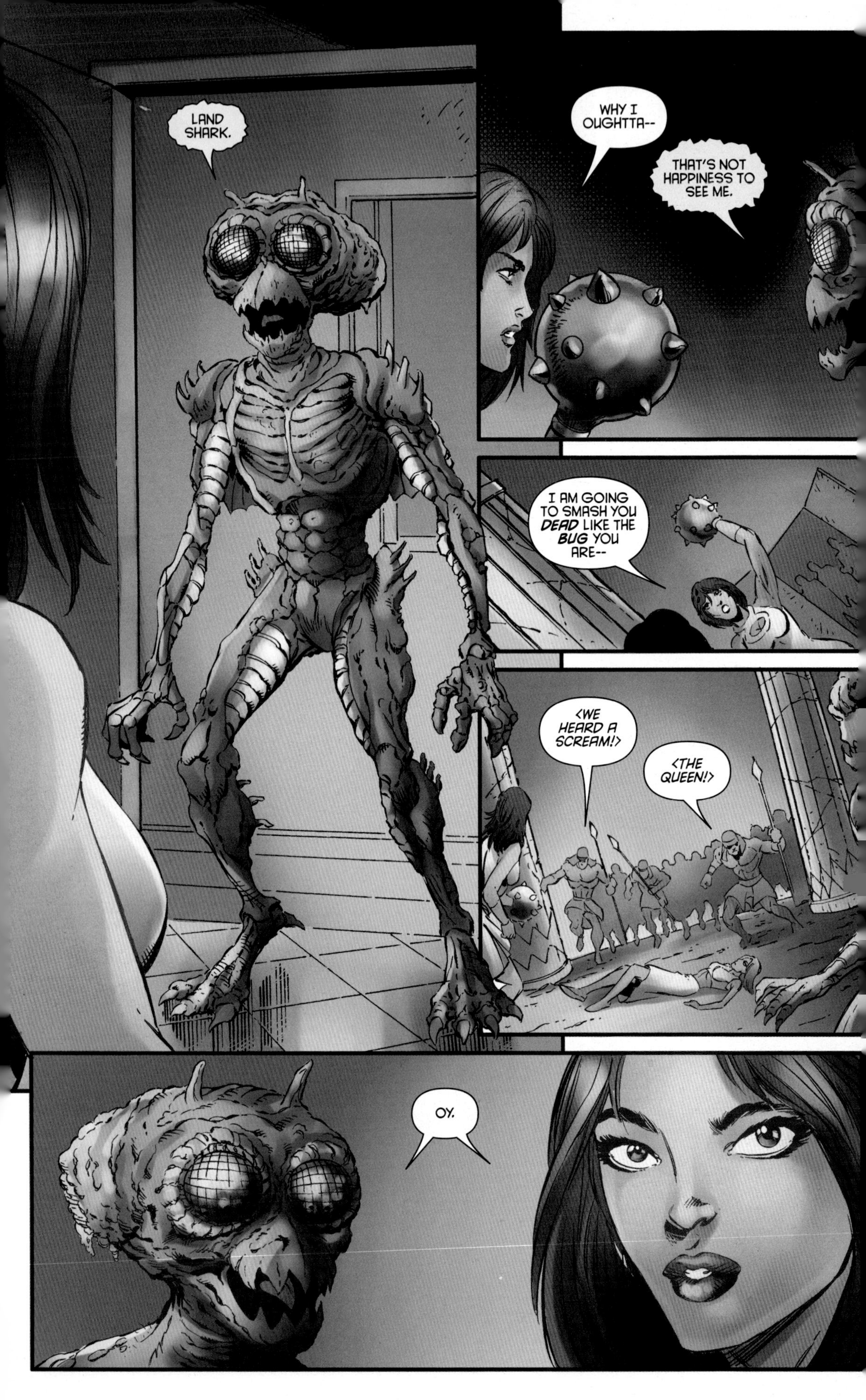
LAND SHARK.
WHY I OUGHTTA--
THAT'S NOT HAPPINESS TO SEE ME.
I AM GOING TO SMASH YOU *DEAD* LIKE THE *BUG* YOU ARE--
<WE HEARD A SCREAM!>
<THE QUEEN!>
OY.

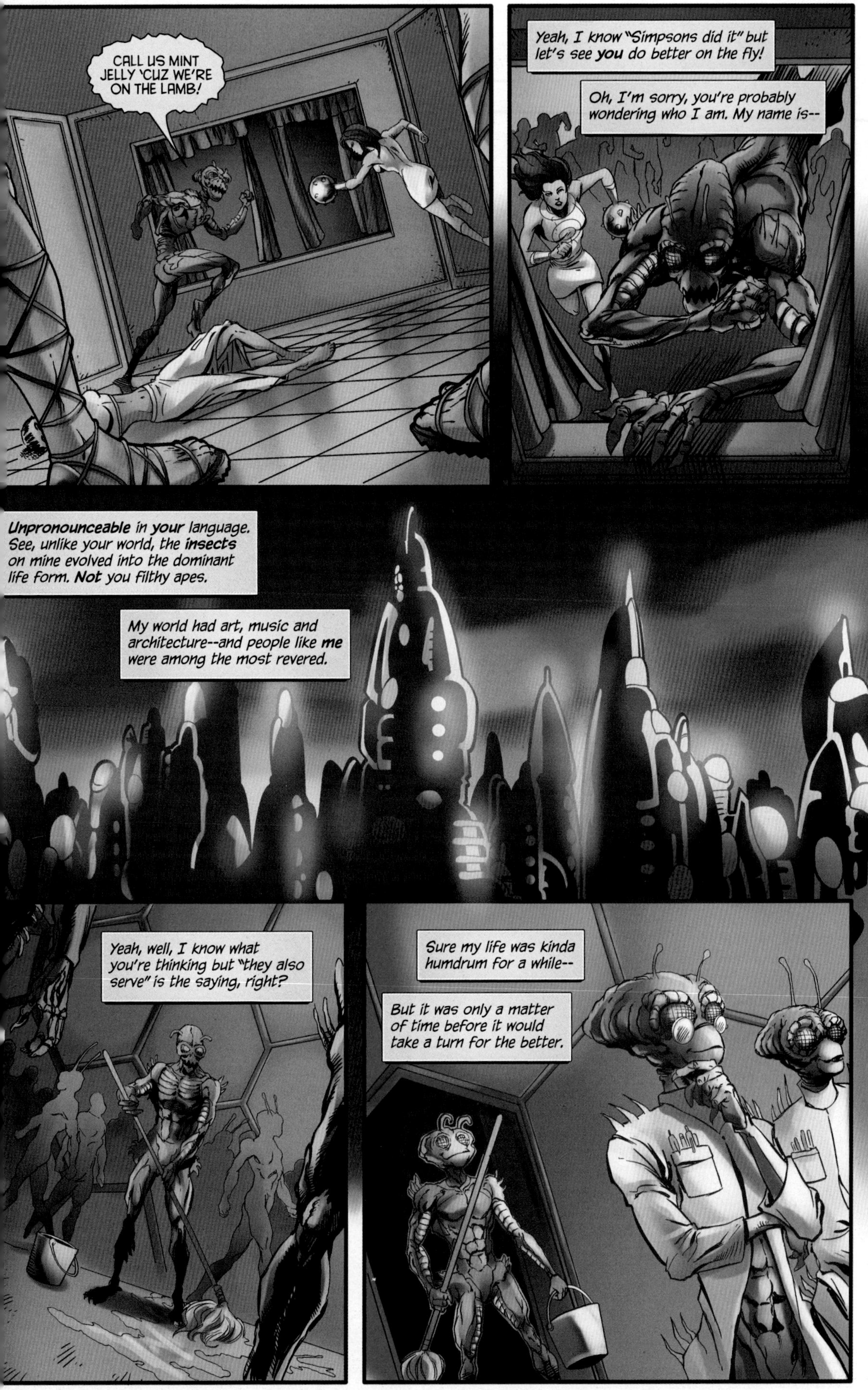
CALL US MINT JELLY 'CUZ WE'RE ON THE LAMB!
Yeah, I know "Simpsons did it" but let's see **you** do better on the fly!
Oh, I'm sorry, you're probably wondering who I am. My name is--
Unpronounceable in **your** language. See, unlike your world, the **insects** on mine evolved into the dominant life form. **Not** you filthy apes.
My world had art, music and architecture--and people like **me** were among the most revered.
Yeah, well, I know what you're thinking but "they also serve" is the saying, right?
Sure my life was kinda humdrum for a while--
But it was only a matter of time before it would take a turn for the better.

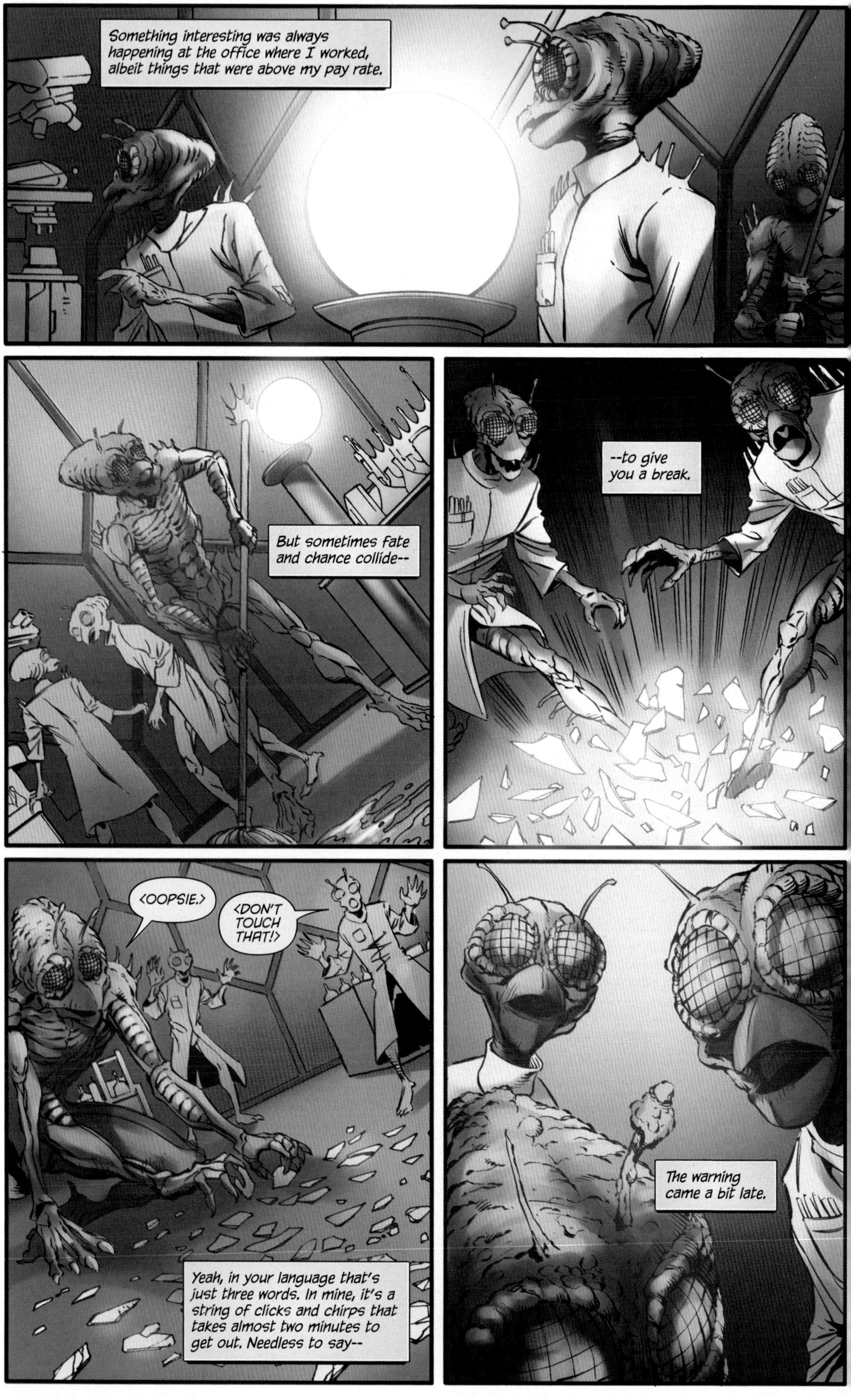

Something interesting was always happening at the office where I worked, albeit things that were above my pay rate.
But sometimes fate and chance collide--
--to give you a break.
<OOPSIE.>
<DON'T TOUCH THAT!>
Yeah, in your language that's just three words. In mine, it's a string of clicks and chirps that takes almost two minutes to get out. Needless to say--
The warning came a bit late.

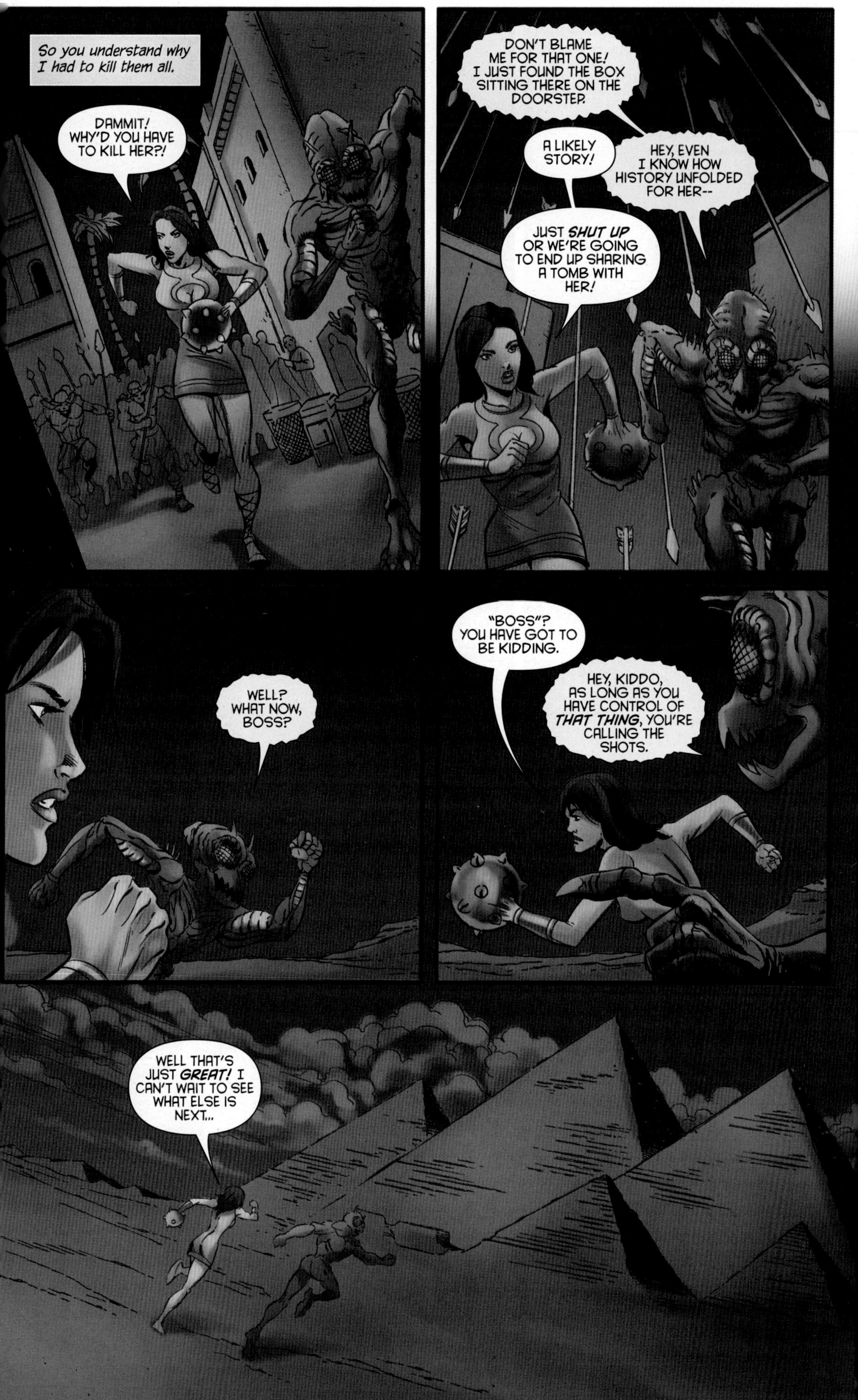
So you understand why I had to kill them all.
DAMMIT! WHY'D YOU HAVE TO KILL HER?!
DON'T BLAME ME FOR THAT ONE! I JUST FOUND THE BOX SITTING THERE ON THE DOORSTEP.
A LIKELY STORY!
HEY, EVEN I KNOW HOW HISTORY UNFOLDED FOR HER--
JUST SHUT UP OR WE'RE GOING TO END UP SHARING A TOMB WITH HER!
WELL? WHAT NOW, BOSS?
"BOSS"? YOU HAVE GOT TO BE KIDDING.
HEY, KIDDO, AS LONG AS YOU HAVE CONTROL OF THAT THING, YOU'RE CALLING THE SHOTS.
WELL THAT'S JUST GREAT! I CAN'T WAIT TO SEE WHAT ELSE IS NEXT...

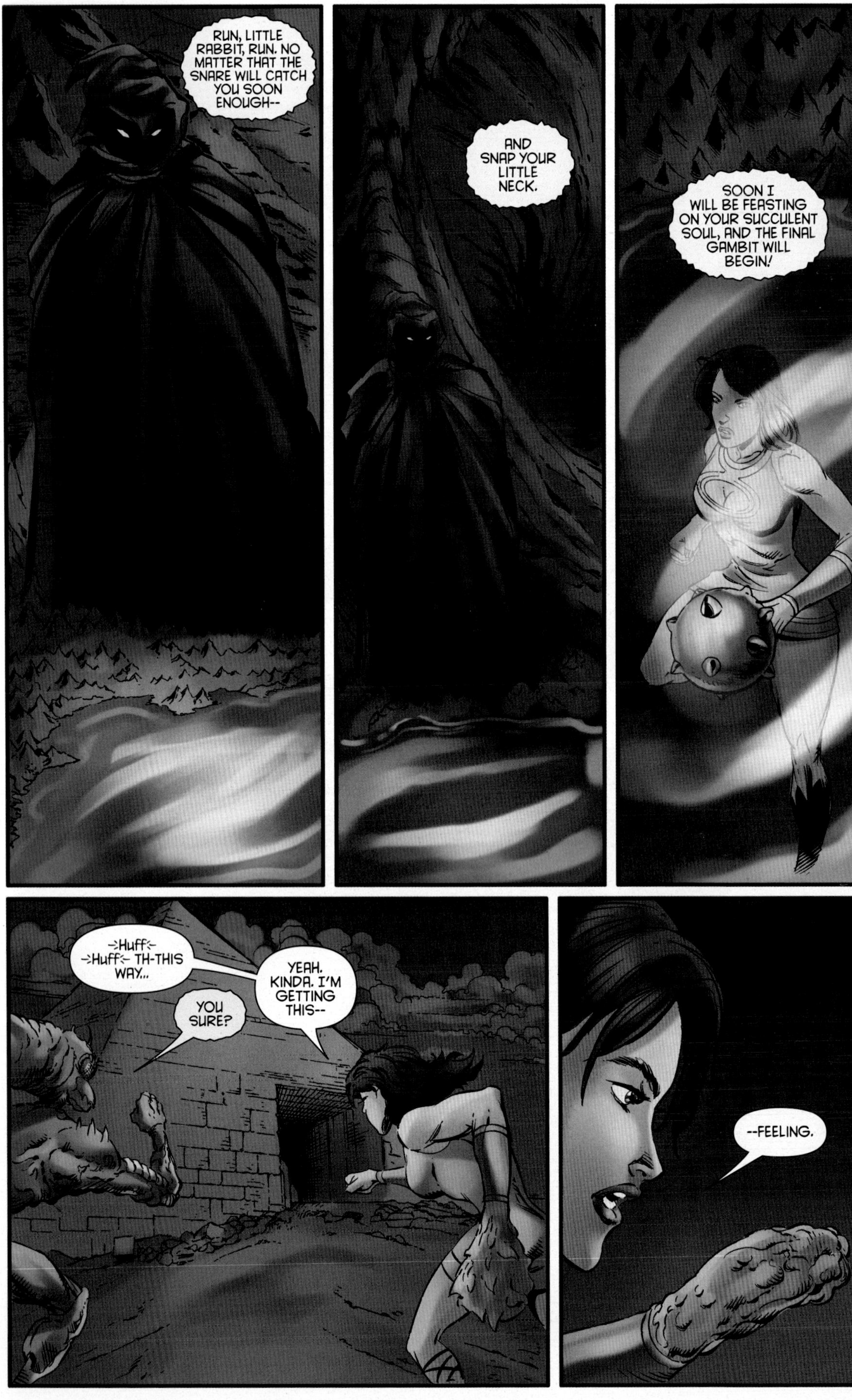
RUN, LITTLE RABBIT, RUN. NO MATTER THAT THE SNARE WILL CATCH YOU SOON ENOUGH--
AND SNAP YOUR LITTLE NECK.
SOON I WILL BE FEASTING ON YOUR SUCCULENT SOUL, AND THE FINAL GAMBIT WILL BEGIN!
-Huff- -Huff- TH-THIS WAY...
YOU SURE?
YEAH. KINDA. I'M GETTING THIS--
--FEELING.

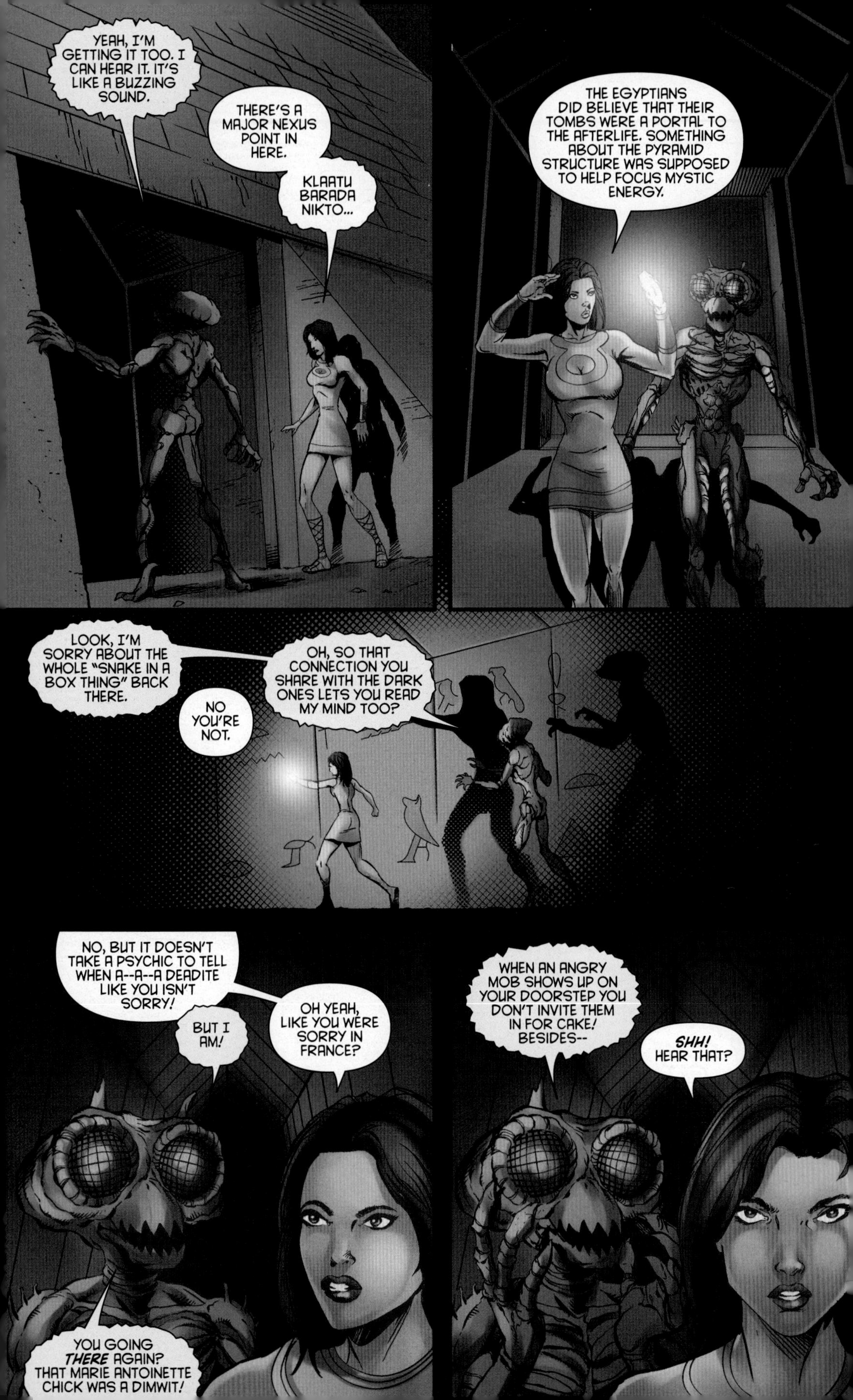
YEAH, I'M GETTING IT TOO. I CAN HEAR IT. IT'S LIKE A BUZZING SOUND.
THERE'S A MAJOR NEXUS POINT IN HERE.
KLAATU BARADA NIKTO...
THE EGYPTIANS DID BELIEVE THAT THEIR TOMBS WERE A PORTAL TO THE AFTERLIFE. SOMETHING ABOUT THE PYRAMID STRUCTURE WAS SUPPOSED TO HELP FOCUS MYSTIC ENERGY.
LOOK, I'M SORRY ABOUT THE WHOLE "SNAKE IN A BOX THING" BACK THERE.
NO YOU'RE NOT.
OH, SO THAT CONNECTION YOU SHARE WITH THE DARK ONES LETS YOU READ MY MIND TOO?
NO, BUT IT DOESN'T TAKE A PSYCHIC TO TELL WHEN A--A--A DEADITE LIKE YOU ISN'T SORRY!
BUT I AM!
OH YEAH, LIKE YOU WERE SORRY IN FRANCE?
YOU GOING *THERE* AGAIN? THAT MARIE ANTOINETTE CHICK WAS A DIMWIT!
WHEN AN ANGRY MOB SHOWS UP ON YOUR DOORSTEP YOU DON'T INVITE THEM IN FOR CAKE! BESIDES--
SHH! HEAR THAT?

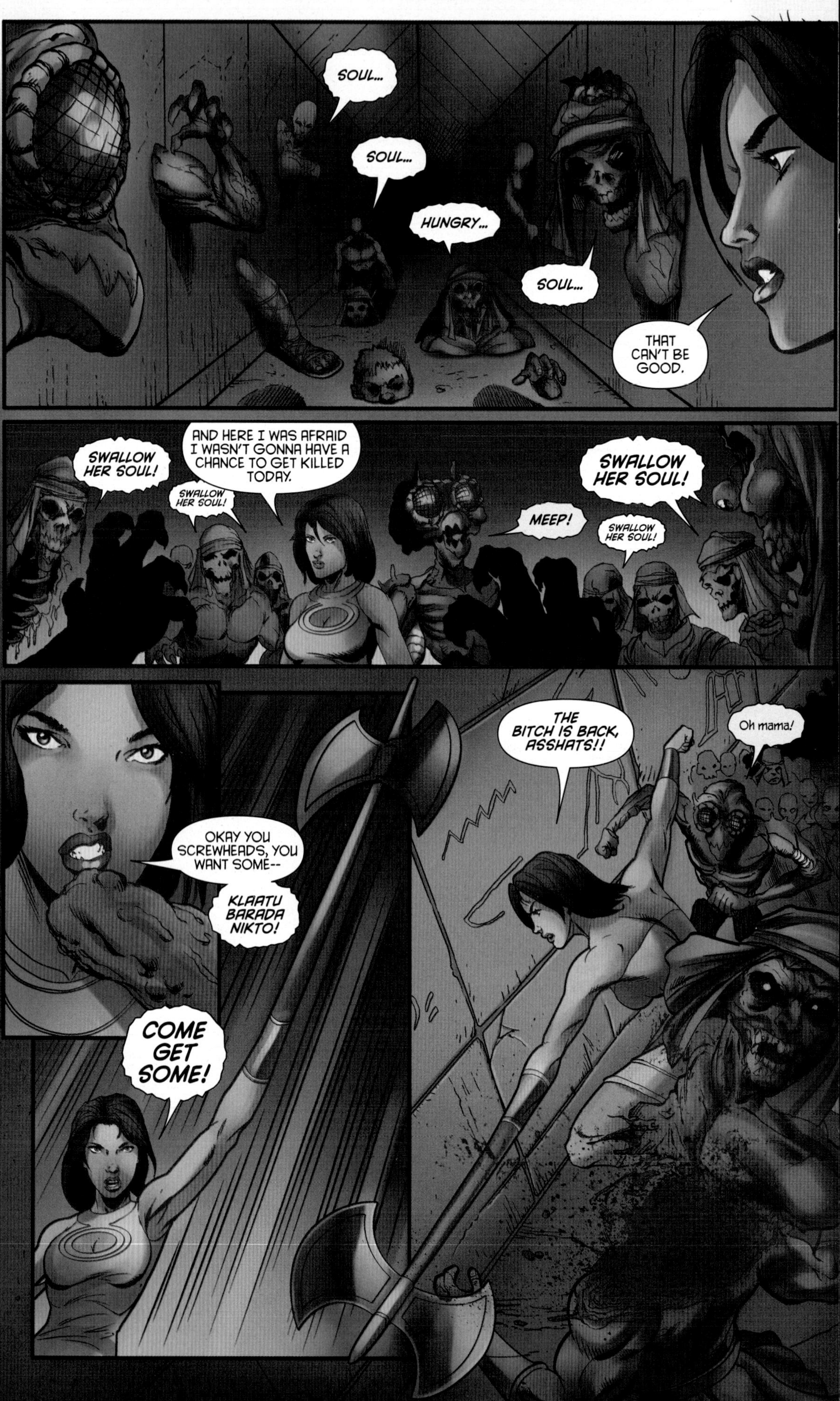
SOUL...
SOUL...
HUNGRY...
SOUL...
THAT CAN'T BE GOOD.
SWALLOW HER SOUL!
AND HERE I WAS AFRAID I WASN'T GONNA HAVE A CHANCE TO GET KILLED TODAY.
SWALLOW HER SOUL!
MEEP!
SWALLOW HER SOUL!
SWALLOW HER SOUL!
OKAY YOU SCREWHEADS, YOU WANT SOME--
KLAATU BARADA NIKTO!
COME GET SOME!
THE BITCH IS BACK, ASSHATS!!
Oh mama!

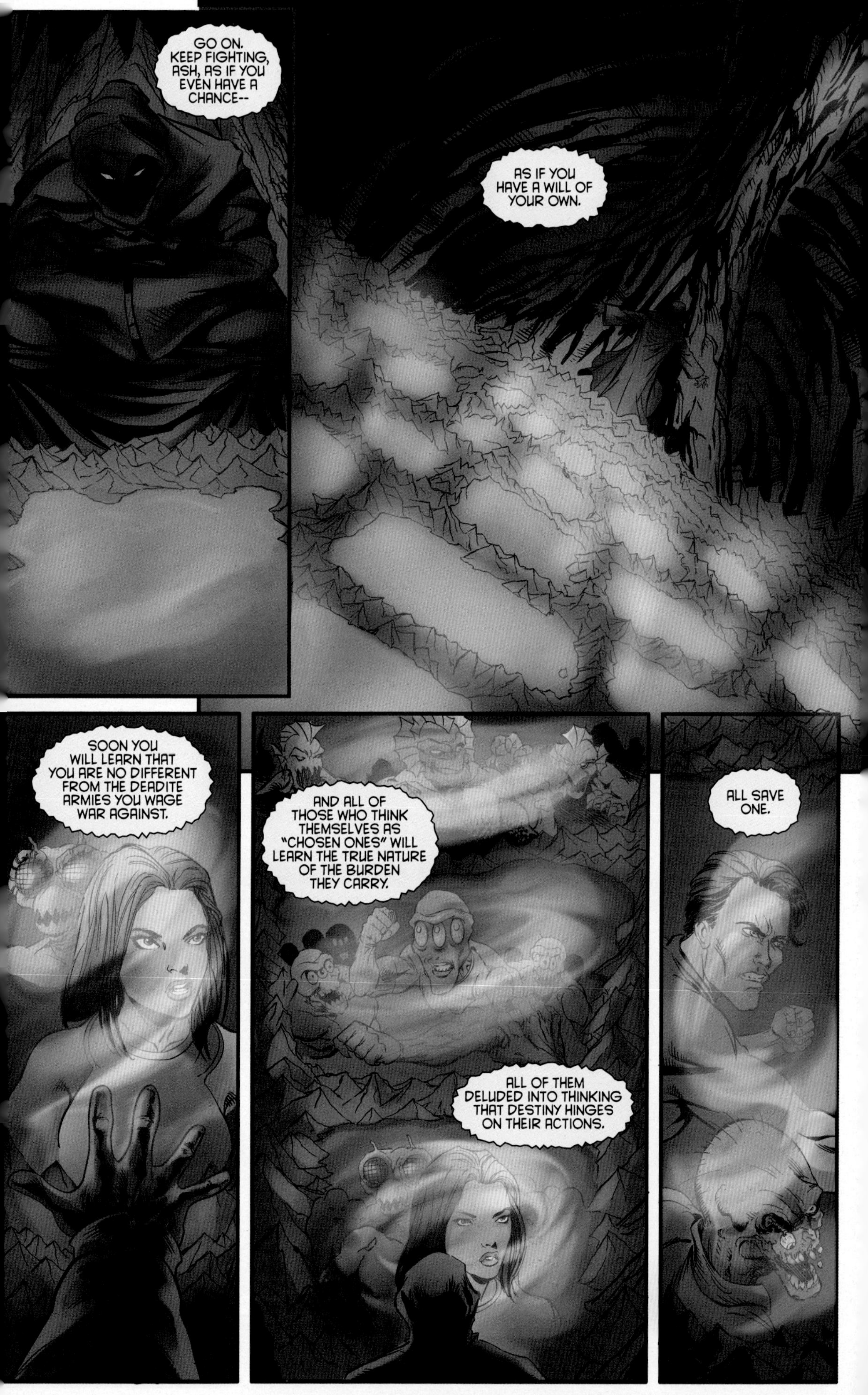
GO ON. KEEP FIGHTING, ASH, AS IF YOU EVEN HAVE A CHANCE--
AS IF YOU HAVE A WILL OF YOUR OWN.
SOON YOU WILL LEARN THAT YOU ARE NO DIFFERENT FROM THE DEADITE ARMIES YOU WAGE WAR AGAINST.
AND ALL OF THOSE WHO THINK THEMSELVES AS "CHOSEN ONES" WILL LEARN THE TRUE NATURE OF THE BURDEN THEY CARRY.
ALL OF THEM DELUDED INTO THINKING THAT DESTINY HINGES ON THEIR ACTIONS.
ALL SAVE ONE.

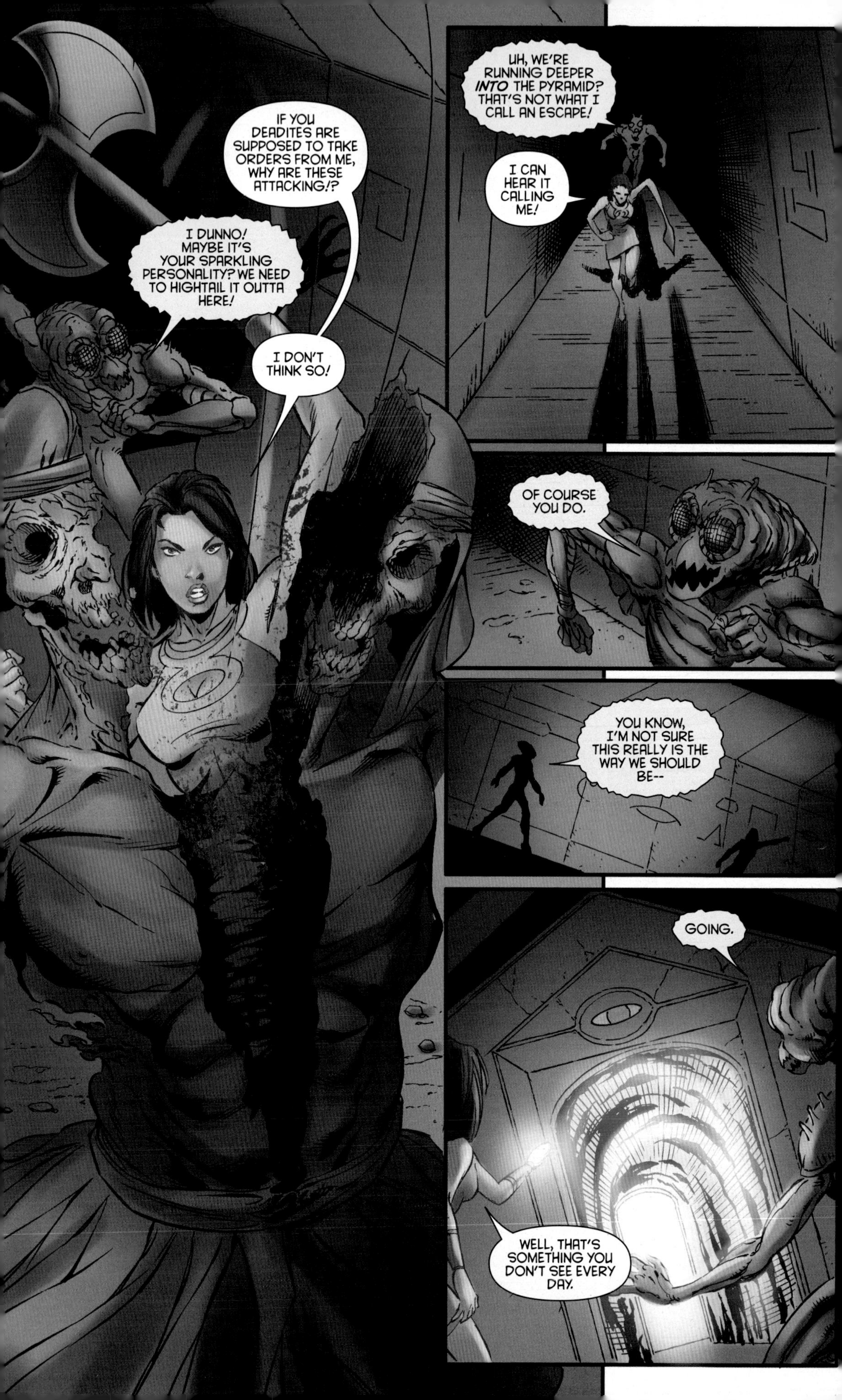
IF YOU DEADITES ARE SUPPOSED TO TAKE ORDERS FROM ME, WHY ARE THESE ATTACKING!?
I DUNNO! MAYBE IT'S YOUR SPARKLING PERSONALITY? WE NEED TO HIGHTAIL IT OUTTA HERE!
I DON'T THINK SO!
UH, WE'RE RUNNING DEEPER INTO THE PYRAMID? THAT'S NOT WHAT I CALL AN ESCAPE!
I CAN HEAR IT CALLING ME!
OF COURSE YOU DO.
YOU KNOW, I'M NOT SURE THIS REALLY IS THE WAY WE SHOULD BE--
GOING.
WELL, THAT'S SOMETHING YOU DON'T SEE EVERY DAY.

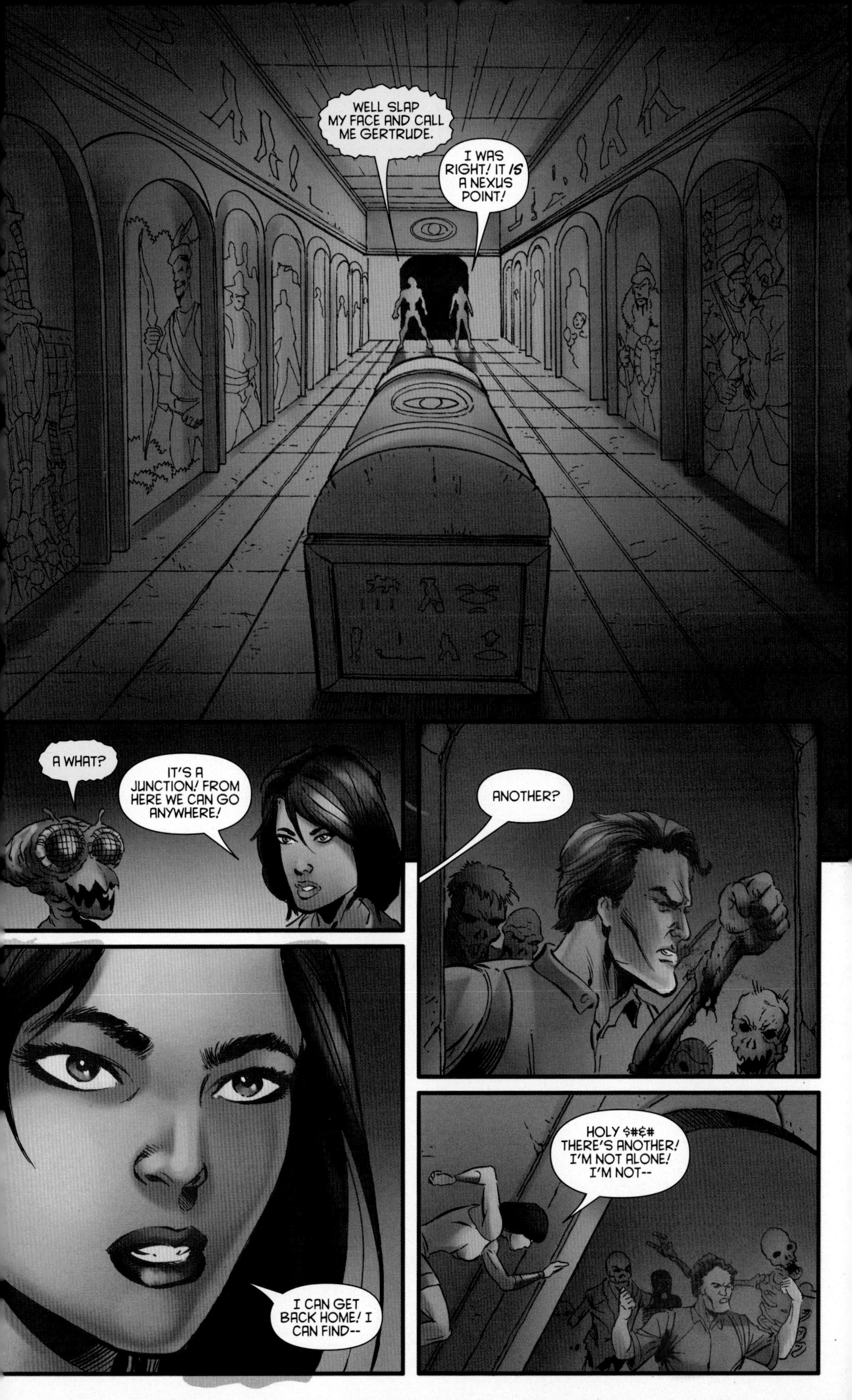
WELL SLAP MY FACE AND CALL ME GERTRUDE.
I WAS RIGHT! IT IS A NEXUS POINT!
A WHAT?
IT'S A JUNCTION! FROM HERE WE CAN GO ANYWHERE!
I CAN GET BACK HOME! I CAN FIND--
ANOTHER?
HOLY $#&# THERE'S ANOTHER! I'M NOT ALONE! I'M NOT--

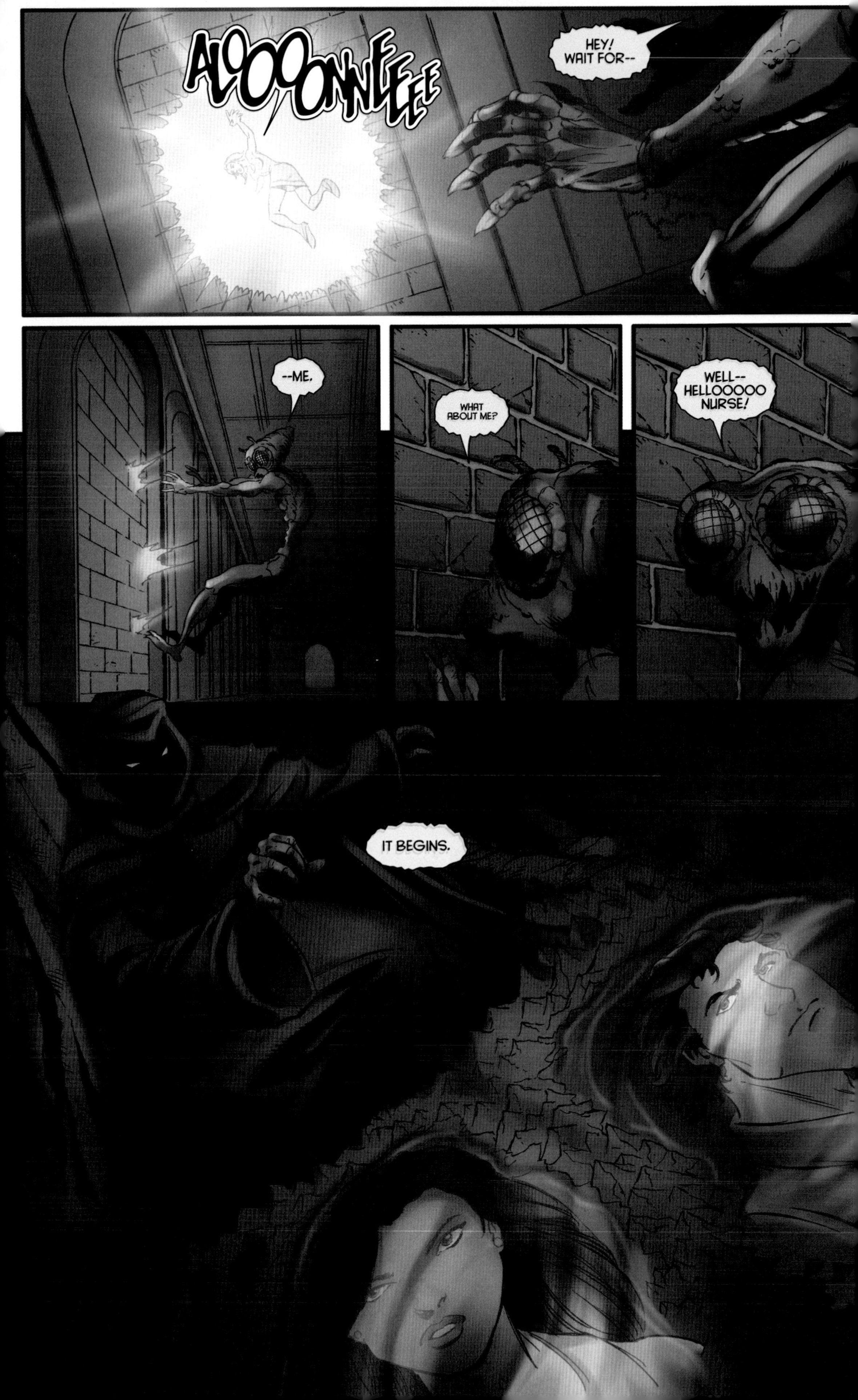

ALOOOONNNEEEE
HEY! WAIT FOR--
--ME.
WHAT ABOUT ME?
WELL-- HELLOOOOO NURSE!
IT BEGINS.

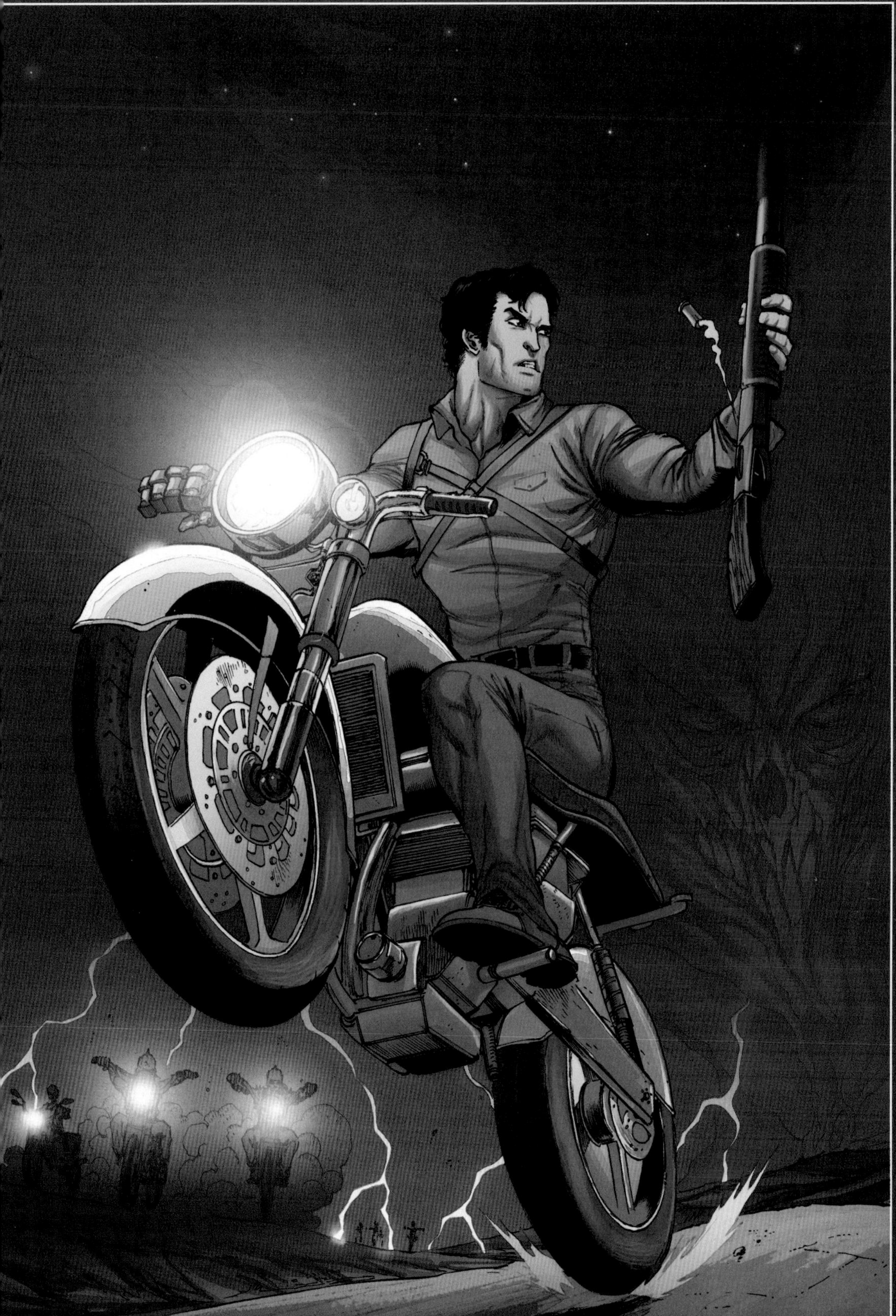

cover to issue #2 by TIM SEELEY, colors by ADRIANO LUCAS

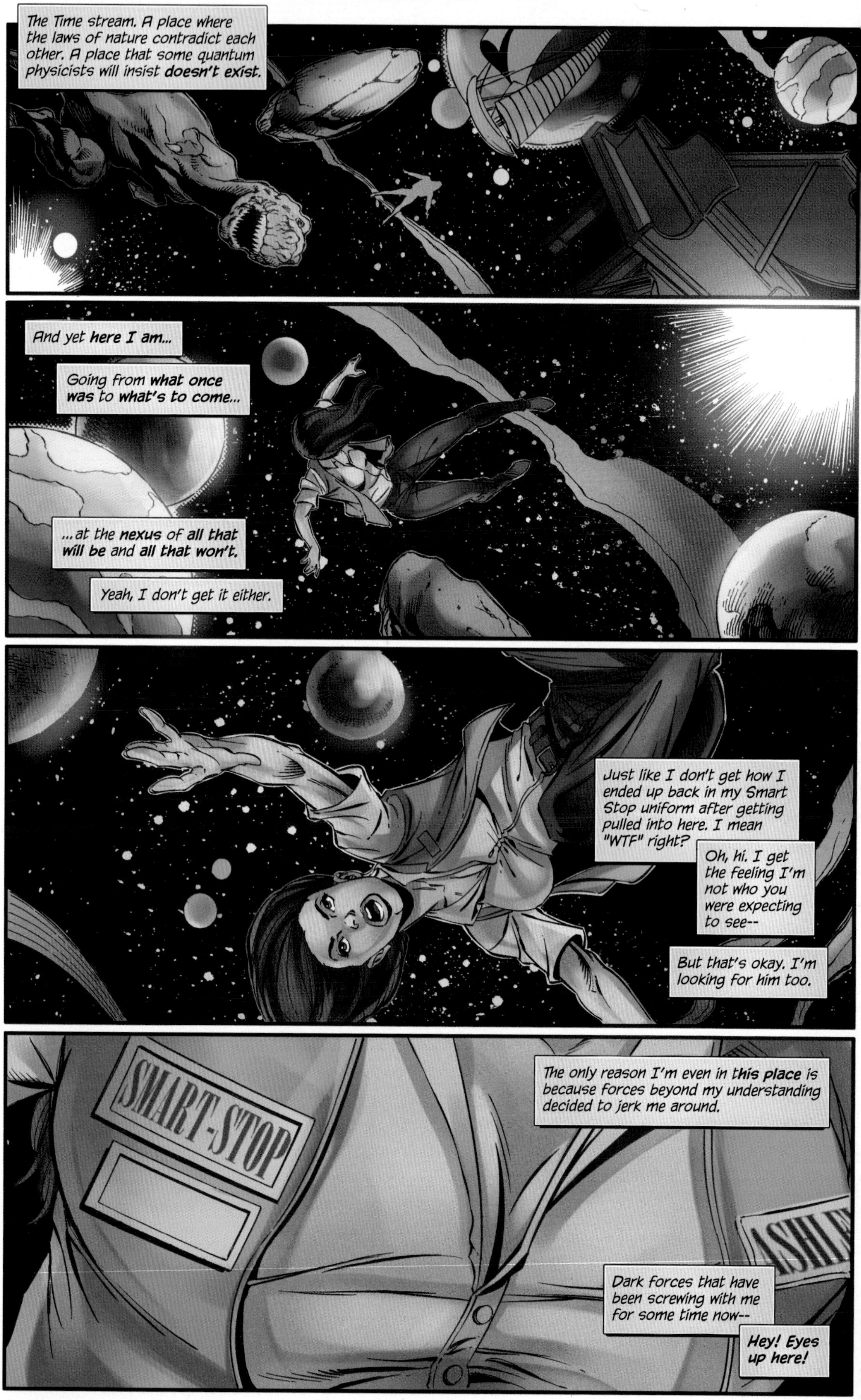
The Time stream. A place where the laws of nature contradict each other. A place that some quantum physicists will insist doesn't exist.
And yet here I am...
Going from what once was to what's to come...
...at the nexus of all that will be and all that won't.
Yeah, I don't get it either.
Just like I don't get how I ended up back in my Smart Stop uniform after getting pulled into here. I mean "WTF" right?
Oh, hi. I get the feeling I'm not who you were expecting to see--
But that's okay. I'm looking for him too.
SMART-STOP
The only reason I'm even in this place is because forces beyond my understanding decided to jerk me around.
Dark forces that have been screwing with me for some time now--
Hey! Eyes up here!

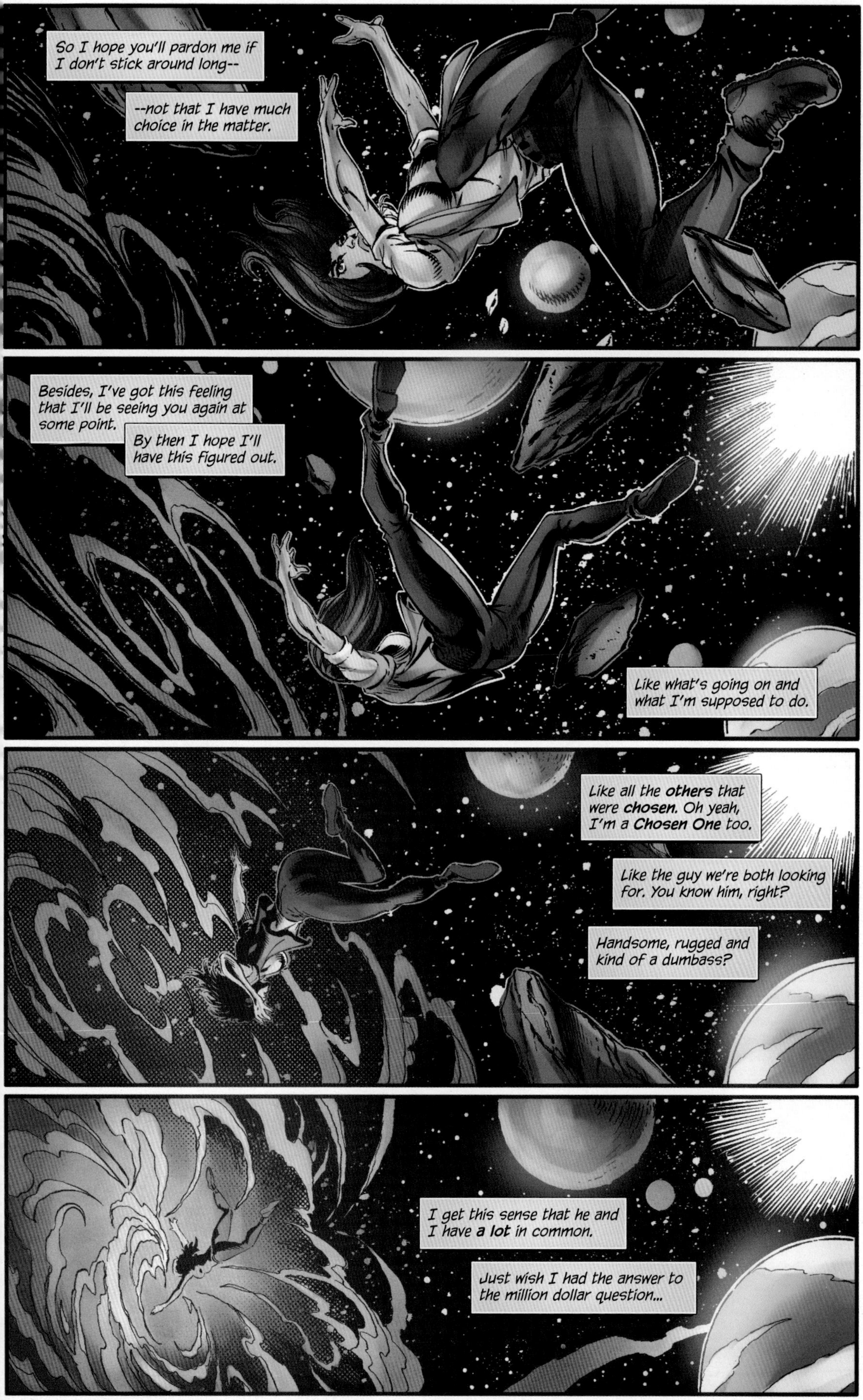
So I hope you'll pardon me if I don't stick around long--
--not that I have much choice in the matter.
Besides, I've got this feeling that I'll be seeing you again at some point.
By then I hope I'll have this figured out.
Like what's going on and what I'm supposed to do.
Like all the **others** that were **chosen**. Oh yeah, I'm a **Chosen One** too.
Like the guy we're both looking for. You know him, right?
Handsome, rugged and kind of a dumbass?
I get this sense that he and I have **a lot** in common.
Just wish I had the answer to the million dollar question...

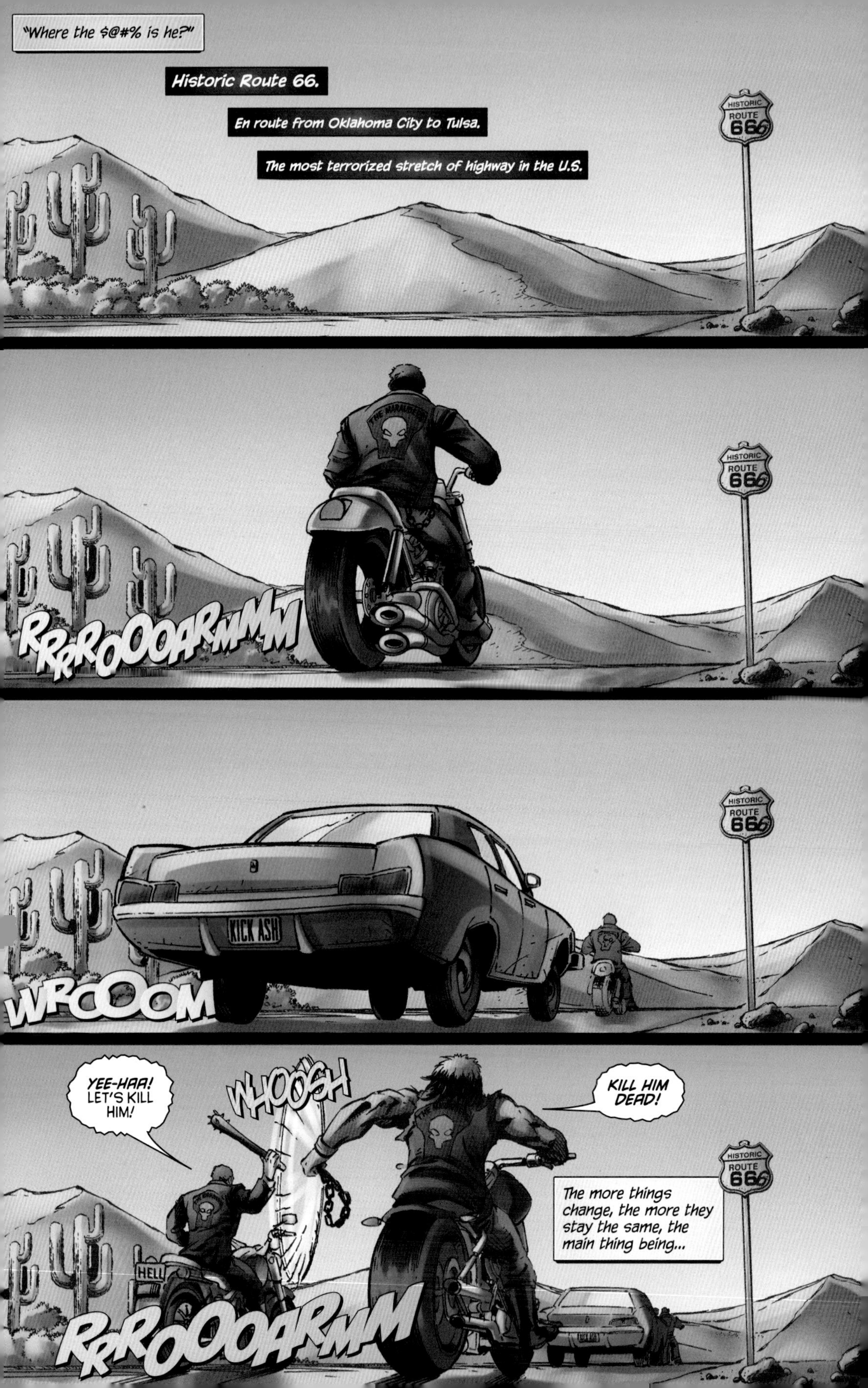
"Where the $@#% is he?"
Historic Route 66.
En route from Oklahoma City to Tulsa.
The most terrorized stretch of highway in the U.S.
HISTORIC ROUTE 666
RRRROOOOARMMM
KICK ASH
WROOOM
YEE-HAA! LET'S KILL HIM!
WHOOSH
KILL HIM DEAD!
The more things change, the more they stay the same, the main thing being...
HELL
RRROOOOARMM

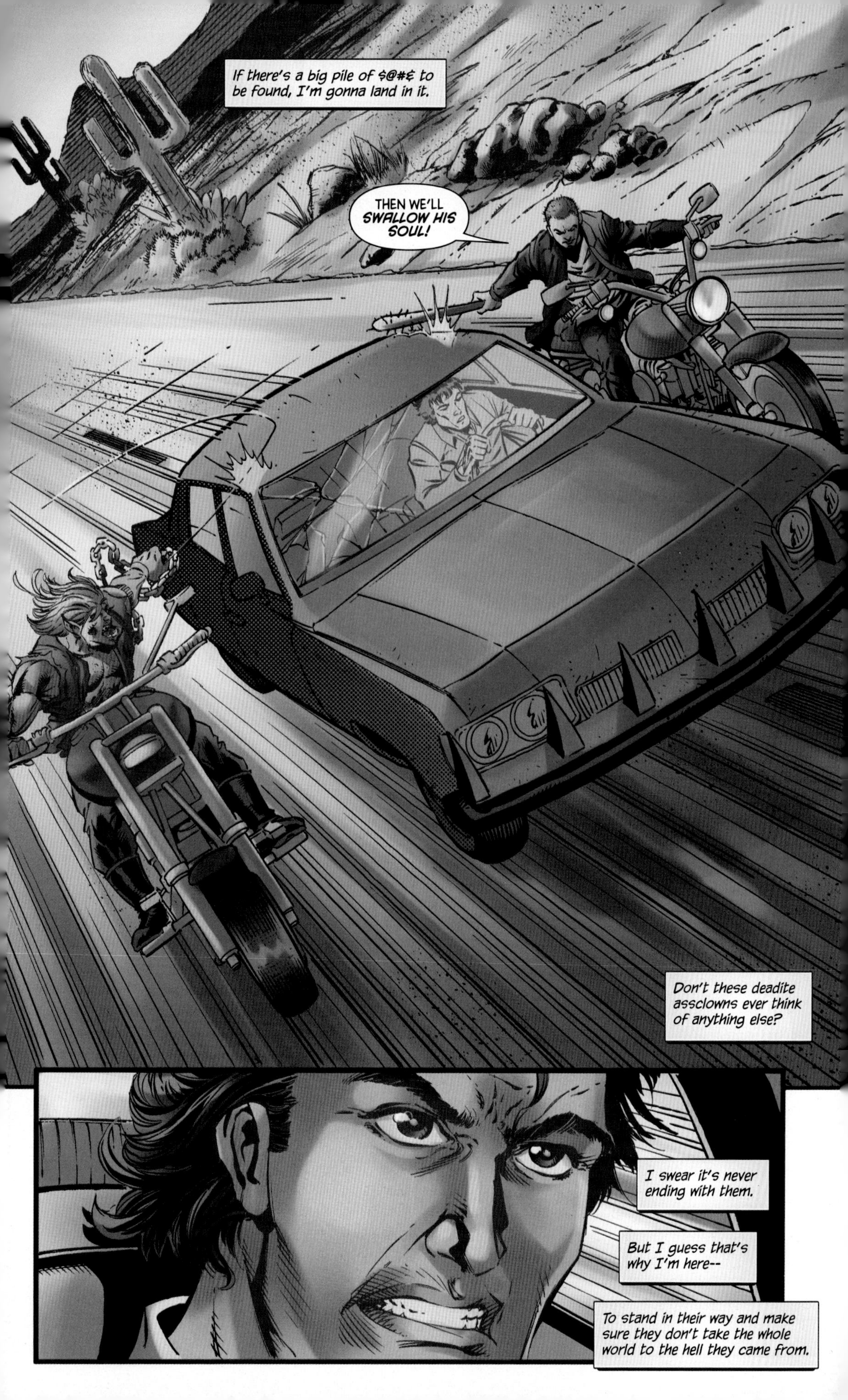
If there's a big pile of $@#& to be found, I'm gonna land in it.
THEN WE'LL SWALLOW HIS SOUL!
Don't these deadite assclowns ever think of anything else?
I swear it's never ending with them.
But I guess that's why I'm here--
To stand in their way and make sure they don't take the whole world to the hell they came from.

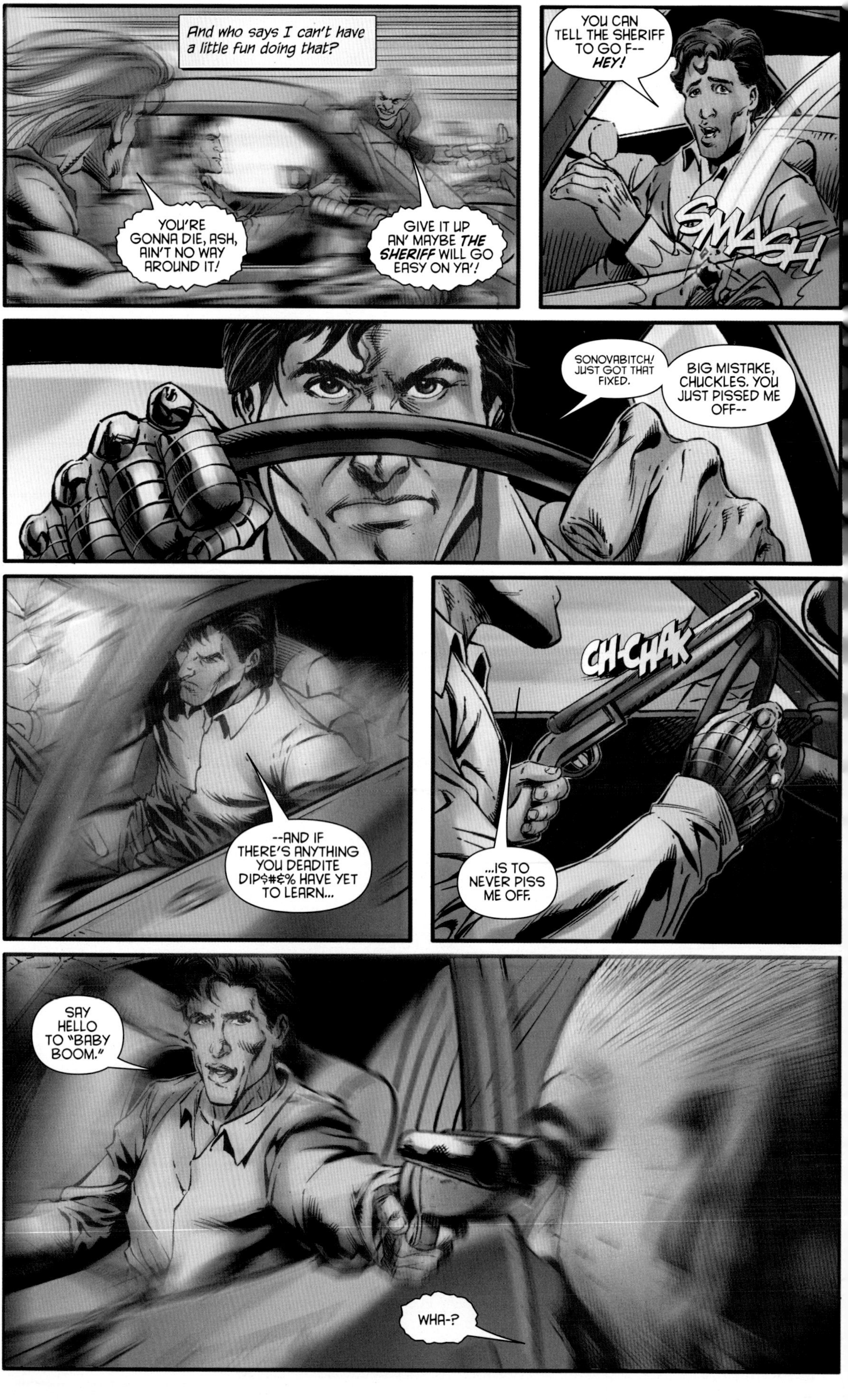
And who says I can't have a little fun doing that?
YOU'RE GONNA DIE, ASH, AIN'T NO WAY AROUND IT!
GIVE IT UP AN' MAYBE THE SHERIFF WILL GO EASY ON YA'!
YOU CAN TELL THE SHERIFF TO GO F-- HEY!
SMASH
SONOVABITCH! JUST GOT THAT FIXED.
BIG MISTAKE, CHUCKLES. YOU JUST PISSED ME OFF--
--AND IF THERE'S ANYTHING YOU DEADITE DIP$#&% HAVE YET TO LEARN...
CH-CHAK
...IS TO NEVER PISS ME OFF.
SAY HELLO TO "BABY BOOM."
WHA-?

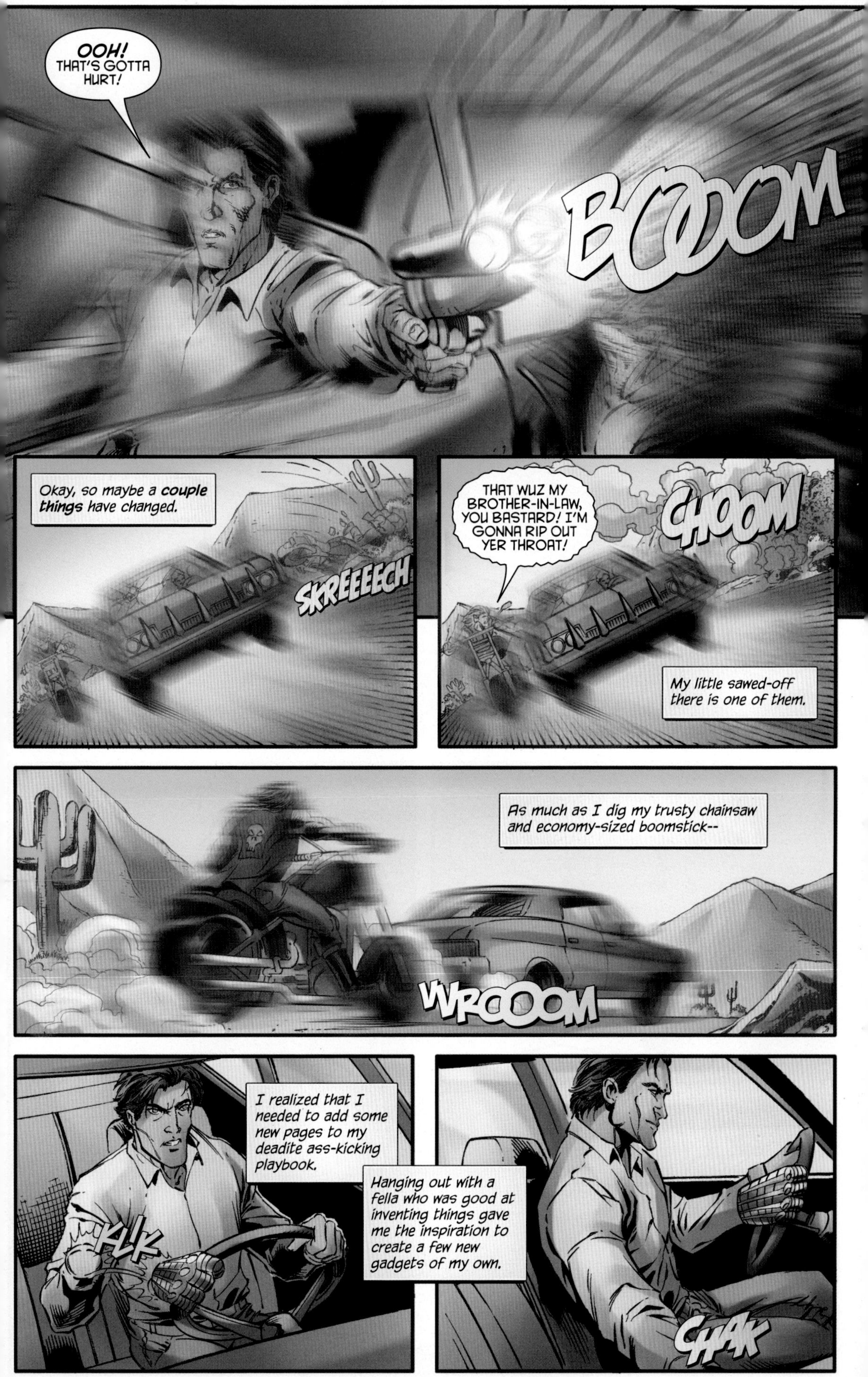
OOH! THAT'S GOTTA HURT!
BOOOM
Okay, so maybe a **couple things** have changed.
SKREEEECH
THAT WUZ MY BROTHER-IN-LAW, YOU BASTARD! I'M GONNA RIP OUT YER THROAT!
CHOOM
My little sawed-off there is one of them.
As much as I dig my trusty chainsaw and economy-sized boomstick--
VVROOOM
I realized that I needed to add some new pages to my deadite ass-kicking playbook.
KLIK
Hanging out with a fella who was good at inventing things gave me the inspiration to create a few new gadgets of my own.
CHAK

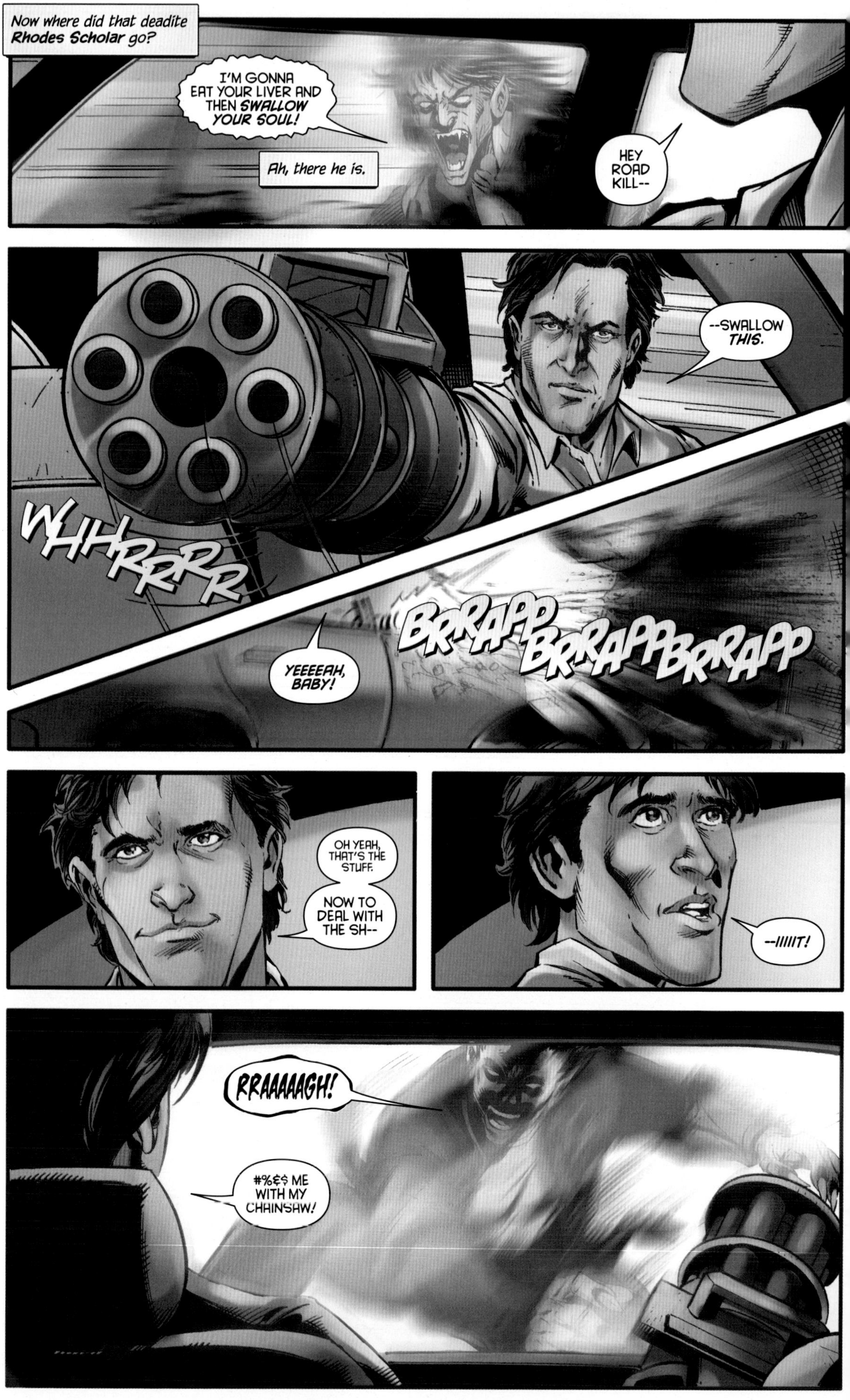
Now where did that deadite Rhodes Scholar go?
I'M GONNA EAT YOUR LIVER AND THEN SWALLOW YOUR SOUL!
Ah, there he is.
HEY ROAD KILL--
--SWALLOW THIS.
WHHRRRR
YEEEEAH, BABY!
BRRAPP BRRAPP BRRAPP
OH YEAH, THAT'S THE STUFF.
NOW TO DEAL WITH THE SH--
--IIIIIT!
RRAAAAAGH!
#%&$ ME WITH MY CHAINSAW!

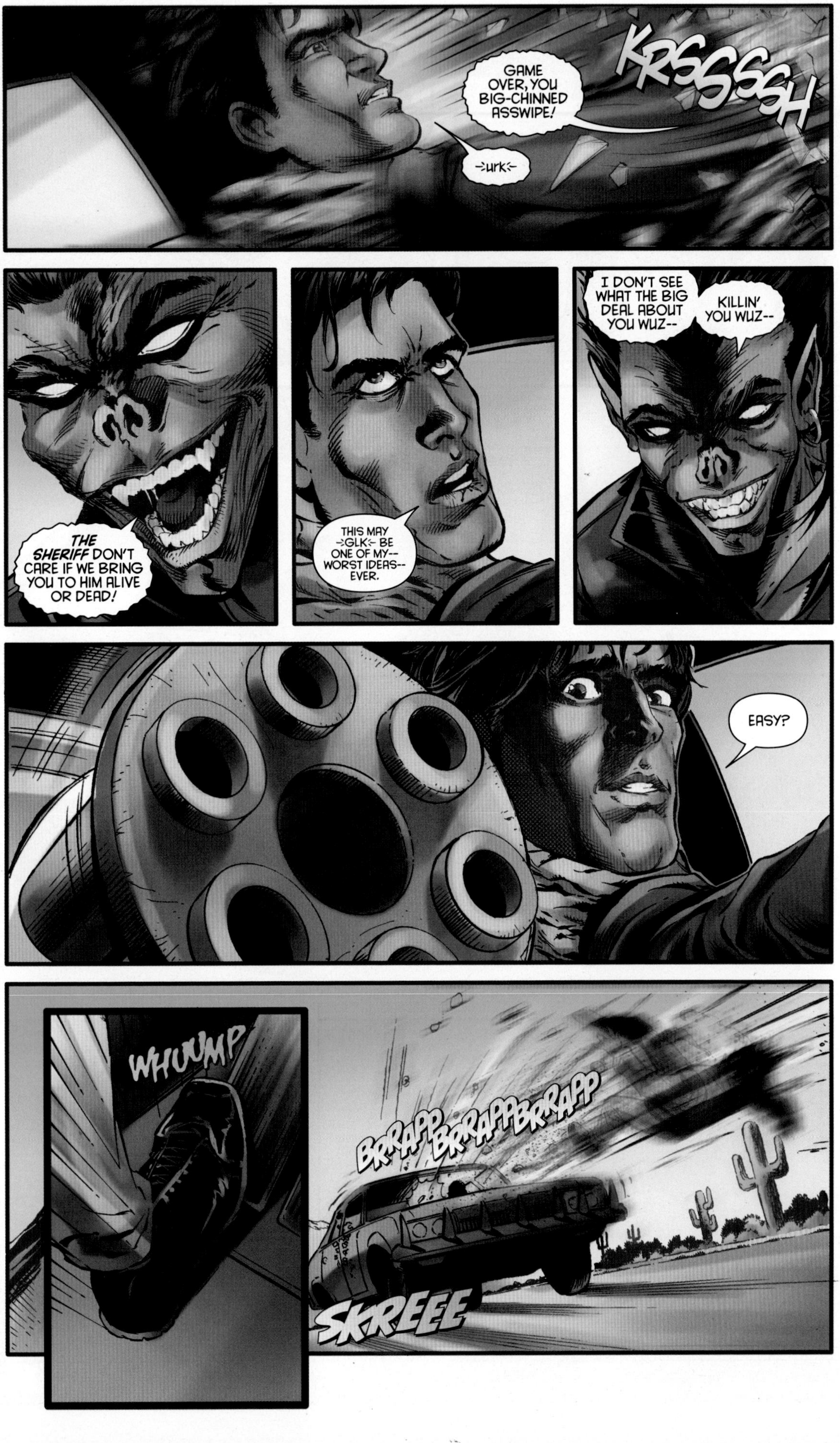
KRSSSSH
GAME OVER, YOU BIG-CHINNED ASSWIPE!
-urk-
THE SHERIFF DON'T CARE IF WE BRING YOU TO HIM ALIVE OR DEAD!
THIS MAY -GLK- BE ONE OF MY-- WORST IDEAS-- EVER.
I DON'T SEE WHAT THE BIG DEAL ABOUT YOU WUZ--
KILLIN' YOU WUZ--
EASY?
WHUUMP
BRRAPP BRRAPP BRRAPP
SKREEE

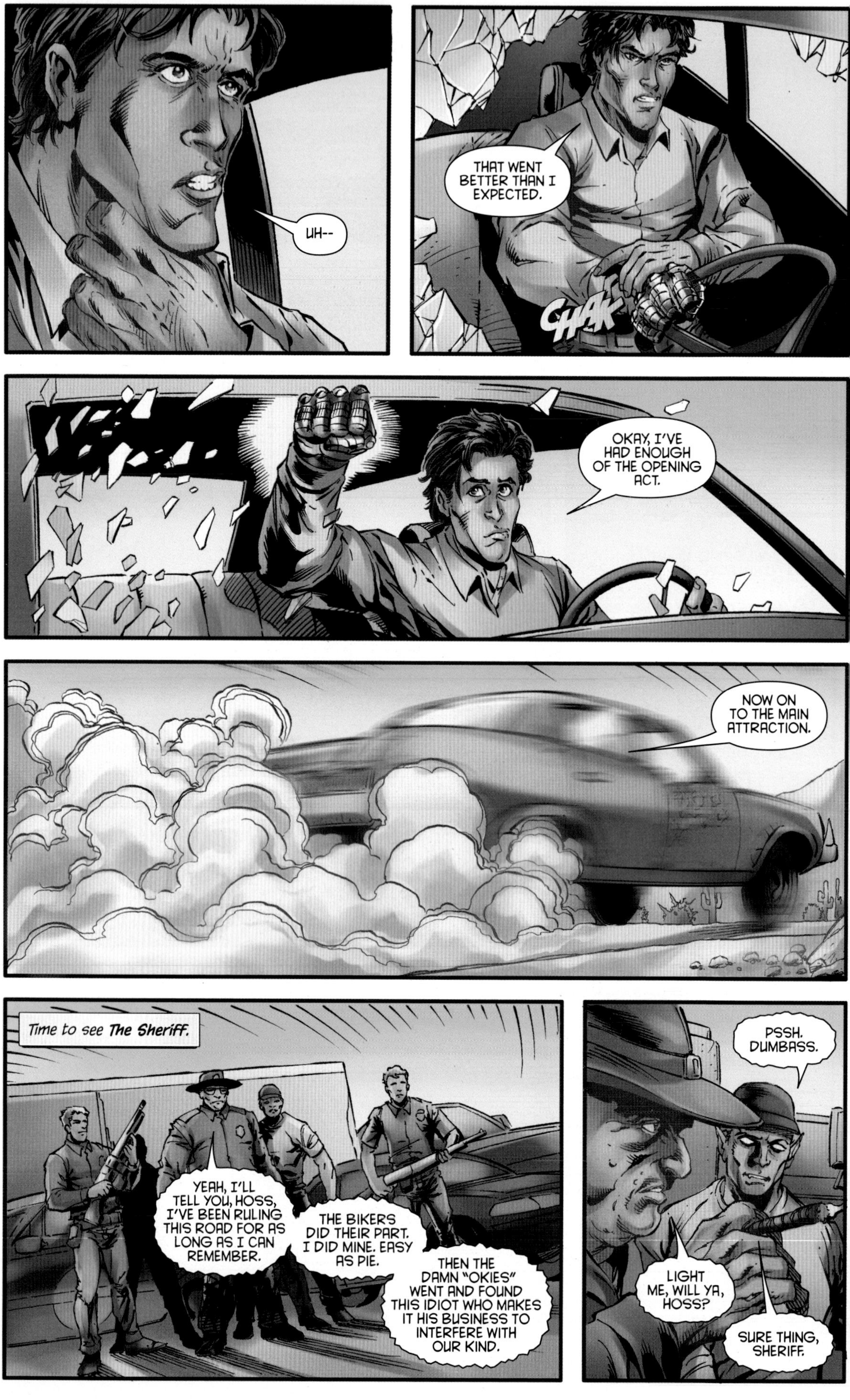
UH--
THAT WENT BETTER THAN I EXPECTED.
CHAK
OKAY, I'VE HAD ENOUGH OF THE OPENING ACT.
NOW ON TO THE MAIN ATTRACTION.
Time to see The Sheriff.
YEAH, I'LL TELL YOU, HOSS, I'VE BEEN RULING THIS ROAD FOR AS LONG AS I CAN REMEMBER.
THE BIKERS DID THEIR PART. I DID MINE. EASY AS PIE.
THEN THE DAMN "OKIES" WENT AND FOUND THIS IDIOT WHO MAKES IT HIS BUSINESS TO INTERFERE WITH OUR KIND.
PSSH. DUMBASS.
LIGHT ME, WILL YA, HOSS?
SURE THING, SHERIFF.

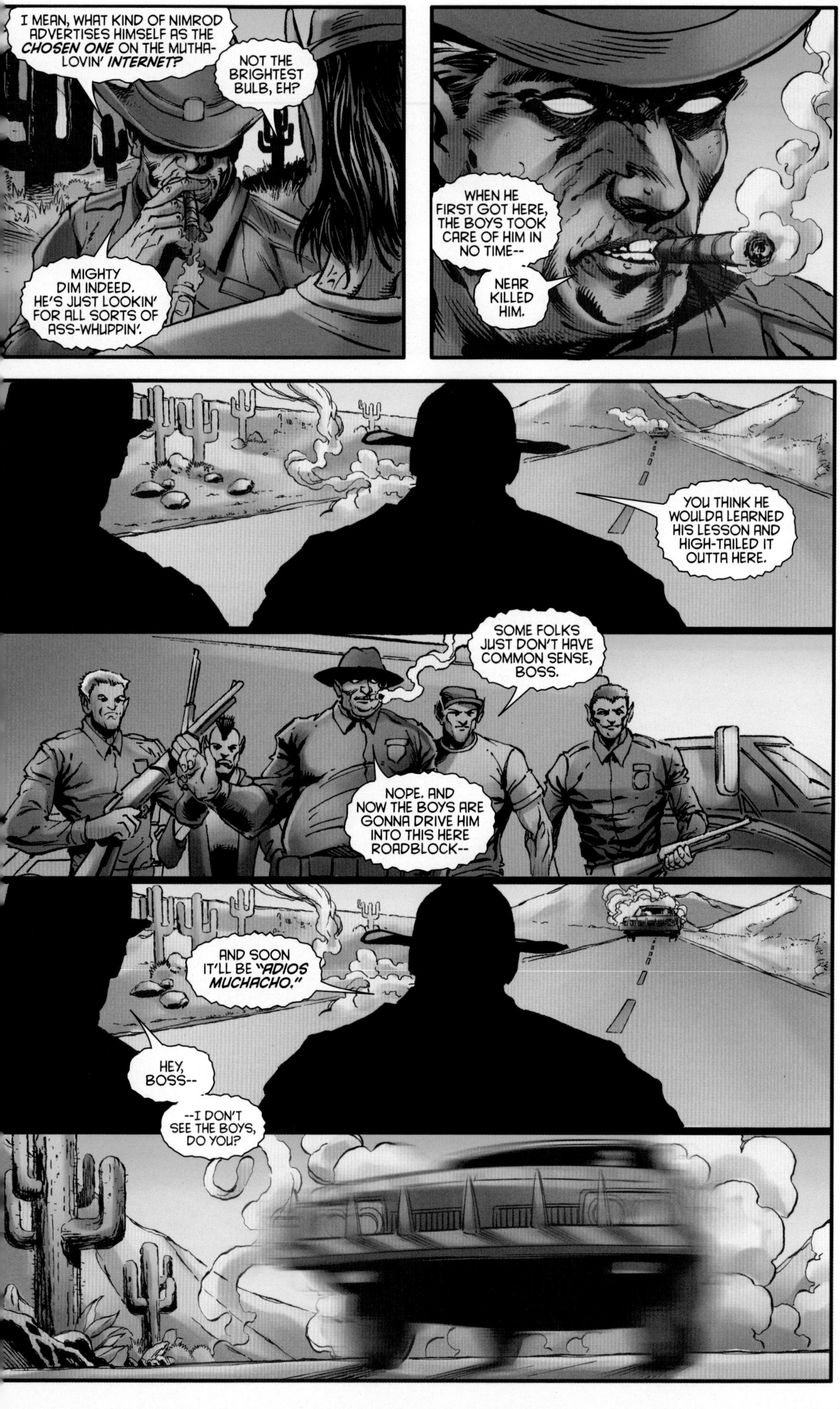
I MEAN, WHAT KIND OF NIMROD ADVERTISES HIMSELF AS THE *CHOSEN ONE* ON THE MUTHA-LOVIN' *INTERNET?*
NOT THE BRIGHTEST BULB, EH?
MIGHTY DIM INDEED. HE'S JUST LOOKIN' FOR ALL SORTS OF ASS-WHUPPIN'.
WHEN HE FIRST GOT HERE, THE BOYS TOOK CARE OF HIM IN NO TIME--
NEAR KILLED HIM.
YOU THINK HE WOULDA LEARNED HIS LESSON AND HIGH-TAILED IT OUTTA HERE.
SOME FOLKS JUST DON'T HAVE COMMON SENSE, BOSS.
NOPE. AND NOW THE BOYS ARE GONNA DRIVE HIM INTO THIS HERE ROADBLOCK--
AND SOON IT'LL BE *"ADIOS MUCHACHO."*
HEY, BOSS--
--I DON'T SEE THE BOYS, DO YOU?

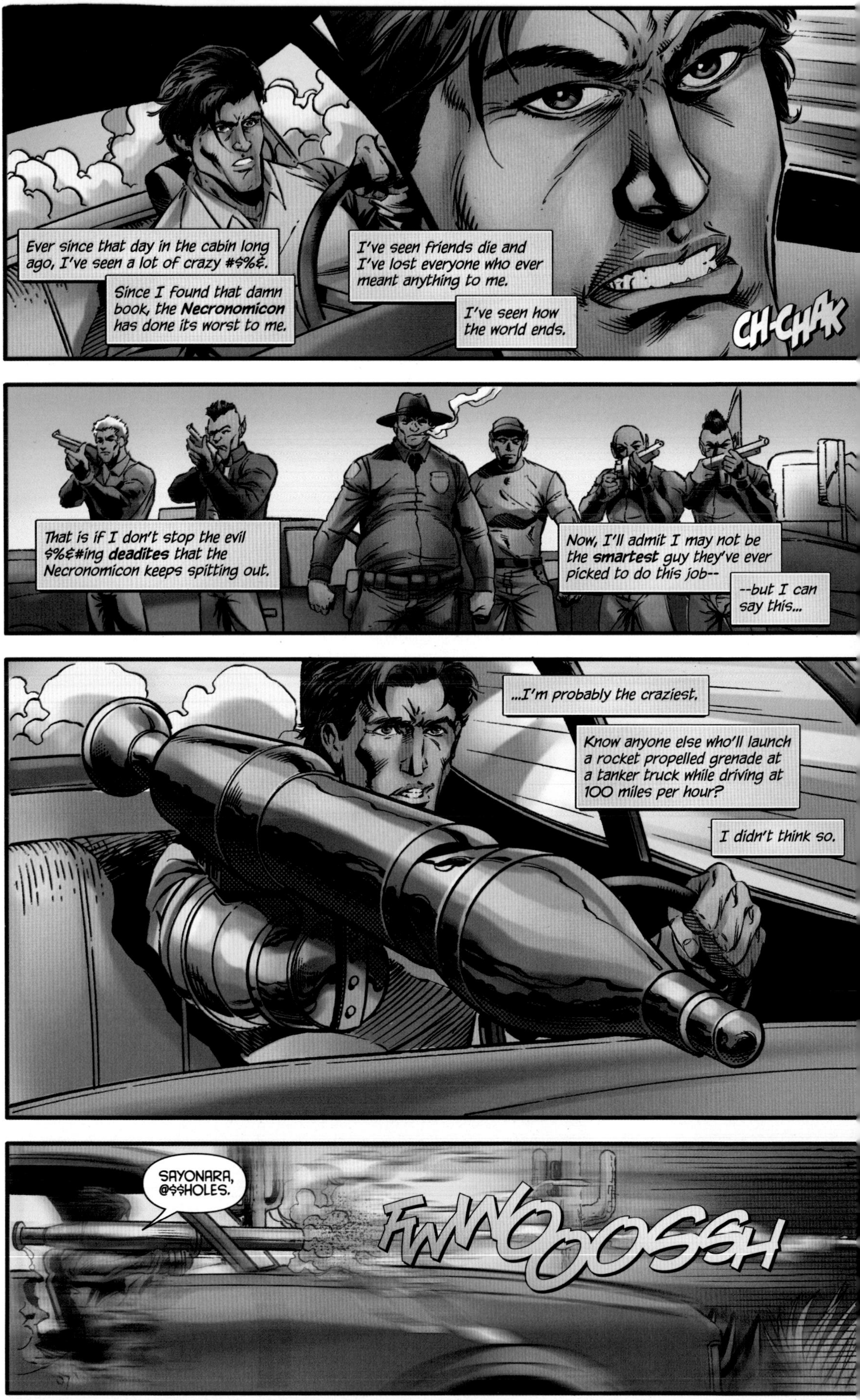

Ever since that day in the cabin long ago, I've seen a lot of crazy #$%&.
Since I found that damn book, the **Necronomicon** has done its worst to me.
I've seen friends die and I've lost everyone who ever meant anything to me.
I've seen how the world ends.
CH-CHAK
That is if I don't stop the evil $%&#ing **deadites** that the Necronomicon keeps spitting out.
Now, I'll admit I may not be the **smartest** guy they've ever picked to do this job--
--but I can say this...
...I'm probably the craziest.
Know anyone else who'll launch a rocket propelled grenade at a tanker truck while driving at 100 miles per hour?
I didn't think so.
SAYONARA, @$$HOLES.
FWWOOOSSH

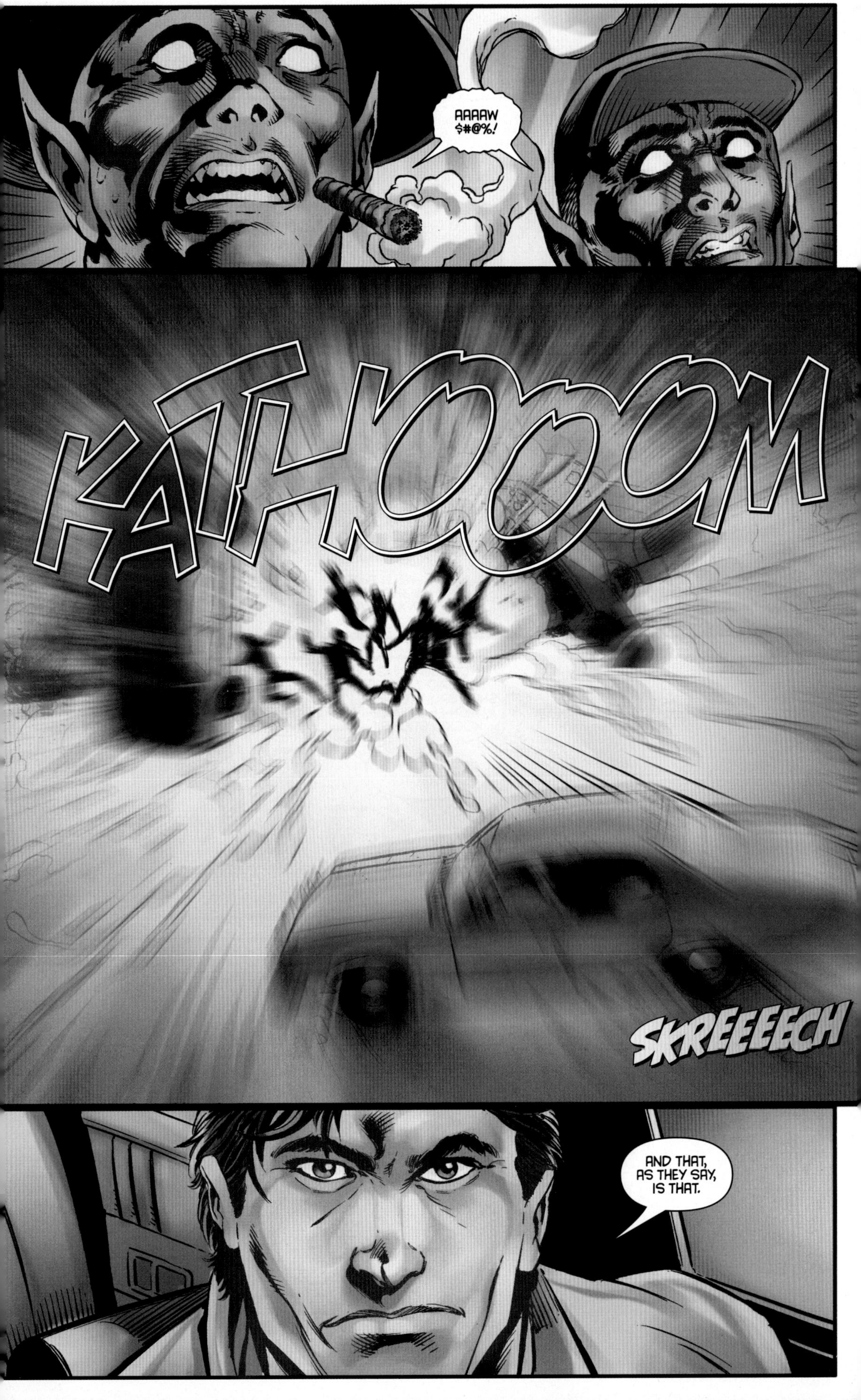
AAAAW
$#@%!
KATHOOOM
SKREEEECH
AND THAT, AS THEY SAY, IS THAT.

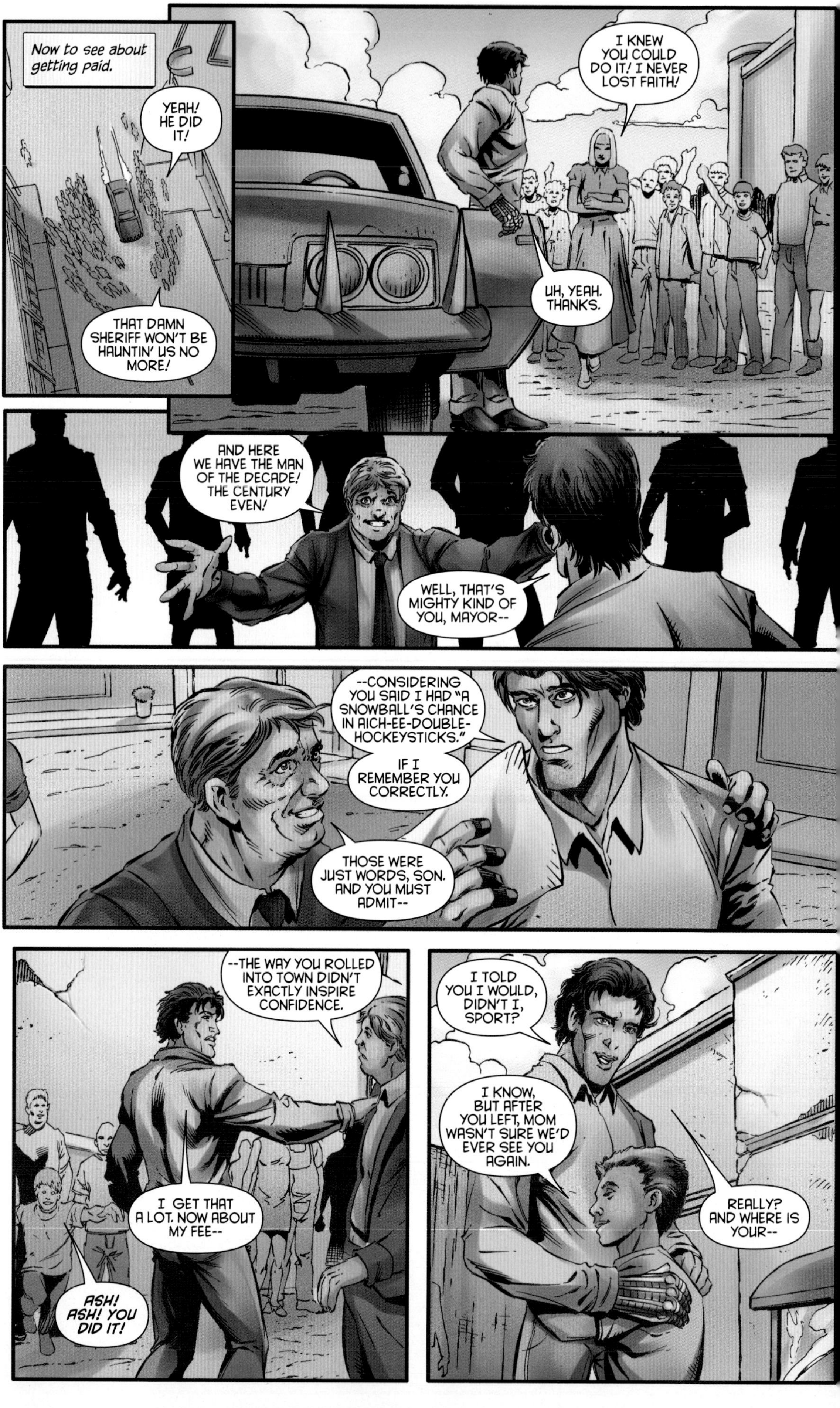
Now to see about getting paid.
YEAH! HE DID IT!
THAT DAMN SHERIFF WON'T BE HAUNTIN' US NO MORE!
I KNEW YOU COULD DO IT! I NEVER LOST FAITH!
UH, YEAH. THANKS.
AND HERE WE HAVE THE MAN OF THE DECADE! THE CENTURY EVEN!
WELL, THAT'S MIGHTY KIND OF YOU, MAYOR--
--CONSIDERING YOU SAID I HAD "A SNOWBALL'S CHANCE IN AICH-EE-DOUBLE-HOCKEYSTICKS."
IF I REMEMBER YOU CORRECTLY.
THOSE WERE JUST WORDS, SON. AND YOU MUST ADMIT--
--THE WAY YOU ROLLED INTO TOWN DIDN'T EXACTLY INSPIRE CONFIDENCE.
I GET THAT A LOT. NOW ABOUT MY FEE--
ASH! ASH! YOU DID IT!
I TOLD YOU I WOULD, DIDN'T I, SPORT?
I KNOW, BUT AFTER YOU LEFT, MOM WASN'T SURE WE'D EVER SEE YOU AGAIN.
REALLY? AND WHERE IS YOUR--

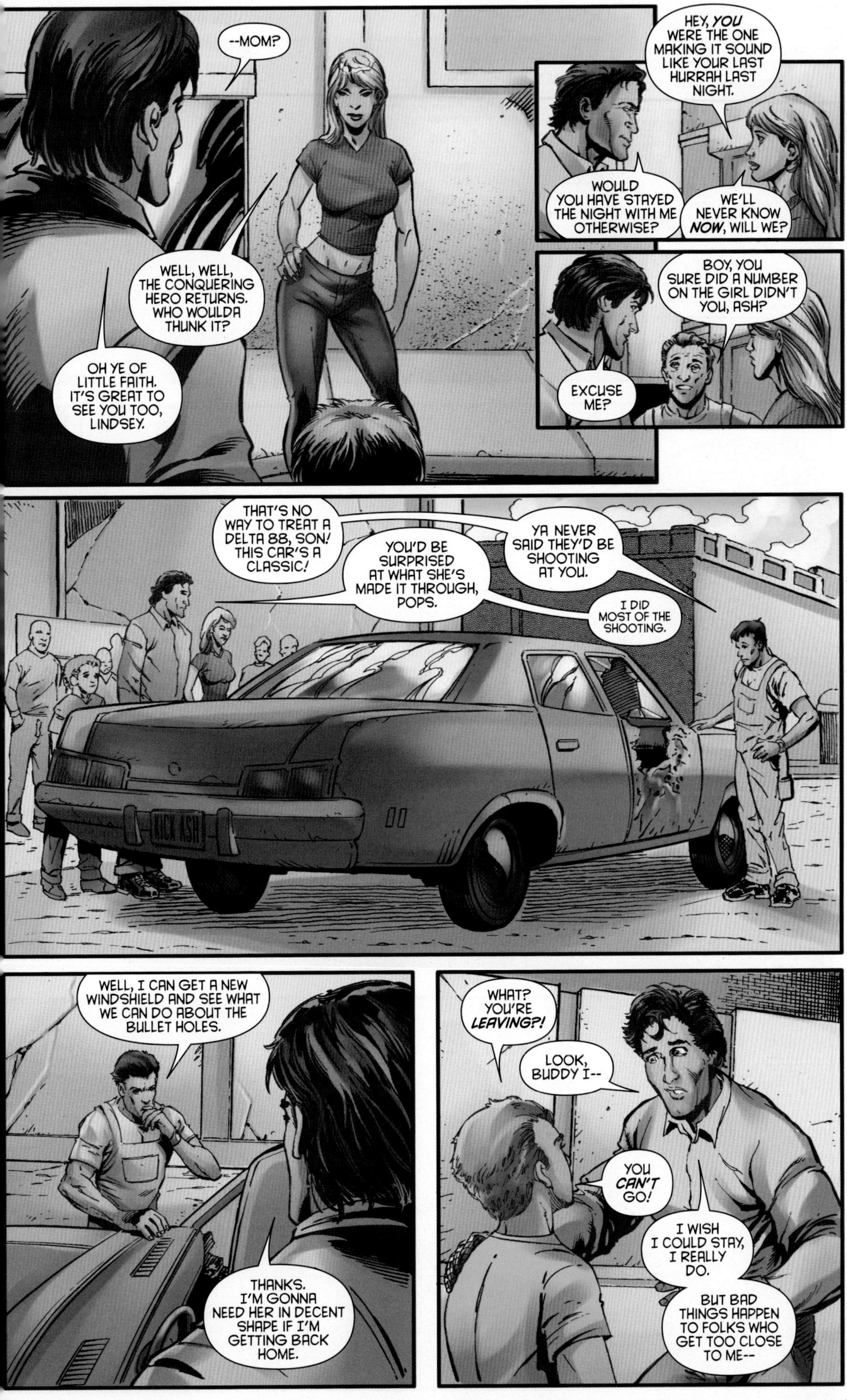
--MOM?
WELL, WELL, THE CONQUERING HERO RETURNS. WHO WOULDA THUNK IT?
OH YE OF LITTLE FAITH. IT'S GREAT TO SEE YOU TOO, LINDSEY.
HEY, YOU WERE THE ONE MAKING IT SOUND LIKE YOUR LAST HURRAH LAST NIGHT.
WOULD YOU HAVE STAYED THE NIGHT WITH ME OTHERWISE?
WE'LL NEVER KNOW NOW, WILL WE?
BOY, YOU SURE DID A NUMBER ON THE GIRL DIDN'T YOU, ASH?
EXCUSE ME?
THAT'S NO WAY TO TREAT A DELTA 88, SON! THIS CAR'S A CLASSIC!
YOU'D BE SURPRISED AT WHAT SHE'S MADE IT THROUGH, POPS.
YA NEVER SAID THEY'D BE SHOOTING AT YOU.
I DID MOST OF THE SHOOTING.
KICK ASH
WELL, I CAN GET A NEW WINDSHIELD AND SEE WHAT WE CAN DO ABOUT THE BULLET HOLES.
THANKS. I'M GONNA NEED HER IN DECENT SHAPE IF I'M GETTING BACK HOME.
WHAT? YOU'RE LEAVING?!
LOOK, BUDDY I--
YOU CAN'T GO!
I WISH I COULD STAY, I REALLY DO.
BUT BAD THINGS HAPPEN TO FOLKS WHO GET TOO CLOSE TO ME--

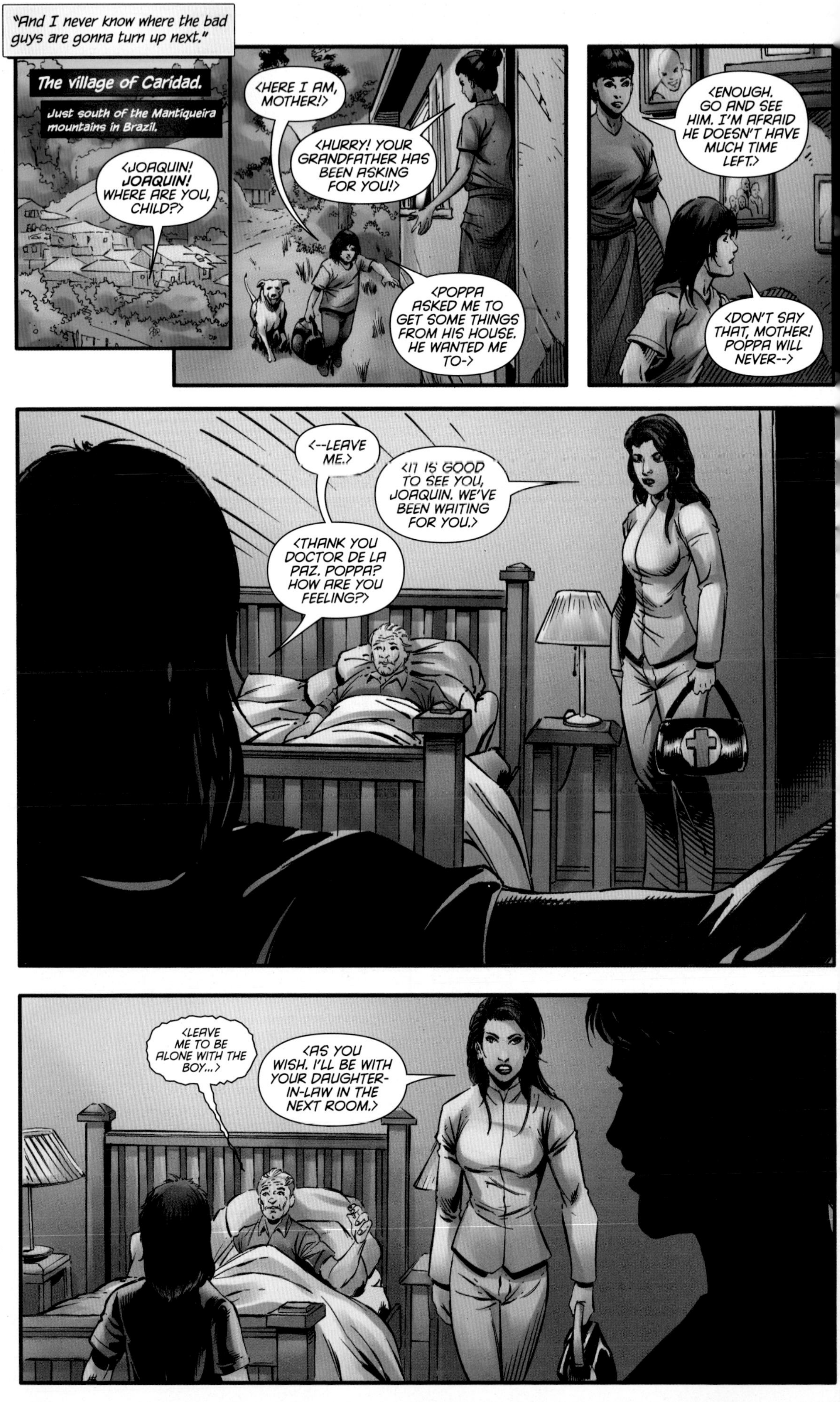
"And I never know where the bad guys are gonna turn up next."
The village of Caridad.
Just south of the Mantiqueira mountains in Brazil.
<JOAQUIN! **JOAQUIN!** WHERE ARE YOU, CHILD?>
<HERE I AM, MOTHER!>
<HURRY! YOUR GRANDFATHER HAS BEEN ASKING FOR YOU!>
<POPPA ASKED ME TO GET SOME THINGS FROM HIS HOUSE. HE WANTED ME TO->
<ENOUGH. GO AND SEE HIM. I'M AFRAID HE DOESN'T HAVE MUCH TIME LEFT.>
<DON'T SAY THAT, MOTHER! POPPA WILL NEVER-->
<--LEAVE ME.>
<IT IS GOOD TO SEE YOU, JOAQUIN. WE'VE BEEN WAITING FOR YOU.>
<THANK YOU DOCTOR DE LA PAZ. POPPA? HOW ARE YOU FEELING?>
<LEAVE ME TO BE ALONE WITH THE BOY...>
<AS YOU WISH. I'LL BE WITH YOUR DAUGHTER-IN-LAW IN THE NEXT ROOM.>

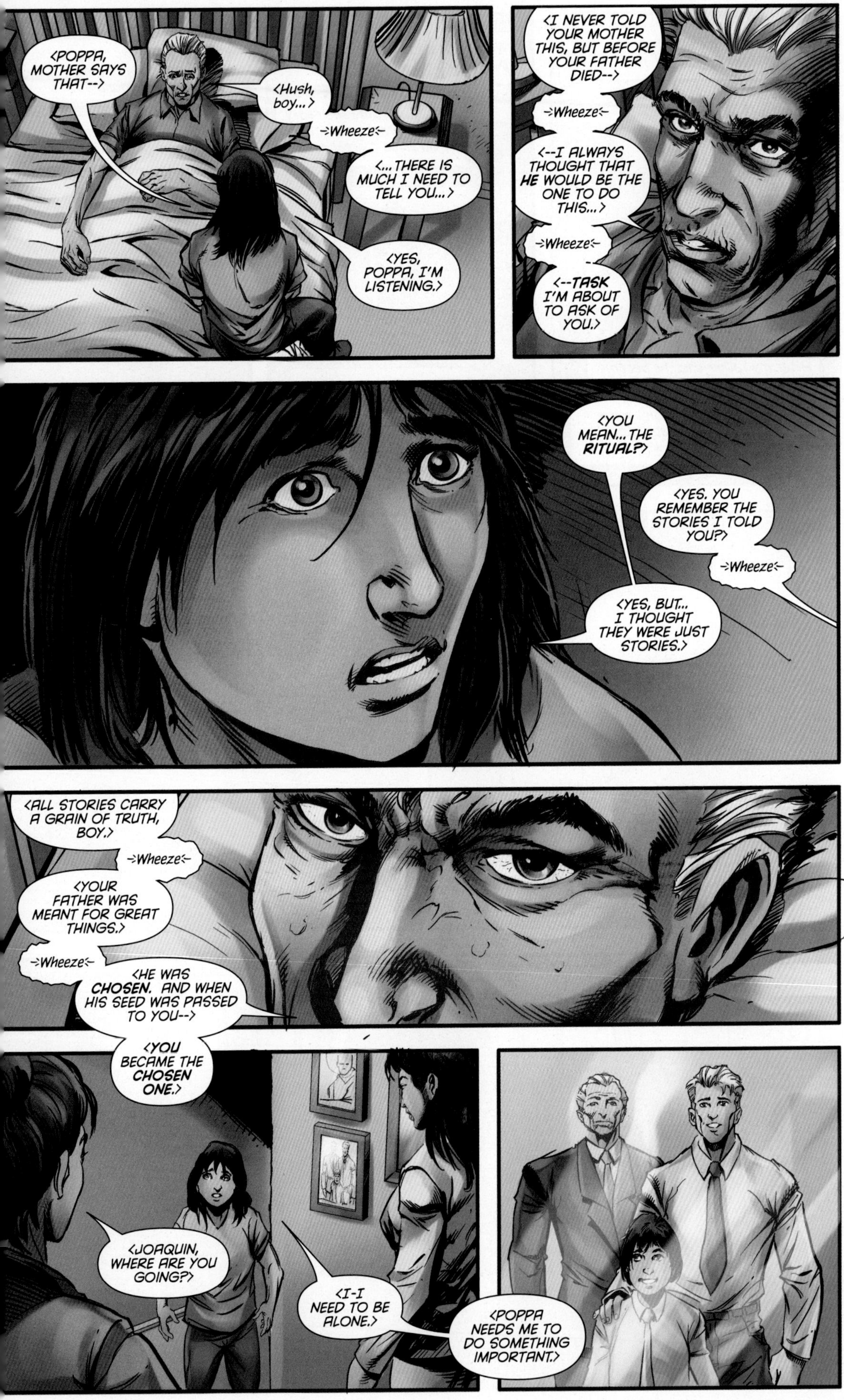
<POPPA, MOTHER SAYS THAT-->
<Hush, boy...>
->Wheeze<-
<...THERE IS MUCH I NEED TO TELL YOU...>
<YES, POPPA, I'M LISTENING.>
<I NEVER TOLD YOUR MOTHER THIS, BUT BEFORE YOUR FATHER DIED-->
->Wheeze<-
<--I ALWAYS THOUGHT THAT **HE** WOULD BE THE ONE TO DO THIS...>
->Wheeze<-
<--**TASK** I'M ABOUT TO ASK OF YOU.>
<YOU MEAN... THE **RITUAL?**>
<YES. YOU REMEMBER THE STORIES I TOLD YOU?>
->Wheeze<-
<YES, BUT... I THOUGHT THEY WERE JUST STORIES.>
<ALL STORIES CARRY A GRAIN OF TRUTH, BOY.>
->Wheeze<-
<YOUR FATHER WAS MEANT FOR GREAT THINGS.>
->Wheeze<-
<HE WAS **CHOSEN.** AND WHEN HIS SEED WAS PASSED TO YOU-->
<**YOU** BECAME THE **CHOSEN ONE.**>
<JOAQUIN, WHERE ARE YOU GOING?>
<I-I NEED TO BE ALONE.>
<POPPA NEEDS ME TO DO SOMETHING IMPORTANT.>

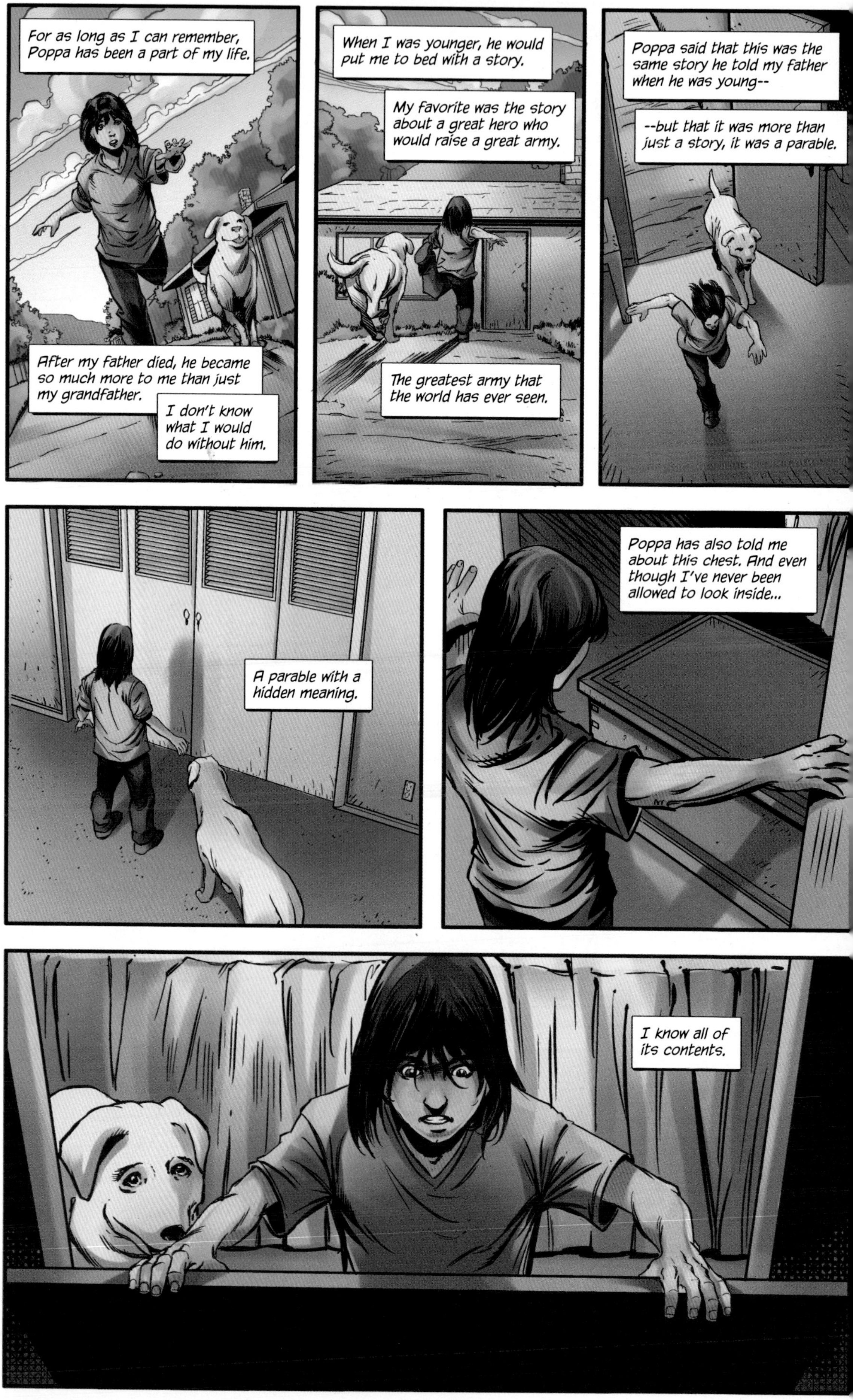
For as long as I can remember, Poppa has been a part of my life.
After my father died, he became so much more to me than just my grandfather.
I don't know what I would do without him.
When I was younger, he would put me to bed with a story.
My favorite was the story about a great hero who would raise a great army.
The greatest army that the world has ever seen.
Poppa said that this was the same story he told my father when he was young--
--but that it was more than just a story, it was a parable.
A parable with a hidden meaning.
Poppa has also told me about this chest. And even though I've never been allowed to look inside...
I know all of its contents.

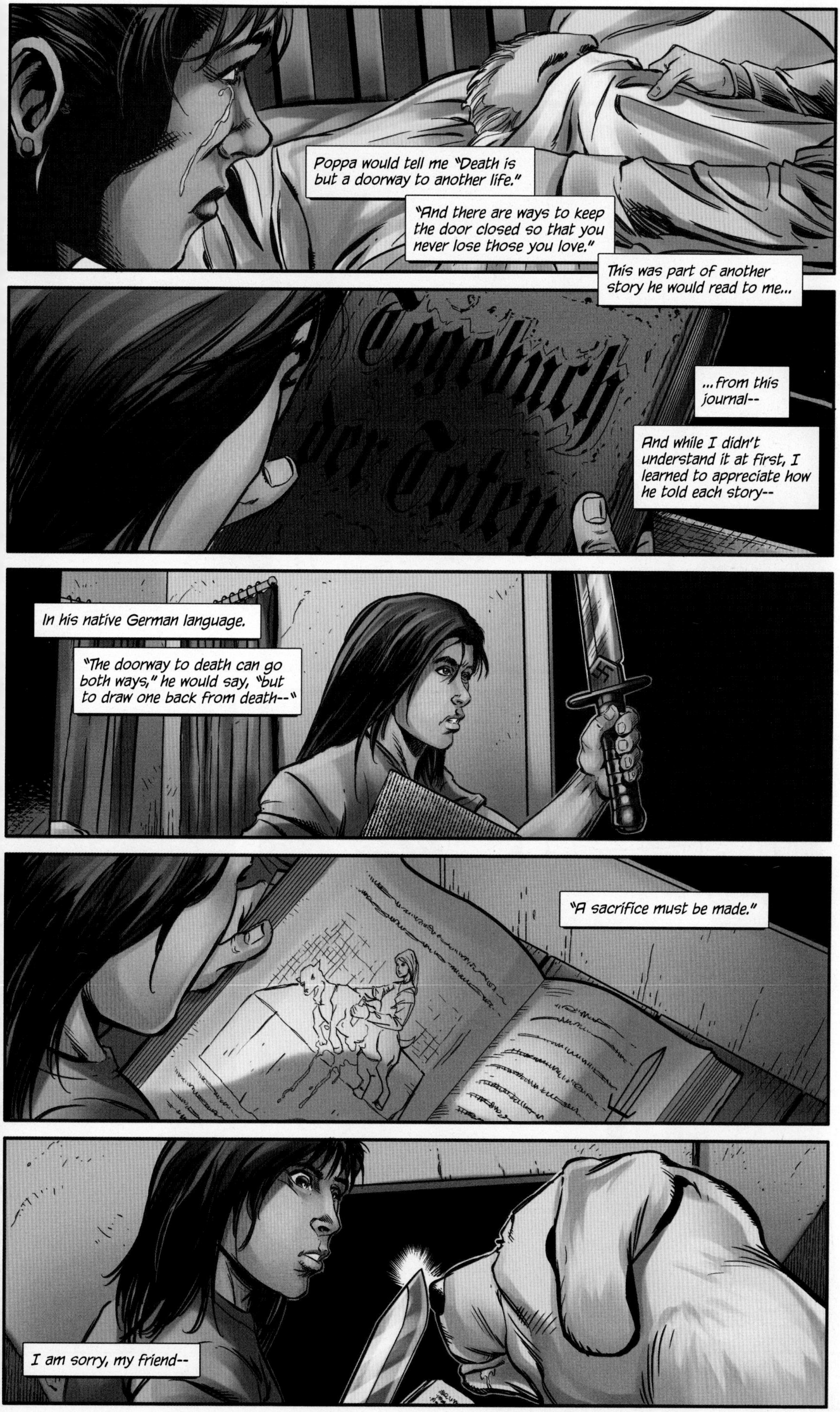
Poppa would tell me "Death is but a doorway to another life."
"And there are ways to keep the door closed so that you never lose those you love."
This was part of another story he would read to me...
...from this journal--
And while I didn't understand it at first, I learned to appreciate how he told each story--
In his native German language.
"The doorway to death can go both ways," he would say, "but to draw one back from death--"
"A sacrifice must be made."
I am sorry, my friend--

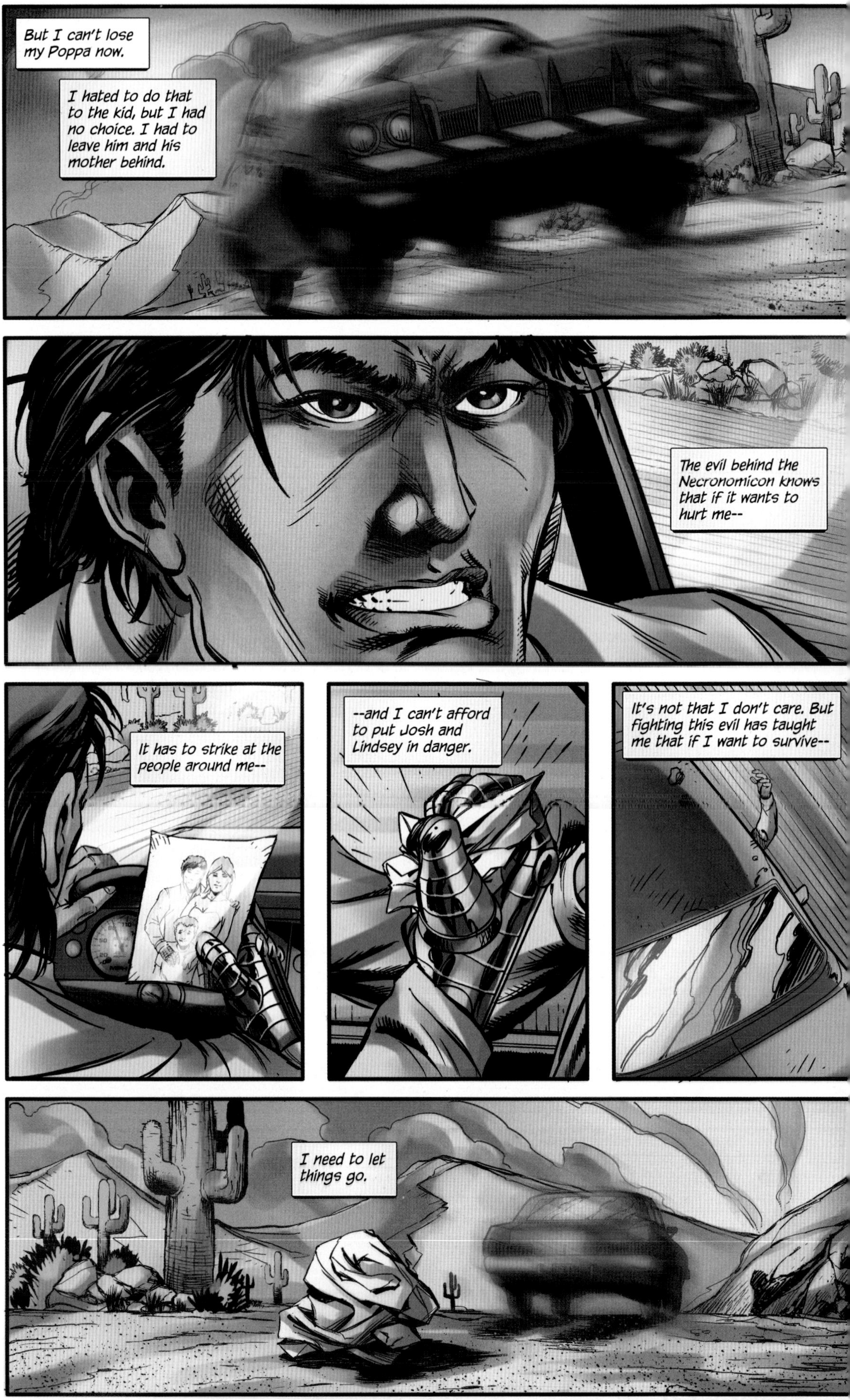

But I can't lose my Poppa now.
I hated to do that to the kid, but I had no choice. I had to leave him and his mother behind.
The evil behind the Necronomicon knows that if it wants to hurt me--
It has to strike at the people around me--
--and I can't afford to put Josh and Lindsey in danger.
It's not that I don't care. But fighting this evil has taught me that if I want to survive--
I need to let things go.

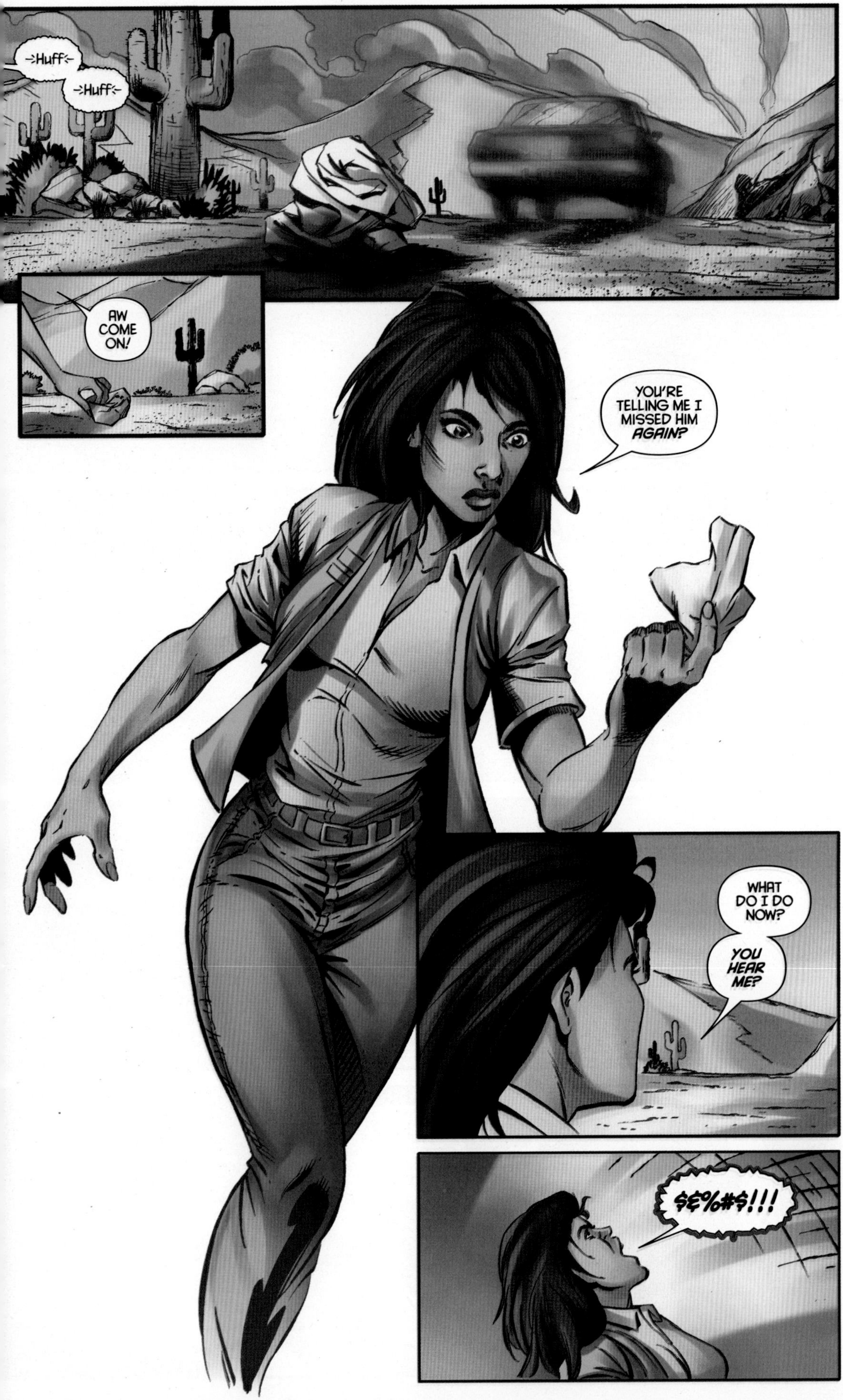

-=Huff=-
-=Huff=-
AW COME ON!
YOU'RE TELLING ME I MISSED HIM *AGAIN?*
WHAT DO I DO NOW?
YOU HEAR ME?
$€%#$!!!

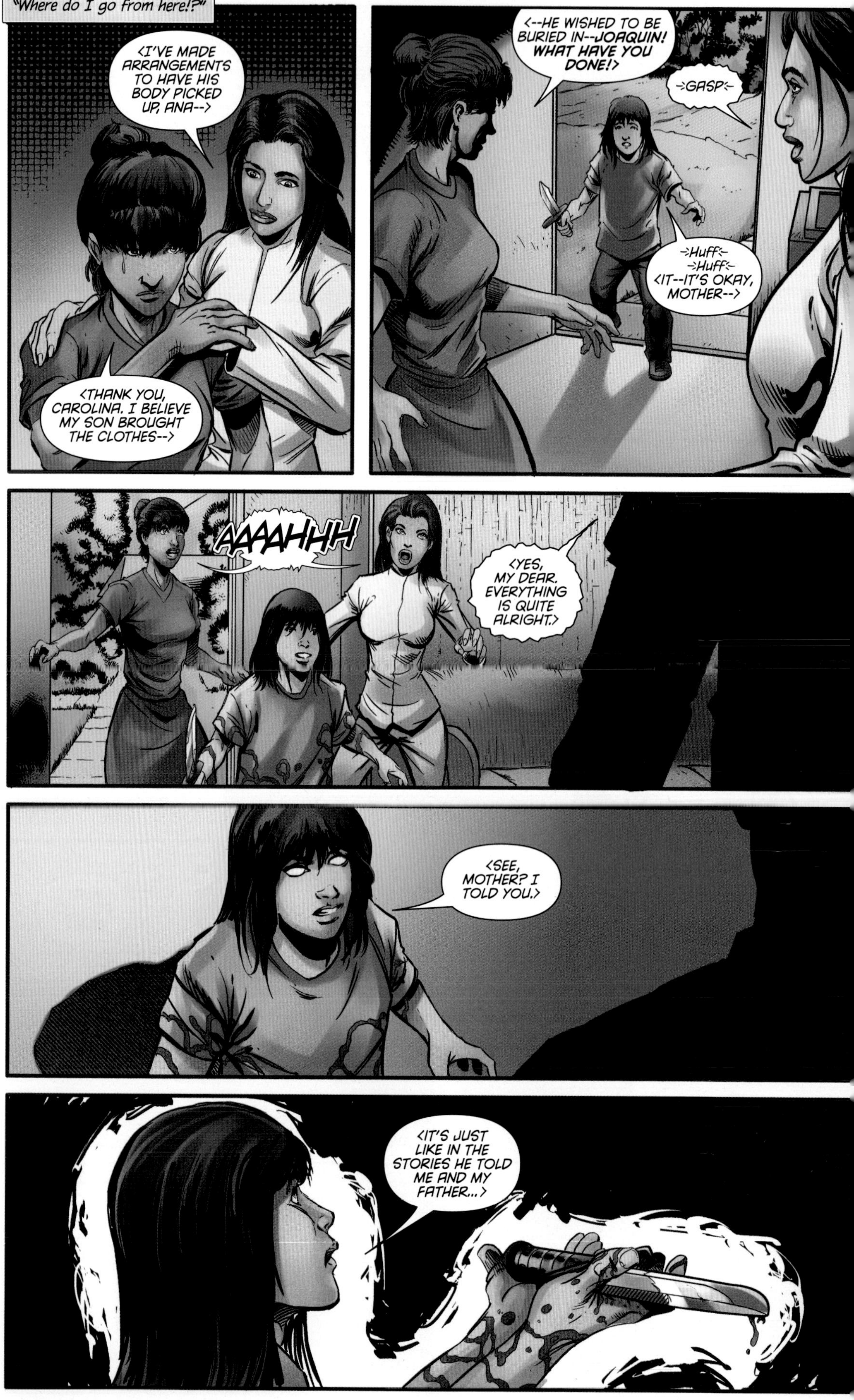
"Where do I go from here!?"
<I'VE MADE ARRANGEMENTS TO HAVE HIS BODY PICKED UP, ANA-->
<THANK YOU, CAROLINA. I BELIEVE MY SON BROUGHT THE CLOTHES-->
<--HE WISHED TO BE BURIED IN--JOAQUIN! WHAT HAVE YOU DONE!>
-GASP-
-Huff- -Huff- <IT--IT'S OKAY, MOTHER-->
AAAAHHH
<YES, MY DEAR. EVERYTHING IS QUITE ALRIGHT.>
<SEE, MOTHER? I TOLD YOU.>
<IT'S JUST LIKE IN THE STORIES HE TOLD ME AND MY FATHER...>

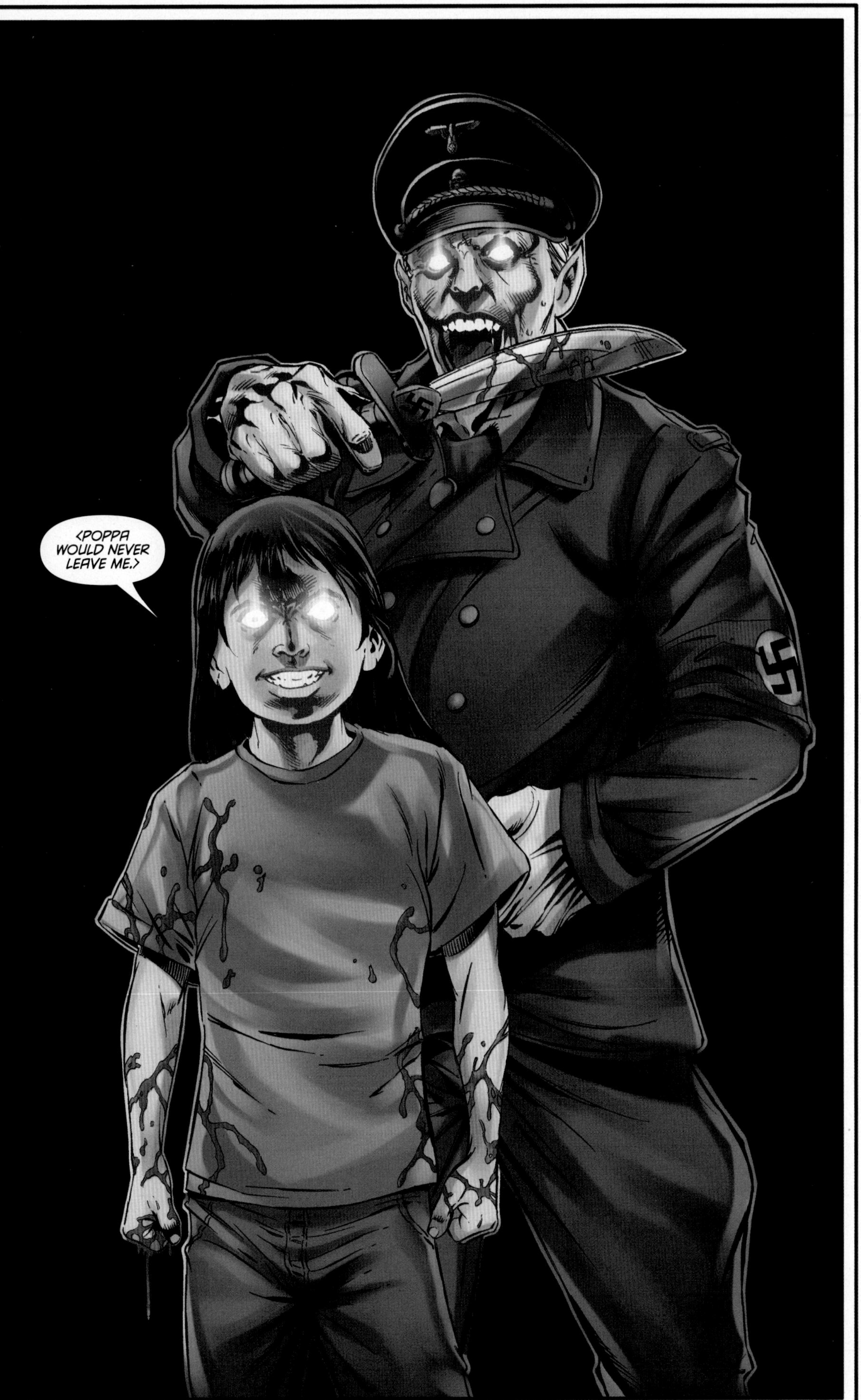
<POPPA WOULD NEVER LEAVE ME.>

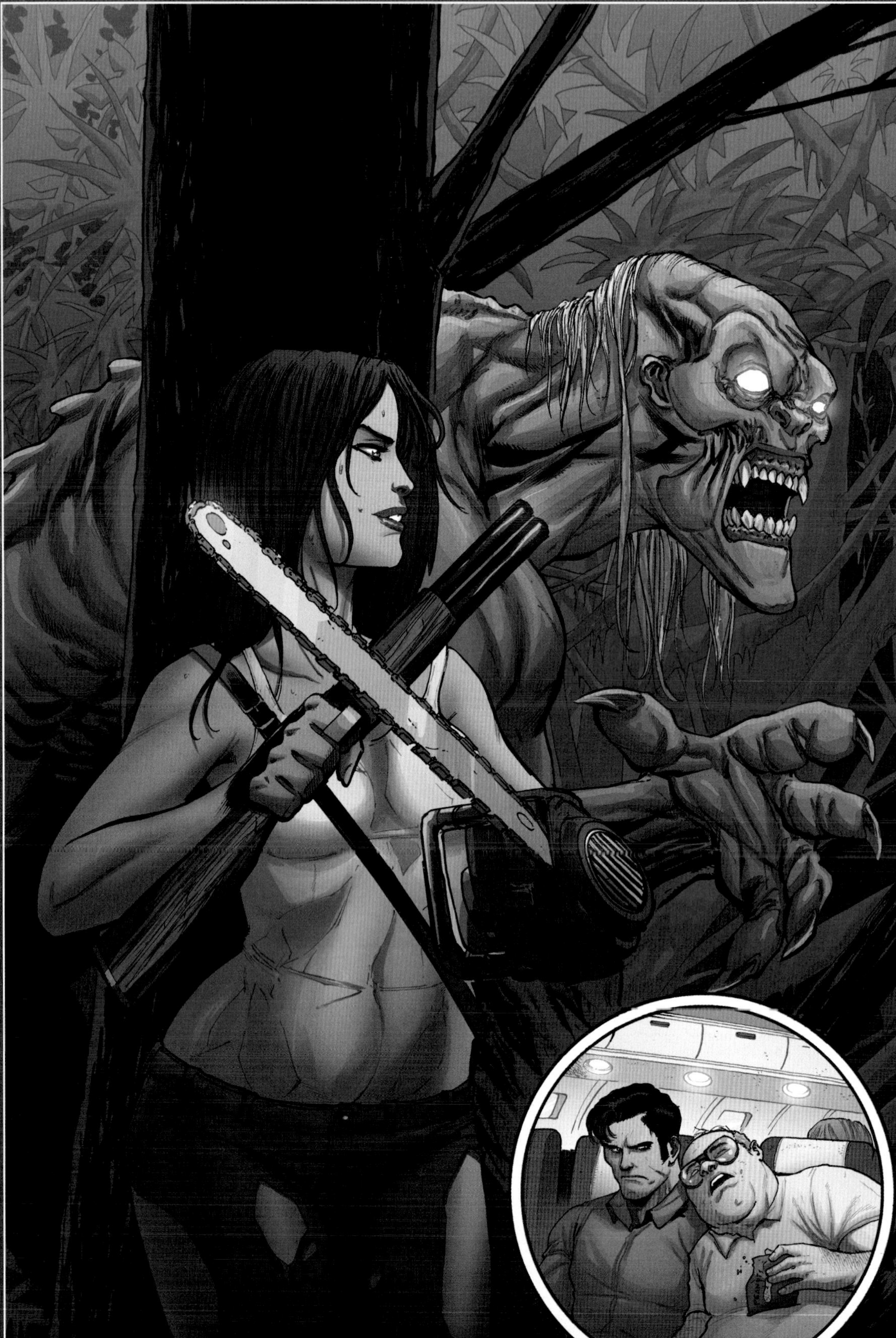

cover to issue #3 by TIM SEELEY, colors by ADRIANO LUCAS

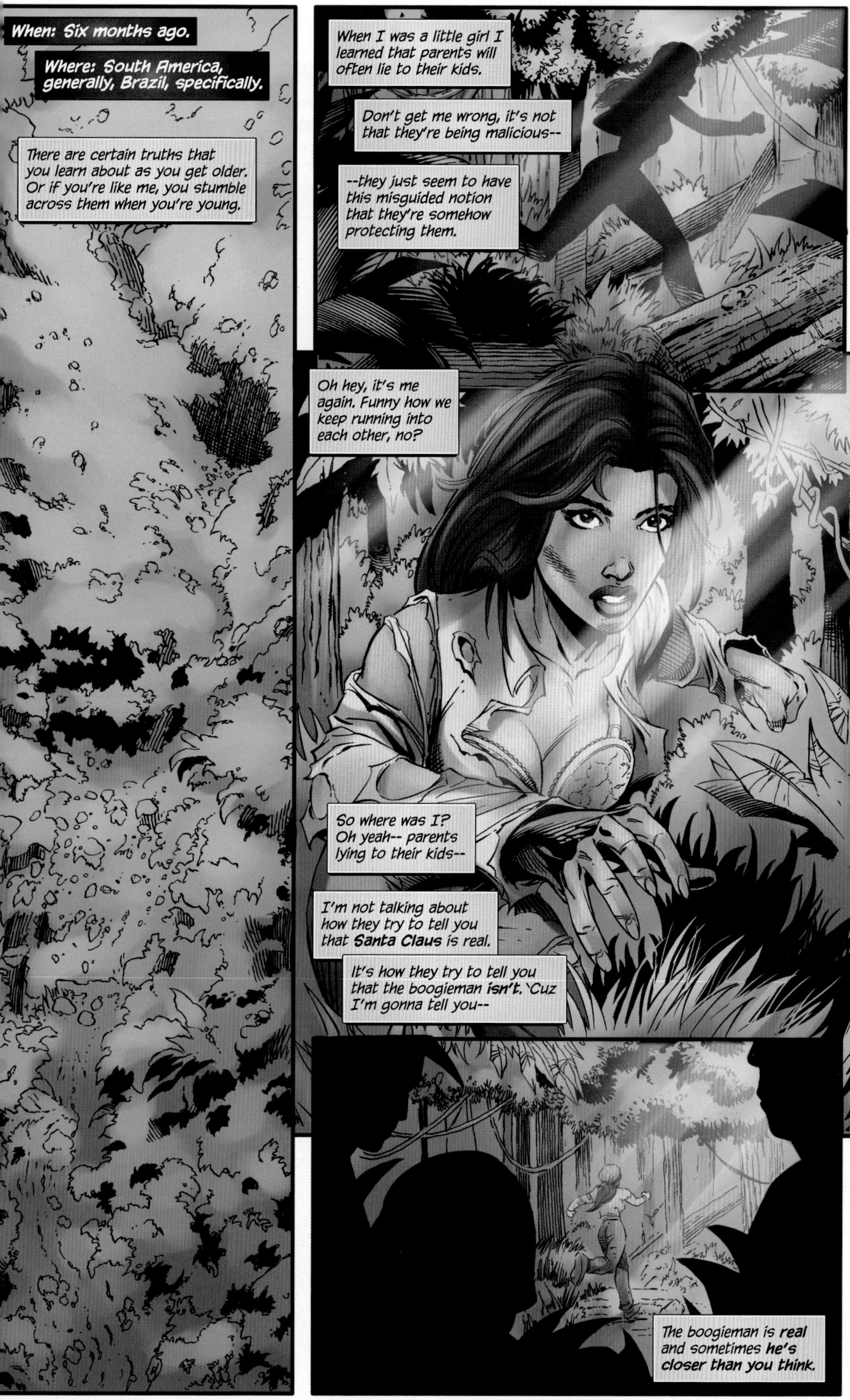
When: Six months ago.
Where: South America, generally, Brazil, specifically.
There are certain truths that you learn about as you get older. Or if you're like me, you stumble across them when you're young.
When I was a little girl I learned that parents will often lie to their kids.
Don't get me wrong, it's not that they're being malicious--
--they just seem to have this misguided notion that they're somehow protecting them.
Oh hey, it's me again. Funny how we keep running into each other, no?
So where was I? Oh yeah-- parents lying to their kids--
I'm not talking about how they try to tell you that **Santa Claus** is real.
It's how they try to tell you that the boogieman ***isn't.*** 'Cuz I'm gonna tell you--
The boogieman is ***real*** and sometimes ***he's closer than you think.***

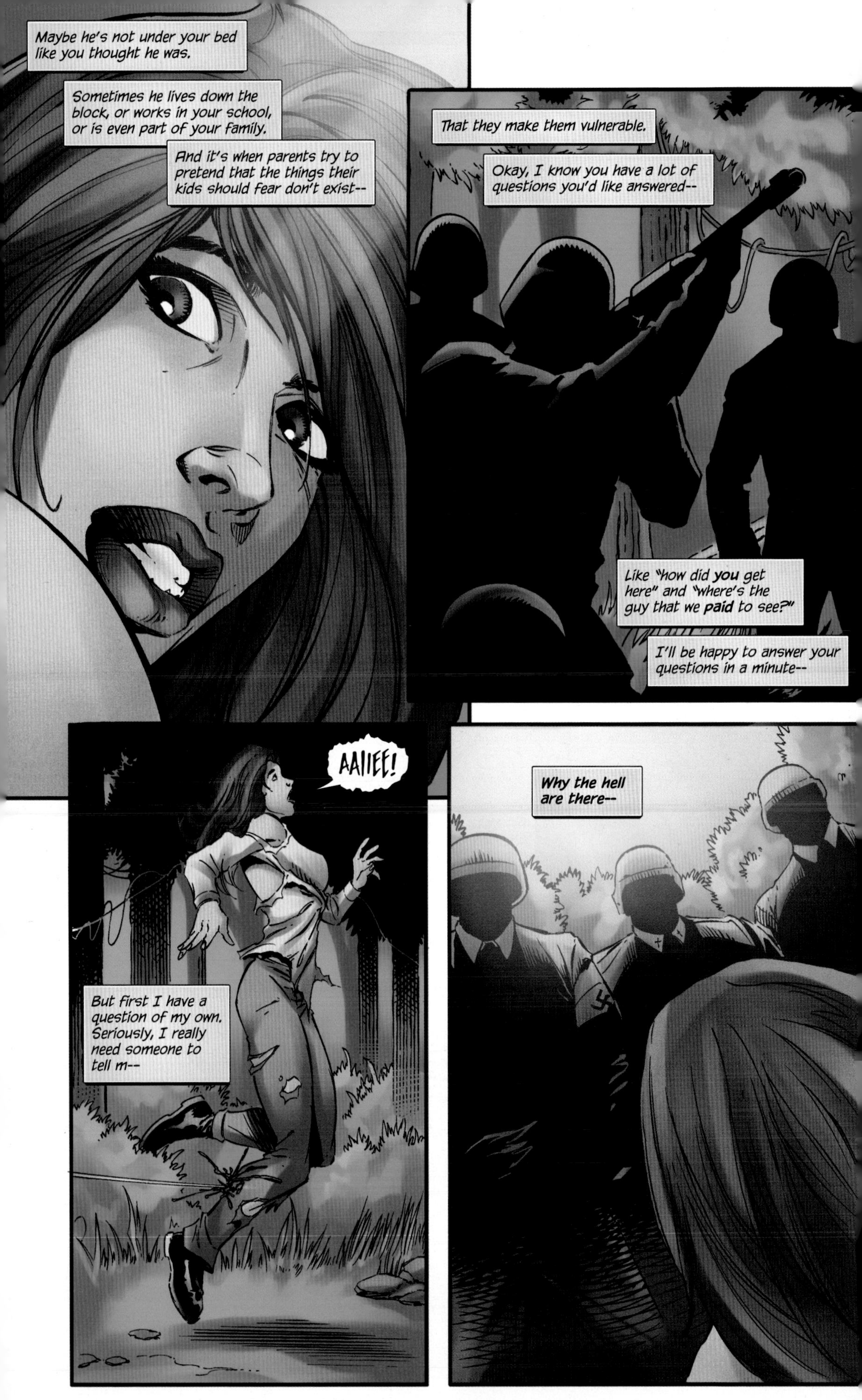
Maybe he's not under your bed like you thought he was.
Sometimes he lives down the block, or works in your school, or is even part of your family.
And it's when parents try to pretend that the things their kids should fear don't exist--
That they make them vulnerable.
Okay, I know you have a lot of questions you'd like answered--
Like "how did **you** get here" and "where's the guy that we **paid** to see?"
I'll be happy to answer your questions in a minute--
AAIIEE!
But first I have a question of my own. Seriously, I really need someone to tell m--
Why the hell are there--

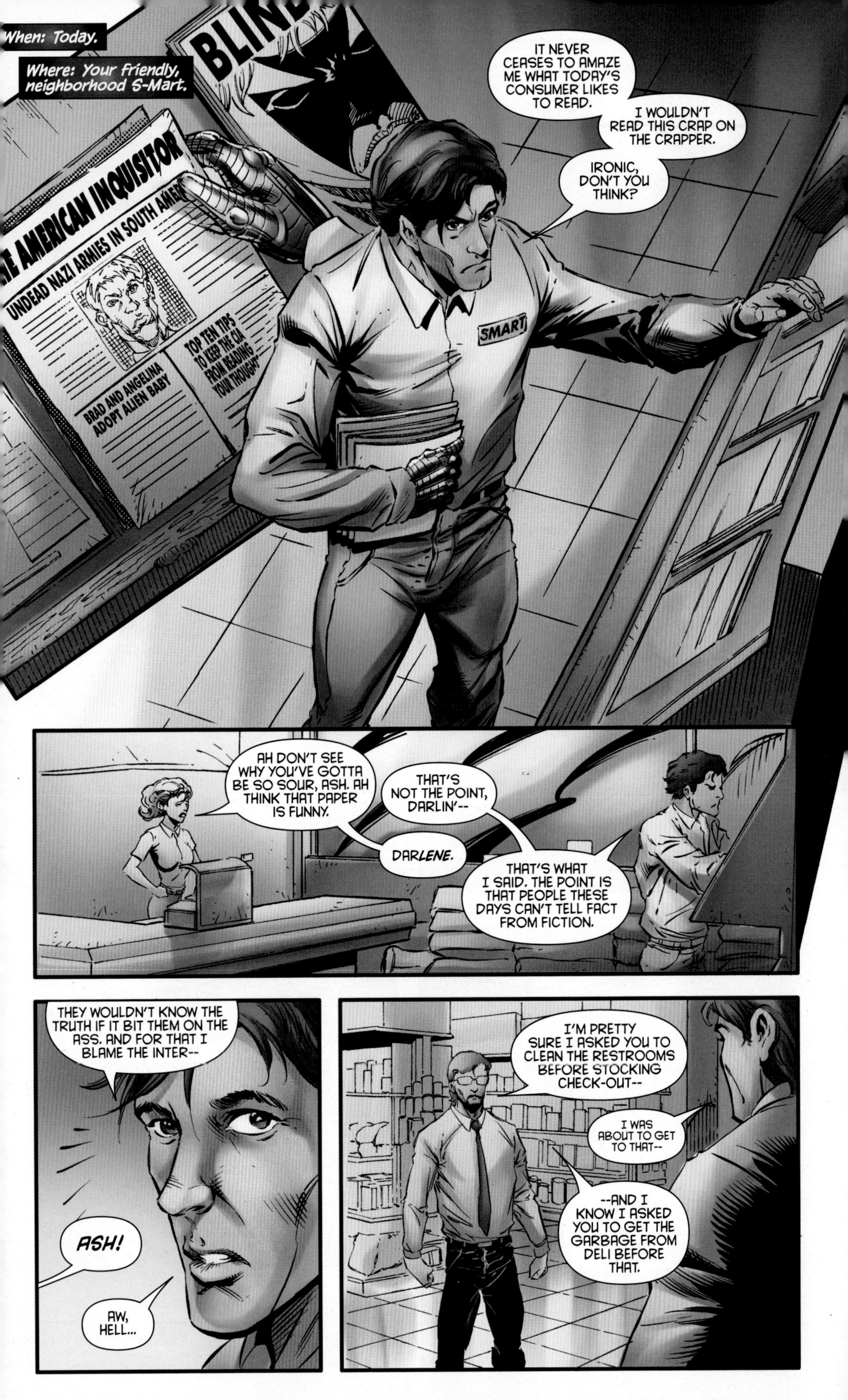
When: Today.
Where: Your friendly, neighborhood S-Mart.
BLIN
THE AMERICAN INQUISITOR
UNDEAD NAZI ARMIES IN SOUTH AME
BRAD AND ANGELINA ADOPT ALIEN BABY
TOP TEN TIPS TO KEEP THE CIA FROM READING YOUR THOUGHT
SMART
IT NEVER CEASES TO AMAZE ME WHAT TODAY'S CONSUMER LIKES TO READ.
I WOULDN'T READ THIS CRAP ON THE CRAPPER.
IRONIC, DON'T YOU THINK?
AH DON'T SEE WHY YOU'VE GOTTA BE SO SOUR, ASH. AH THINK THAT PAPER IS FUNNY.
THAT'S NOT THE POINT, DARLIN'--
DARLENE.
THAT'S WHAT I SAID. THE POINT IS THAT PEOPLE THESE DAYS CAN'T TELL FACT FROM FICTION.
THEY WOULDN'T KNOW THE TRUTH IF IT BIT THEM ON THE ASS. AND FOR THAT I BLAME THE INTER--
ASH!
AW, HELL...
I'M PRETTY SURE I ASKED YOU TO CLEAN THE RESTROOMS BEFORE STOCKING CHECK-OUT--
I WAS ABOUT TO GET TO THAT--
--AND I KNOW I ASKED YOU TO GET THE GARBAGE FROM DELI BEFORE THAT.

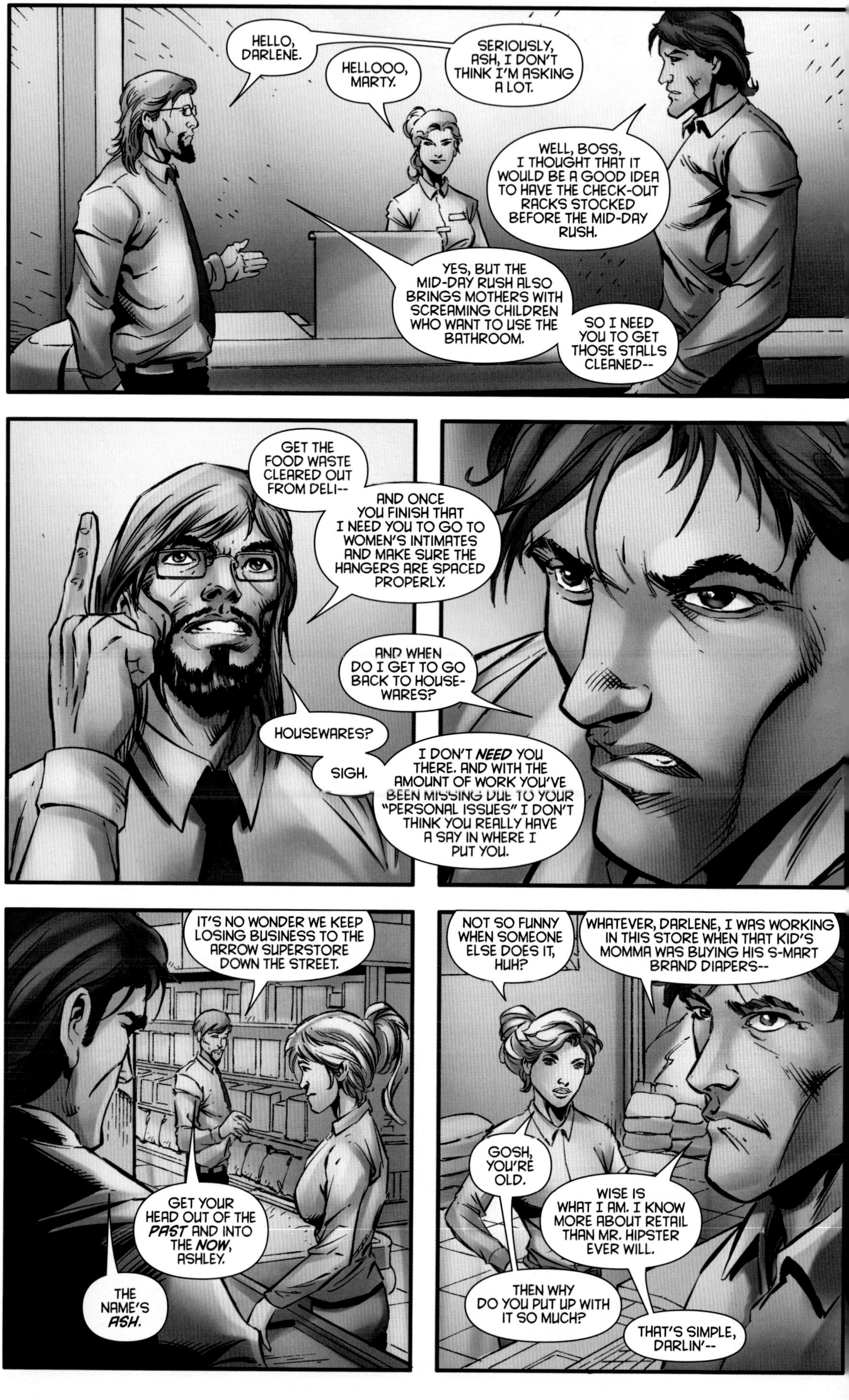
HELLO, DARLENE.
HELLOOO, MARTY.
SERIOUSLY, ASH, I DON'T THINK I'M ASKING A LOT.
WELL, BOSS, I THOUGHT THAT IT WOULD BE A GOOD IDEA TO HAVE THE CHECK-OUT RACKS STOCKED BEFORE THE MID-DAY RUSH.
YES, BUT THE MID-DAY RUSH ALSO BRINGS MOTHERS WITH SCREAMING CHILDREN WHO WANT TO USE THE BATHROOM.
SO I NEED YOU TO GET THOSE STALLS CLEANED--
GET THE FOOD WASTE CLEARED OUT FROM DELI--
AND ONCE YOU FINISH THAT I NEED YOU TO GO TO WOMEN'S INTIMATES AND MAKE SURE THE HANGERS ARE SPACED PROPERLY.
AND WHEN DO I GET TO GO BACK TO HOUSE-WARES?
HOUSEWARES?
SIGH.
I DON'T NEED YOU THERE. AND WITH THE AMOUNT OF WORK YOU'VE BEEN MISSING DUE TO YOUR "PERSONAL ISSUES" I DON'T THINK YOU REALLY HAVE A SAY IN WHERE I PUT YOU.
IT'S NO WONDER WE KEEP LOSING BUSINESS TO THE ARROW SUPERSTORE DOWN THE STREET.
GET YOUR HEAD OUT OF THE PAST AND INTO THE NOW, ASHLEY.
THE NAME'S ASH.
NOT SO FUNNY WHEN SOMEONE ELSE DOES IT, HUH?
WHATEVER, DARLENE, I WAS WORKING IN THIS STORE WHEN THAT KID'S MOMMA WAS BUYING HIS S-MART BRAND DIAPERS--
GOSH, YOU'RE OLD.
WISE IS WHAT I AM. I KNOW MORE ABOUT RETAIL THAN MR. HIPSTER EVER WILL.
THEN WHY DO YOU PUT UP WITH IT SO MUCH?
THAT'S SIMPLE, DARLIN'--

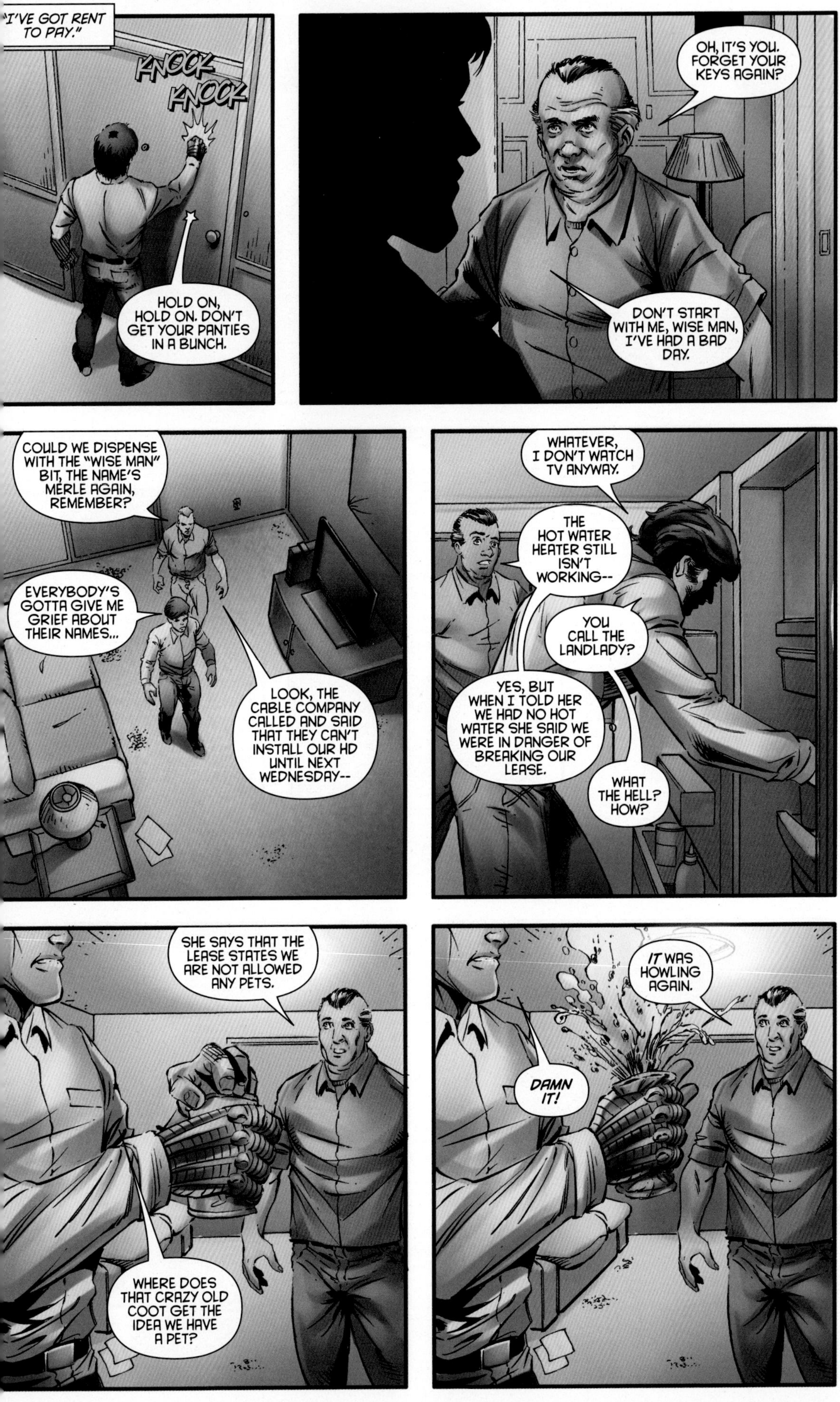
"I'VE GOT RENT TO PAY."
KNOCK KNOCK
HOLD ON, HOLD ON. DON'T GET YOUR PANTIES IN A BUNCH.
OH, IT'S YOU. FORGET YOUR KEYS AGAIN?
DON'T START WITH ME, WISE MAN, I'VE HAD A BAD DAY.
COULD WE DISPENSE WITH THE "WISE MAN" BIT, THE NAME'S MERLE AGAIN, REMEMBER?
EVERYBODY'S GOTTA GIVE ME GRIEF ABOUT THEIR NAMES...
LOOK, THE CABLE COMPANY CALLED AND SAID THAT THEY CAN'T INSTALL OUR HD UNTIL NEXT WEDNESDAY--
WHATEVER, I DON'T WATCH TV ANYWAY.
THE HOT WATER HEATER STILL ISN'T WORKING--
YOU CALL THE LANDLADY?
YES, BUT WHEN I TOLD HER WE HAD NO HOT WATER SHE SAID WE WERE IN DANGER OF BREAKING OUR LEASE.
WHAT THE HELL? HOW?
SHE SAYS THAT THE LEASE STATES WE ARE NOT ALLOWED ANY PETS.
WHERE DOES THAT CRAZY OLD COOT GET THE IDEA WE HAVE A PET?
IT WAS HOWLING AGAIN.
DAMN IT!

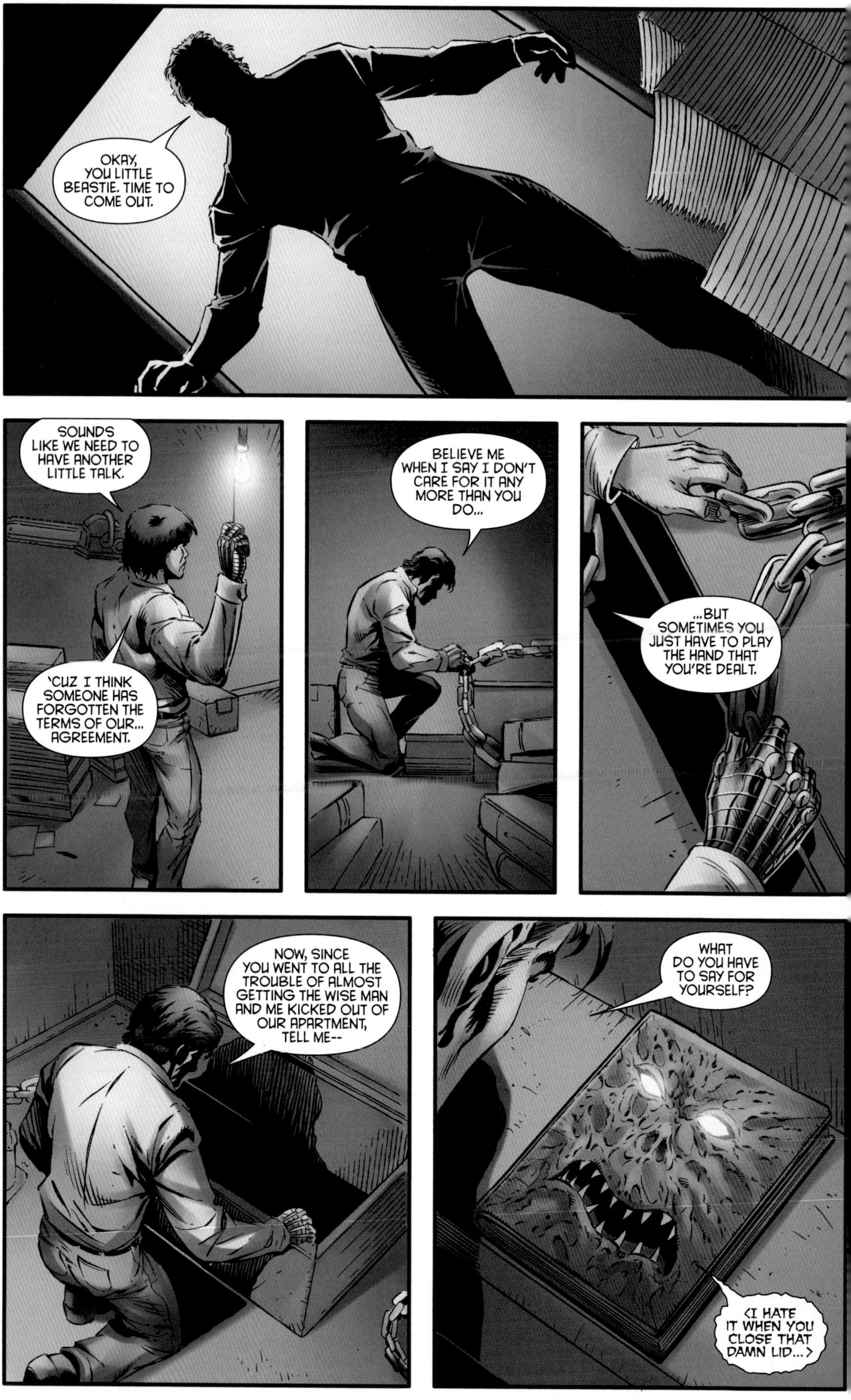
OKAY, YOU LITTLE BEASTIE. TIME TO COME OUT.
SOUNDS LIKE WE NEED TO HAVE ANOTHER LITTLE TALK.
'CUZ I THINK SOMEONE HAS FORGOTTEN THE TERMS OF OUR... AGREEMENT.
BELIEVE ME WHEN I SAY I DON'T CARE FOR IT ANY MORE THAN YOU DO...
...BUT SOMETIMES YOU JUST HAVE TO PLAY THE HAND THAT YOU'RE DEALT.
NOW, SINCE YOU WENT TO ALL THE TROUBLE OF ALMOST GETTING THE WISE MAN AND ME KICKED OUT OF OUR APARTMENT, TELL ME--
WHAT DO YOU HAVE TO SAY FOR YOURSELF?
<I HATE IT WHEN YOU CLOSE THAT DAMN LID...>

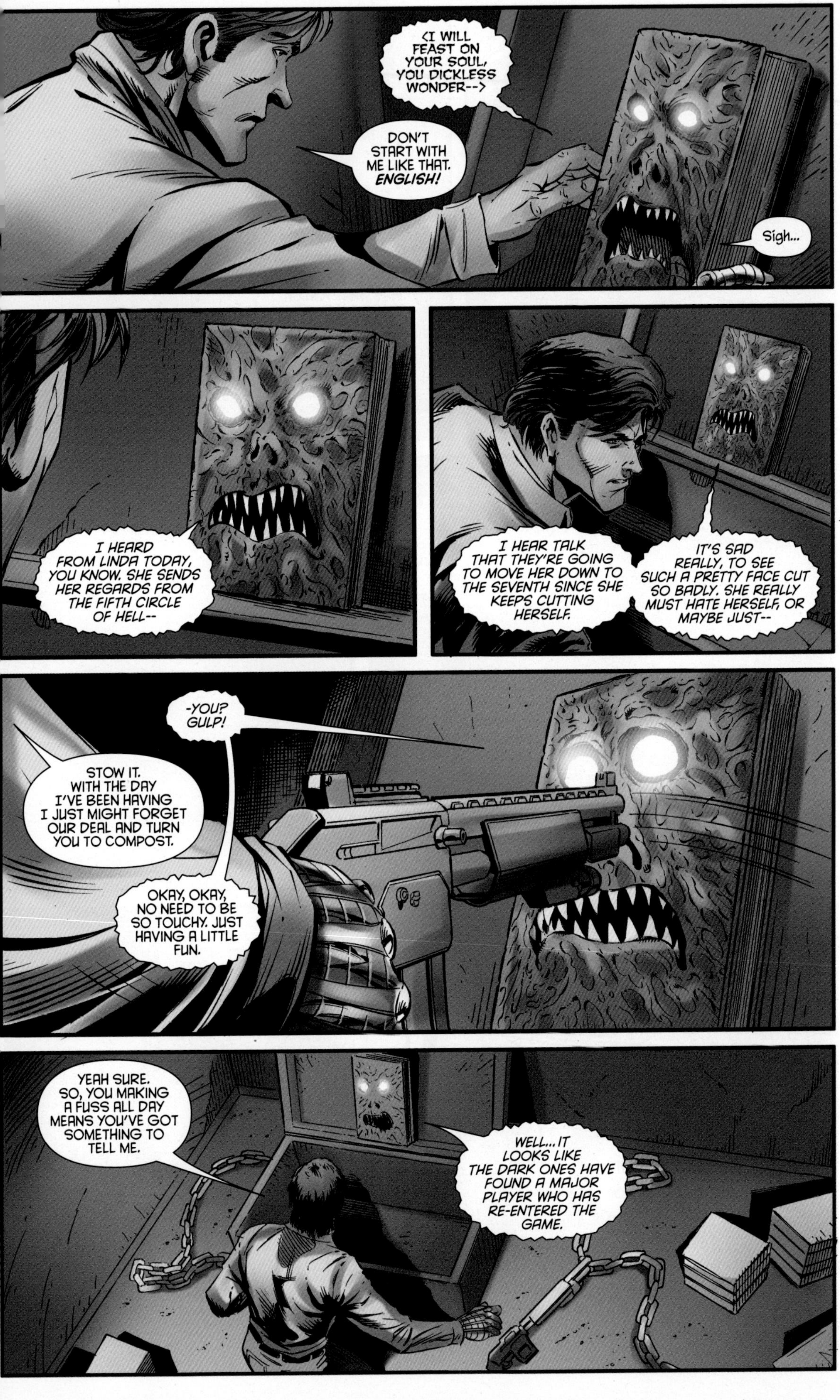
<I WILL FEAST ON YOUR SOUL, YOU DICKLESS WONDER-->
DON'T START WITH ME LIKE THAT. *ENGLISH!*
Sigh...
I HEARD FROM LINDA TODAY, YOU KNOW. SHE SENDS HER REGARDS FROM THE FIFTH CIRCLE OF HELL--
I HEAR TALK THAT THEY'RE GOING TO MOVE HER DOWN TO THE SEVENTH SINCE SHE KEEPS CUTTING HERSELF.
IT'S SAD REALLY, TO SEE SUCH A PRETTY FACE CUT SO BADLY. SHE REALLY MUST HATE HERSELF, OR MAYBE JUST--
-YOU? GULP!
STOW IT. WITH THE DAY I'VE BEEN HAVING I JUST MIGHT FORGET OUR DEAL AND TURN YOU TO COMPOST.
OKAY, OKAY, NO NEED TO BE SO TOUCHY. JUST HAVING A LITTLE FUN.
YEAH SURE. SO, YOU MAKING A FUSS ALL DAY MEANS YOU'VE GOT SOMETHING TO TELL ME.
WELL... IT LOOKS LIKE THE DARK ONES HAVE FOUND A MAJOR PLAYER WHO HAS RE-ENTERED THE GAME.

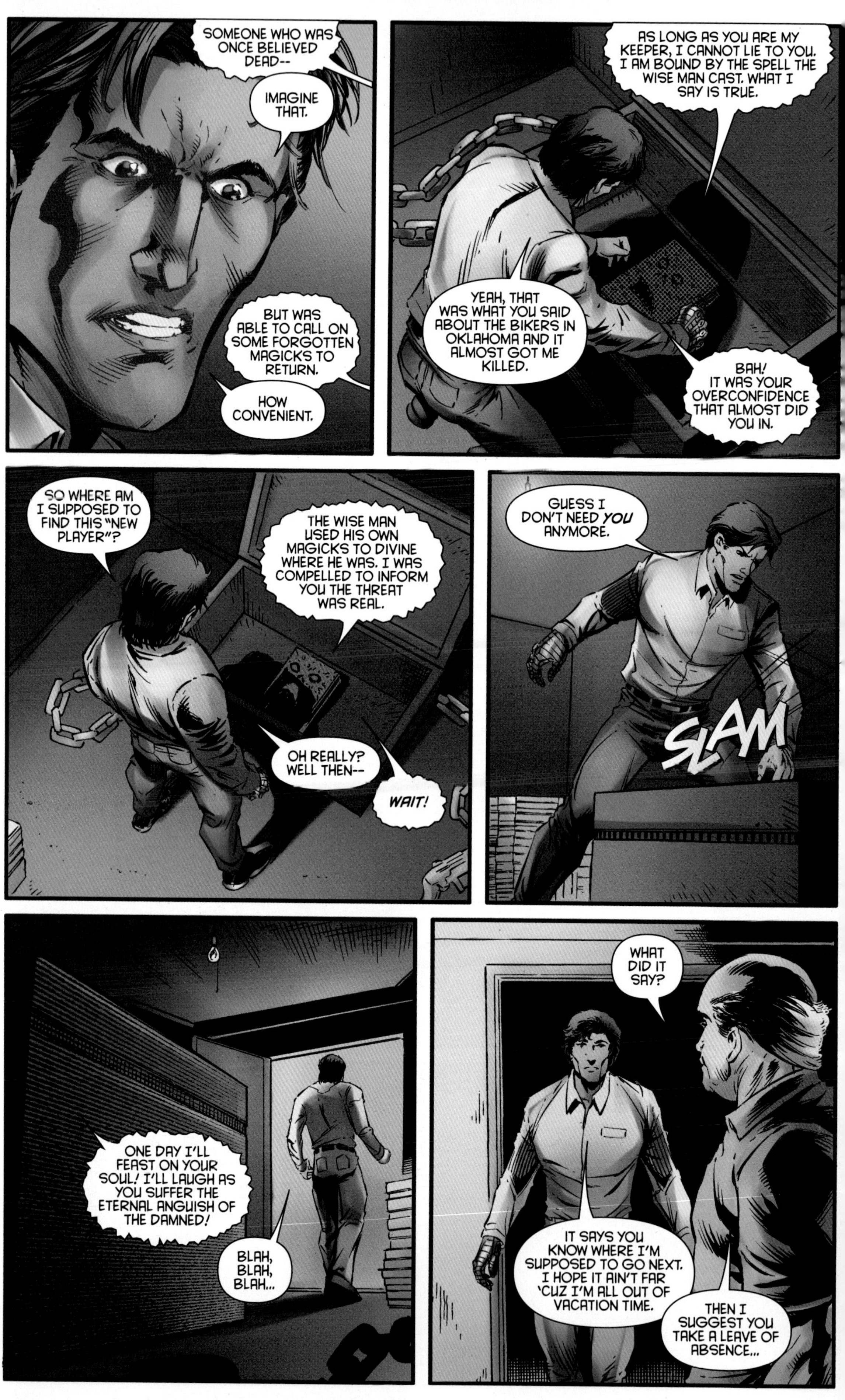
SOMEONE WHO WAS ONCE BELIEVED DEAD--
IMAGINE THAT.
BUT WAS ABLE TO CALL ON SOME FORGOTTEN MAGICKS TO RETURN.
HOW CONVENIENT.
AS LONG AS YOU ARE MY KEEPER, I CANNOT LIE TO YOU. I AM BOUND BY THE SPELL THE WISE MAN CAST. WHAT I SAY IS TRUE.
YEAH, THAT WAS WHAT YOU SAID ABOUT THE BIKERS IN OKLAHOMA AND IT ALMOST GOT ME KILLED.
BAH! IT WAS YOUR OVERCONFIDENCE THAT ALMOST DID YOU IN.
SO WHERE AM I SUPPOSED TO FIND THIS "NEW PLAYER"?
THE WISE MAN USED HIS OWN MAGICKS TO DIVINE WHERE HE WAS. I WAS COMPELLED TO INFORM YOU THE THREAT WAS REAL.
OH REALLY? WELL THEN--
WAIT!
GUESS I DON'T NEED YOU ANYMORE.
SLAM
ONE DAY I'LL FEAST ON YOUR SOUL! I'LL LAUGH AS YOU SUFFER THE ETERNAL ANGUISH OF THE DAMNED!
BLAH, BLAH, BLAH...
WHAT DID IT SAY?
IT SAYS YOU KNOW WHERE I'M SUPPOSED TO GO NEXT. I HOPE IT AIN'T FAR 'CUZ I'M ALL OUT OF VACATION TIME.
THEN I SUGGEST YOU TAKE A LEAVE OF ABSENCE...

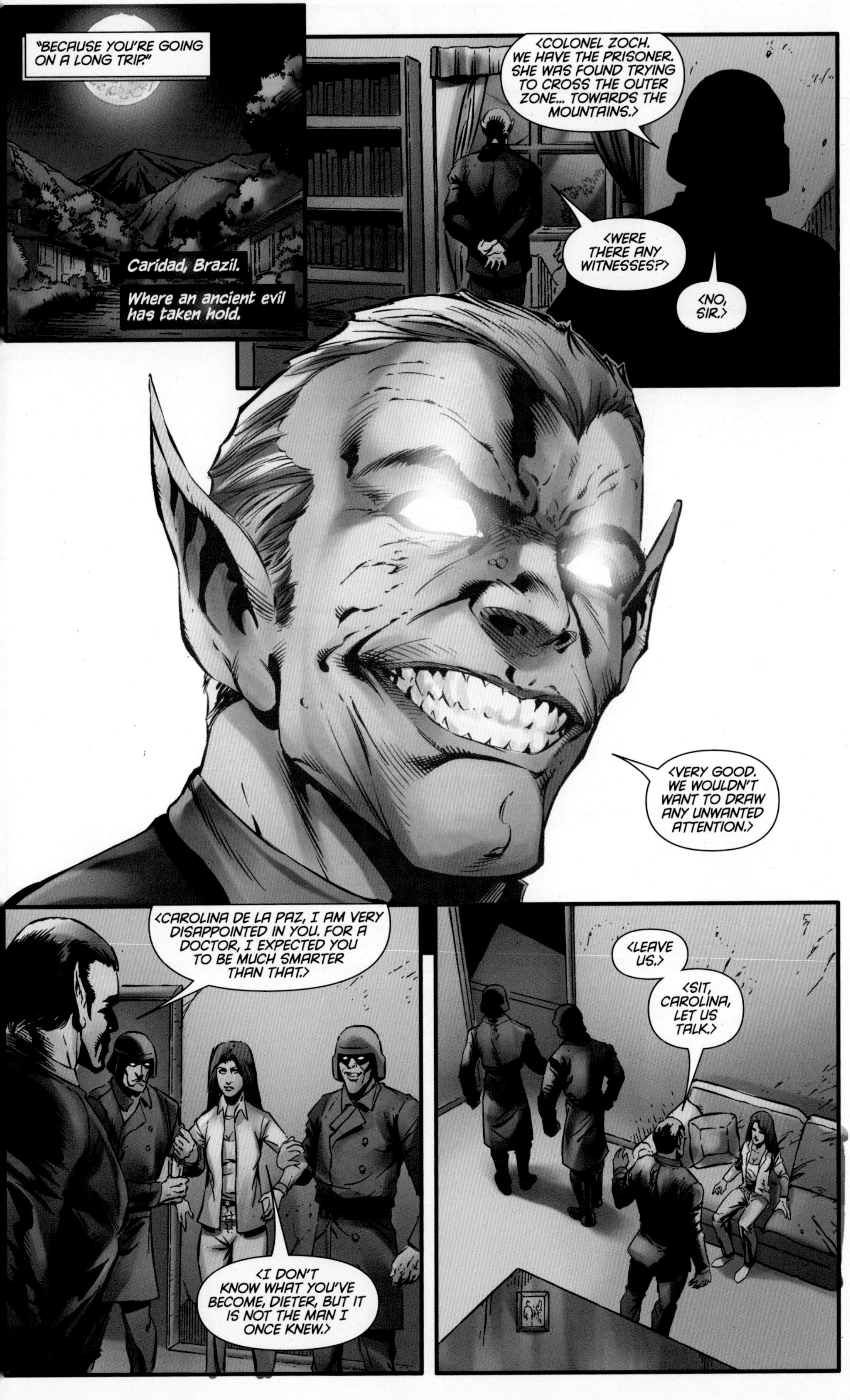
"BECAUSE YOU'RE GOING ON A LONG TRIP."
Caridad, Brazil.
Where an ancient evil has taken hold.
<COLONEL ZOCH. WE HAVE THE PRISONER. SHE WAS FOUND TRYING TO CROSS THE OUTER ZONE... TOWARDS THE MOUNTAINS.>
<WERE THERE ANY WITNESSES?>
<NO, SIR.>
<VERY GOOD. WE WOULDN'T WANT TO DRAW ANY UNWANTED ATTENTION.>
<CAROLINA DE LA PAZ, I AM VERY DISAPPOINTED IN YOU. FOR A DOCTOR, I EXPECTED YOU TO BE MUCH SMARTER THAN THAT.>
<I DON'T KNOW WHAT YOU'VE BECOME, DIETER, BUT IT IS NOT THE MAN I ONCE KNEW.>
<LEAVE US.>
<SIT, CAROLINA, LET US TALK.>

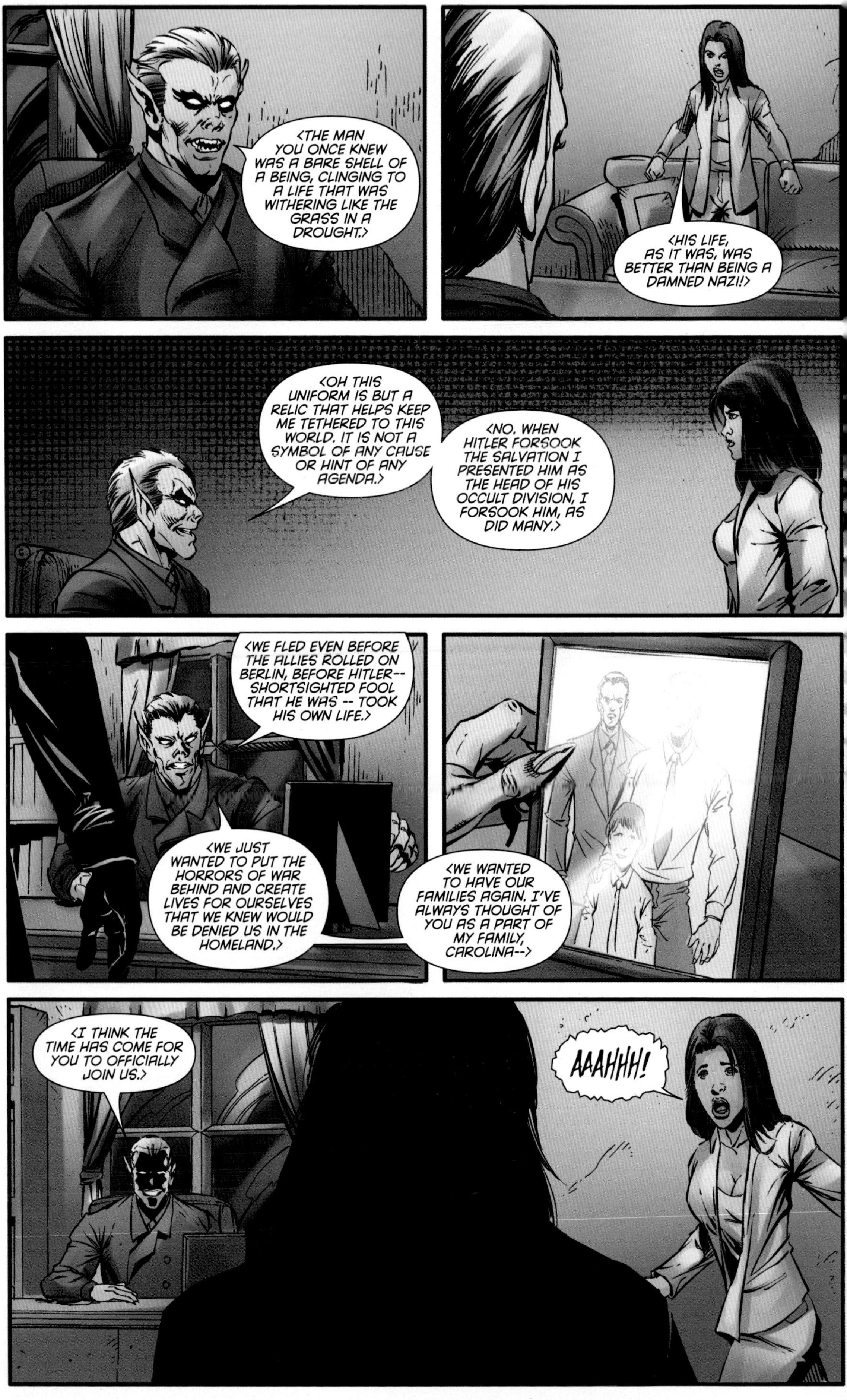
<THE MAN YOU ONCE KNEW WAS A BARE SHELL OF A BEING, CLINGING TO A LIFE THAT WAS WITHERING LIKE THE GRASS IN A DROUGHT.>
<HIS LIFE, AS IT WAS, WAS BETTER THAN BEING A DAMNED NAZI!>
<OH THIS UNIFORM IS BUT A RELIC THAT HELPS KEEP ME TETHERED TO THIS WORLD. IT IS NOT A SYMBOL OF ANY CAUSE OR HINT OF ANY AGENDA.>
<NO. WHEN HITLER FORSOOK THE SALVATION I PRESENTED HIM AS THE HEAD OF HIS OCCULT DIVISION, I FORSOOK HIM, AS DID MANY.>
<WE FLED EVEN BEFORE THE ALLIES ROLLED ON BERLIN, BEFORE HITLER-- SHORTSIGHTED FOOL THAT HE WAS -- TOOK HIS OWN LIFE.>
<WE JUST WANTED TO PUT THE HORRORS OF WAR BEHIND AND CREATE LIVES FOR OURSELVES THAT WE KNEW WOULD BE DENIED US IN THE HOMELAND.>
<WE WANTED TO HAVE OUR FAMILIES AGAIN. I'VE ALWAYS THOUGHT OF YOU AS A PART OF MY FAMILY, CAROLINA-->
<I THINK THE TIME HAS COME FOR YOU TO OFFICIALLY JOIN US.>
AAAHHH!

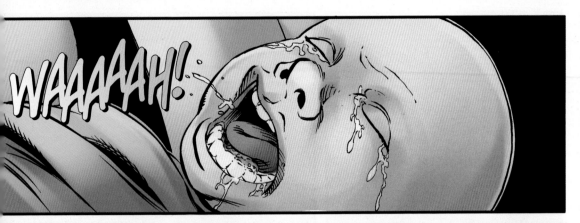

WAAAAAH!

Oh God, I've been to **Hell** and this is still **worse**.

Goddamn Merle and his cheap travel websites!

Okay, Williams, think about it. Hell is a pit of torment. Fire and brimstone everywhere with the souls of the damned wailing in eternal anguish.

Can a flight from Detroit to Miami, before moving on to Brazil, really be worse?

Yeah, I'd still prefer Hell.

PLEASE KEEP YOUR ARMS RAISED, SIR.

When: One hour on the runway and another Three in the air later.

Where: Miami International Airport.

....

I'M SORRY SIR--

OH, WHAT NOW?

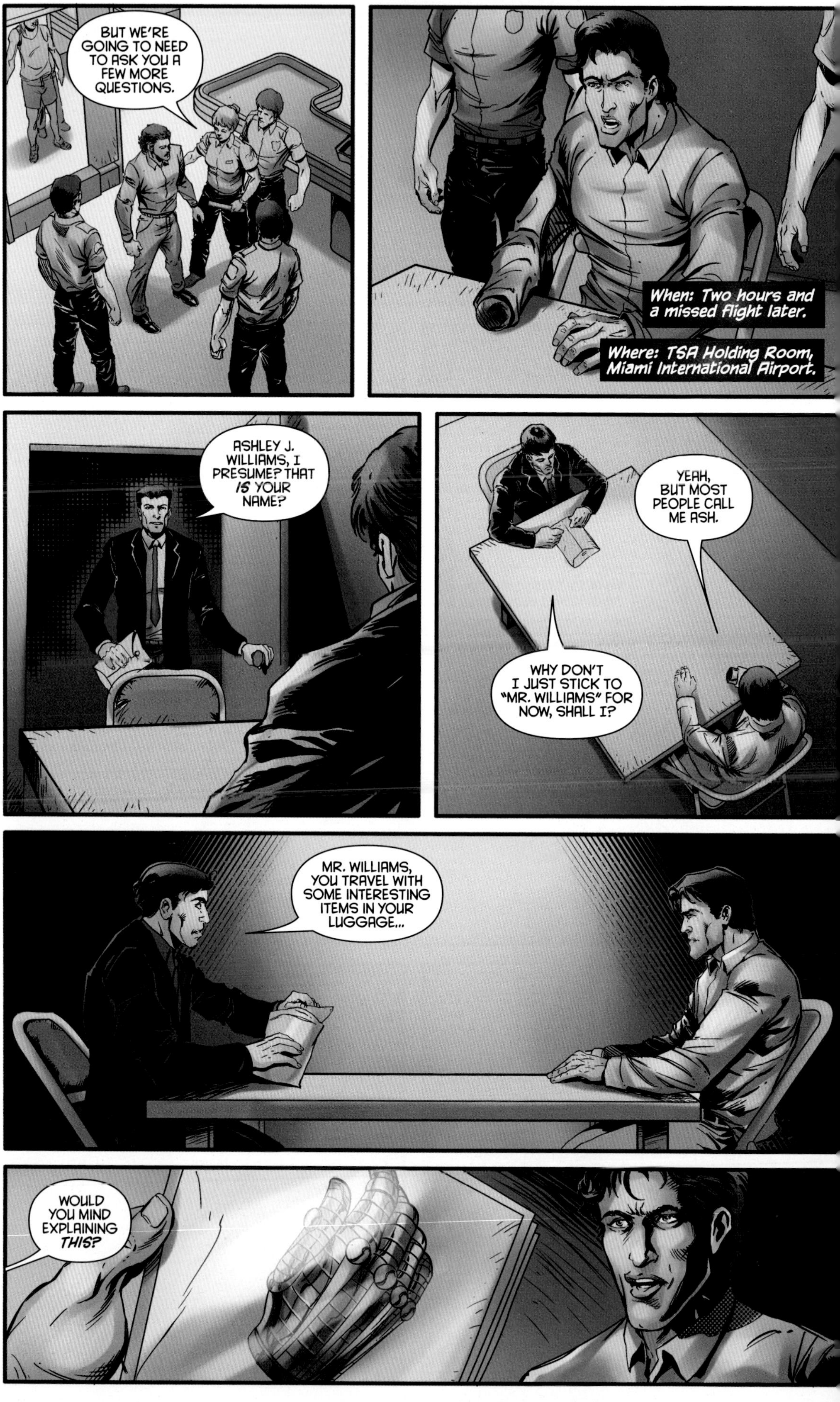
BUT WE'RE GOING TO NEED TO ASK YOU A FEW MORE QUESTIONS.
When: Two hours and a missed flight later.
Where: TSA Holding Room, Miami International Airport.
ASHLEY J. WILLIAMS, I PRESUME? THAT IS YOUR NAME?
YEAH, BUT MOST PEOPLE CALL ME ASH.
WHY DON'T I JUST STICK TO "MR. WILLIAMS" FOR NOW, SHALL I?
MR. WILLIAMS, YOU TRAVEL WITH SOME INTERESTING ITEMS IN YOUR LUGGAGE...
WOULD YOU MIND EXPLAINING THIS?

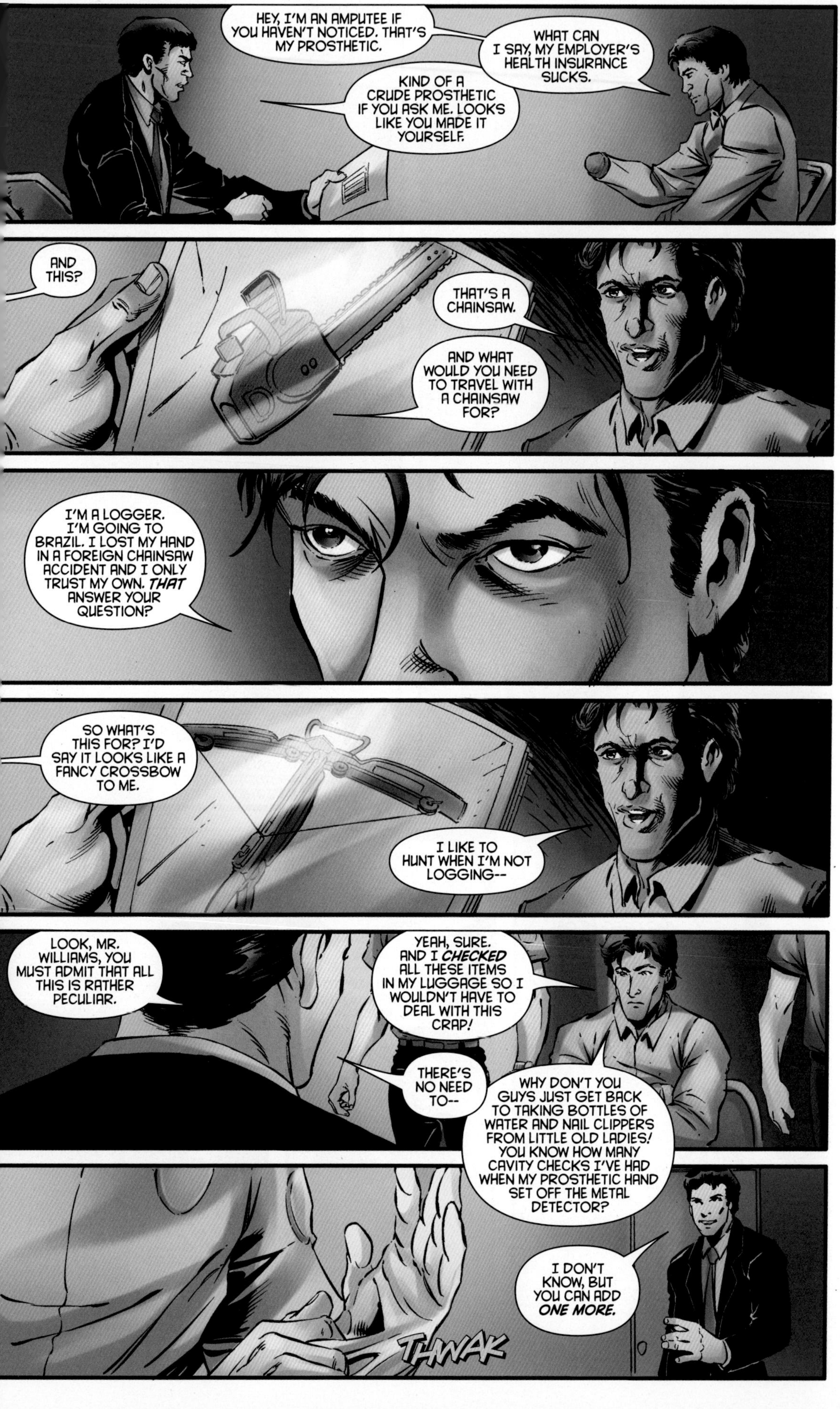
HEY, I'M AN AMPUTEE IF YOU HAVEN'T NOTICED. THAT'S MY PROSTHETIC.
WHAT CAN I SAY, MY EMPLOYER'S HEALTH INSURANCE SUCKS.
KIND OF A CRUDE PROSTHETIC IF YOU ASK ME. LOOKS LIKE YOU MADE IT YOURSELF.
AND THIS?
THAT'S A CHAINSAW.
AND WHAT WOULD YOU NEED TO TRAVEL WITH A CHAINSAW FOR?
I'M A LOGGER. I'M GOING TO BRAZIL. I LOST MY HAND IN A FOREIGN CHAINSAW ACCIDENT AND I ONLY TRUST MY OWN. *THAT* ANSWER YOUR QUESTION?
SO WHAT'S THIS FOR? I'D SAY IT LOOKS LIKE A FANCY CROSSBOW TO ME.
I LIKE TO HUNT WHEN I'M NOT LOGGING--
LOOK, MR. WILLIAMS, YOU MUST ADMIT THAT ALL THIS IS RATHER PECULIAR.
YEAH, SURE. AND I ***CHECKED*** ALL THESE ITEMS IN MY LUGGAGE SO I WOULDN'T HAVE TO DEAL WITH THIS CRAP!
THERE'S NO NEED TO--
WHY DON'T YOU GUYS JUST GET BACK TO TAKING BOTTLES OF WATER AND NAIL CLIPPERS FROM LITTLE OLD LADIES! YOU KNOW HOW MANY CAVITY CHECKS I'VE HAD WHEN MY PROSTHETIC HAND SET OFF THE METAL DETECTOR?
I DON'T KNOW, BUT YOU CAN ADD ***ONE MORE.***
THWAK

<IT'S FUNNY, I'VE LOST COUNT OF HOW MANY TIMES I'VE DONE THIS MYSELF-->

<--MAYBE ONE DAY THIS WILL BE AS COMMON TO YOU AS IT'S BECOME FOR ME.>

<I CAN ONLY HOPE TO ONE DAY BE AS GOOD AS YOU ARE, POPPA.>

<YOU ARE DESTINED TO BE GREATER THAN I, MY BOY.>

<WHAT IS IT THAT YOU NEED TO DO NOW? ANOTHER SPELL TO HIDE THE VILLAGE?>

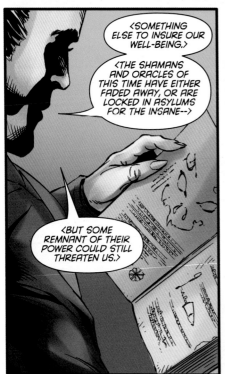

<SOMETHING ELSE TO INSURE OUR WELL-BEING.>

<THE SHAMANS AND ORACLES OF THIS TIME HAVE EITHER FADED AWAY, OR ARE LOCKED IN ASYLUMS FOR THE INSANE-->

<BUT SOME REMNANT OF THEIR POWER COULD STILL THREATEN US.>

CLOAKED IN DARKNESS YOUR SERVANT LIES, HIDING FROM LIGHT'S PRYING EYES--

IF YOUR WILL IS TO BE DONE, DRAW TO ME THEIR CHOSEN ONE.

<WHAT DID THOSE WORDS MEAN, POPPA?>

<IT'S JUST PART OF THE GAME WE'RE PLAYING, MY BOY-->

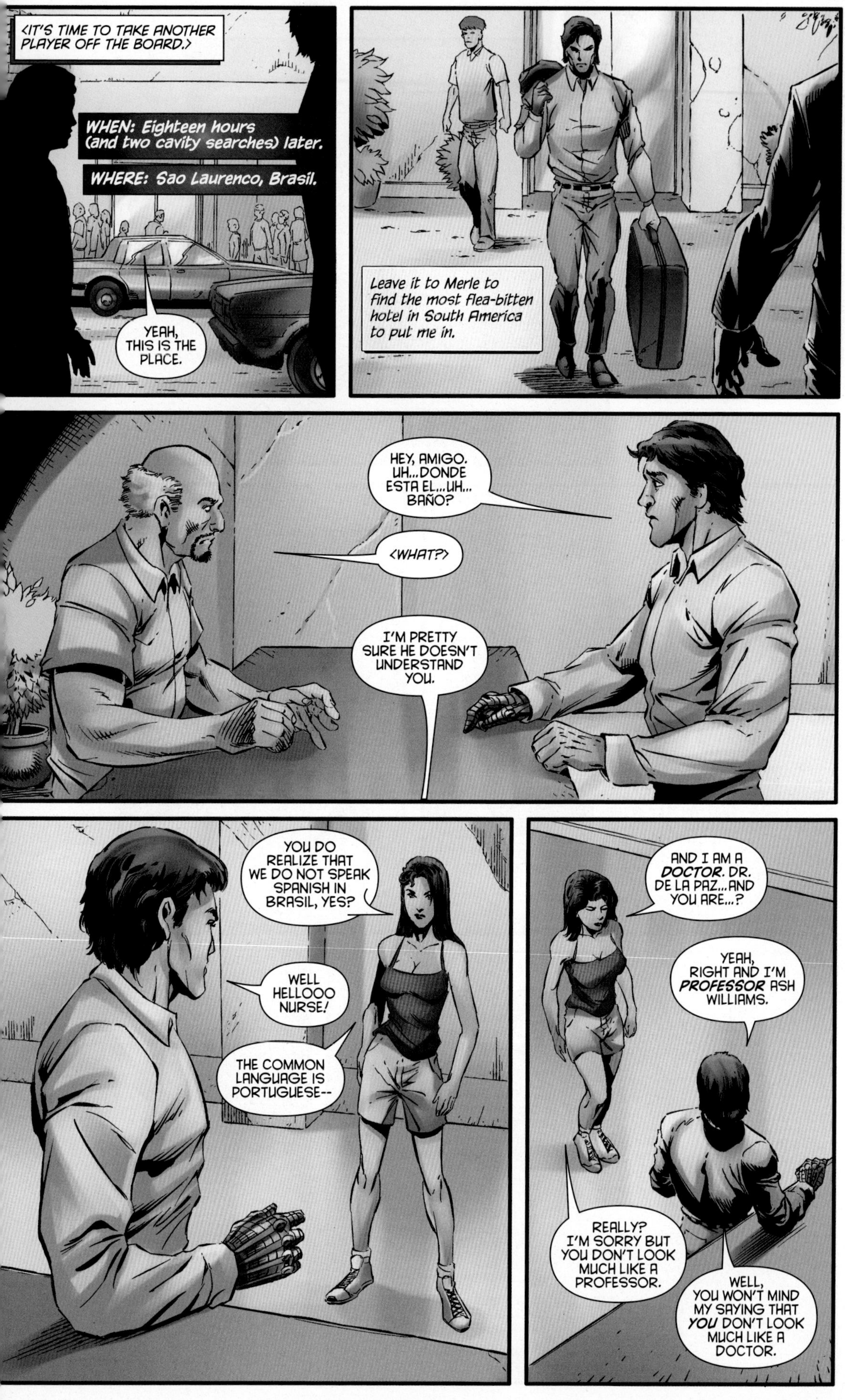

<IT'S TIME TO TAKE ANOTHER PLAYER OFF THE BOARD.>
WHEN: Eighteen hours (and two cavity searches) later.
WHERE: Sao Laurenco, Brasil.
YEAH, THIS IS THE PLACE.
Leave it to Merle to find the most flea-bitten hotel in South America to put me in.
HEY, AMIGO. UH...DONDE ESTA EL...UH... BAÑO?
<WHAT?>
I'M PRETTY SURE HE DOESN'T UNDERSTAND YOU.
YOU DO REALIZE THAT WE DO NOT SPEAK SPANISH IN BRASIL, YES?
WELL HELLOOO NURSE!
THE COMMON LANGUAGE IS PORTUGUESE--
AND I AM A *DOCTOR*. DR. DE LA PAZ...AND YOU ARE...?
YEAH, RIGHT AND I'M *PROFESSOR* ASH WILLIAMS.
REALLY? I'M SORRY BUT YOU DON'T LOOK MUCH LIKE A PROFESSOR.
WELL, YOU WON'T MIND MY SAYING THAT *YOU* DON'T LOOK MUCH LIKE A DOCTOR.

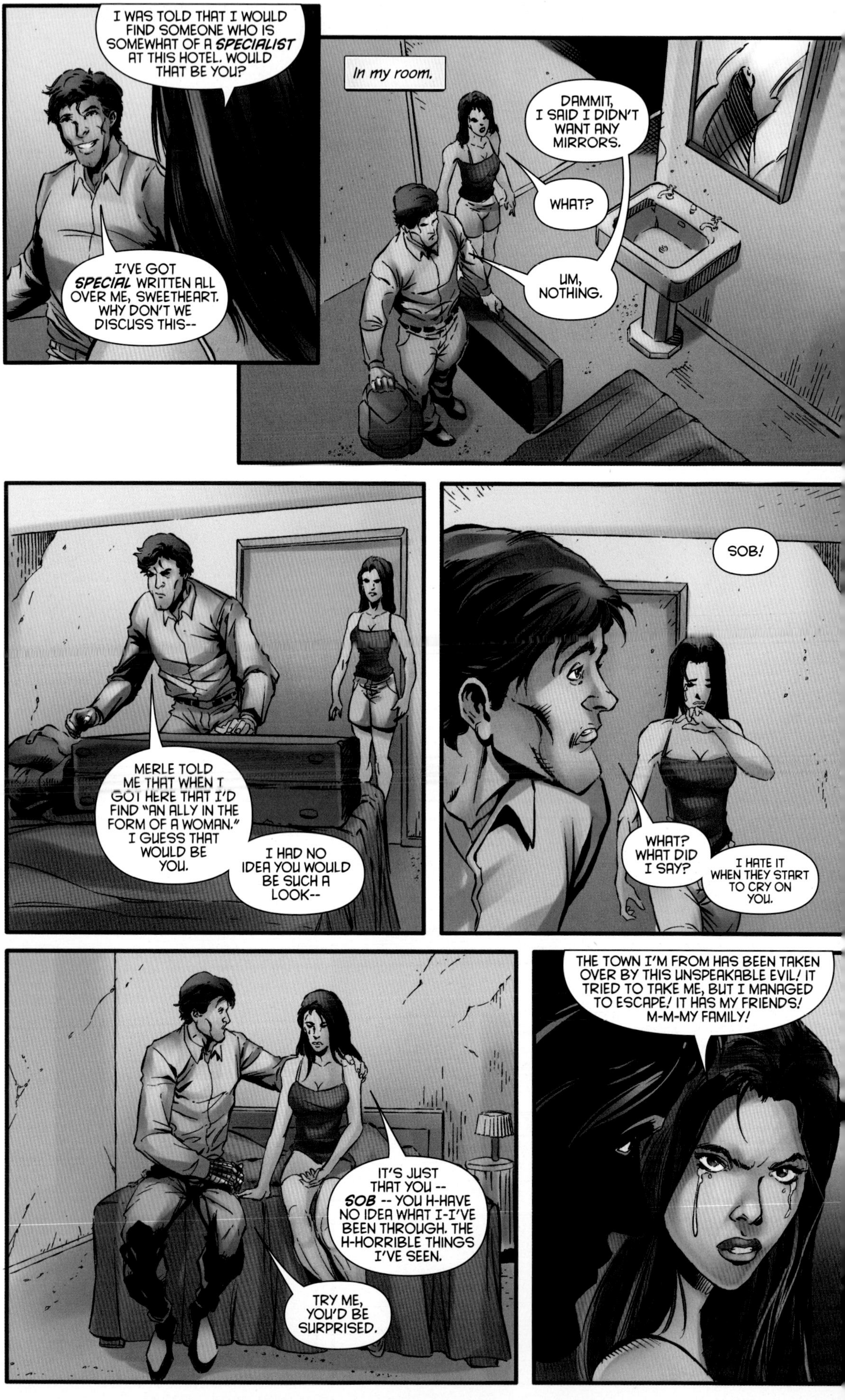

I WAS TOLD THAT I WOULD FIND SOMEONE WHO IS SOMEWHAT OF A *SPECIALIST* AT THIS HOTEL. WOULD THAT BE YOU?
I'VE GOT *SPECIAL* WRITTEN ALL OVER ME, SWEETHEART. WHY DON'T WE DISCUSS THIS--
In my room.
DAMMIT, I SAID I DIDN'T WANT ANY MIRRORS.
WHAT?
UM, NOTHING.
MERLE TOLD ME THAT WHEN I GOT HERE THAT I'D FIND "AN ALLY IN THE FORM OF A WOMAN." I GUESS THAT WOULD BE YOU.
I HAD NO IDEA YOU WOULD BE SUCH A LOOK--
SOB!
WHAT? WHAT DID I SAY?
I HATE IT WHEN THEY START TO CRY ON YOU.
IT'S JUST THAT YOU -- *SOB* -- YOU H-HAVE NO IDEA WHAT I-I'VE BEEN THROUGH. THE H-HORRIBLE THINGS I'VE SEEN.
TRY ME, YOU'D BE SURPRISED.
THE TOWN I'M FROM HAS BEEN TAKEN OVER BY THIS UNSPEAKABLE EVIL! IT TRIED TO TAKE ME, BUT I MANAGED TO ESCAPE! IT HAS MY FRIENDS! M-M-MY FAMILY!

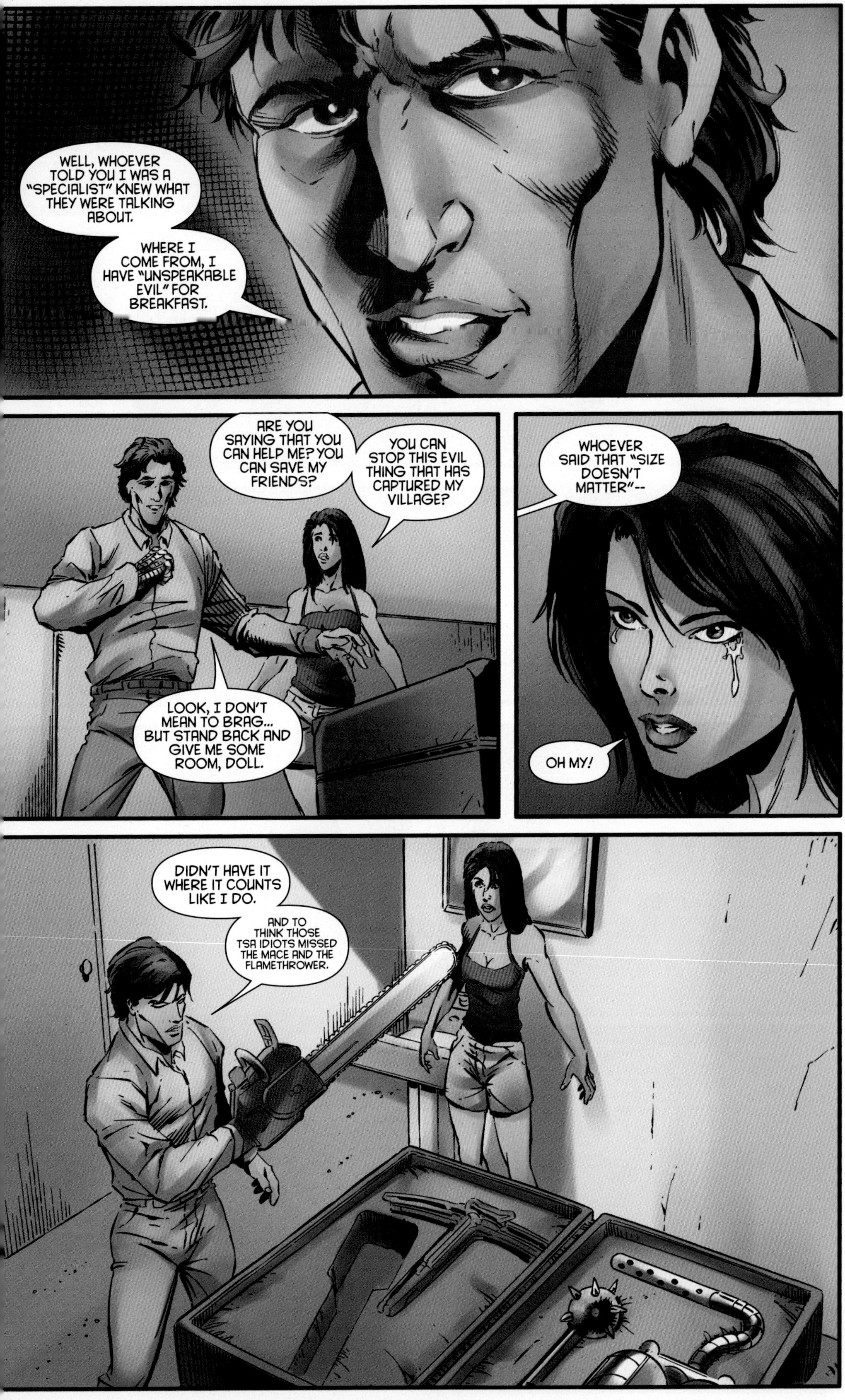
WELL, WHOEVER TOLD YOU I WAS A "SPECIALIST" KNEW WHAT THEY WERE TALKING ABOUT.
WHERE I COME FROM, I HAVE "UNSPEAKABLE EVIL" FOR BREAKFAST.
ARE YOU SAYING THAT YOU CAN HELP ME? YOU CAN SAVE MY FRIENDS?
YOU CAN STOP THIS EVIL THING THAT HAS CAPTURED MY VILLAGE?
LOOK, I DON'T MEAN TO BRAG... BUT STAND BACK AND GIVE ME SOME ROOM, DOLL.
WHOEVER SAID THAT "SIZE DOESN'T MATTER"--
OH MY!
DIDN'T HAVE IT WHERE IT COUNTS LIKE I DO.
AND TO THINK THOSE TSA IDIOTS MISSED THE MACE AND THE FLAMETHROWER.

Three hours and a tire change later.

WE'RE ALMOST THERE.

TELL ME, HOW IS IT THAT YOU'VE COME TO DO THIS KIND OF WORK?

IT'S A LONG STORY. THE FUNNY THING IS, I DON'T EVEN CONSIDER THIS MY JOB. I GET PAID TO WORK AT A DEPARTMENT STORE. THIS SORT OF THING BARELY COVERS EXPENSES.

YOU CHARGE PEOPLE?

ONLY IF THEY CAN HELP GET ME TO WHERE I NEED TO GO. LATELY IT SEEMS THAT I'M NEEDED *EVERY-WHERE.*

WHEN WISE MAN -- I MEAN *MERLE* -- SET UP THIS WEB SITE TO LET FOLKS CONTACT ME --

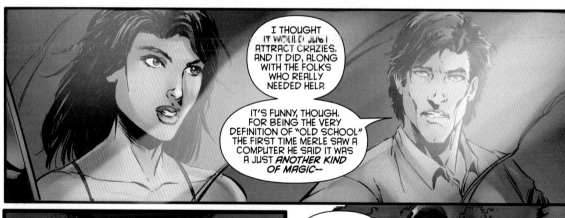

I THOUGHT IT WOULD JUST ATTRACT CRAZIES. AND IT DID, ALONG WITH THE FOLKS WHO REALLY NEEDED HELP.

IT'S FUNNY, THOUGH. FOR BEING THE VERY DEFINITION OF "OLD SCHOOL" THE FIRST TIME MERLE SAW A COMPUTER HE SAID IT WAS A JUST *ANOTHER KIND OF MAGIC* --

THEN I SAW HIM WITH A COPY OF "HTML FOR DUMMIES." HE CALLED IT A "NEW SPELL BOOK TO LEARN." NOW HE'S MY WEBMASTER.

WE'RE HERE.

FOLLOW ME. WE'LL BE ABLE TO SEE THE VILLAGE FROM THE TOP OF THIS HILL.

RIGHT BEHIND YOU.

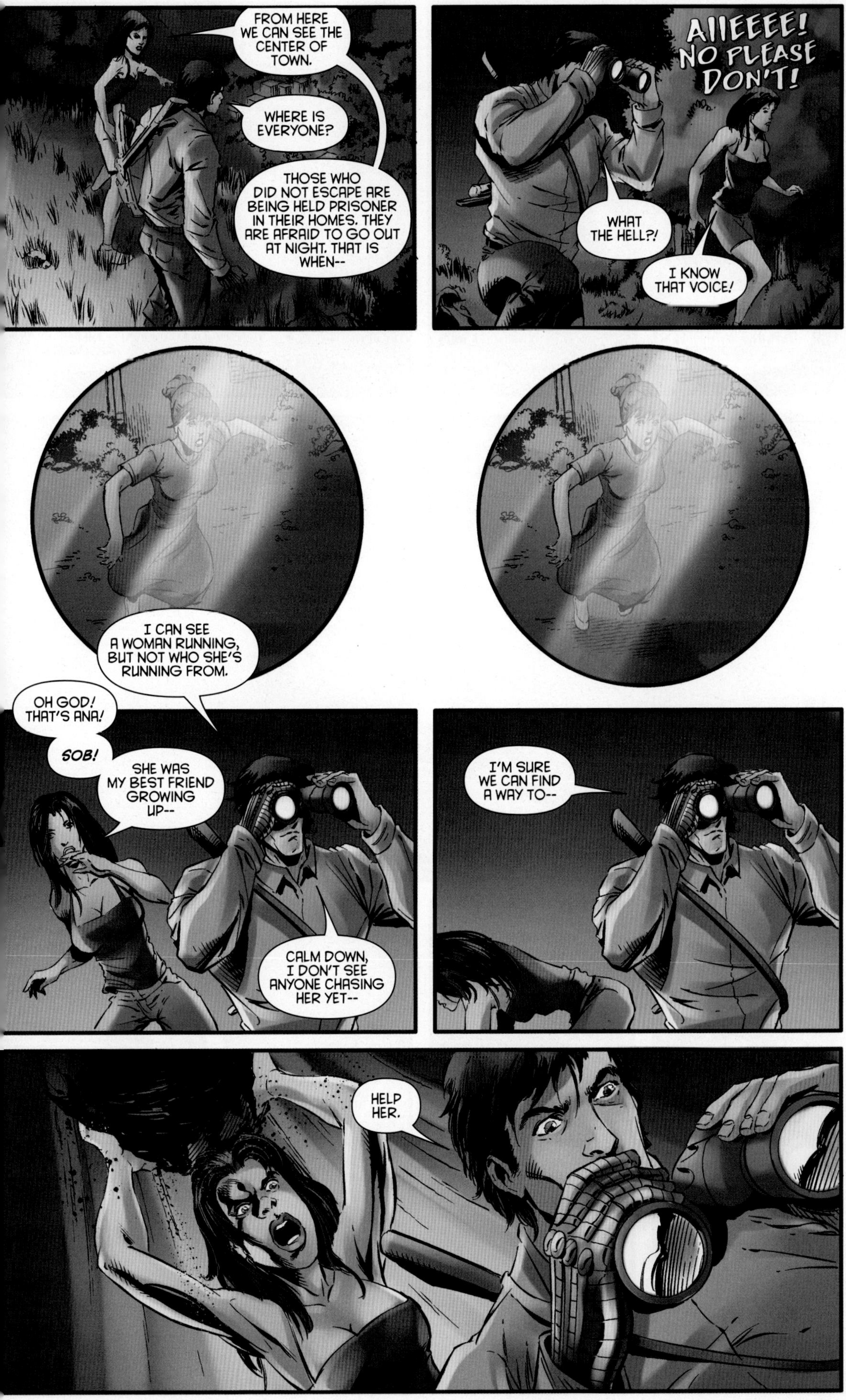
FROM HERE WE CAN SEE THE CENTER OF TOWN.
WHERE IS EVERYONE?
THOSE WHO DID NOT ESCAPE ARE BEING HELD PRISONER IN THEIR HOMES. THEY ARE AFRAID TO GO OUT AT NIGHT. THAT IS WHEN--
AIIEEEE! NO PLEASE DON'T!
WHAT THE HELL?!
I KNOW THAT VOICE!
I CAN SEE A WOMAN RUNNING, BUT NOT WHO SHE'S RUNNING FROM.
OH GOD! THAT'S ANA!
SOB!
SHE WAS MY BEST FRIEND GROWING UP--
CALM DOWN, I DON'T SEE ANYONE CHASING HER YET--
I'M SURE WE CAN FIND A WAY TO--
HELP HER.

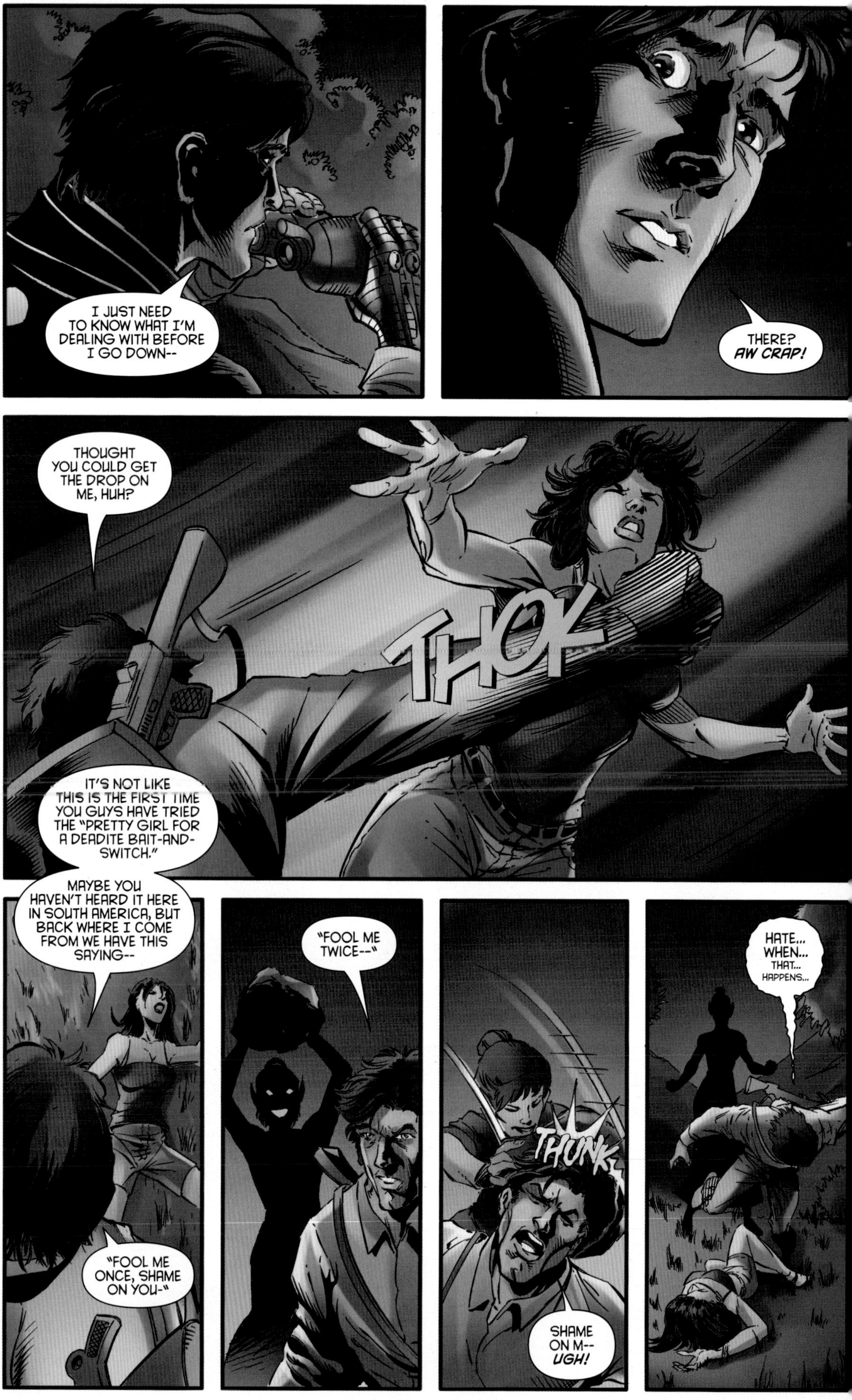
I JUST NEED TO KNOW WHAT I'M DEALING WITH BEFORE I GO DOWN--
THERE? *AW CRAP!*
THOUGHT YOU COULD GET THE DROP ON ME, HUH?
THOK
IT'S NOT LIKE THIS IS THE FIRST TIME YOU GUYS HAVE TRIED THE "PRETTY GIRL FOR A DEADITE BAIT-AND-SWITCH."
MAYBE YOU HAVEN'T HEARD IT HERE IN SOUTH AMERICA, BUT BACK WHERE I COME FROM WE HAVE THIS SAYING--
"FOOL ME ONCE, SHAME ON YOU-"
"FOOL ME TWICE--"
THUNK
SHAME ON M-- *UGH!*
HATE... WHEN... THAT... HAPPENS...

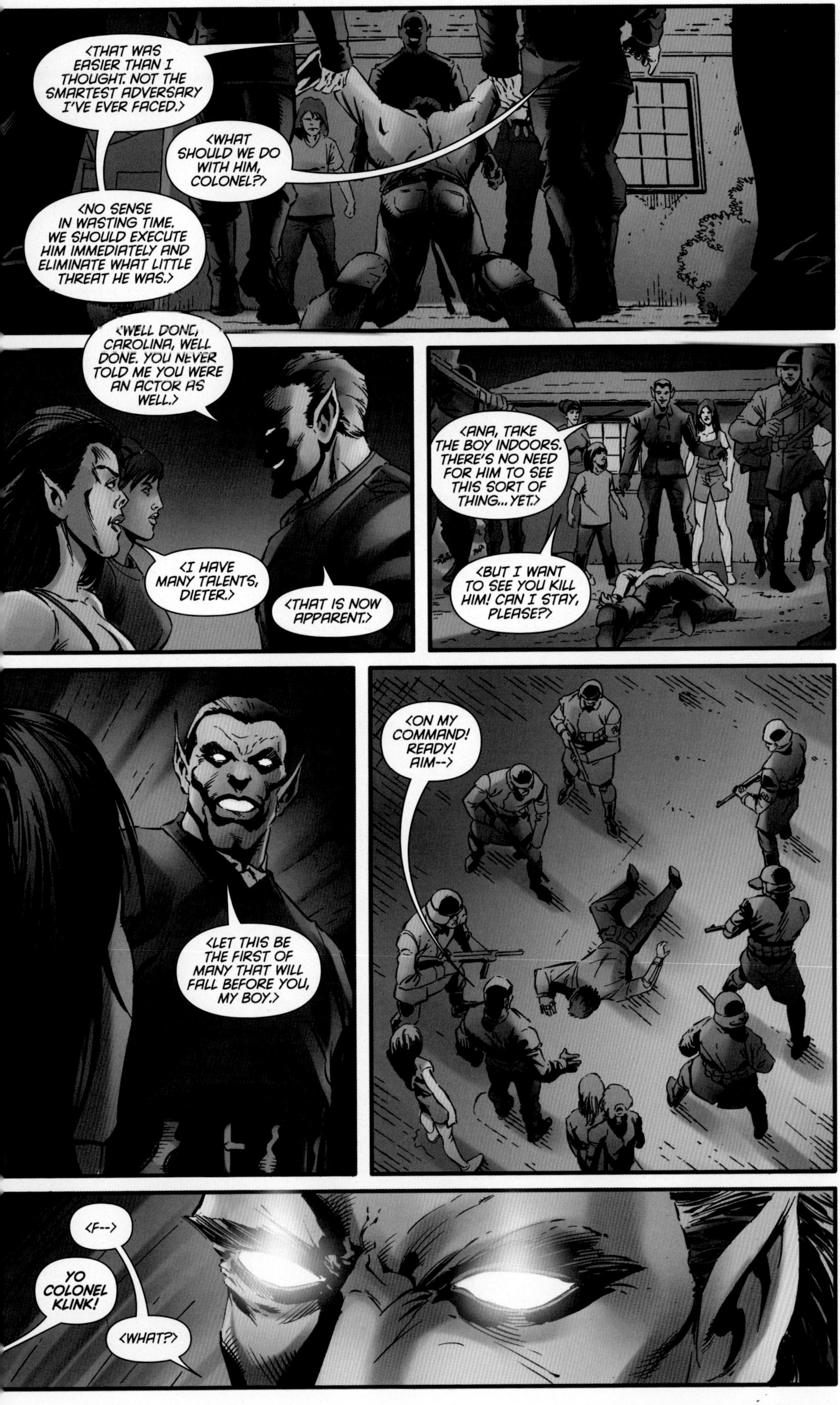
<THAT WAS EASIER THAN I THOUGHT. NOT THE SMARTEST ADVERSARY I'VE EVER FACED.>
<WHAT SHOULD WE DO WITH HIM, COLONEL?>
<NO SENSE IN WASTING TIME. WE SHOULD EXECUTE HIM IMMEDIATELY AND ELIMINATE WHAT LITTLE THREAT HE WAS.>
<WELL DONE, CAROLINA, WELL DONE. YOU NEVER TOLD ME YOU WERE AN ACTOR AS WELL.>
<I HAVE MANY TALENTS, DIETER.>
<THAT IS NOW APPARENT.>
<ANA, TAKE THE BOY INDOORS. THERE'S NO NEED FOR HIM TO SEE THIS SORT OF THING... YET.>
<BUT I WANT TO SEE YOU KILL HIM! CAN I STAY, PLEASE?>
<LET THIS BE THE FIRST OF MANY THAT WILL FALL BEFORE YOU, MY BOY.>
<ON MY COMMAND! READY! AIM-->
<F-->
YO COLONEL KLINK!
<WHAT?>

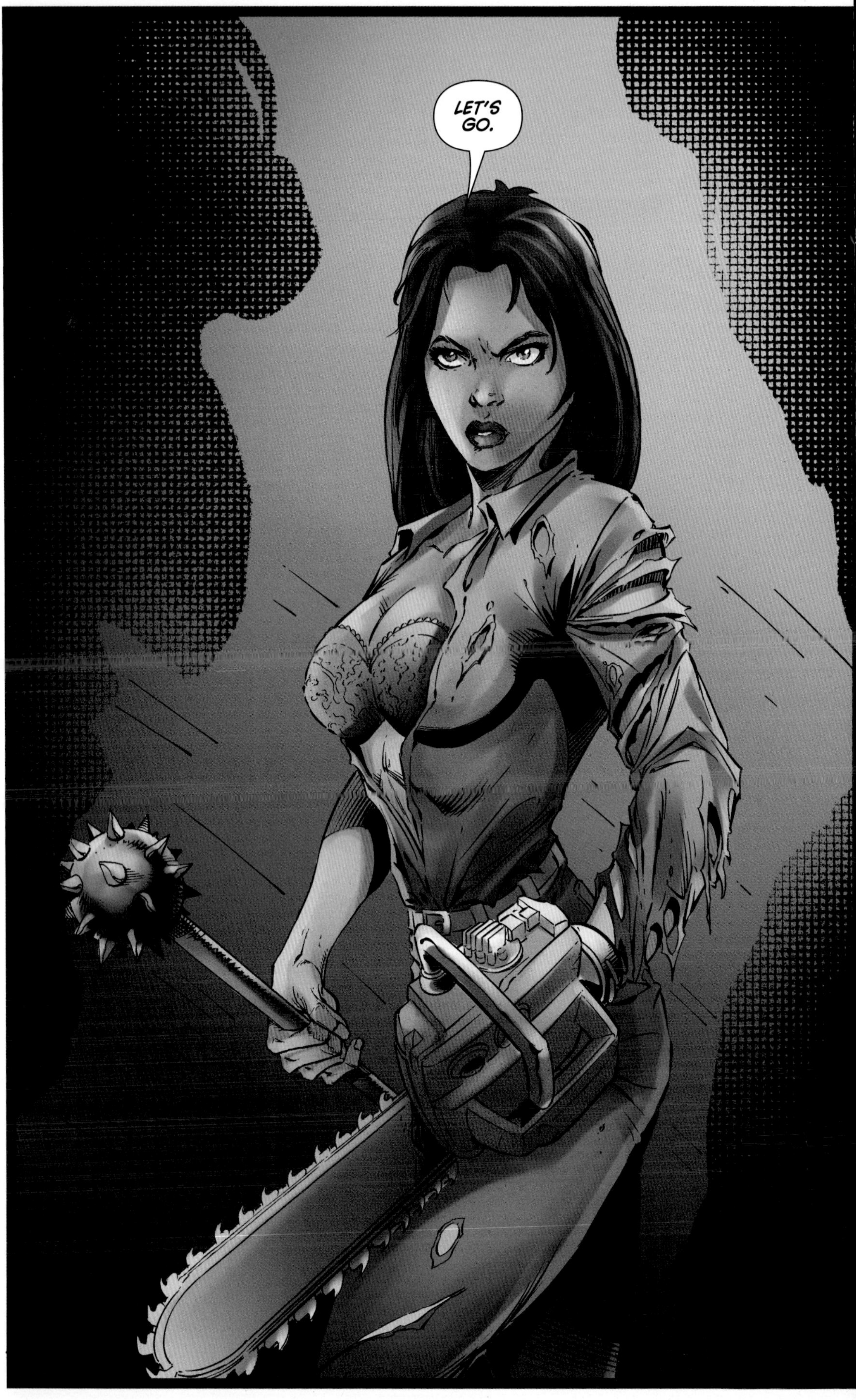
LET'S GO.

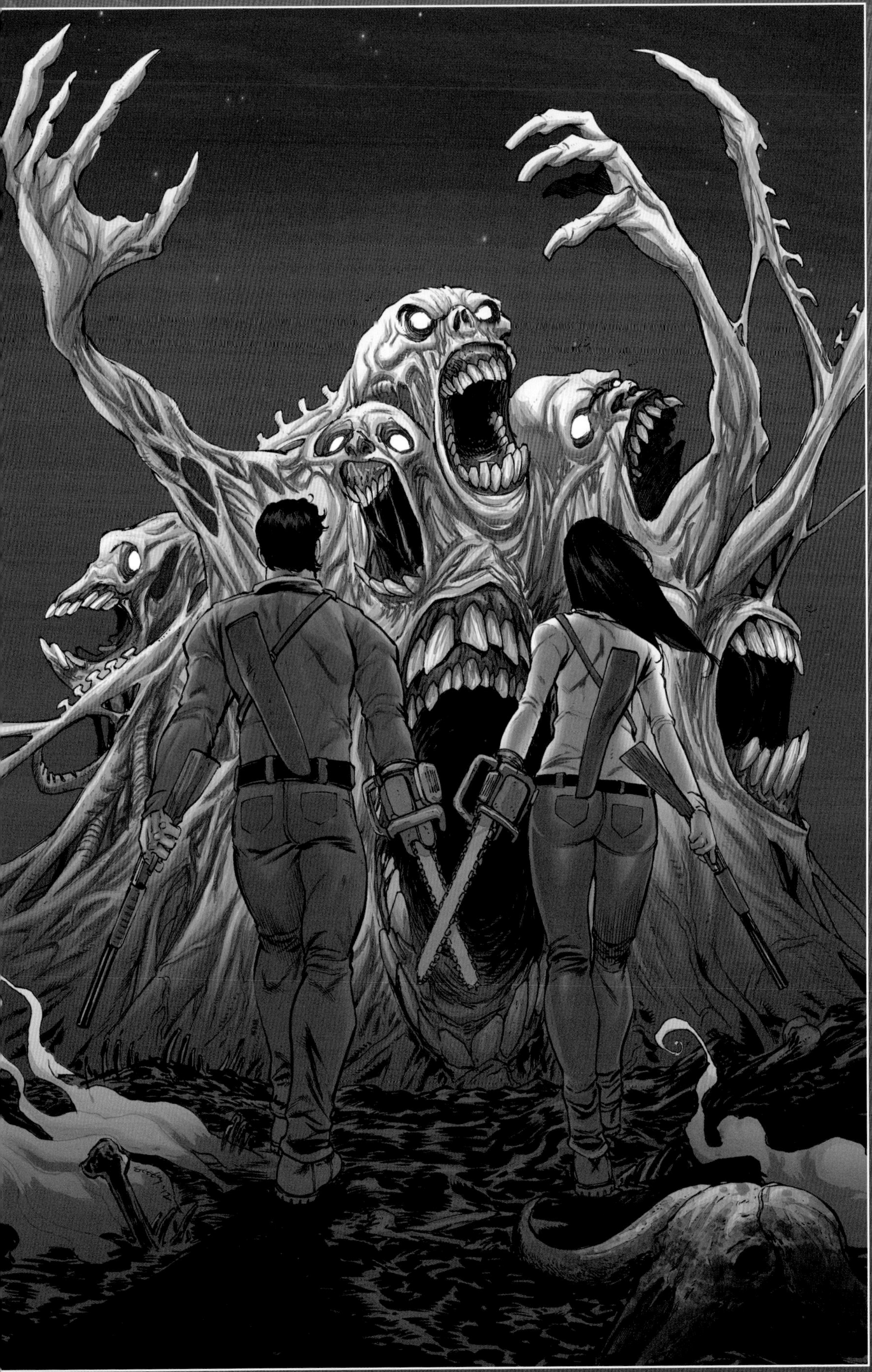

cover to issue #4 by TIM SEELEY, colors by ADRIANO LUCAS

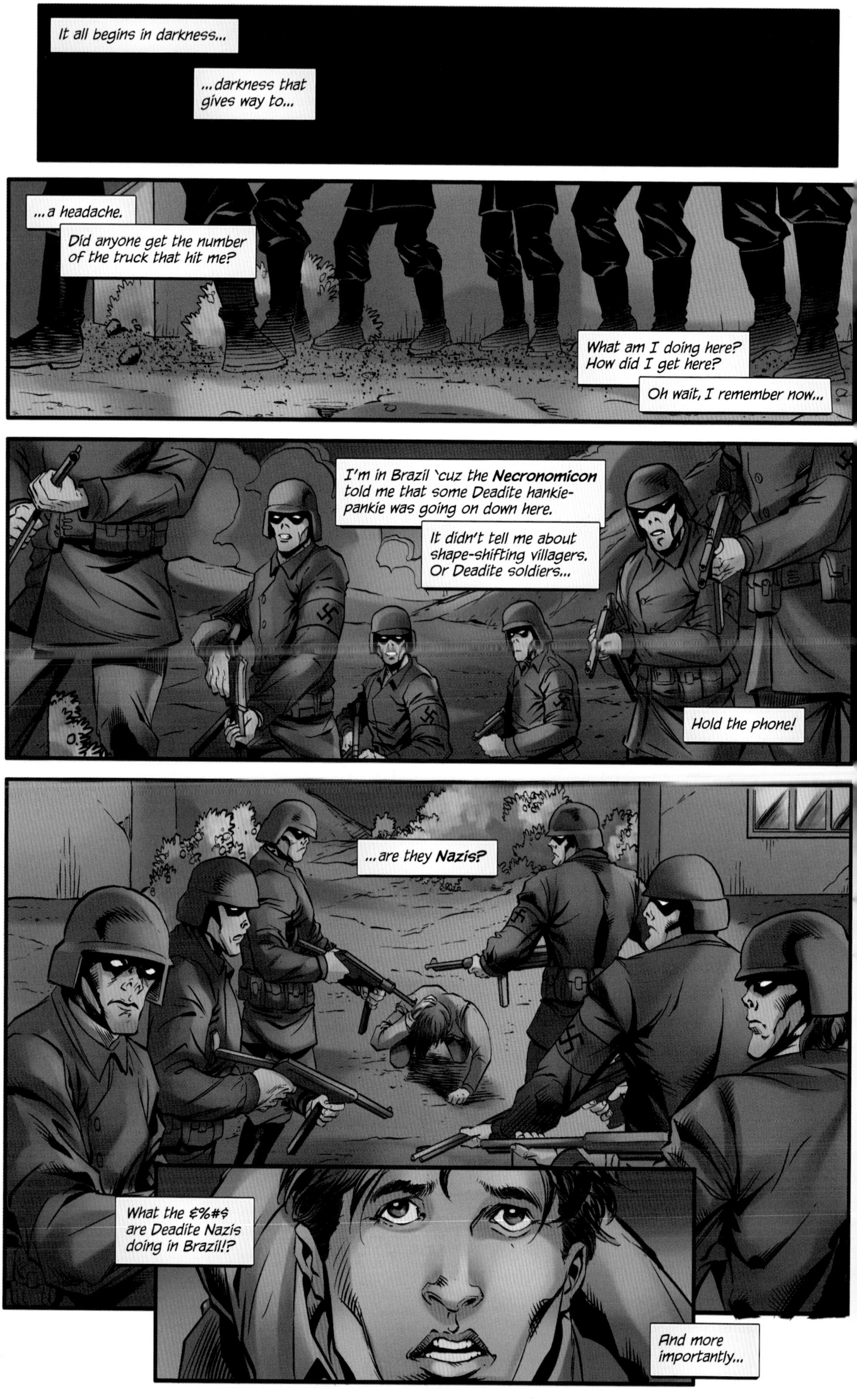
It all begins in darkness...
...darkness that gives way to...
...a headache.
Did anyone get the number of the truck that hit me?
What am I doing here? How did I get here?
Oh wait, I remember now...
I'm in Brazil 'cuz the **Necronomicon** told me that some Deadite hankie-pankie was going on down here.
It didn't tell me about shape-shifting villagers. Or Deadite soldiers...
Hold the phone!
...are they **Nazis?**
What the &%#$ are Deadite Nazis doing in Brazil!?
And more importantly...

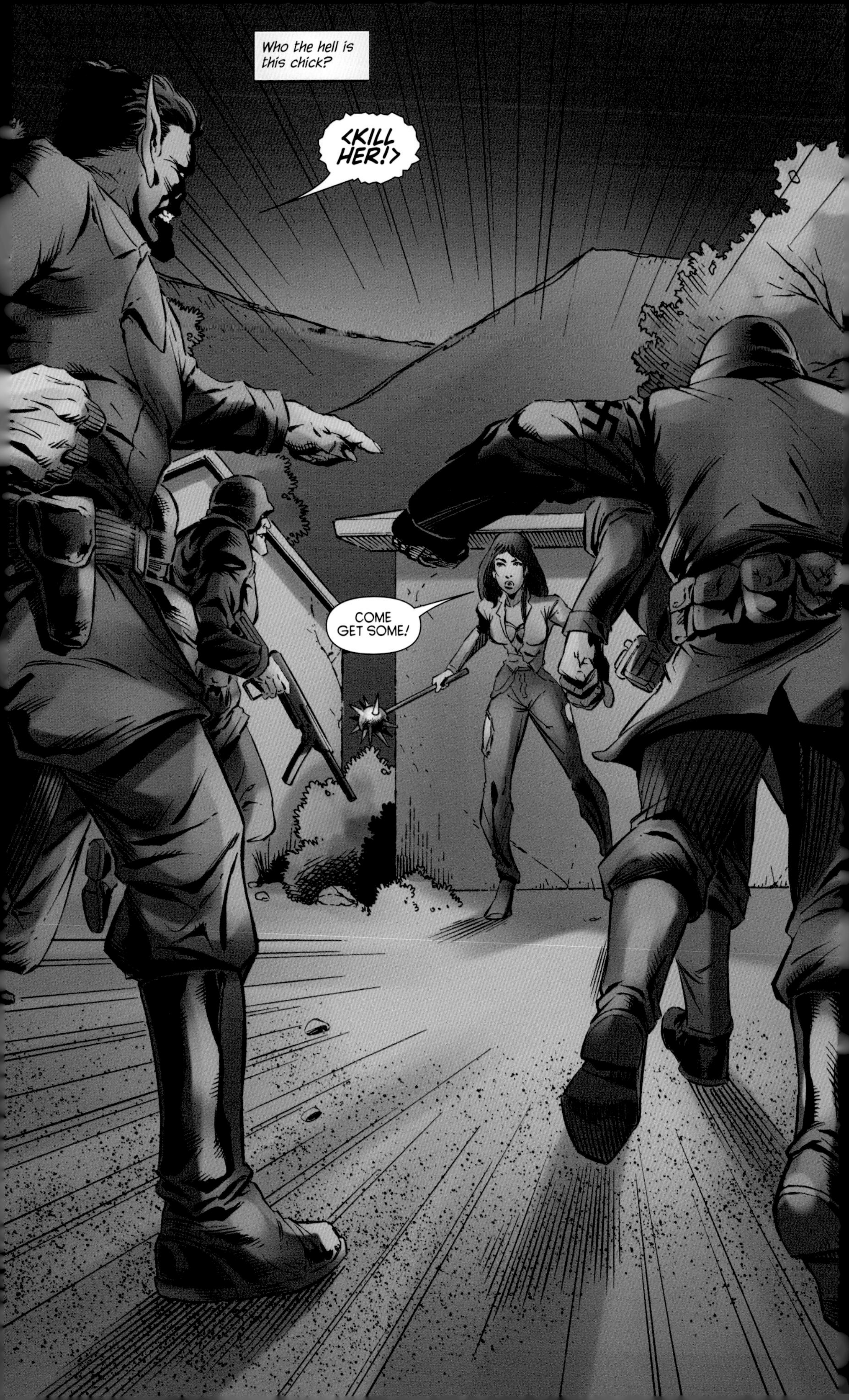
Who the hell is this chick?
<KILL HER!>
COME GET SOME!

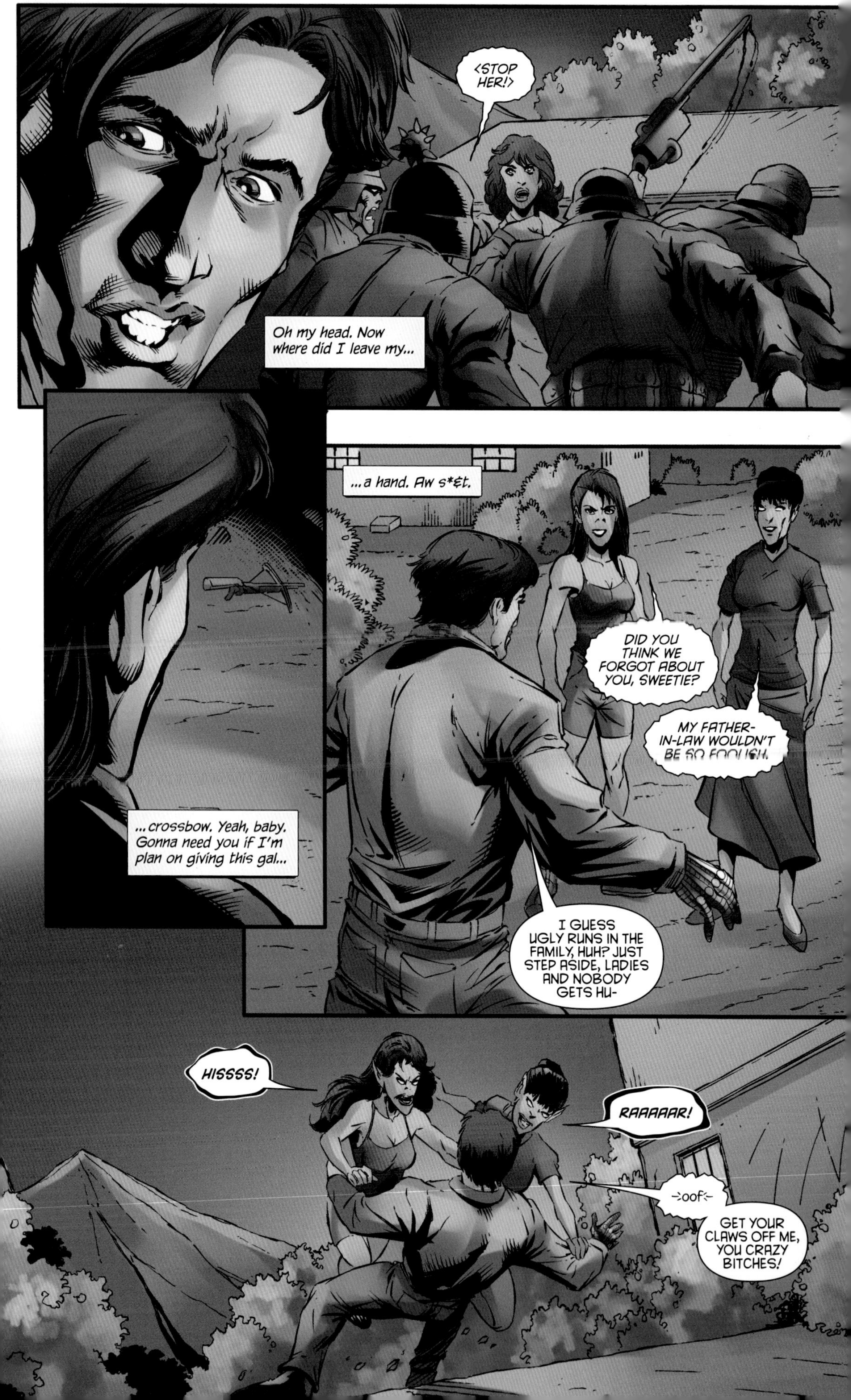

<STOP HER!>
Oh my head. Now where did I leave my...
...crossbow. Yeah, baby. Gonna need you if I'm plan on giving this gal...
...a hand. Aw s*&t.
DID YOU THINK WE FORGOT ABOUT YOU, SWEETIE?
MY FATHER-IN-LAW WOULDN'T BE SO FOOLISH.
I GUESS UGLY RUNS IN THE FAMILY, HUH? JUST STEP ASIDE, LADIES AND NOBODY GETS HU-
HISSSS!
RAAAAAR!
-oof-
GET YOUR CLAWS OFF ME, YOU CRAZY BITCHES!

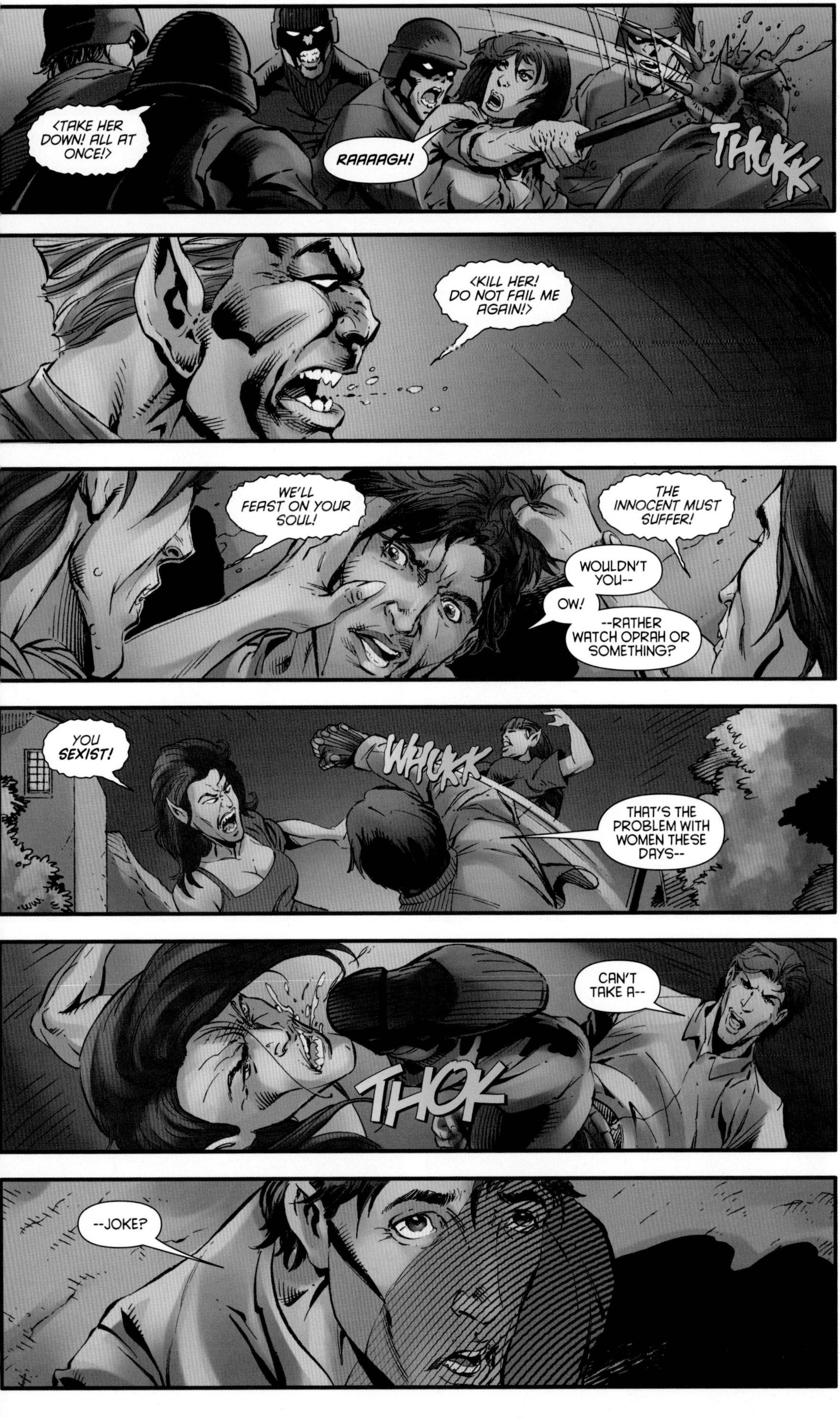
<TAKE HER DOWN! ALL AT ONCE!>
RAAAAGH!
THUKK
<KILL HER! DO NOT FAIL ME AGAIN!>
WE'LL FEAST ON YOUR SOUL!
THE INNOCENT MUST SUFFER!
WOULDN'T YOU--
OW!
--RATHER WATCH OPRAH OR SOMETHING?
YOU SEXIST!
WHUKK
THAT'S THE PROBLEM WITH WOMEN THESE DAYS--
CAN'T TAKE A--
THOK
--JOKE?

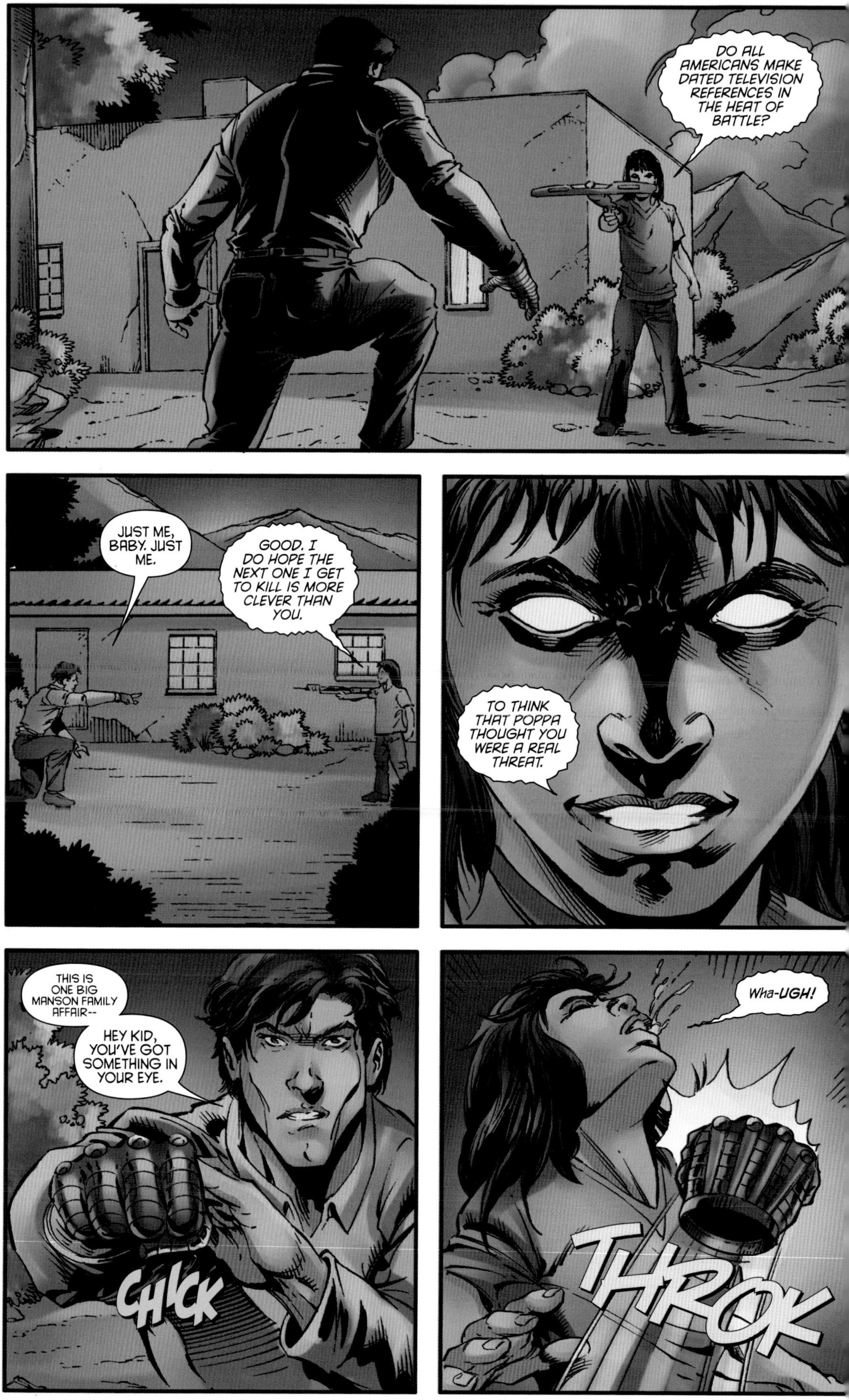
DO ALL AMERICANS MAKE DATED TELEVISION REFERENCES IN THE HEAT OF BATTLE?
JUST ME, BABY. JUST ME.
GOOD. I DO HOPE THE NEXT ONE I GET TO KILL IS MORE CLEVER THAN YOU.
TO THINK THAT POPPA THOUGHT YOU WERE A REAL THREAT.
THIS IS ONE BIG MANSON FAMILY AFFAIR--
HEY KID, YOU'VE GOT SOMETHING IN YOUR EYE.
CHICK
Wha-UGH!
THROK

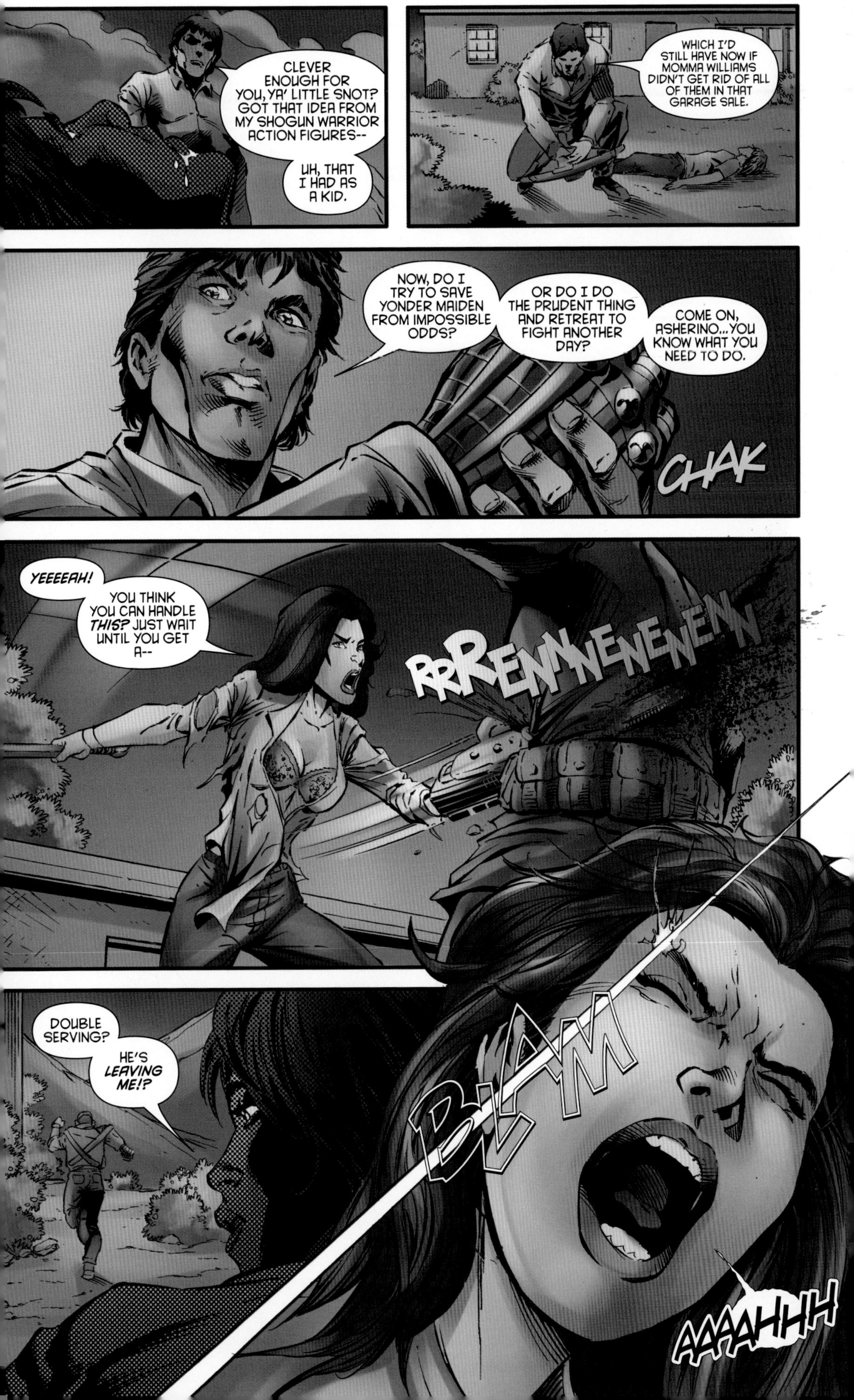

CLEVER ENOUGH FOR YOU, YA' LITTLE SNOT? GOT THAT IDEA FROM MY SHOGUN WARRIOR ACTION FIGURES--
UH, THAT I HAD AS A KID.
WHICH I'D STILL HAVE NOW IF MOMMA WILLIAMS DIDN'T GET RID OF ALL OF THEM IN THAT GARAGE SALE.
NOW, DO I TRY TO SAVE YONDER MAIDEN FROM IMPOSSIBLE ODDS?
OR DO I DO THE PRUDENT THING AND RETREAT TO FIGHT ANOTHER DAY?
COME ON, ASHERINO...YOU KNOW WHAT YOU NEED TO DO.
CHAK
YEEEEAH!
YOU THINK YOU CAN HANDLE *THIS?* JUST WAIT UNTIL YOU GET A--
RRRENNNENENENN
DOUBLE SERVING?
HE'S *LEAVING ME!?*
BLAM
AAAAHHH

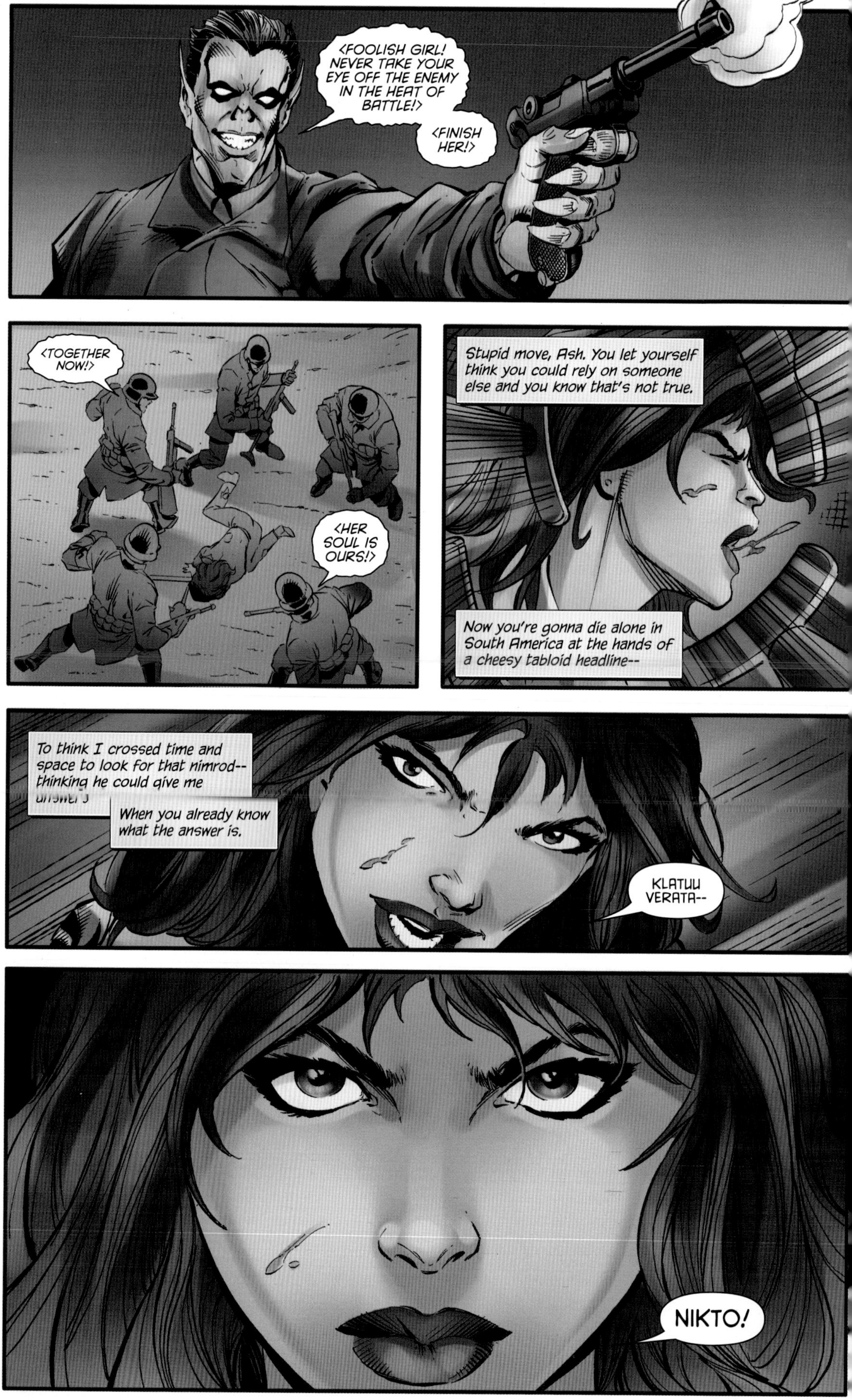
<FOOLISH GIRL! NEVER TAKE YOUR EYE OFF THE ENEMY IN THE HEAT OF BATTLE!>
<FINISH HER!>
<TOGETHER NOW!>
<HER SOUL IS OURS!>
Stupid move, Ash. You let yourself think you could rely on someone else and you know that's not true.
Now you're gonna die alone in South America at the hands of a cheesy tabloid headline--
To think I crossed time and space to look for that nimrod--thinking he could give me
When you already know what the answer is.
KLATUU VERATA--
NIKTO!

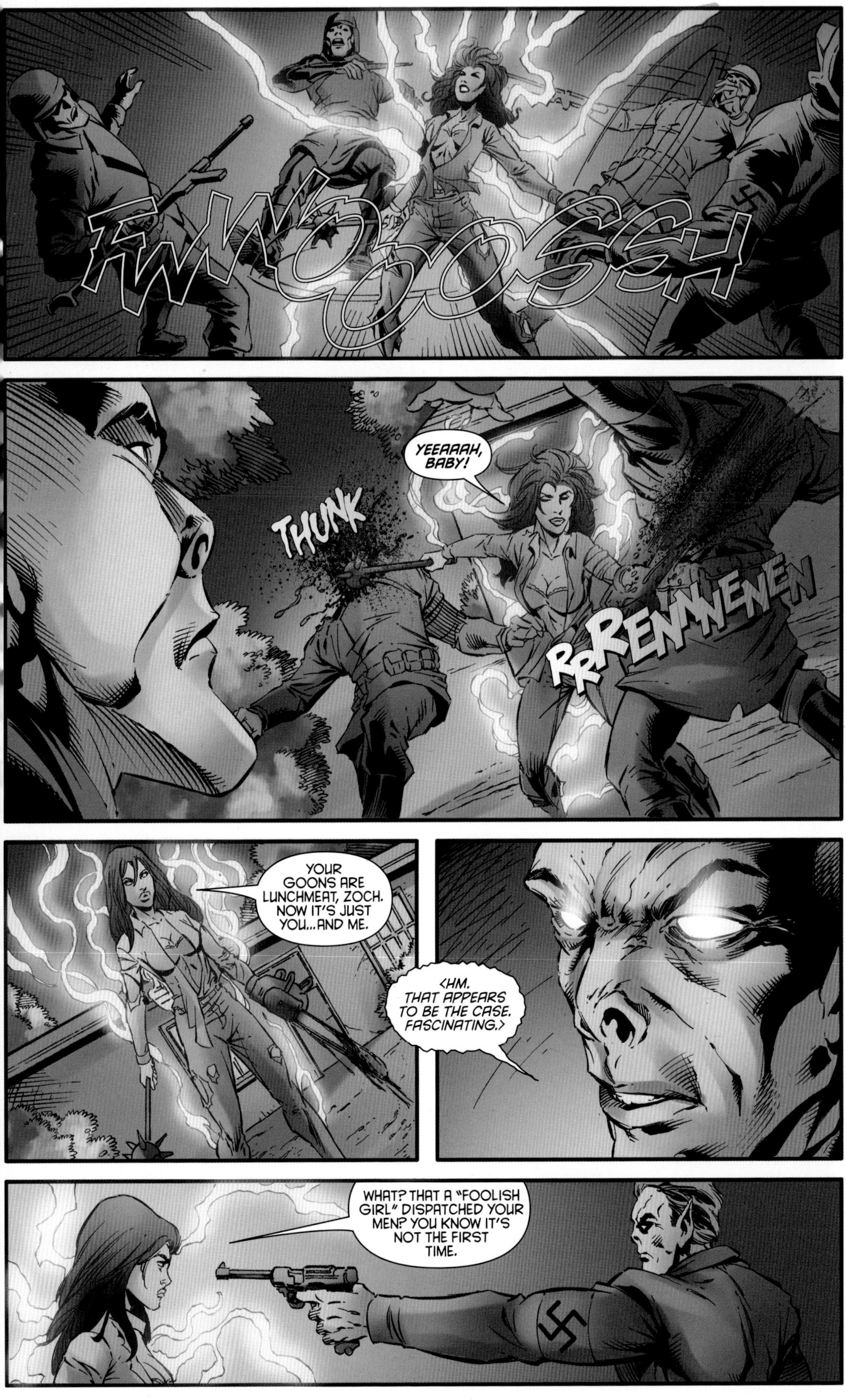
FWWOOOSSH
YEEAAAH, BABY!
THUNK
RRRENNNNENEN
YOUR GOONS ARE LUNCHMEAT, ZOCH. NOW IT'S JUST YOU...AND ME.
<HM. THAT APPEARS TO BE THE CASE. FASCINATING.>
WHAT? THAT A "FOOLISH GIRL" DISPATCHED YOUR MEN? YOU KNOW IT'S NOT THE FIRST TIME.

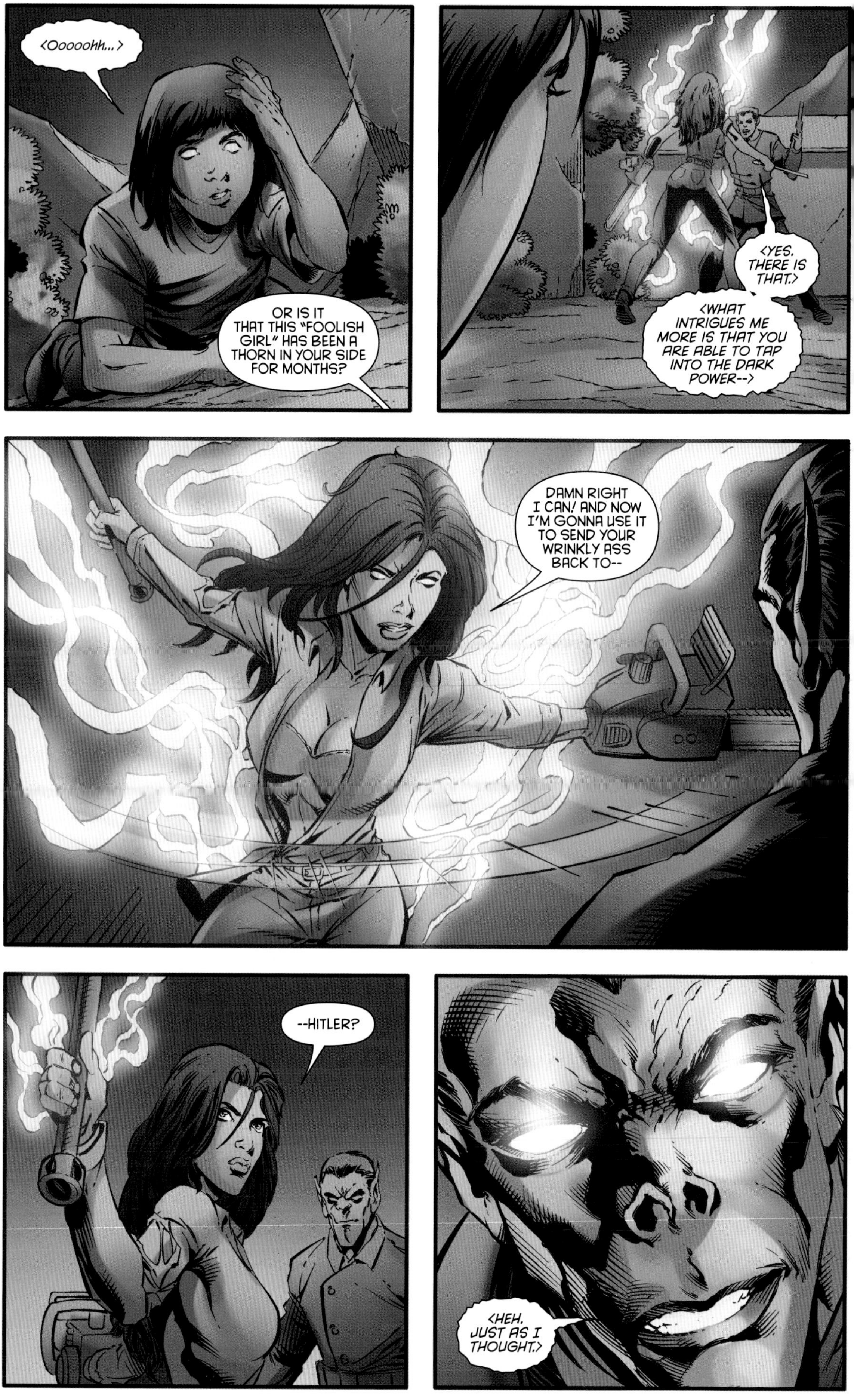
<Ooooohh...>
OR IS IT THAT THIS "FOOLISH GIRL" HAS BEEN A THORN IN YOUR SIDE FOR MONTHS?
<YES. THERE IS THAT.>
<WHAT INTRIGUES ME MORE IS THAT YOU ARE ABLE TO TAP INTO THE DARK POWER-->
DAMN RIGHT I CAN! AND NOW I'M GONNA USE IT TO SEND YOUR WRINKLY ASS BACK TO--
--HITLER?
<HEH. JUST AS I THOUGHT.>

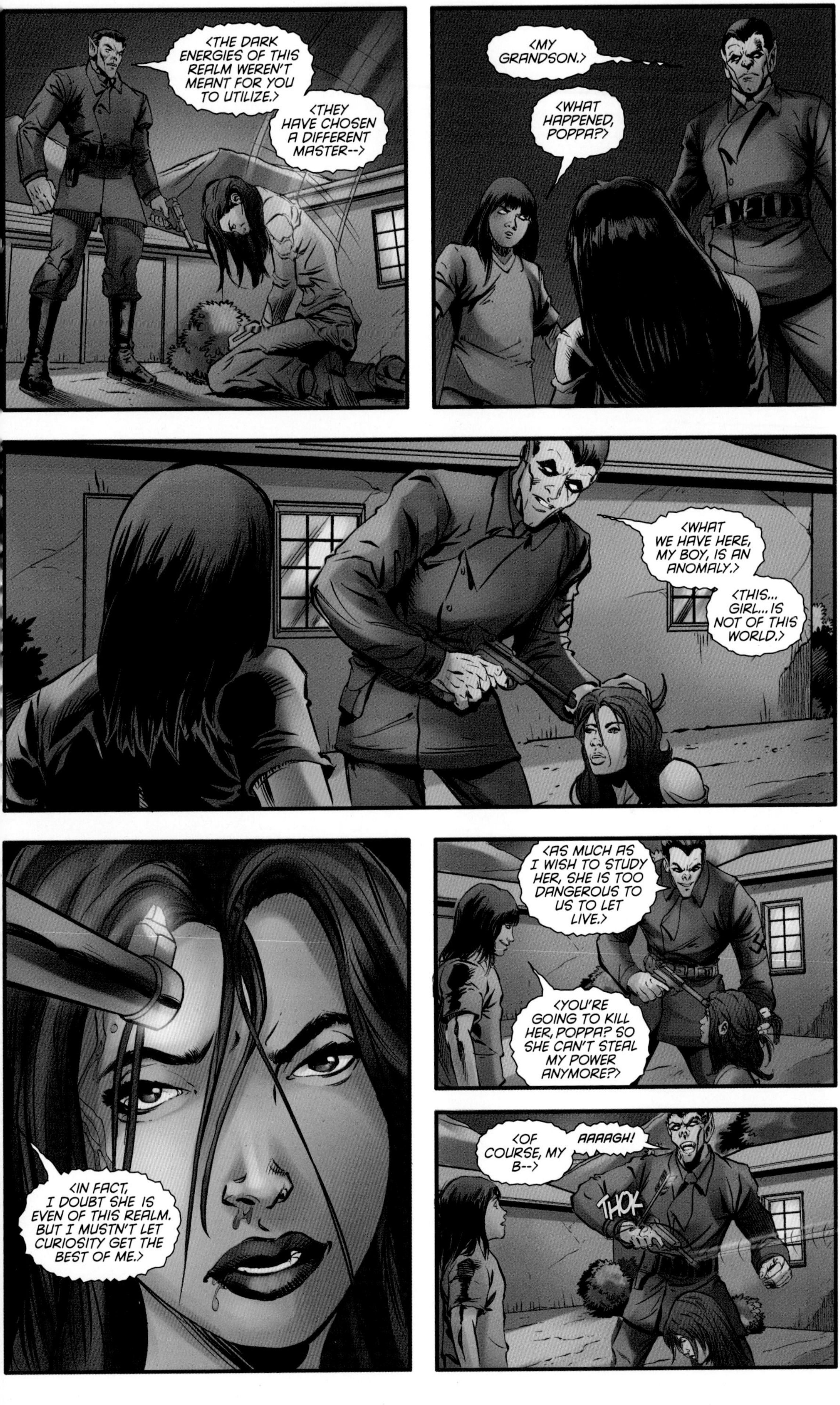
<THE DARK ENERGIES OF THIS REALM WEREN'T MEANT FOR YOU TO UTILIZE.>
<THEY HAVE CHOSEN A DIFFERENT MASTER-->
<MY GRANDSON.>
<WHAT HAPPENED, POPPA?>
<WHAT WE HAVE HERE, MY BOY, IS AN ANOMALY.>
<THIS... GIRL... IS NOT OF THIS WORLD.>
<IN FACT, I DOUBT SHE IS EVEN OF THIS REALM. BUT I MUSTN'T LET CURIOSITY GET THE BEST OF ME.>
<AS MUCH AS I WISH TO STUDY HER, SHE IS TOO DANGEROUS TO US TO LET LIVE.>
<YOU'RE GOING TO KILL HER, POPPA? SO SHE CAN'T STEAL MY POWER ANYMORE?>
<OF COURSE, MY B-->
AAAAGH!
THOK

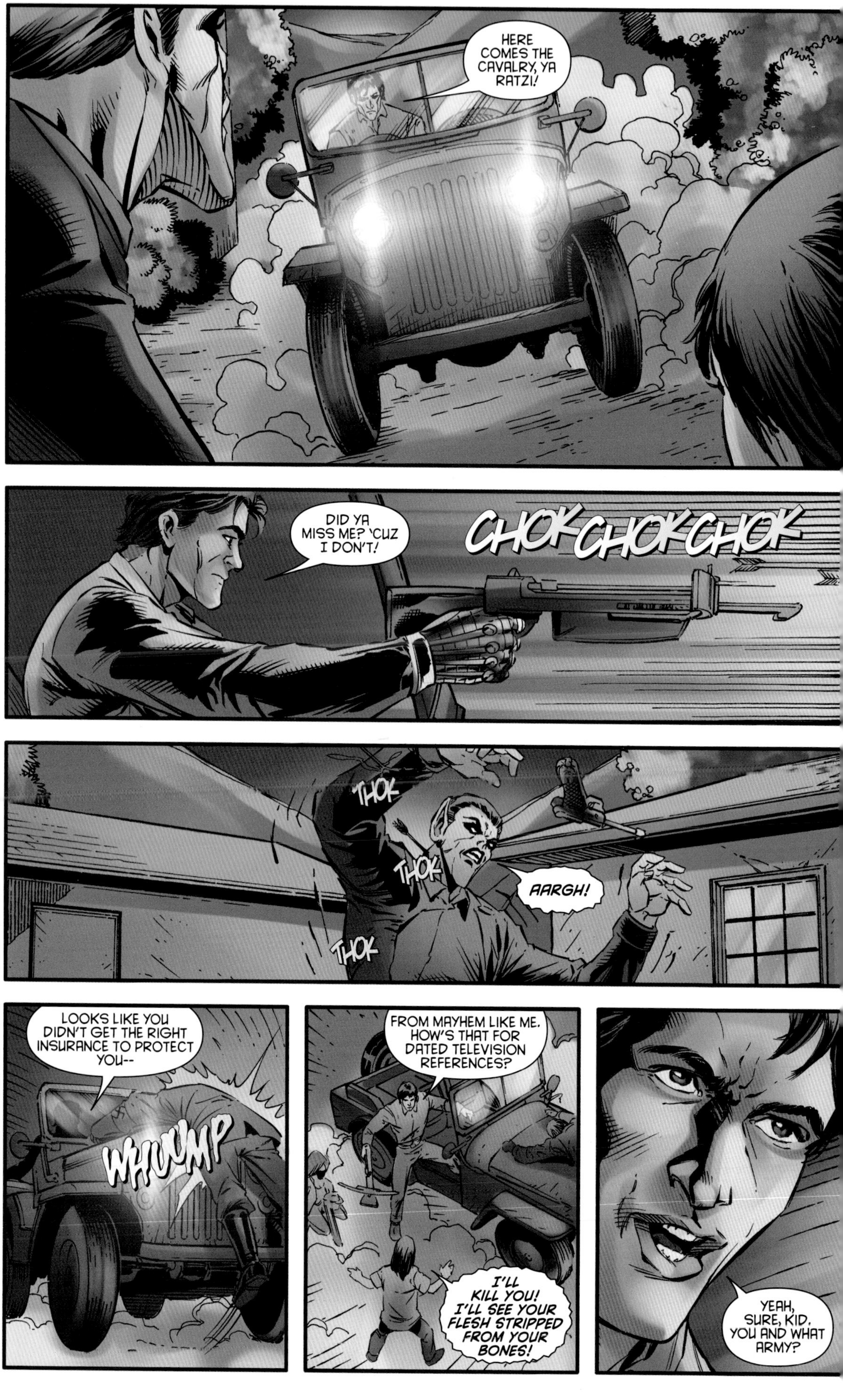
HERE COMES THE CAVALRY, YA RATZI!
DID YA MISS ME? 'CUZ I DON'T!
CHOK CHOK CHOK
THOK
THOK
AARGH!
THOK
LOOKS LIKE YOU DIDN'T GET THE RIGHT INSURANCE TO PROTECT YOU--
WHUUMP
FROM MAYHEM LIKE ME. HOW'S THAT FOR DATED TELEVISION REFERENCES?
I'LL KILL YOU! I'LL SEE YOUR FLESH STRIPPED FROM YOUR BONES!
YEAH, SURE, KID. YOU AND WHAT ARMY?

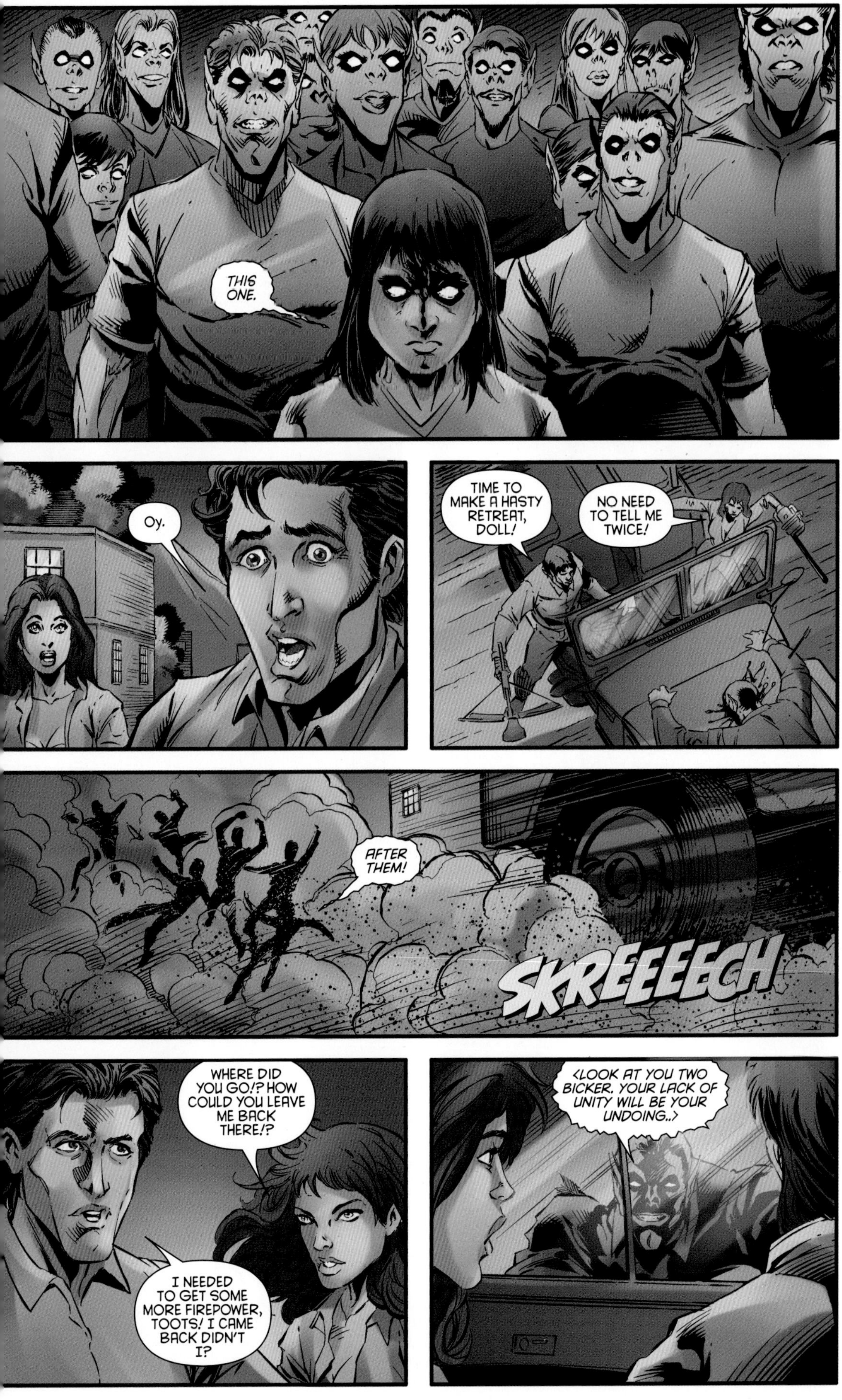
THIS ONE.
Oy.
TIME TO MAKE A HASTY RETREAT, DOLL!
NO NEED TO TELL ME TWICE!
AFTER THEM!
SKREEEECH
WHERE DID YOU GO!? HOW COULD YOU LEAVE ME BACK THERE!?
I NEEDED TO GET SOME MORE FIREPOWER, TOOTS! I CAME BACK DIDN'T I?
<LOOK AT YOU TWO BICKER. YOUR LACK OF UNITY WILL BE YOUR UNDOING..>

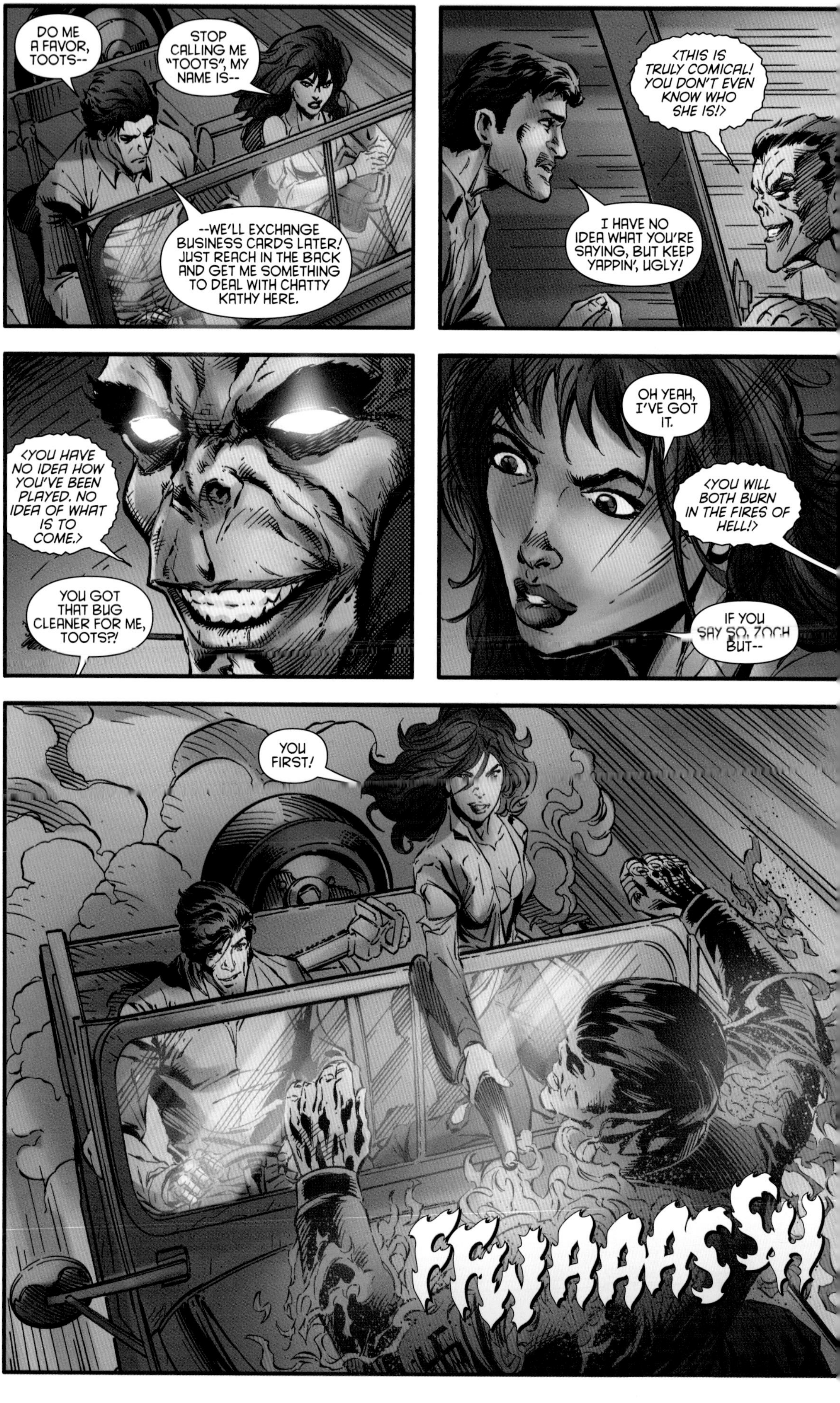
DO ME A FAVOR, TOOTS--
STOP CALLING ME "TOOTS", MY NAME IS--
--WE'LL EXCHANGE BUSINESS CARDS LATER! JUST REACH IN THE BACK AND GET ME SOMETHING TO DEAL WITH CHATTY KATHY HERE.
<THIS IS TRULY COMICAL! YOU DON'T EVEN KNOW WHO SHE IS!>
I HAVE NO IDEA WHAT YOU'RE SAYING, BUT KEEP YAPPIN', UGLY!
<YOU HAVE NO IDEA HOW YOU'VE BEEN PLAYED. NO IDEA OF WHAT IS TO COME.>
YOU GOT THAT BUG CLEANER FOR ME, TOOTS?!
OH YEAH, I'VE GOT IT.
<YOU WILL BOTH BURN IN THE FIRES OF HELL!>
IF YOU SAY SO, ZOCH BUT--
YOU FIRST!
FWAAASH

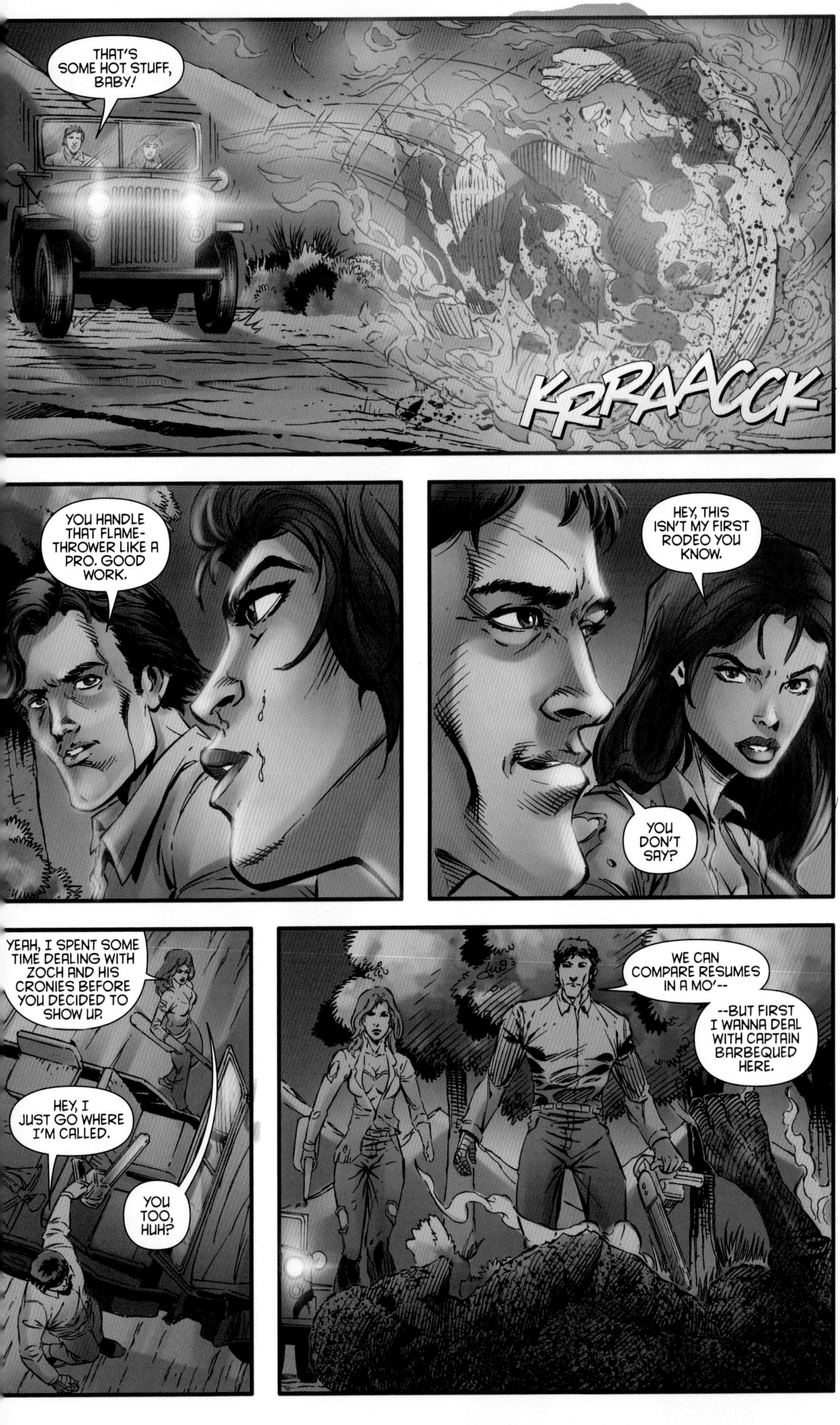
THAT'S SOME HOT STUFF, BABY!
KRRAACCK
YOU HANDLE THAT FLAME-THROWER LIKE A PRO. GOOD WORK.
HEY, THIS ISN'T MY FIRST RODEO YOU KNOW.
YOU DON'T SAY?
YEAH, I SPENT SOME TIME DEALING WITH ZOCH AND HIS CRONIES BEFORE YOU DECIDED TO SHOW UP.
HEY, I JUST GO WHERE I'M CALLED.
YOU TOO, HUH?
WE CAN COMPARE RESUMES IN A MO'--
--BUT FIRST I WANNA DEAL WITH CAPTAIN BARBEQUED HERE.

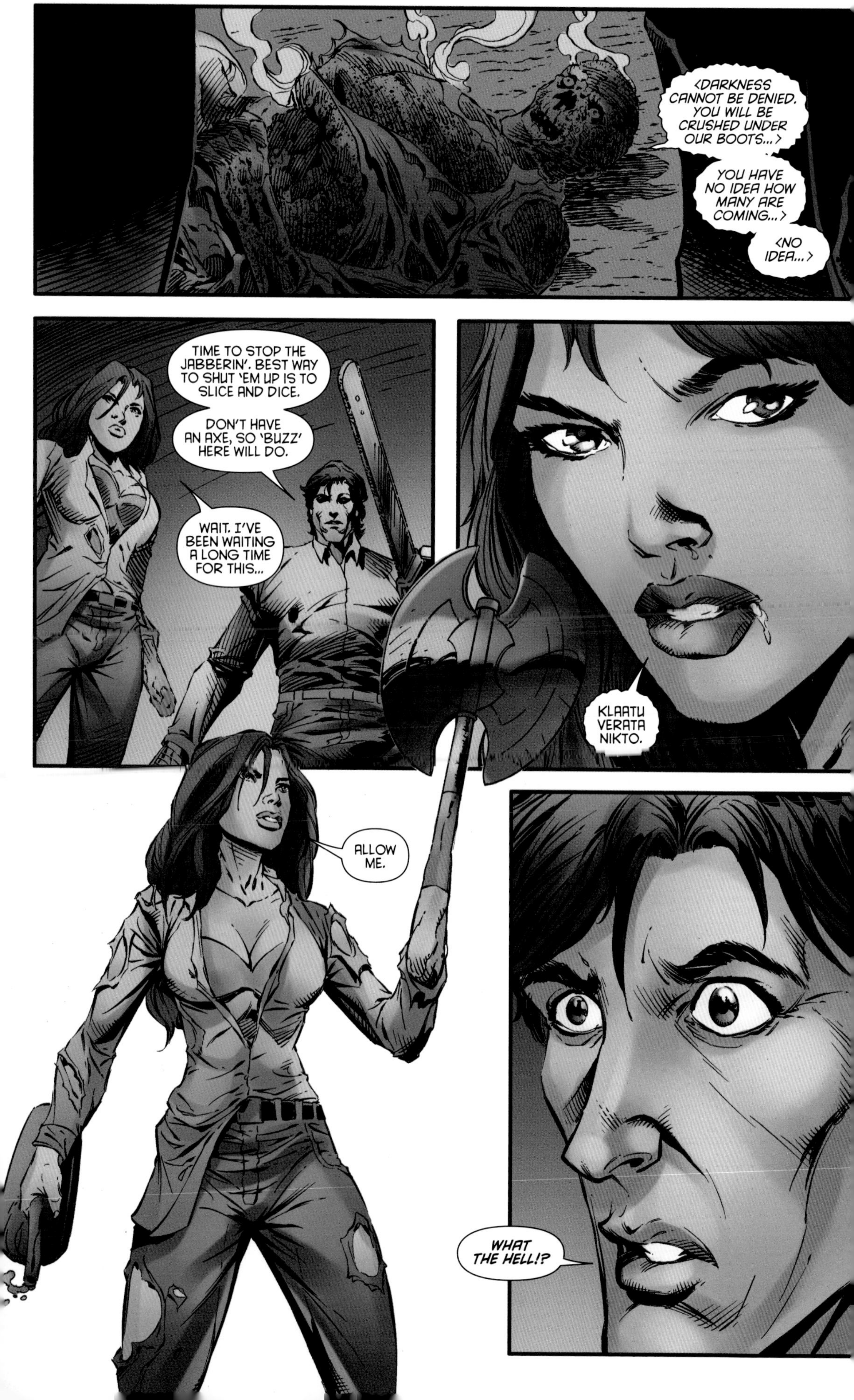
<DARKNESS CANNOT BE DENIED. YOU WILL BE CRUSHED UNDER OUR BOOTS...>
YOU HAVE NO IDEA HOW MANY ARE COMING...>
<NO IDEA...>
TIME TO STOP THE JABBERIN'. BEST WAY TO SHUT 'EM UP IS TO SLICE AND DICE.
DON'T HAVE AN AXE, SO 'BUZZ' HERE WILL DO.
WAIT. I'VE BEEN WAITING A LONG TIME FOR THIS...
KLAATU VERATA NIKTO.
ALLOW ME.
WHAT THE HELL!?

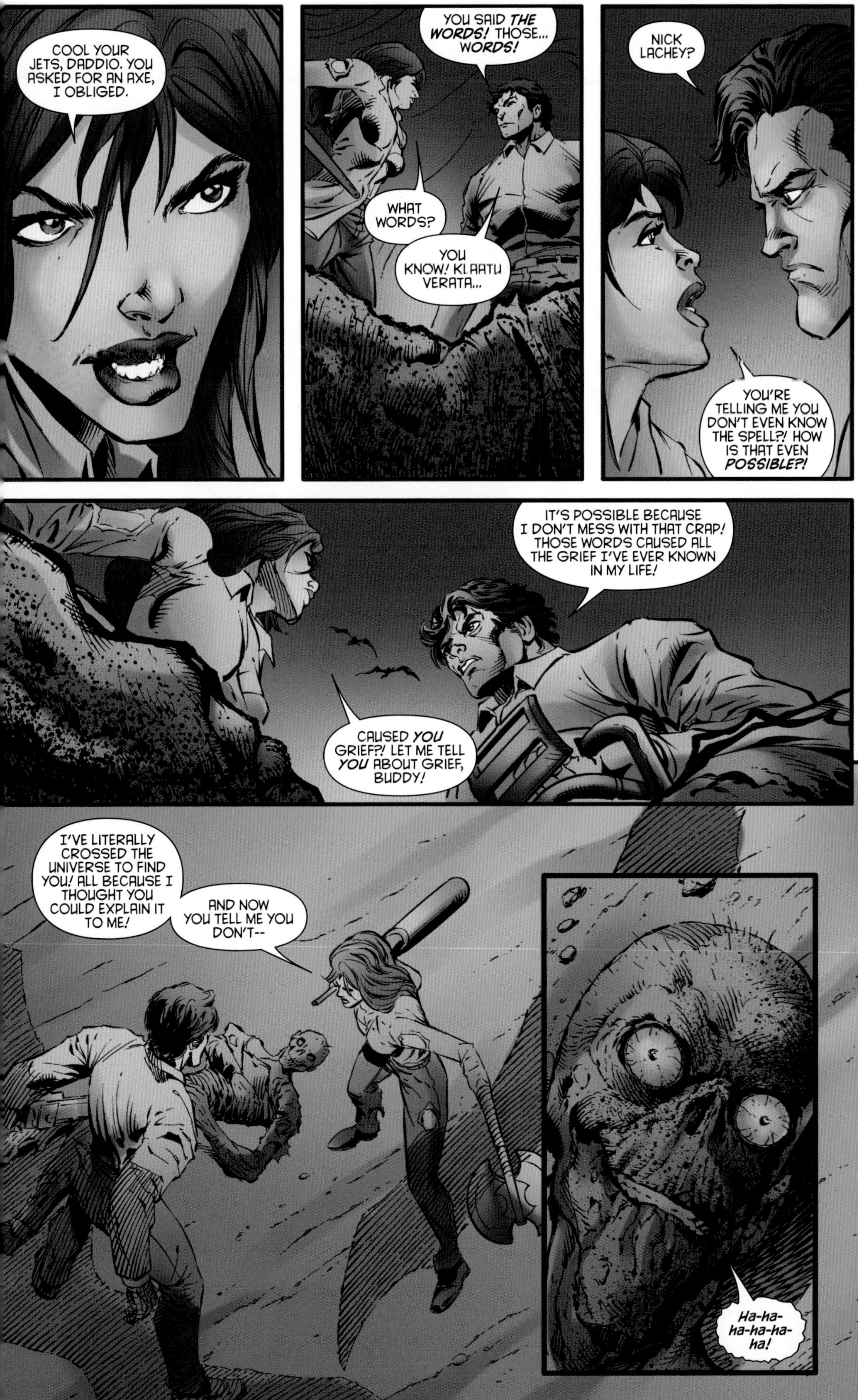
COOL YOUR JETS, DADDIO. YOU ASKED FOR AN AXE, I OBLIGED.
YOU SAID *THE WORDS!* THOSE... *WORDS!*
WHAT WORDS?
YOU KNOW! KLAATU VERATA...
NICK LACHEY?
YOU'RE TELLING ME YOU DON'T EVEN KNOW THE SPELL?! HOW IS THAT EVEN *POSSIBLE?!*
IT'S POSSIBLE BECAUSE I DON'T MESS WITH THAT CRAP! THOSE WORDS CAUSED ALL THE GRIEF I'VE EVER KNOWN IN MY LIFE!
CAUSED *YOU* GRIEF?! LET ME TELL *YOU* ABOUT GRIEF, BUDDY!
I'VE LITERALLY CROSSED THE UNIVERSE TO FIND YOU! ALL BECAUSE I THOUGHT YOU COULD EXPLAIN IT TO ME!
AND NOW YOU TELL ME YOU DON'T--
Ha-ha-ha-ha-ha-ha!

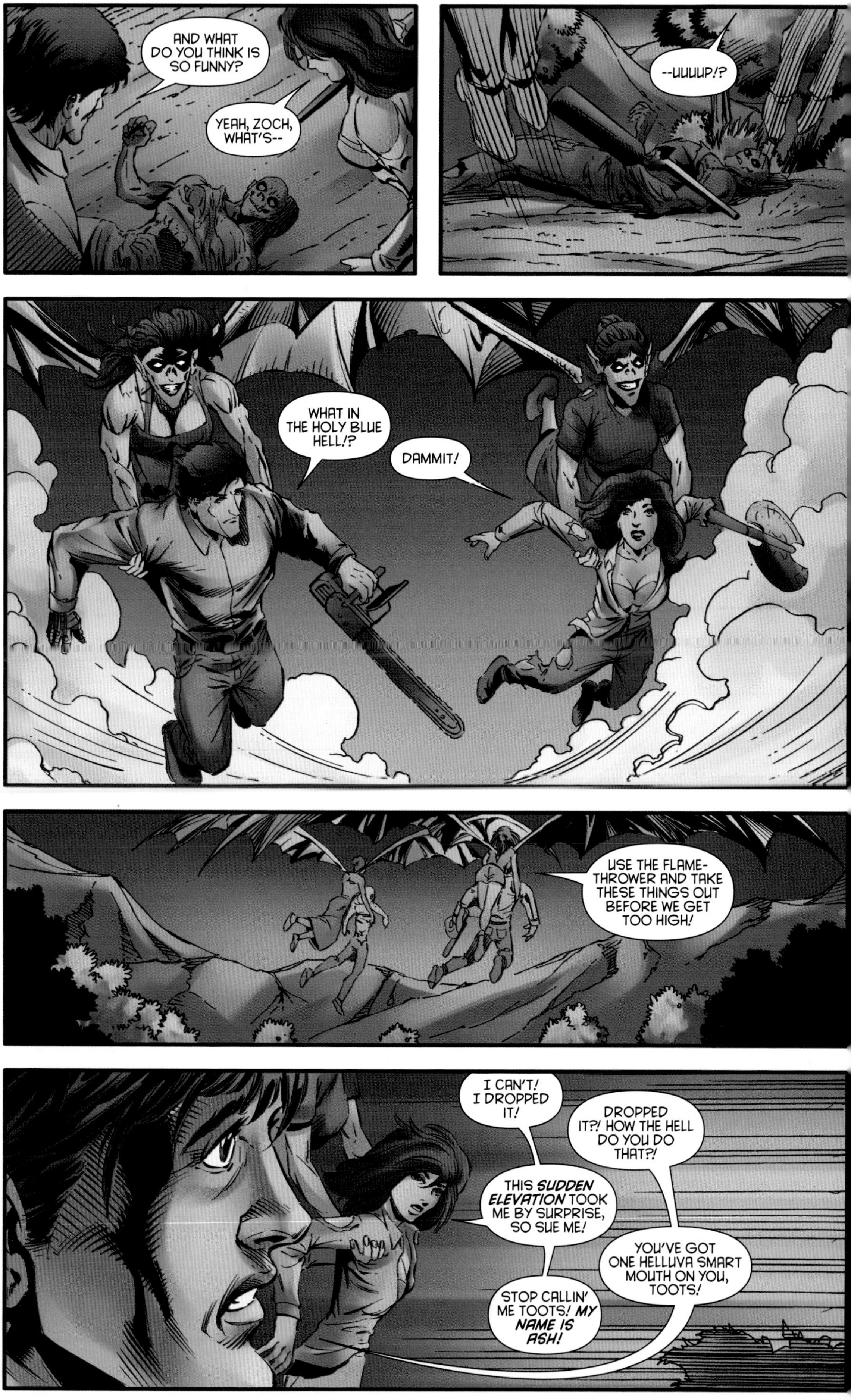
AND WHAT DO YOU THINK IS SO FUNNY?
YEAH, ZOCH, WHAT'S--
--UUUUP!?
WHAT IN THE HOLY BLUE HELL!?
DAMMIT!
USE THE FLAME-THROWER AND TAKE THESE THINGS OUT BEFORE WE GET TOO HIGH!
I CAN'T! I DROPPED IT!
DROPPED IT?! HOW THE HELL DO YOU DO THAT?!
THIS SUDDEN ELEVATION TOOK ME BY SURPRISE, SO SUE ME!
YOU'VE GOT ONE HELLUVA SMART MOUTH ON YOU, TOOTS!
STOP CALLIN' ME TOOTS! MY NAME IS ASH!

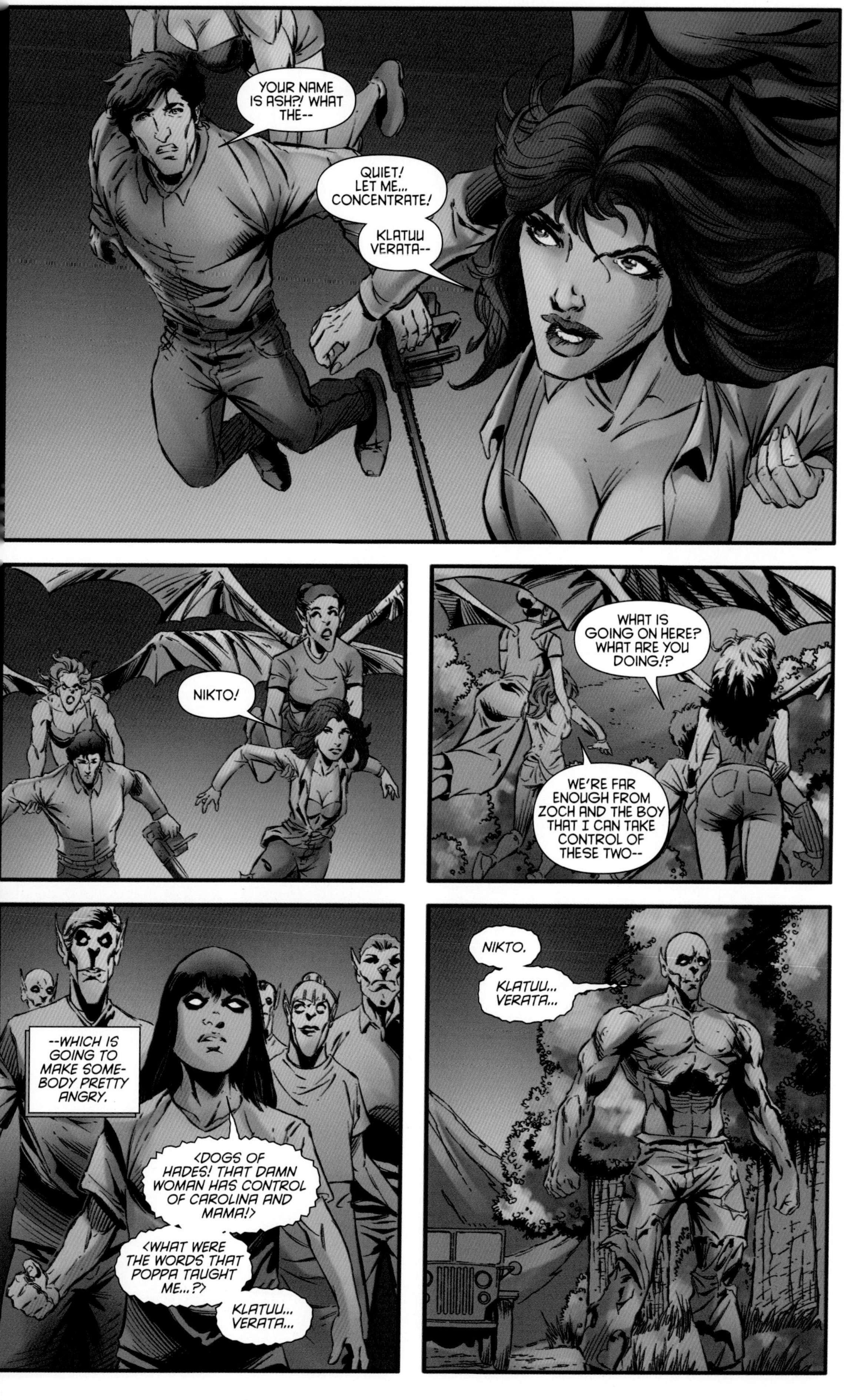
YOUR NAME IS ASH?! WHAT THE--
QUIET! LET ME... CONCENTRATE!
KLATUU VERATA--
NIKTO!
WHAT IS GOING ON HERE? WHAT ARE YOU DOING!?
WE'RE FAR ENOUGH FROM ZOCH AND THE BOY THAT I CAN TAKE CONTROL OF THESE TWO--
--WHICH IS GOING TO MAKE SOME-BODY PRETTY ANGRY.
<DOGS OF HADES! THAT DAMN WOMAN HAS CONTROL OF CAROLINA AND MAMA!>
<WHAT WERE THE WORDS THAT POPPA TAUGHT ME...?>
KLATUU... VERATA...
NIKTO.
KLATUU... VERATA...

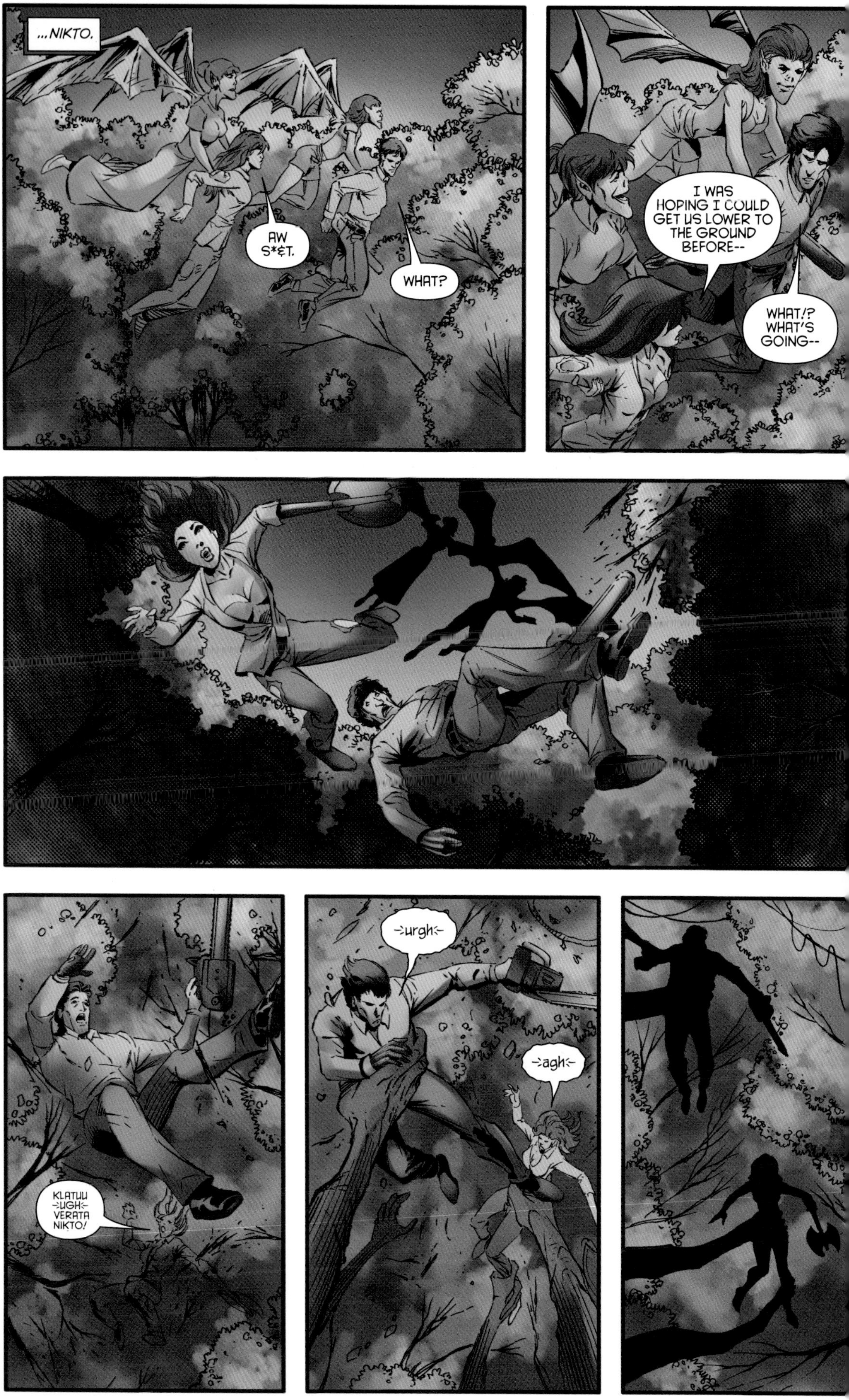
...NIKTO.
AW S*&T.
WHAT?
I WAS HOPING I COULD GET US LOWER TO THE GROUND BEFORE--
WHAT!? WHAT'S GOING--
KLATUU ~UGH~ VERATA NIKTO!
~urgh~
~agh~

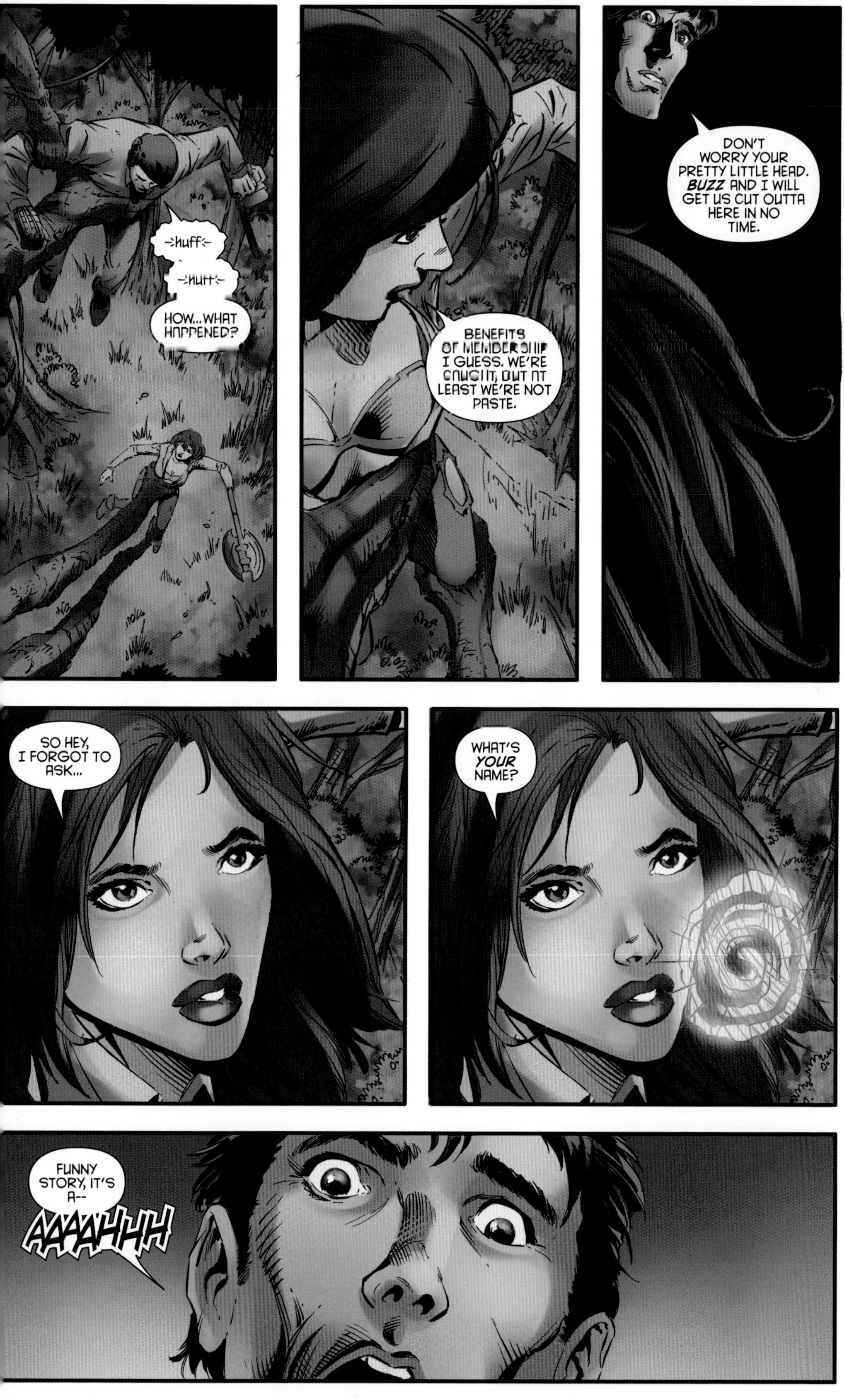
-huff-
-huff-
HOW... WHAT HAPPENED?
BENEFITS OF MEMBERSHIP I GUESS. WE'RE CAUGHT, BUT AT LEAST WE'RE NOT PASTE.
DON'T WORRY YOUR PRETTY LITTLE HEAD. *BUZZ* AND I WILL GET US CUT OUTTA HERE IN NO TIME.
SO HEY, I FORGOT TO ASK...
WHAT'S *YOUR* NAME?
FUNNY STORY, IT'S A--
AAAAHHH

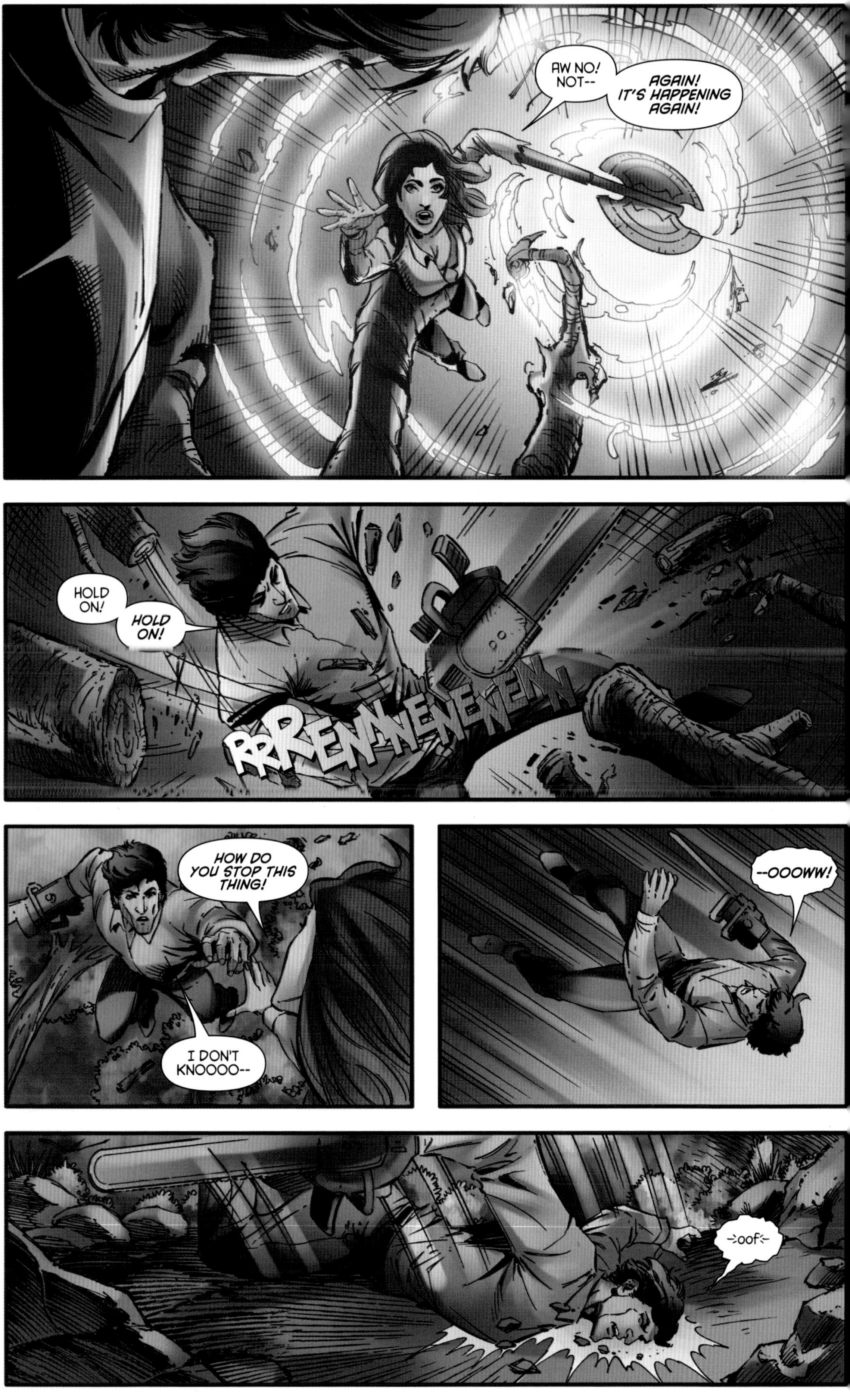
AW NO! NOT--
AGAIN! IT'S HAPPENING AGAIN!
HOLD ON!
HOLD ON!
RRRENNNENENENN
HOW DO YOU STOP THIS THING!
I DON'T KNOOOO--
--OOOWW!
oof

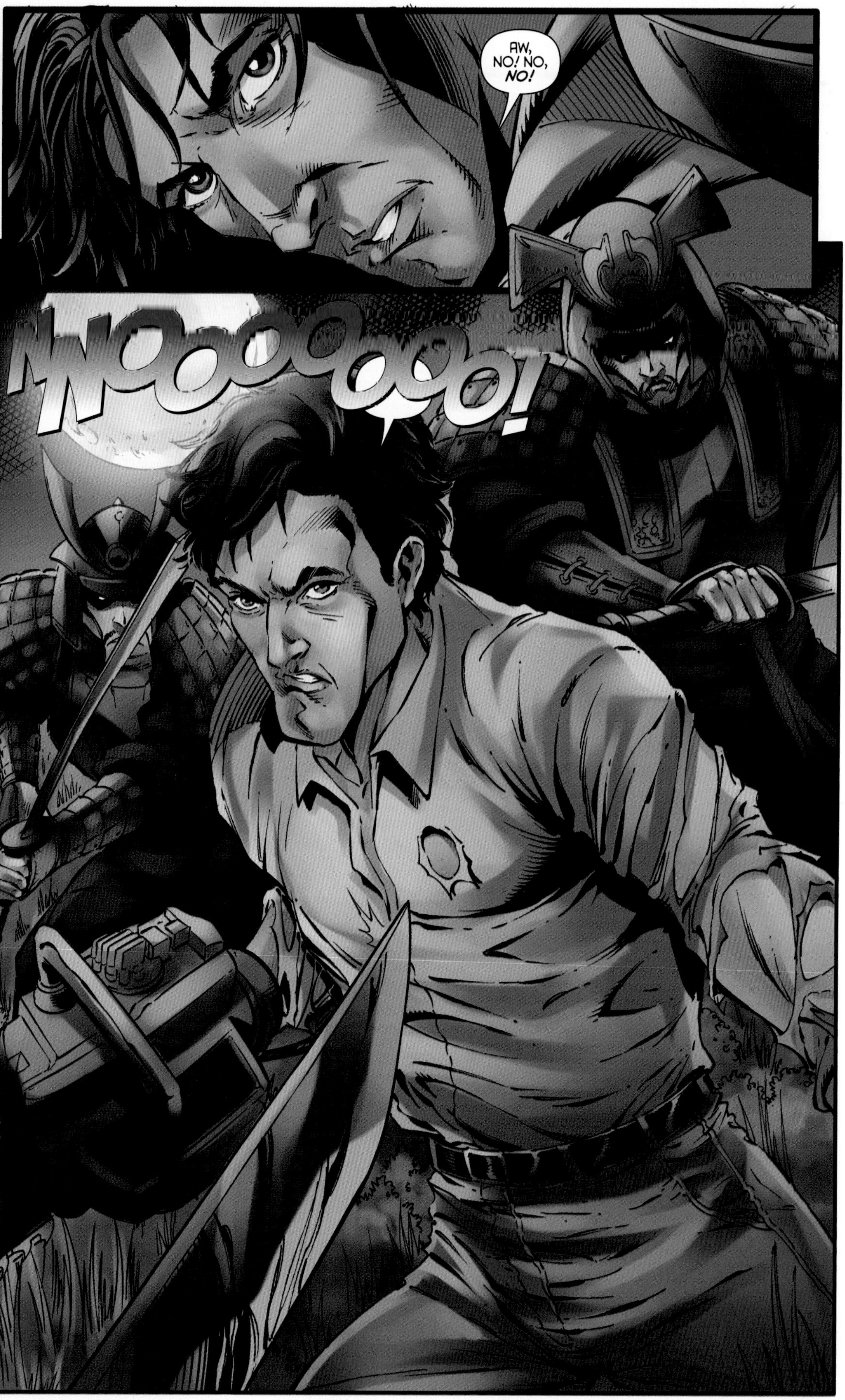

AW, NO! NO, NO!
MNOOOOOOOO!

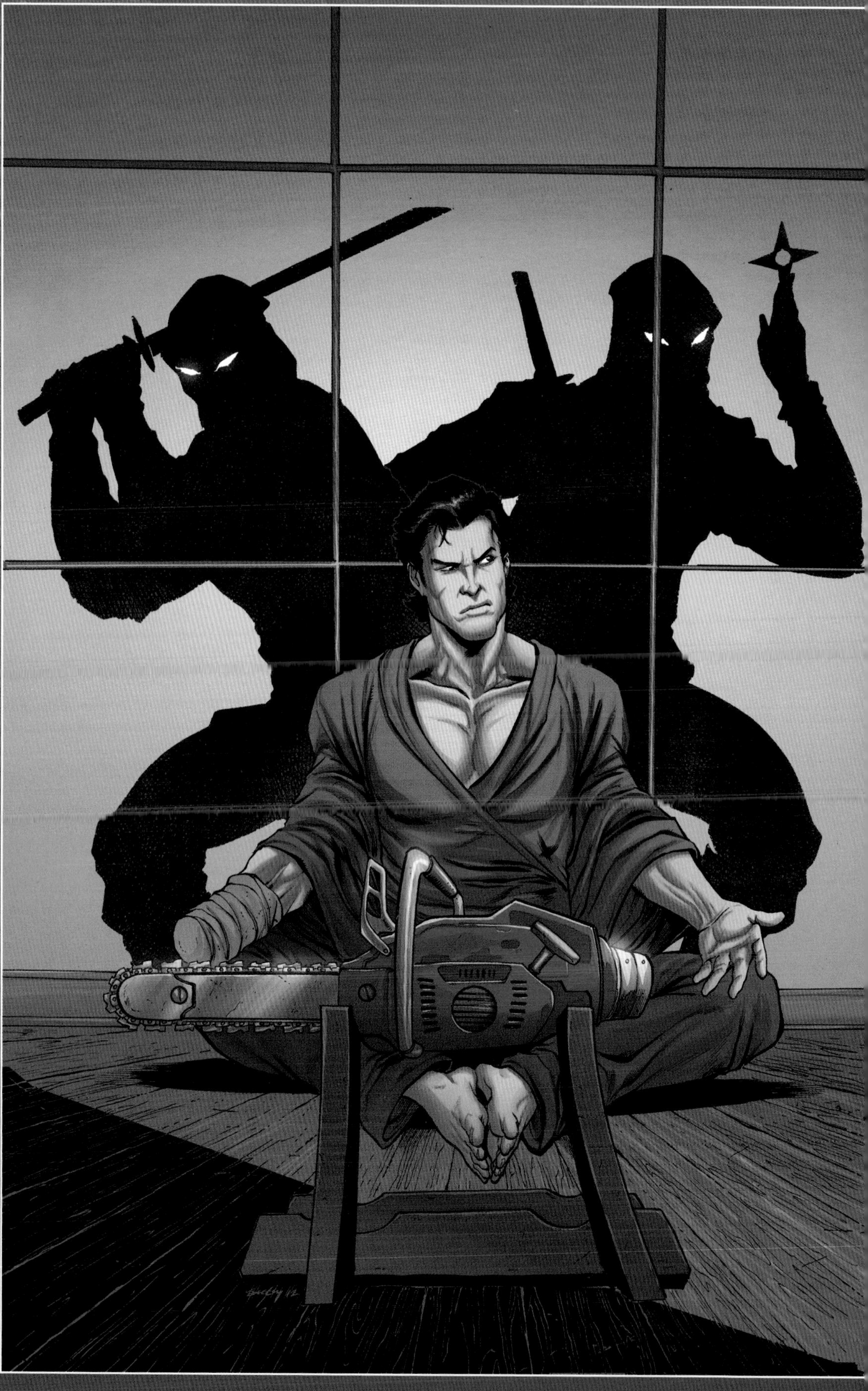

cover to issue #5 by TIM SEELEY, colors by ADRIANO LUCAS

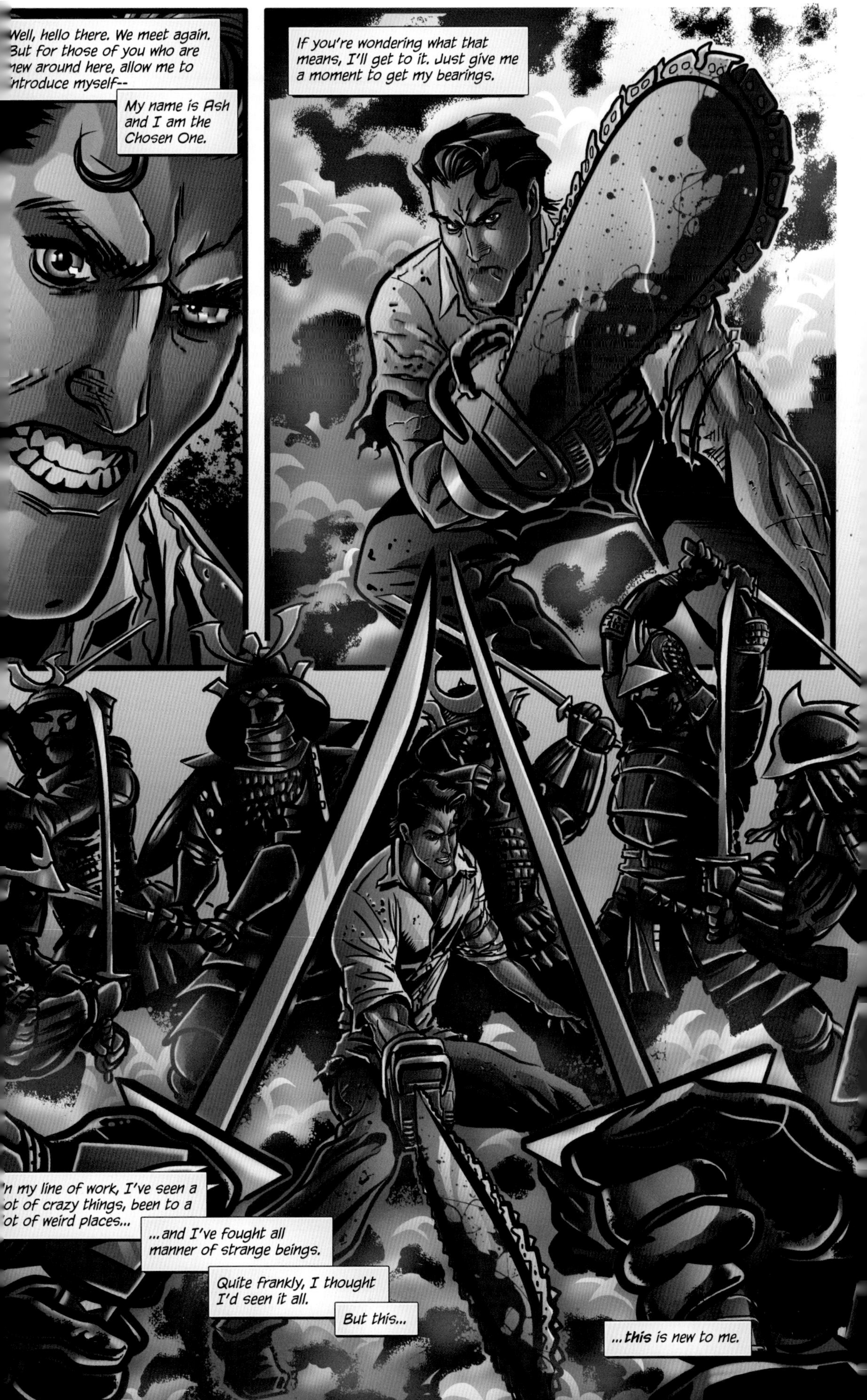

Well, hello there. We meet again. But for those of you who are new around here, allow me to introduce myself--
My name is Ash and I am the Chosen One.
If you're wondering what that means, I'll get to it. Just give me a moment to get my bearings.
In my line of work, I've seen a lot of crazy things, been to a lot of weird places...
...and I've fought all manner of strange beings.
Quite frankly, I thought I'd seen it all.
But this...
...**this** is new to me.

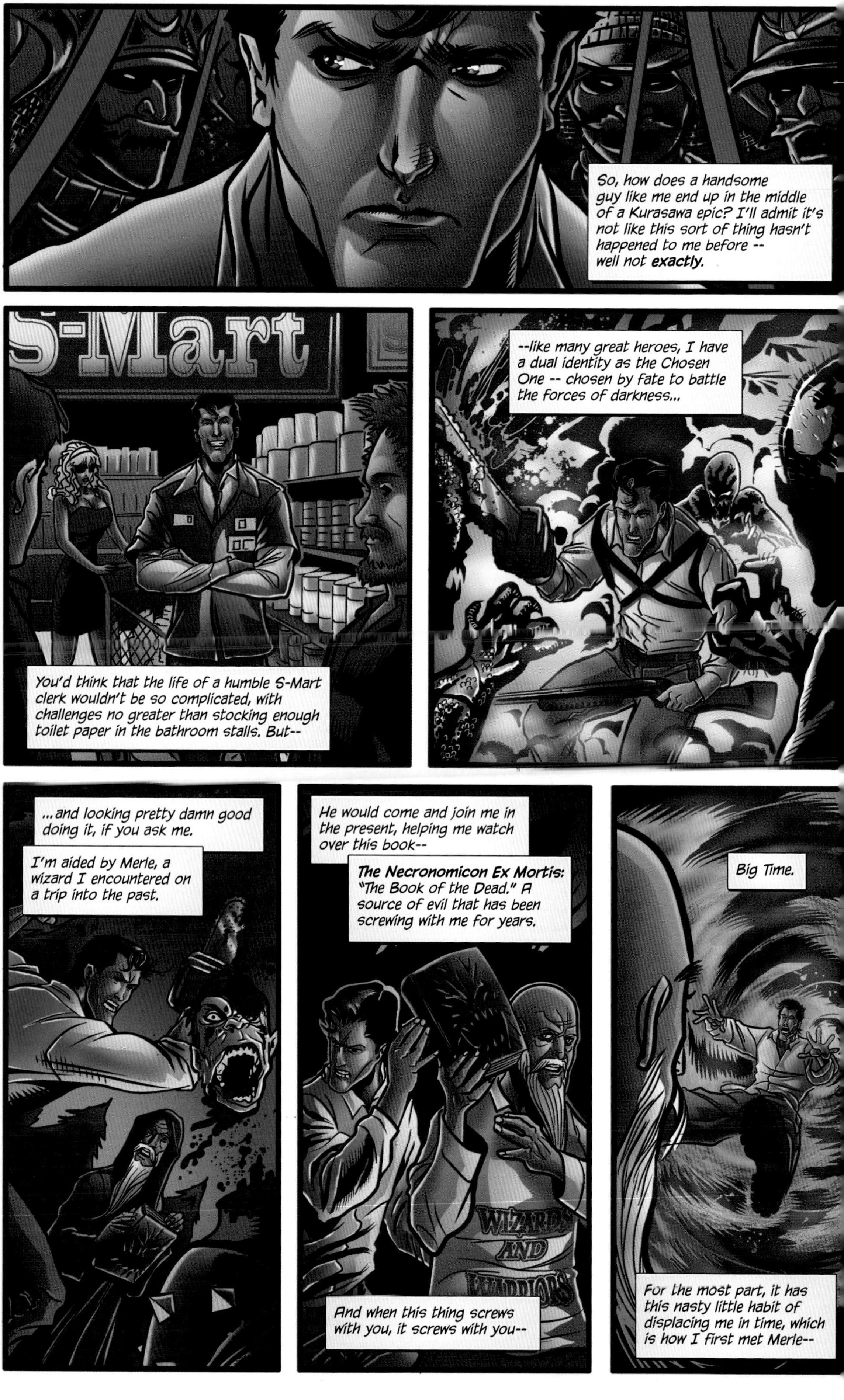
So, how does a handsome guy like me end up in the middle of a Kurasawa epic? I'll admit it's not like this sort of thing hasn't happened to me before -- well not **exactly**.
S-Mart
You'd think that the life of a humble S-Mart clerk wouldn't be so complicated, with challenges no greater than stocking enough toilet paper in the bathroom stalls. But--
--like many great heroes, I have a dual identity as the Chosen One -- chosen by fate to battle the forces of darkness...
...and looking pretty damn good doing it, if you ask me.
I'm aided by Merle, a wizard I encountered on a trip into the past.
He would come and join me in the present, helping me watch over this book--
The Necronomicon Ex Mortis: "The Book of the Dead." A source of evil that has been screwing with me for years.
And when this thing screws with you, it screws with you--
Big Time.
For the most part, it has this nasty little habit of displacing me in time, which is how I first met Merle--

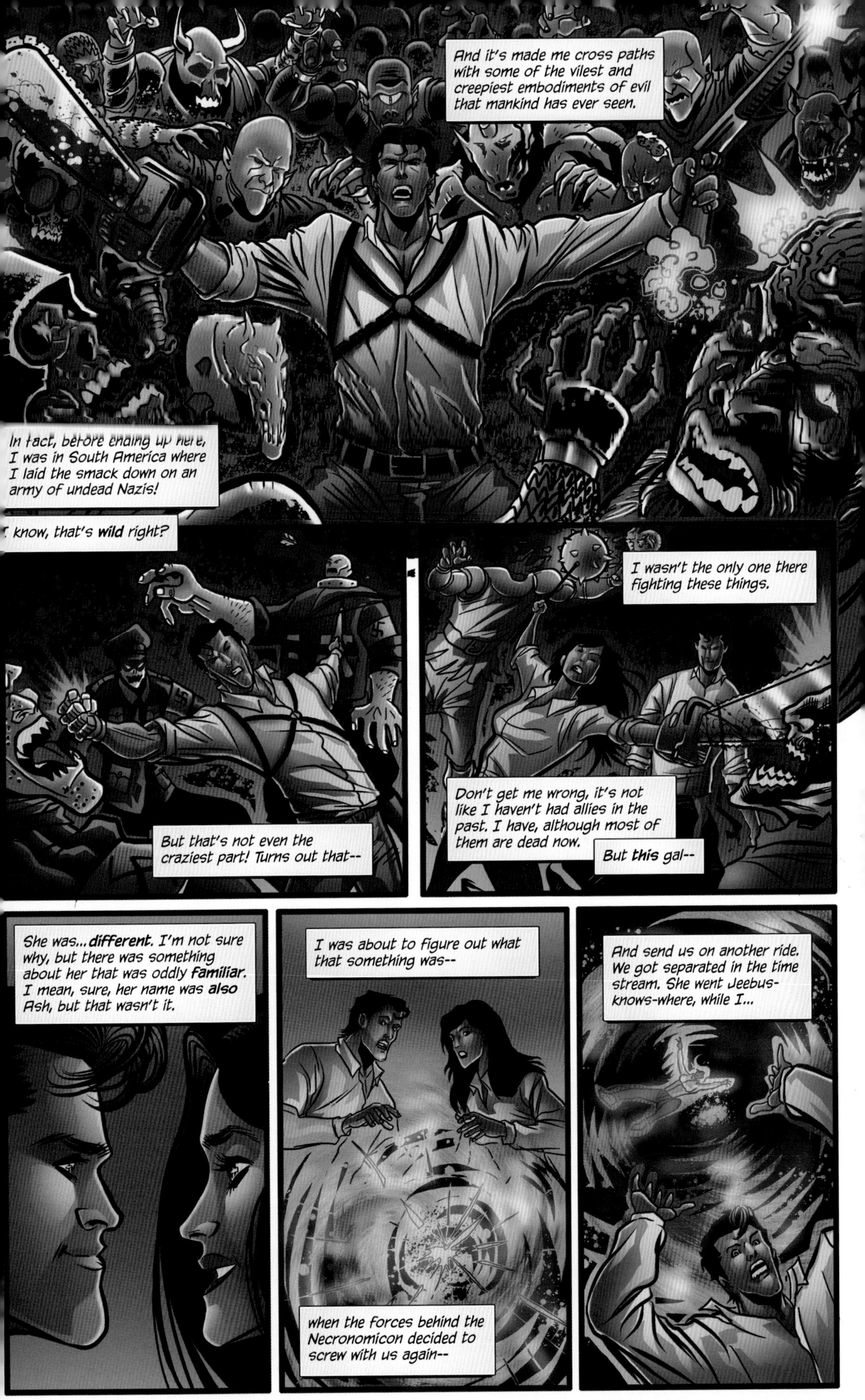
And it's made me cross paths with some of the vilest and creepiest embodiments of evil that mankind has ever seen.
In fact, before ending up here, I was in South America where I laid the smack down on an army of undead Nazis!
I know, that's wild right?
But that's not even the craziest part! Turns out that--
I wasn't the only one there fighting these things.
Don't get me wrong, it's not like I haven't had allies in the past. I have, although most of them are dead now.
But this gal--
She was... different. I'm not sure why, but there was something about her that was oddly familiar. I mean, sure, her name was also Ash, but that wasn't it.
I was about to figure out what that something was--
when the forces behind the Necronomicon decided to screw with us again--
And send us on another ride. We got separated in the time stream. She went Jeebus-knows-where, while I...

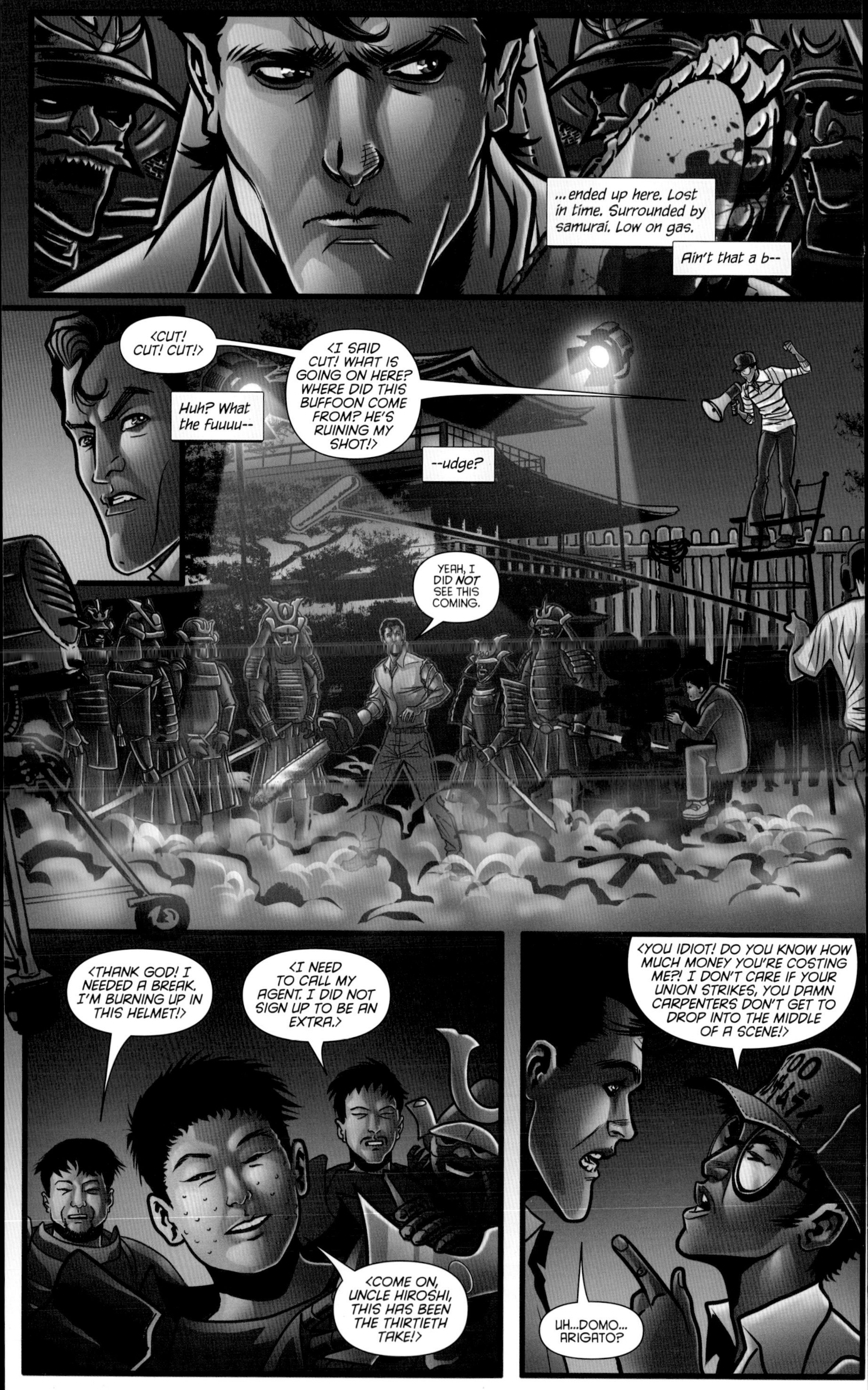
...ended up here. Lost in time. Surrounded by samurai. Low on gas.
Ain't that a b--
<CUT! CUT! CUT!>
Huh? What the fuuuu--
<I SAID CUT! WHAT IS GOING ON HERE? WHERE DID THIS BUFFOON COME FROM? HE'S RUINING MY SHOT!>
--udge?
YEAH, I DID *NOT* SEE THIS COMING.
<THANK GOD! I NEEDED A BREAK. I'M BURNING UP IN THIS HELMET!>
<I NEED TO CALL MY AGENT. I DID NOT SIGN UP TO BE AN EXTRA.>
<COME ON, UNCLE HIROSHI, THIS HAS BEEN THE THIRTIETH TAKE!>
<YOU IDIOT! DO YOU KNOW HOW MUCH MONEY YOU'RE COSTING ME?! I DON'T CARE IF YOUR UNION STRIKES, YOU DAMN CARPENTERS DON'T GET TO DROP INTO THE MIDDLE OF A SCENE!>
UH...DOMO... ARIGATO?

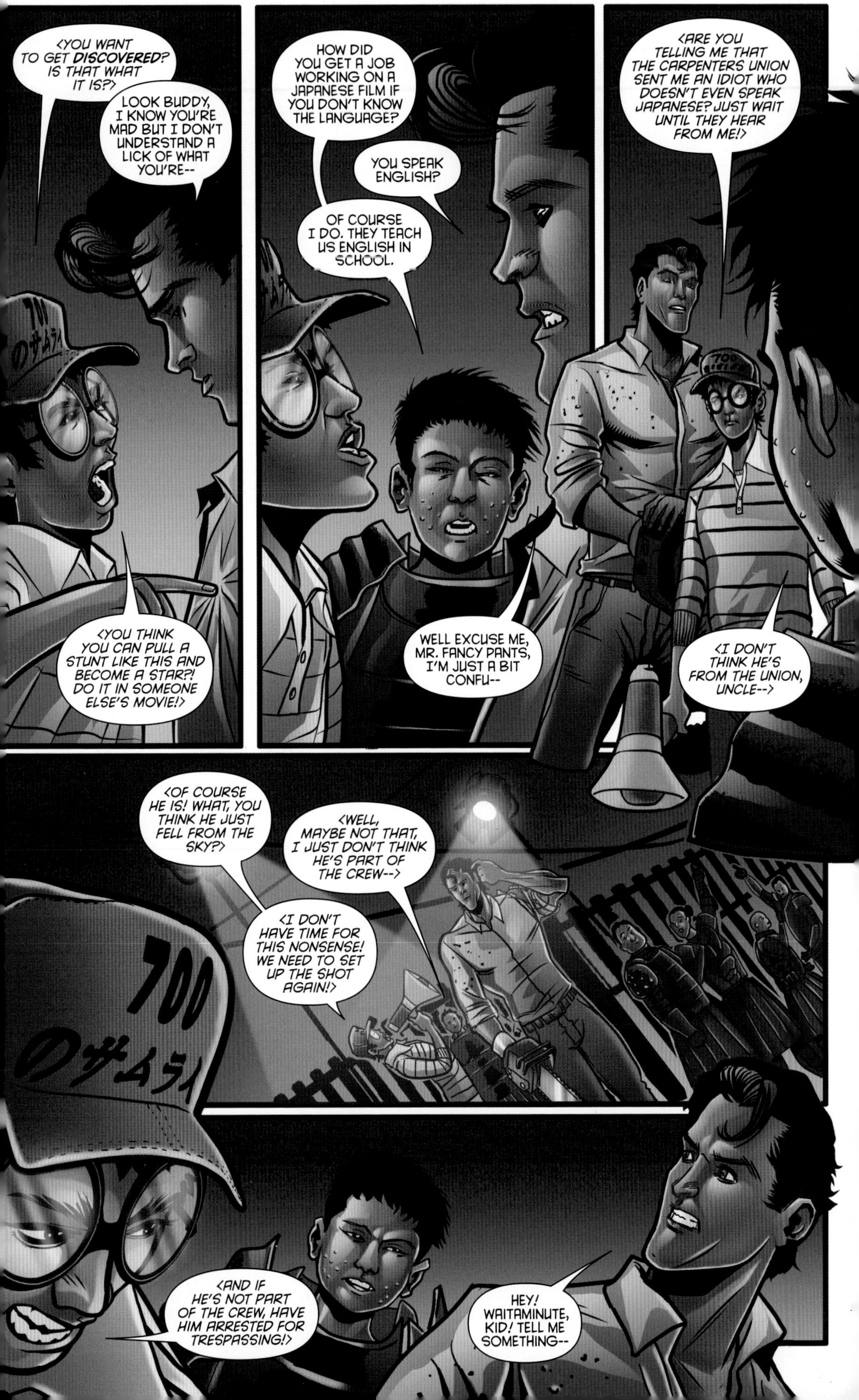

<YOU WANT TO GET **DISCOVERED**? IS THAT WHAT IT IS?>
LOOK BUDDY, I KNOW YOU'RE MAD BUT I DON'T UNDERSTAND A LICK OF WHAT YOU'RE--
<YOU THINK YOU CAN PULL A STUNT LIKE THIS AND BECOME A STAR?! DO IT IN SOMEONE ELSE'S MOVIE!>
HOW DID YOU GET A JOB WORKING ON A JAPANESE FILM IF YOU DON'T KNOW THE LANGUAGE?
YOU SPEAK ENGLISH?
OF COURSE I DO. THEY TEACH US ENGLISH IN SCHOOL.
WELL EXCUSE ME, MR. FANCY PANTS, I'M JUST A BIT CONFU--
<ARE YOU TELLING ME THAT THE CARPENTERS UNION SENT ME AN IDIOT WHO DOESN'T EVEN SPEAK JAPANESE? JUST WAIT UNTIL THEY HEAR FROM ME!>
<I DON'T THINK HE'S FROM THE UNION, UNCLE-->
<OF COURSE HE IS! WHAT, YOU THINK HE JUST FELL FROM THE SKY?>
<WELL, MAYBE NOT THAT, I JUST DON'T THINK HE'S PART OF THE CREW-->
<I DON'T HAVE TIME FOR THIS NONSENSE! WE NEED TO SET UP THE SHOT AGAIN!>
700 のサムライ
<AND IF HE'S NOT PART OF THE CREW, HAVE HIM ARRESTED FOR TRESPASSING!>
HEY! WAITAMINUTE, KID! TELL ME SOMETHING--

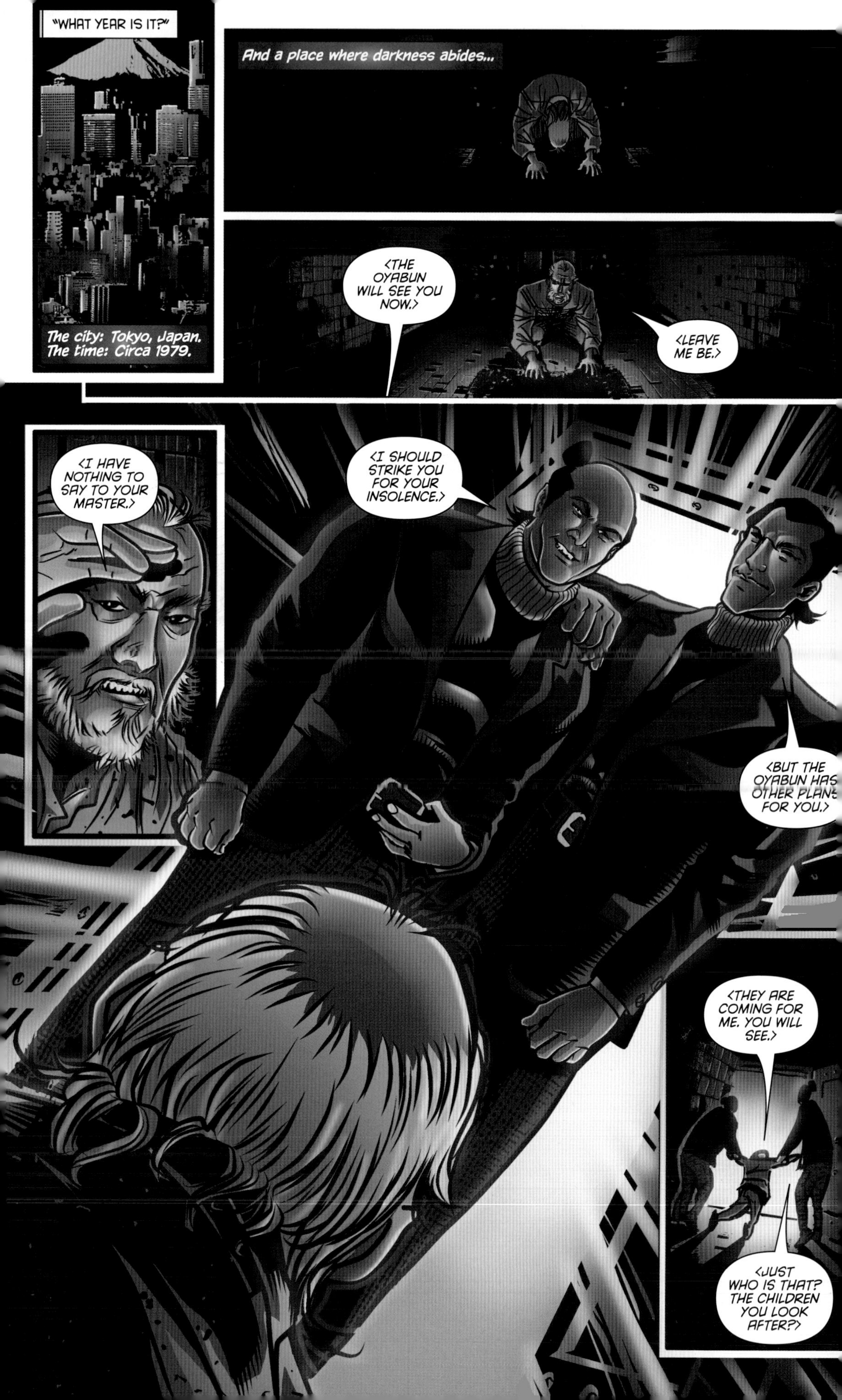
"WHAT YEAR IS IT?"
The city: Tokyo, Japan. The time: Circa 1979.
And a place where darkness abides...
<THE OYABUN WILL SEE YOU NOW.>
<LEAVE ME BE.>
<I HAVE NOTHING TO SAY TO YOUR MASTER.>
<I SHOULD STRIKE YOU FOR YOUR INSOLENCE.>
<BUT THE OYABUN HAS OTHER PLANS FOR YOU.>
<THEY ARE COMING FOR ME. YOU WILL SEE.>
<JUST WHO IS THAT? THE CHILDREN YOU LOOK AFTER?>

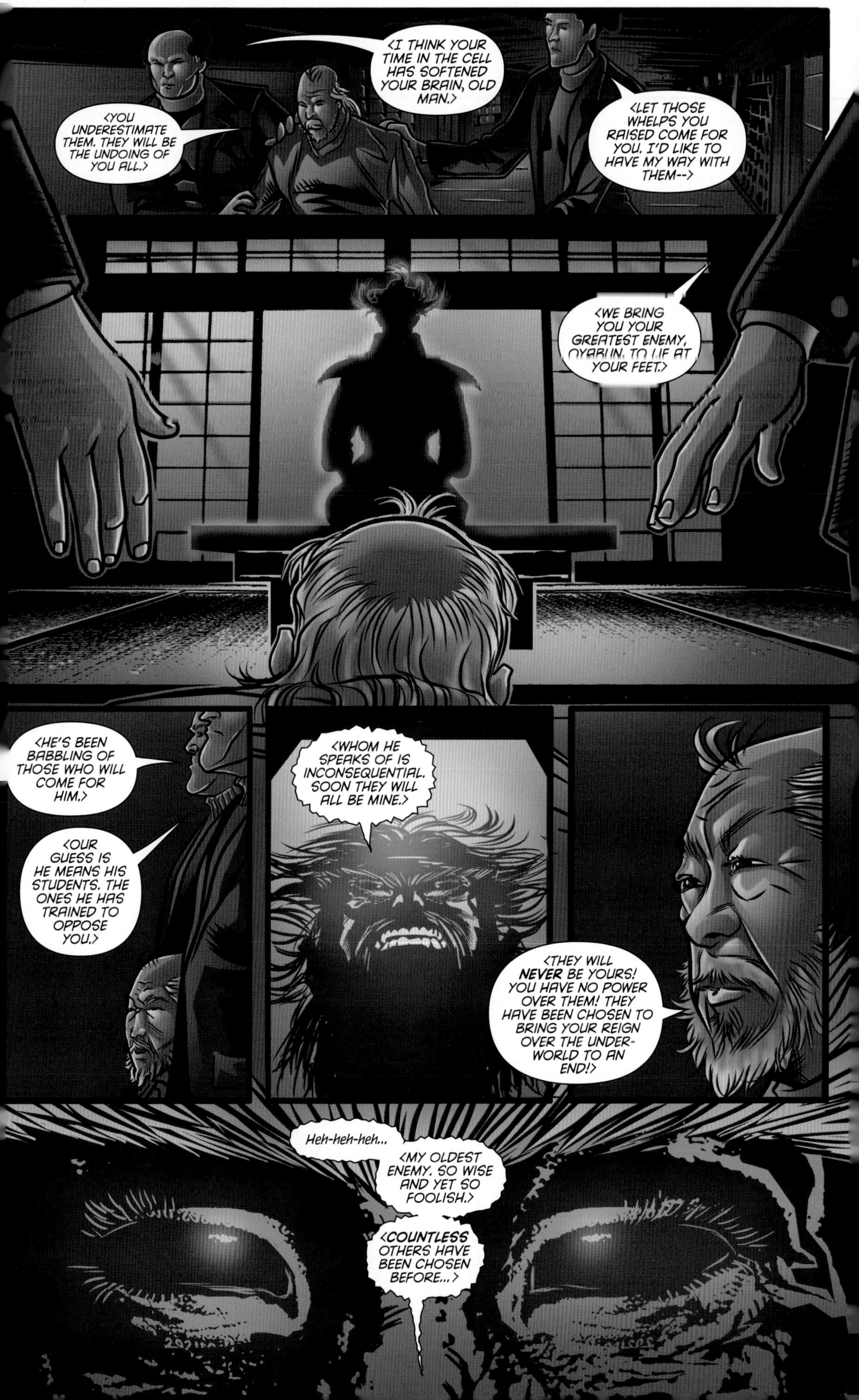
<I THINK YOUR TIME IN THE CELL HAS SOFTENED YOUR BRAIN, OLD MAN.>
<YOU UNDERESTIMATE THEM. THEY WILL BE THE UNDOING OF YOU ALL.>
<LET THOSE WHELPS YOU RAISED COME FOR YOU. I'D LIKE TO HAVE MY WAY WITH THEM-->
<WE BRING YOU YOUR GREATEST ENEMY, OYABUN, TO LIE AT YOUR FEET.>
<HE'S BEEN BABBLING OF THOSE WHO WILL COME FOR HIM.>
<OUR GUESS IS HE MEANS HIS STUDENTS. THE ONES HE HAS TRAINED TO OPPOSE YOU.>
<WHOM HE SPEAKS OF IS INCONSEQUENTIAL. SOON THEY WILL ALL BE MINE.>
<THEY WILL **NEVER** BE YOURS! YOU HAVE NO POWER OVER THEM! THEY HAVE BEEN CHOSEN TO BRING YOUR REIGN OVER THE UNDER-WORLD TO AN END!>
Heh-heh-heh...
<MY OLDEST ENEMY. SO WISE AND YET SO FOOLISH.>
<**COUNTLESS** OTHERS HAVE BEEN CHOSEN BEFORE...>

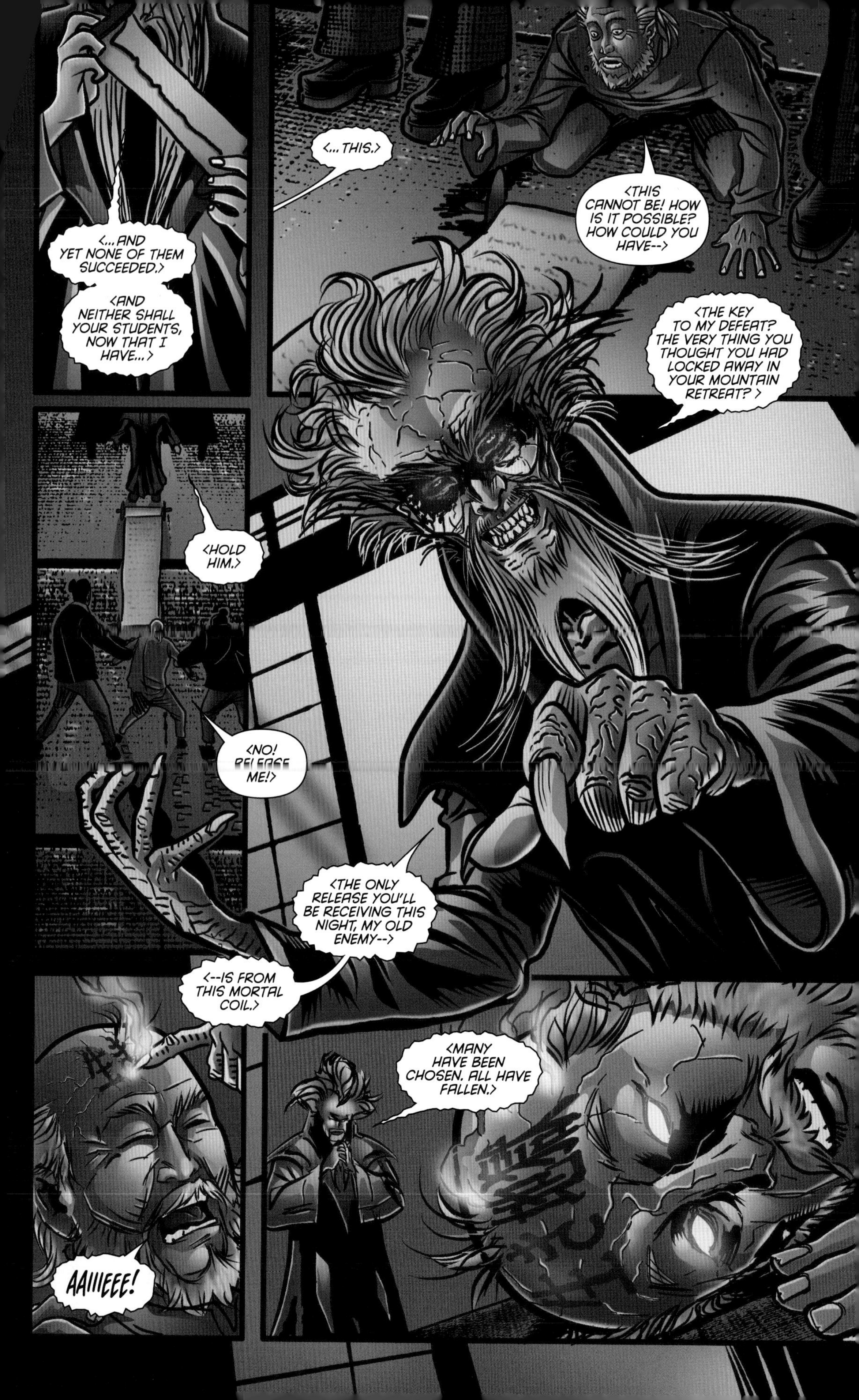

<...AND YET NONE OF THEM SUCCEEDED.>
<AND NEITHER SHALL YOUR STUDENTS, NOW THAT I HAVE...>
<...THIS.>
<THIS CANNOT BE! HOW IS IT POSSIBLE? HOW COULD YOU HAVE-->
<THE KEY TO MY DEFEAT? THE VERY THING YOU THOUGHT YOU HAD LOCKED AWAY IN YOUR MOUNTAIN RETREAT? >
<HOLD HIM.>
<NO! RELEASE ME!>
<THE ONLY RELEASE YOU'LL BE RECEIVING THIS NIGHT, MY OLD ENEMY-->
<--IS FROM THIS MORTAL COIL.>
AAIIIEEE!
<MANY HAVE BEEN CHOSEN. ALL HAVE FALLEN.>

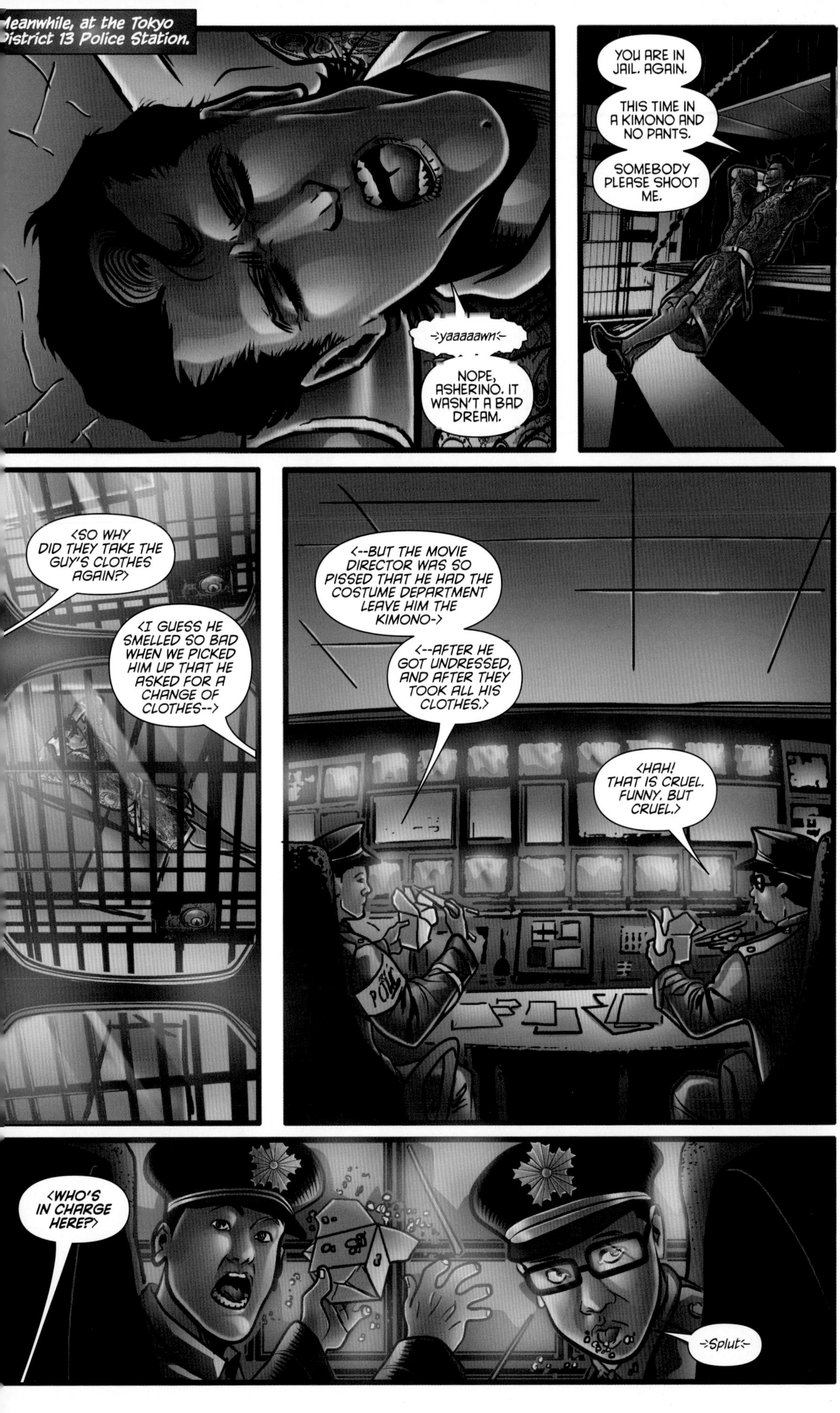
eanwhile, at the Tokyo
istrict 13 Police Station.
->yaaaaawn<-
NOPE, ASHERINO. IT WASN'T A BAD DREAM.
YOU ARE IN JAIL. AGAIN.
THIS TIME IN A KIMONO AND NO PANTS.
SOMEBODY PLEASE SHOOT ME.
<SO WHY DID THEY TAKE THE GUY'S CLOTHES AGAIN?>
<I GUESS HE SMELLED SO BAD WHEN WE PICKED HIM UP THAT HE ASKED FOR A CHANGE OF CLOTHES-->
<--BUT THE MOVIE DIRECTOR WAS SO PISSED THAT HE HAD THE COSTUME DEPARTMENT LEAVE HIM THE KIMONO->
<--AFTER HE GOT UNDRESSED, AND AFTER THEY TOOK ALL HIS CLOTHES.>
<HAH! THAT IS CRUEL. FUNNY. BUT CRUEL.>
<WHO'S IN CHARGE HERE?>
->Splut<-

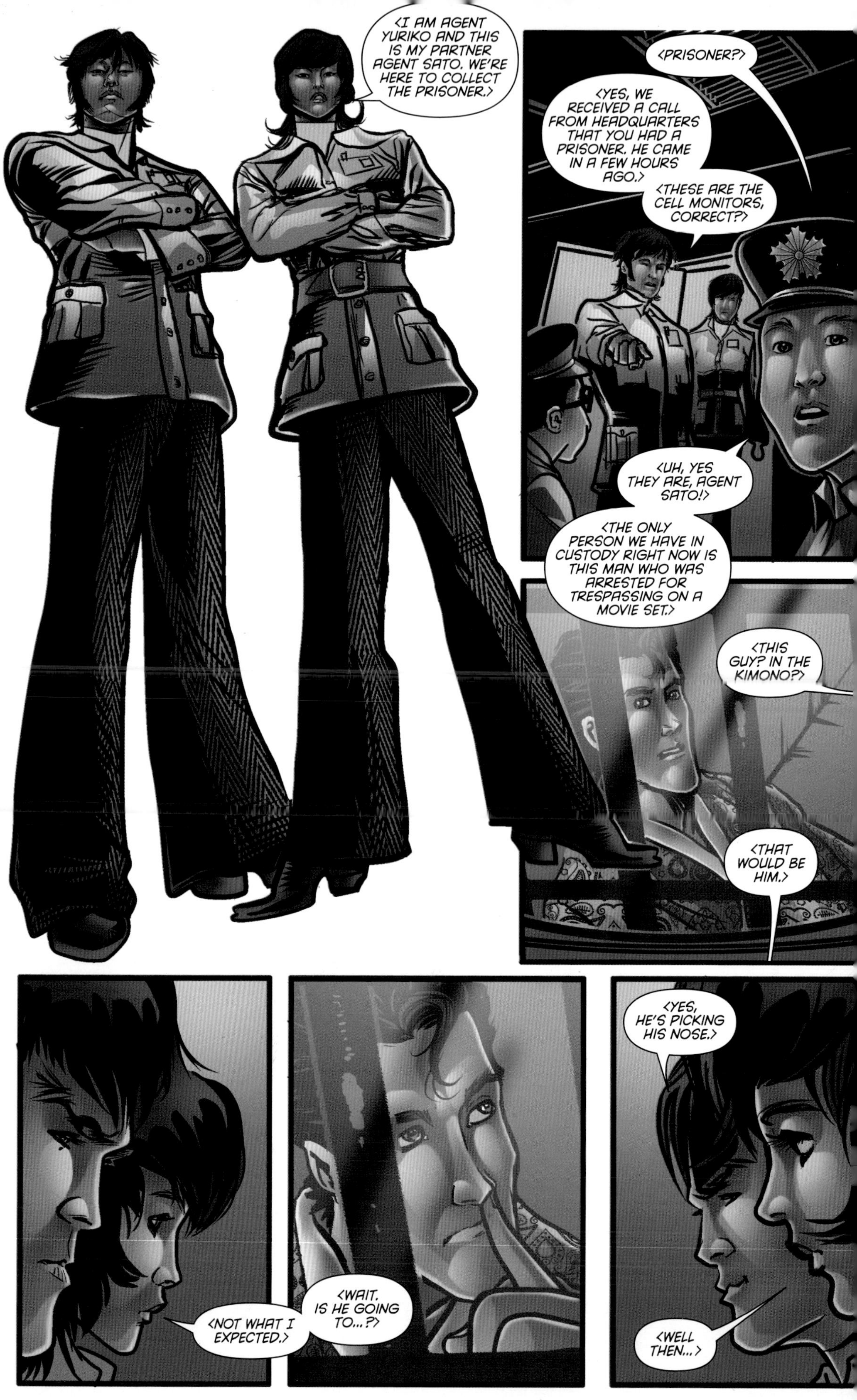

<I AM AGENT YURIKO AND THIS IS MY PARTNER AGENT SATO. WE'RE HERE TO COLLECT THE PRISONER.>
<PRISONER?>
<YES, WE RECEIVED A CALL FROM HEADQUARTERS THAT YOU HAD A PRISONER. HE CAME IN A FEW HOURS AGO.>
<THESE ARE THE CELL MONITORS, CORRECT?>
<UH, YES THEY ARE, AGENT SATO!>
<THE ONLY PERSON WE HAVE IN CUSTODY RIGHT NOW IS THIS MAN WHO WAS ARRESTED FOR TRESPASSING ON A MOVIE SET.>
<THIS GUY? IN THE KIMONO?>
<THAT WOULD BE HIM.>
<NOT WHAT I EXPECTED.>
<WAIT. IS HE GOING TO...?>
<YES, HE'S PICKING HIS NOSE.>
<WELL THEN...>

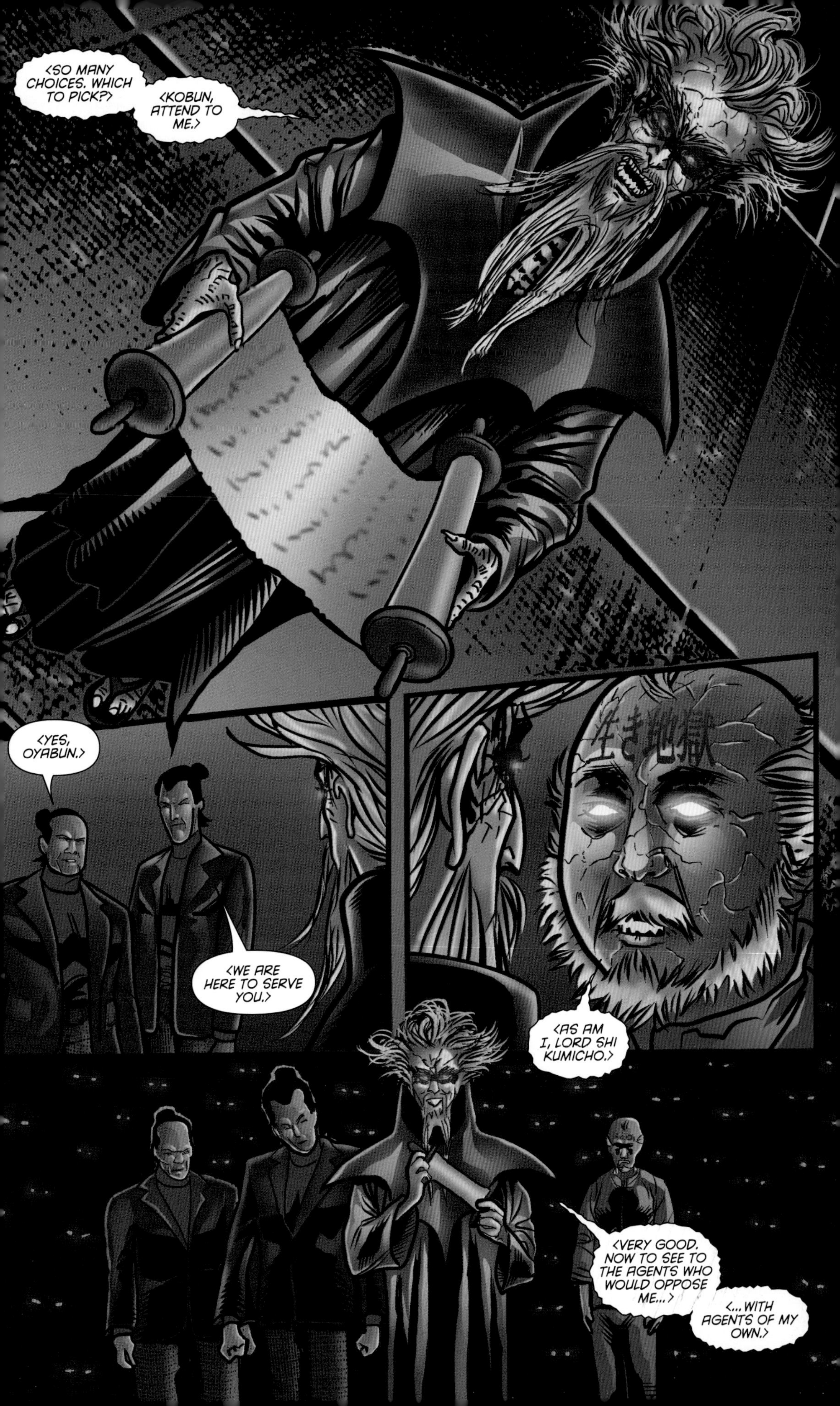
<SO MANY CHOICES. WHICH TO PICK?>
<KOBUN, ATTEND TO ME.>
<YES, OYABUN.>
<WE ARE HERE TO SERVE YOU.>
<AS AM I, LORD SHI KUMICHO.>
<VERY GOOD. NOW TO SEE TO THE AGENTS WHO WOULD OPPOSE ME...>
<...WITH AGENTS OF MY OWN.>

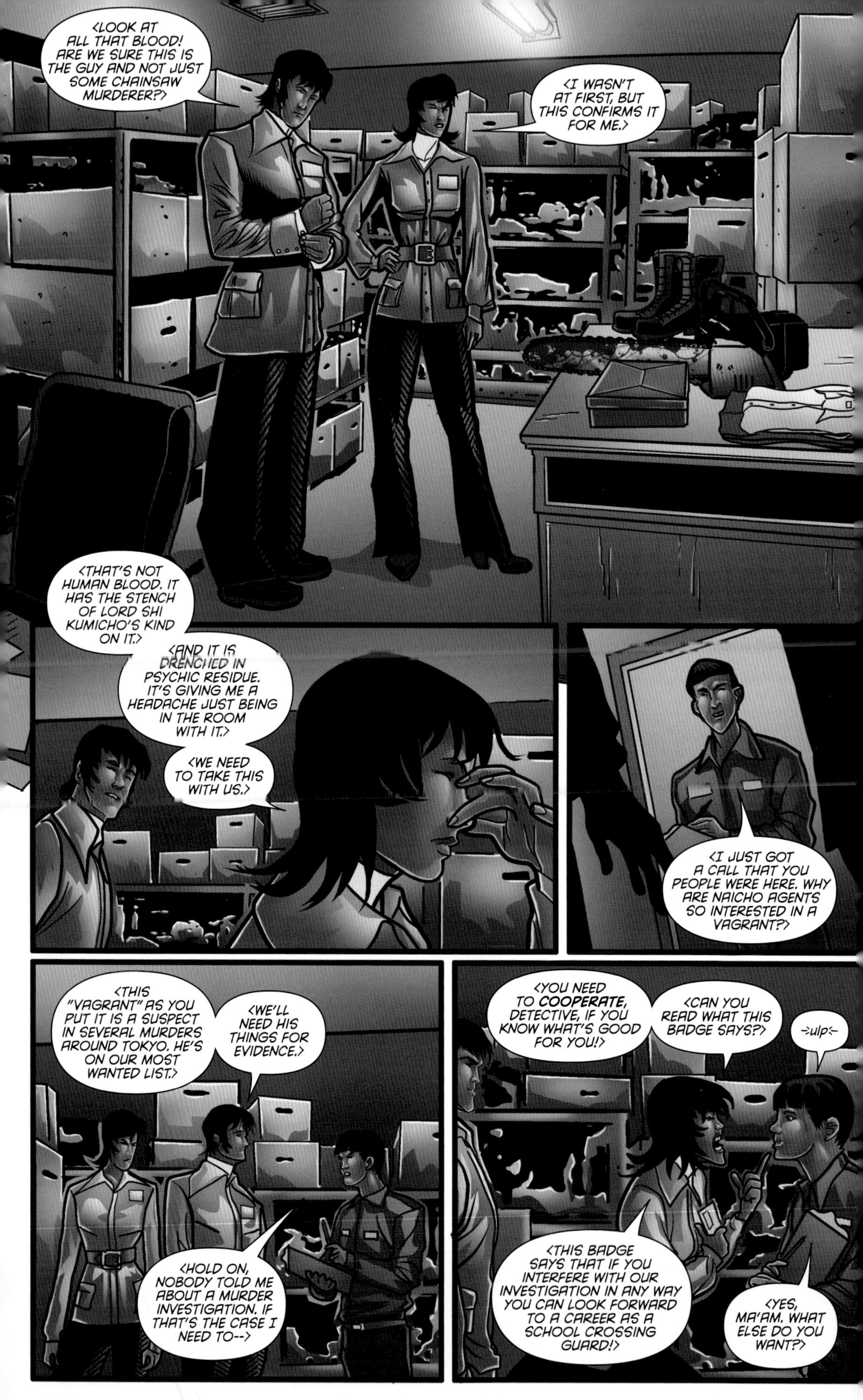
<LOOK AT ALL THAT BLOOD! ARE WE SURE THIS IS THE GUY AND NOT JUST SOME CHAINSAW MURDERER?>
<I WASN'T AT FIRST, BUT THIS CONFIRMS IT FOR ME.>
<THAT'S NOT HUMAN BLOOD. IT HAS THE STENCH OF LORD SHI KUMICHO'S KIND ON IT.>
<AND IT IS DRENCHED IN PSYCHIC RESIDUE. IT'S GIVING ME A HEADACHE JUST BEING IN THE ROOM WITH IT.>
<WE NEED TO TAKE THIS WITH US.>
<I JUST GOT A CALL THAT YOU PEOPLE WERE HERE. WHY ARE NAICHO AGENTS SO INTERESTED IN A VAGRANT?>
<THIS "VAGRANT" AS YOU PUT IT IS A SUSPECT IN SEVERAL MURDERS AROUND TOKYO. HE'S ON OUR MOST WANTED LIST.>
<WE'LL NEED HIS THINGS FOR EVIDENCE.>
<HOLD ON, NOBODY TOLD ME ABOUT A MURDER INVESTIGATION. IF THAT'S THE CASE I NEED TO-->
<YOU NEED TO COOPERATE, DETECTIVE, IF YOU KNOW WHAT'S GOOD FOR YOU!>
<CAN YOU READ WHAT THIS BADGE SAYS?>
-ulp-
<THIS BADGE SAYS THAT IF YOU INTERFERE WITH OUR INVESTIGATION IN ANY WAY YOU CAN LOOK FORWARD TO A CAREER AS A SCHOOL CROSSING GUARD!>
<YES, MA'AM. WHAT ELSE DO YOU WANT?>

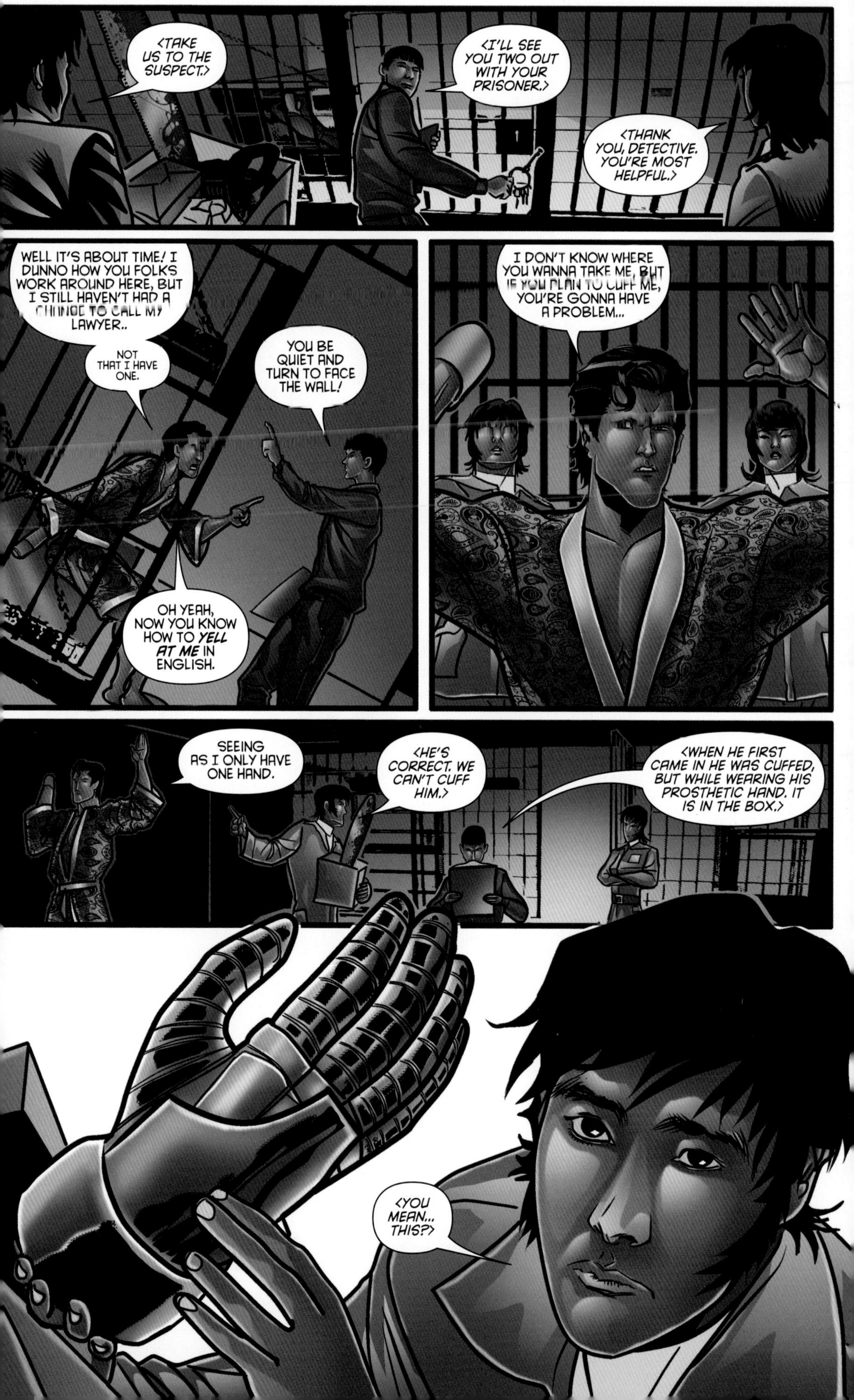
<TAKE US TO THE SUSPECT.>
<I'LL SEE YOU TWO OUT WITH YOUR PRISONER.>
<THANK YOU, DETECTIVE. YOU'RE MOST HELPFUL.>
WELL IT'S ABOUT TIME! I DUNNO HOW YOU FOLKS WORK AROUND HERE, BUT I STILL HAVEN'T HAD A CHANCE TO CALL MY LAWYER..
NOT THAT I HAVE ONE.
YOU BE QUIET AND TURN TO FACE THE WALL!
OH YEAH, NOW YOU KNOW HOW TO *YELL AT ME* IN ENGLISH.
I DON'T KNOW WHERE YOU WANNA TAKE ME, BUT IF YOU PLAN TO CUFF ME, YOU'RE GONNA HAVE A PROBLEM...
SEEING AS I ONLY HAVE ONE HAND.
<HE'S CORRECT. WE CAN'T CUFF HIM.>
<WHEN HE FIRST CAME IN HE WAS CUFFED, BUT WHILE WEARING HIS PROSTHETIC HAND. IT IS IN THE BOX.>
<YOU MEAN... THIS?>

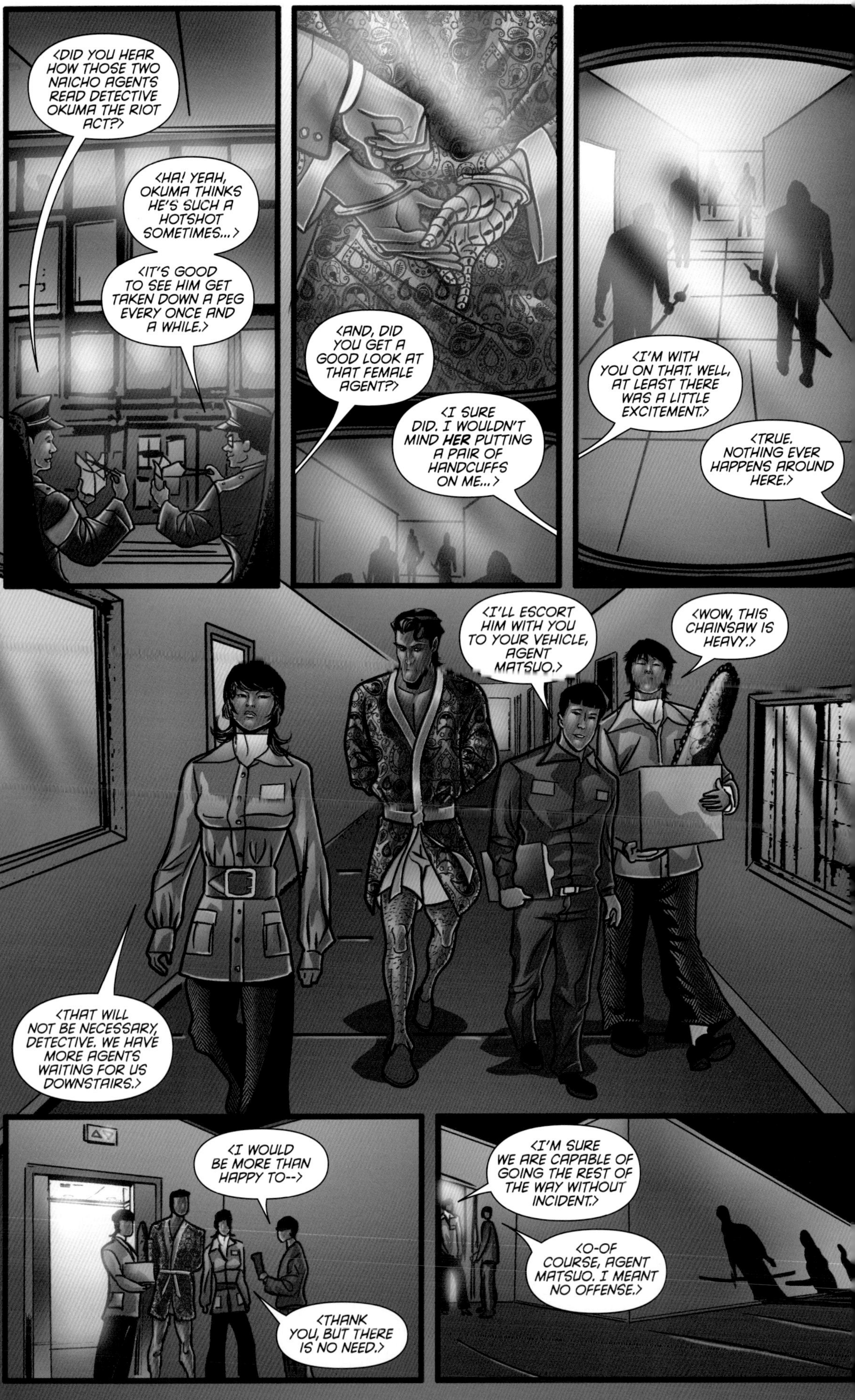
<DID YOU HEAR HOW THOSE TWO NAICHO AGENTS READ DETECTIVE OKUMA THE RIOT ACT?>
<HA! YEAH, OKUMA THINKS HE'S SUCH A HOTSHOT SOMETIMES...>
<IT'S GOOD TO SEE HIM GET TAKEN DOWN A PEG EVERY ONCE AND A WHILE.>
<AND, DID YOU GET A GOOD LOOK AT THAT FEMALE AGENT?>
<I SURE DID. I WOULDN'T MIND **HER** PUTTING A PAIR OF HANDCUFFS ON ME...>
<I'M WITH YOU ON THAT. WELL, AT LEAST THERE WAS A LITTLE EXCITEMENT.>
<TRUE. NOTHING EVER HAPPENS AROUND HERE.>
<I'LL ESCORT HIM WITH YOU TO YOUR VEHICLE, AGENT MATSUO.>
<WOW, THIS CHAINSAW IS HEAVY.>
<THAT WILL NOT BE NECESSARY, DETECTIVE. WE HAVE MORE AGENTS WAITING FOR US DOWNSTAIRS.>
<I WOULD BE MORE THAN HAPPY TO-->
<THANK YOU, BUT THERE IS NO NEED.>
<I'M SURE WE ARE CAPABLE OF GOING THE REST OF THE WAY WITHOUT INCIDENT.>
<O-OF COURSE, AGENT MATSUO. I MEANT NO OFFENSE.>

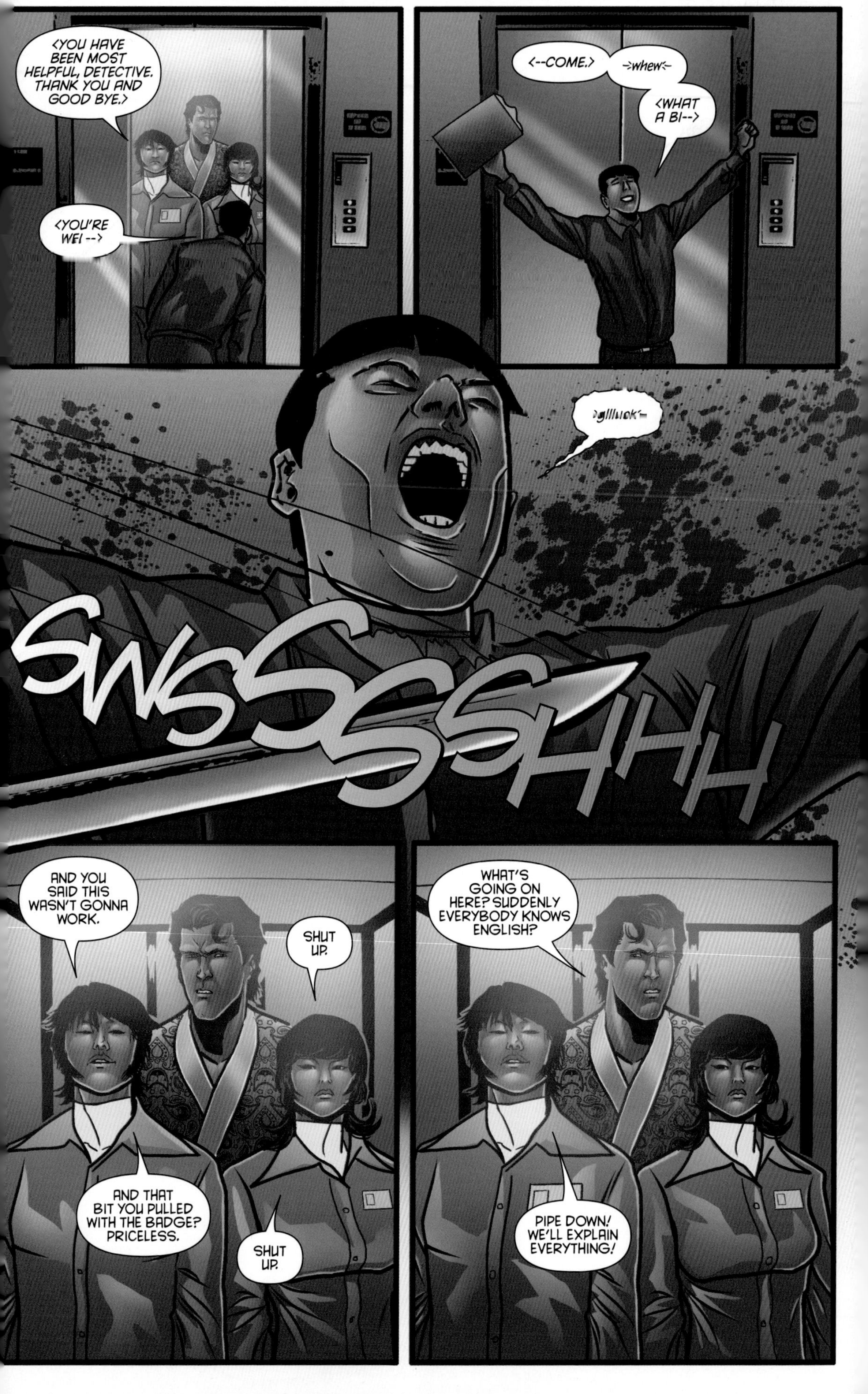

<YOU HAVE BEEN MOST HELPFUL, DETECTIVE. THANK YOU AND GOOD BYE.>
<YOU'RE WEI -->
<--COME.>
~whew~
<WHAT A BI-->
~glllUCK~
SWSSSSHHH
AND YOU SAID THIS WASN'T GONNA WORK.
SHUT UP.
AND THAT BIT YOU PULLED WITH THE BADGE? PRICELESS.
SHUT UP.
WHAT'S GOING ON HERE? SUDDENLY EVERYBODY KNOWS ENGLISH?
PIPE DOWN! WE'LL EXPLAIN EVERYTHING!

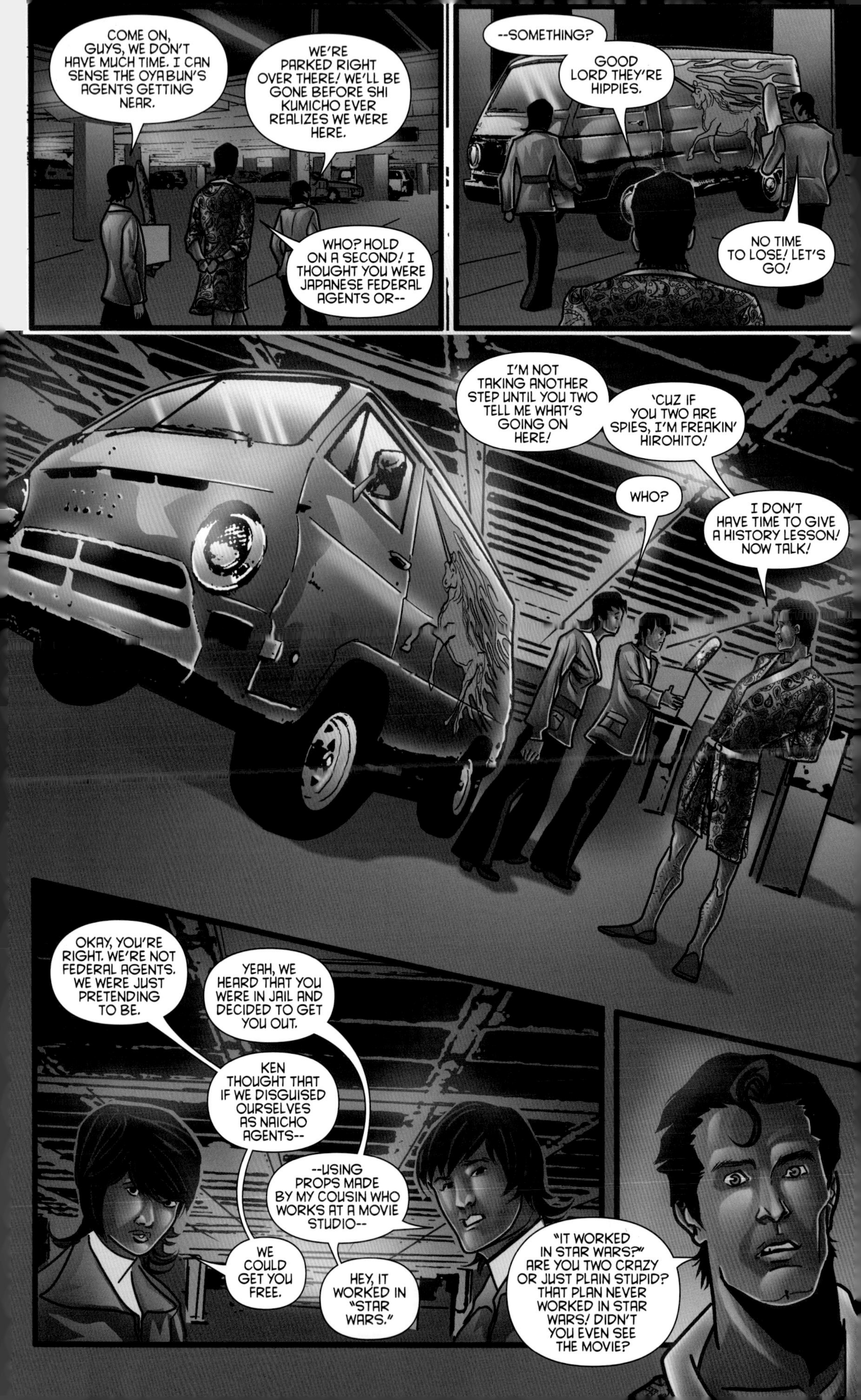
COME ON, GUYS, WE DON'T HAVE MUCH TIME. I CAN SENSE THE OYABUN'S AGENTS GETTING NEAR.
WE'RE PARKED RIGHT OVER THERE! WE'LL BE GONE BEFORE SHI KUMICHO EVER REALIZES WE WERE HERE.
WHO? HOLD ON A SECOND! I THOUGHT YOU WERE JAPANESE FEDERAL AGENTS OR--
--SOMETHING?
GOOD LORD THEY'RE HIPPIES.
NO TIME TO LOSE! LET'S GO!
I'M NOT TAKING ANOTHER STEP UNTIL YOU TWO TELL ME WHAT'S GOING ON HERE!
'CUZ IF YOU TWO ARE SPIES, I'M FREAKIN' HIROHITO!
WHO?
I DON'T HAVE TIME TO GIVE A HISTORY LESSON! NOW TALK!
OKAY, YOU'RE RIGHT. WE'RE NOT FEDERAL AGENTS. WE WERE JUST PRETENDING TO BE.
YEAH, WE HEARD THAT YOU WERE IN JAIL AND DECIDED TO GET YOU OUT.
KEN THOUGHT THAT IF WE DISGUISED OURSELVES AS NAICHO AGENTS--
--USING PROPS MADE BY MY COUSIN WHO WORKS AT A MOVIE STUDIO--
WE COULD GET YOU FREE.
HEY, IT WORKED IN "STAR WARS."
"IT WORKED IN STAR WARS?" ARE YOU TWO CRAZY OR JUST PLAIN STUPID? THAT PLAN NEVER WORKED IN STAR WARS! DIDN'T YOU EVEN SEE THE MOVIE?

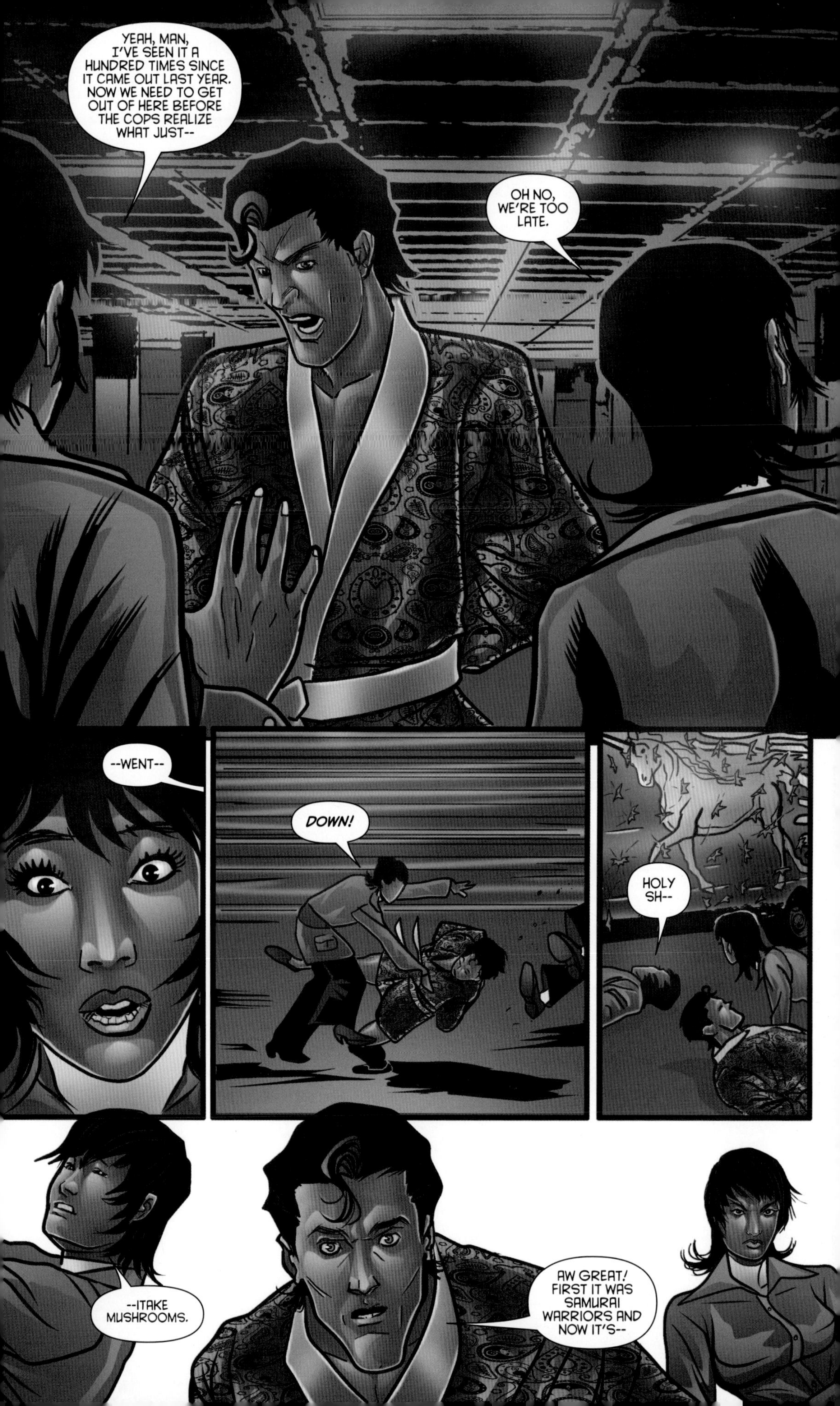
YEAH, MAN, I'VE SEEN IT A HUNDRED TIMES SINCE IT CAME OUT LAST YEAR. NOW WE NEED TO GET OUT OF HERE BEFORE THE COPS REALIZE WHAT JUST--
OH NO, WE'RE TOO LATE.
--WENT--
DOWN!
HOLY SH--
--ITAKE MUSHROOMS.
AW GREAT! FIRST IT WAS SAMURAI WARRIORS AND NOW IT'S--

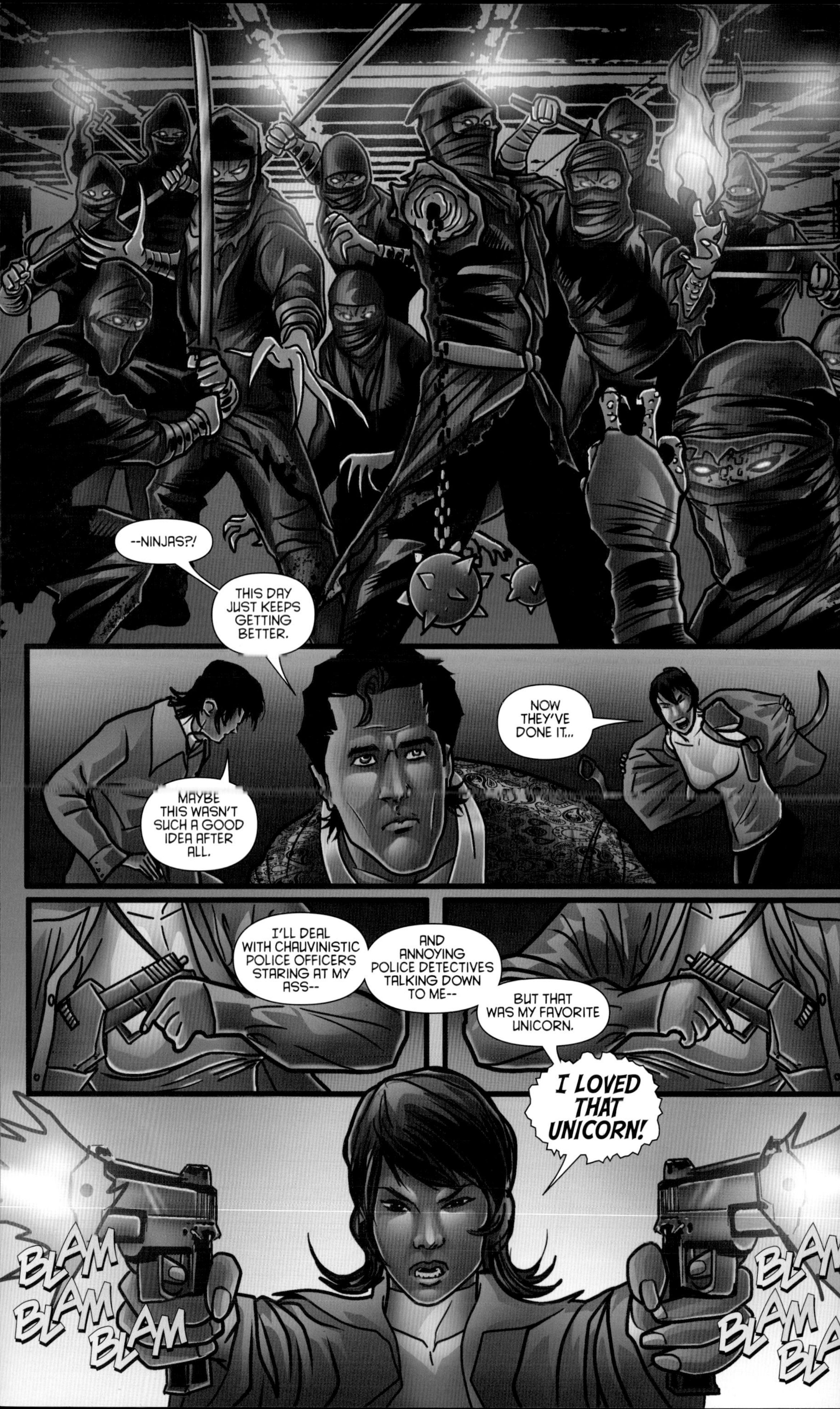
--NINJAS?!
THIS DAY JUST KEEPS GETTING BETTER.
MAYBE THIS WASN'T SUCH A GOOD IDEA AFTER ALL.
NOW THEY'VE DONE IT...
I'LL DEAL WITH CHAUVINISTIC POLICE OFFICERS STARING AT MY ASS--
AND ANNOYING POLICE DETECTIVES TALKING DOWN TO ME--
BUT THAT WAS MY FAVORITE UNICORN.
I LOVED THAT UNICORN!
BLAM BLAM BLAM
BLAM BLAM BLAM

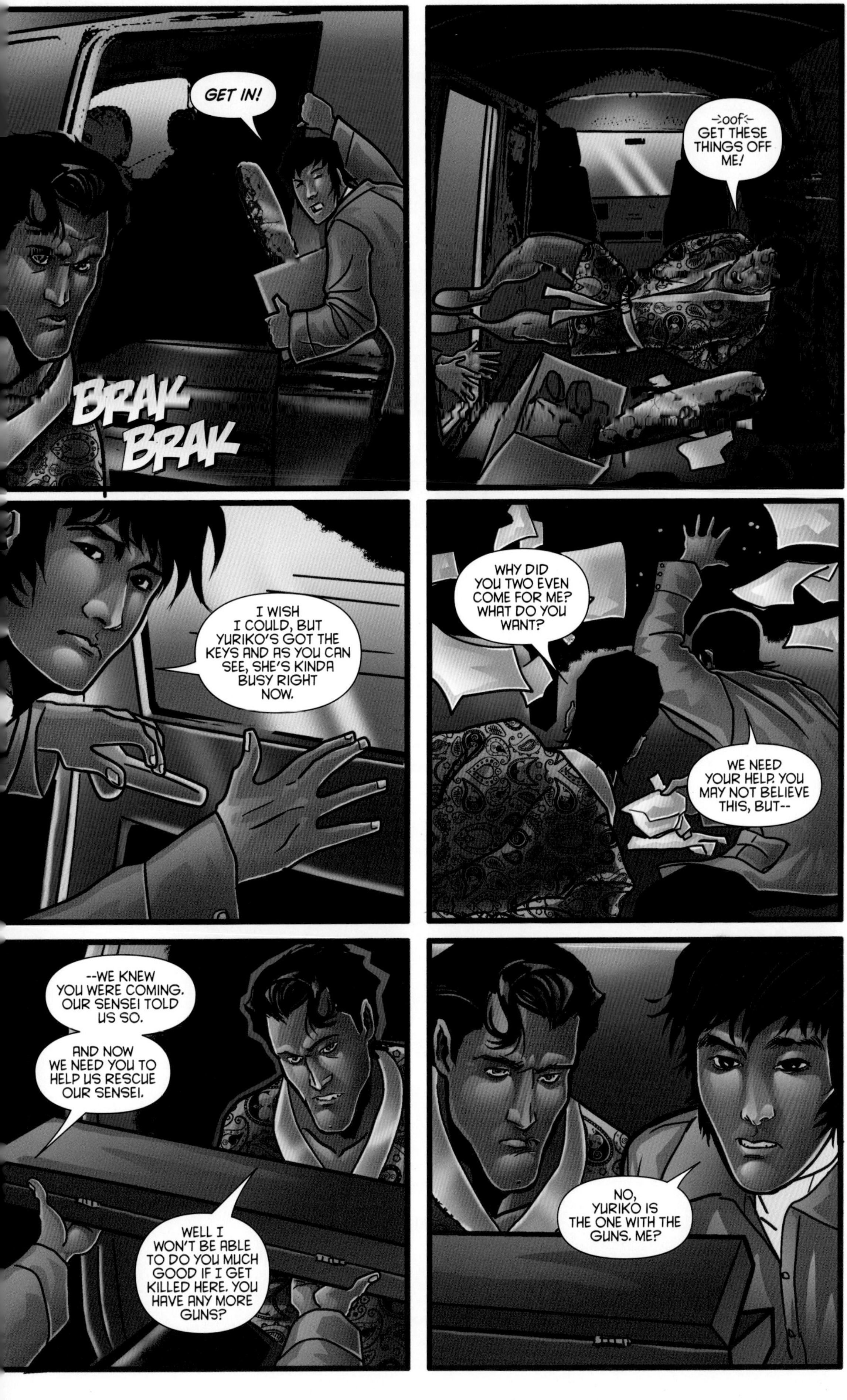
GET IN!
BRAK
BRAK
-oof-
GET THESE THINGS OFF ME!
I WISH I COULD, BUT YURIKO'S GOT THE KEYS AND AS YOU CAN SEE, SHE'S KINDA BUSY RIGHT NOW.
WHY DID YOU TWO EVEN COME FOR ME? WHAT DO YOU WANT?
WE NEED YOUR HELP. YOU MAY NOT BELIEVE THIS, BUT--
--WE KNEW YOU WERE COMING. OUR SENSEI TOLD US SO.
AND NOW WE NEED YOU TO HELP US RESCUE OUR SENSEI.
WELL I WON'T BE ABLE TO DO YOU MUCH GOOD IF I GET KILLED HERE. YOU HAVE ANY MORE GUNS?
NO, YURIKO IS THE ONE WITH THE GUNS. ME?

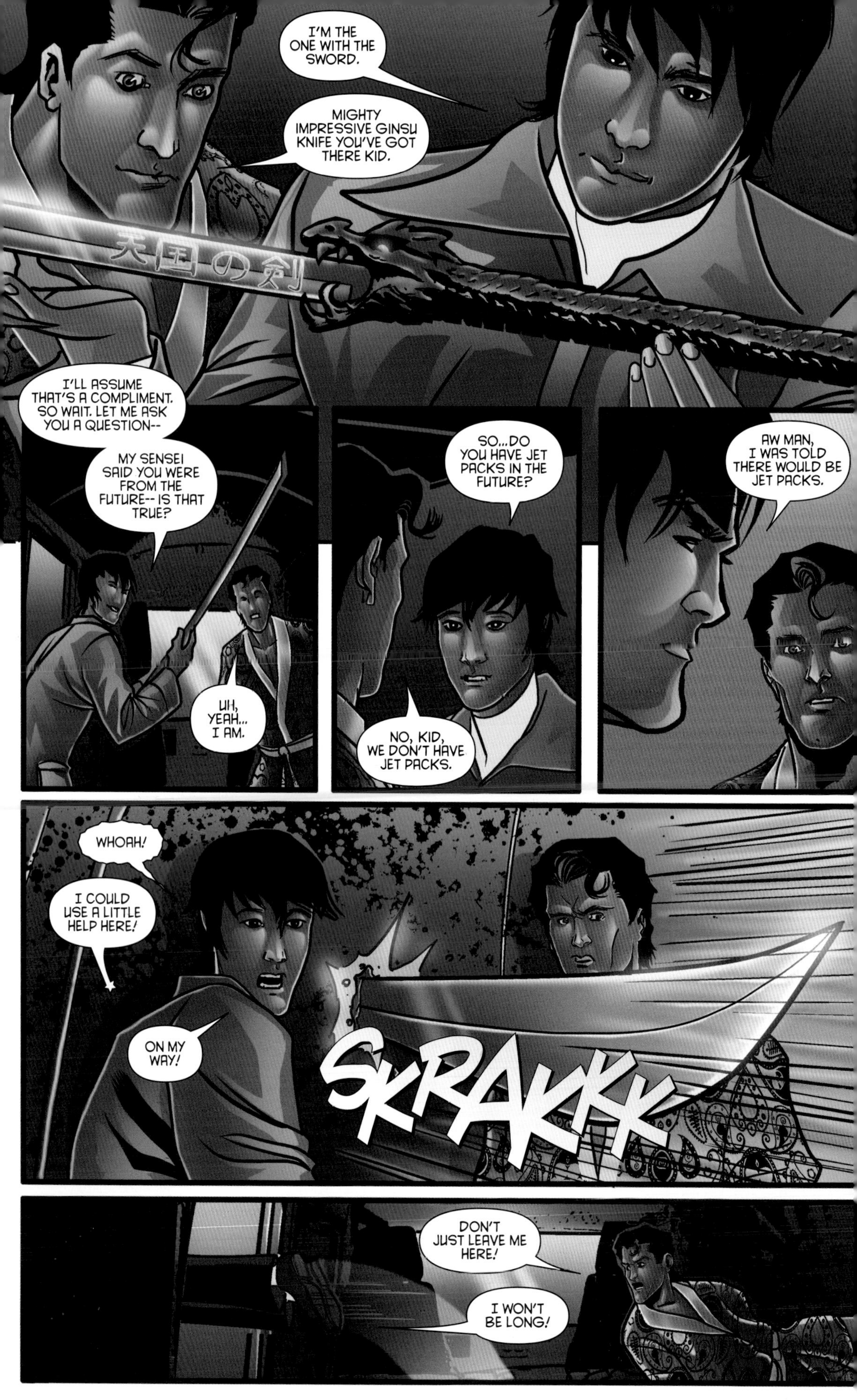

I'M THE ONE WITH THE SWORD.
MIGHTY IMPRESSIVE GINSU KNIFE YOU'VE GOT THERE KID.
天国の剣
I'LL ASSUME THAT'S A COMPLIMENT. SO WAIT. LET ME ASK YOU A QUESTION--
MY SENSEI SAID YOU WERE FROM THE FUTURE-- IS THAT TRUE?
UH, YEAH... I AM.
SO...DO YOU HAVE JET PACKS IN THE FUTURE?
NO, KID, WE DON'T HAVE JET PACKS.
AW MAN, I WAS TOLD THERE WOULD BE JET PACKS.
WHOAH!
I COULD USE A LITTLE HELP HERE!
ON MY WAY!
SKRAKK
DON'T JUST LEAVE ME HERE!
I WON'T BE LONG!

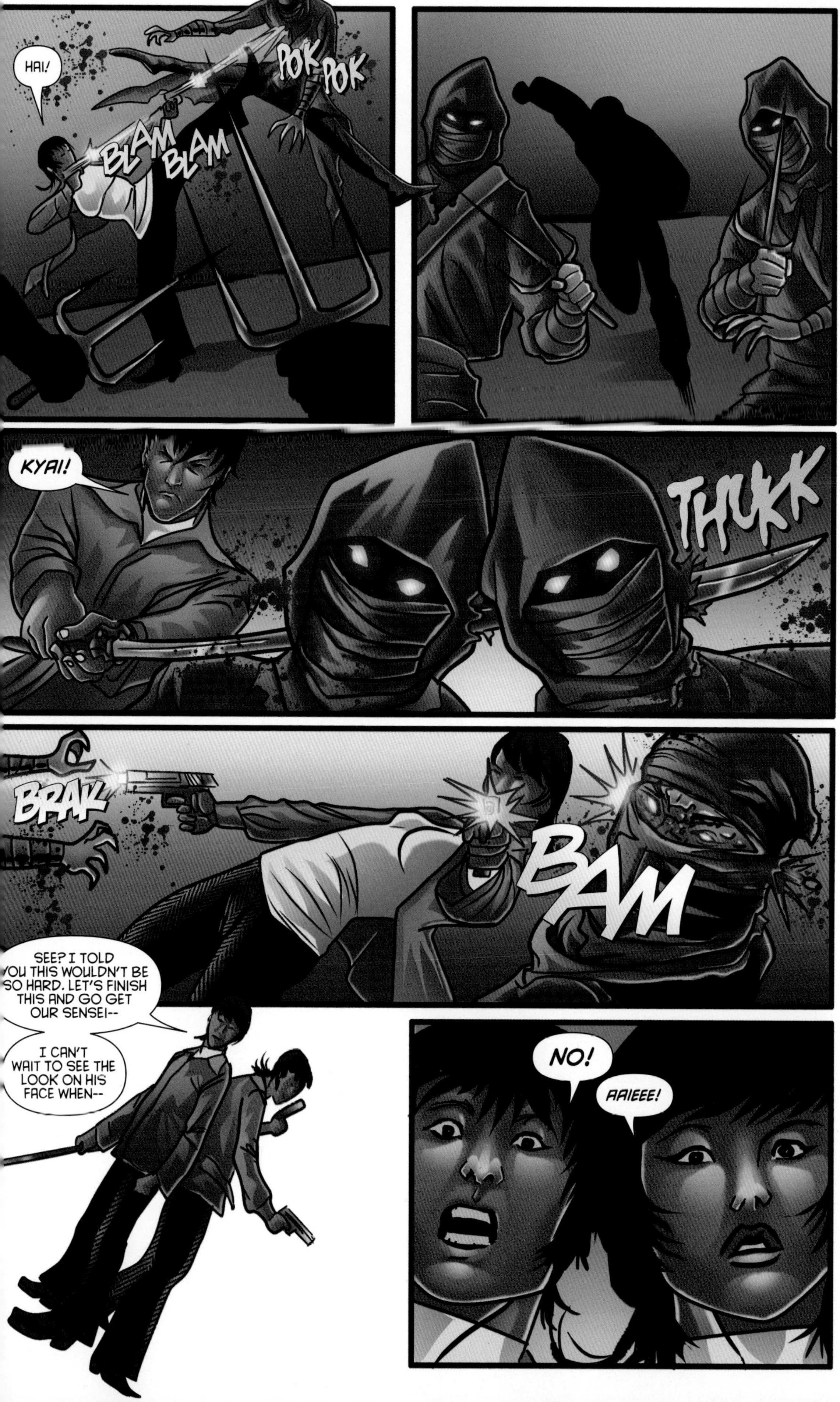
HAI!
POK POK
BLAM BLAM
KYAI!
THUKK
BRAK
BAM
SEE? I TOLD YOU THIS WOULDN'T BE SO HARD. LET'S FINISH THIS AND GO GET OUR SENSEI--
I CAN'T WAIT TO SEE THE LOOK ON HIS FACE WHEN--
NO!
AAIEEE!

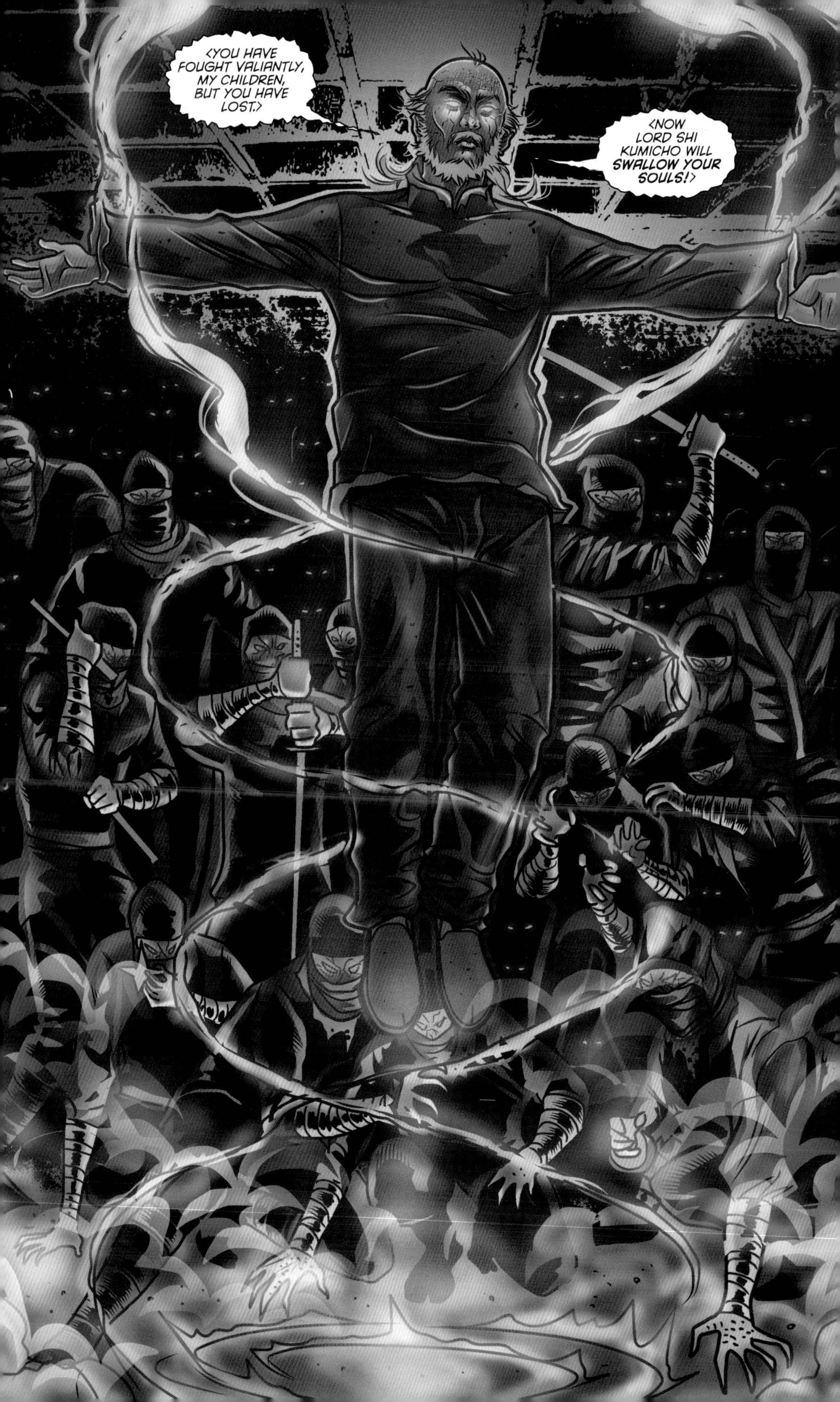
<YOU HAVE FOUGHT VALIANTLY, MY CHILDREN, BUT YOU HAVE LOST.>
<NOW LORD SHI KUMICHO WILL SWALLOW YOUR SOULS!>

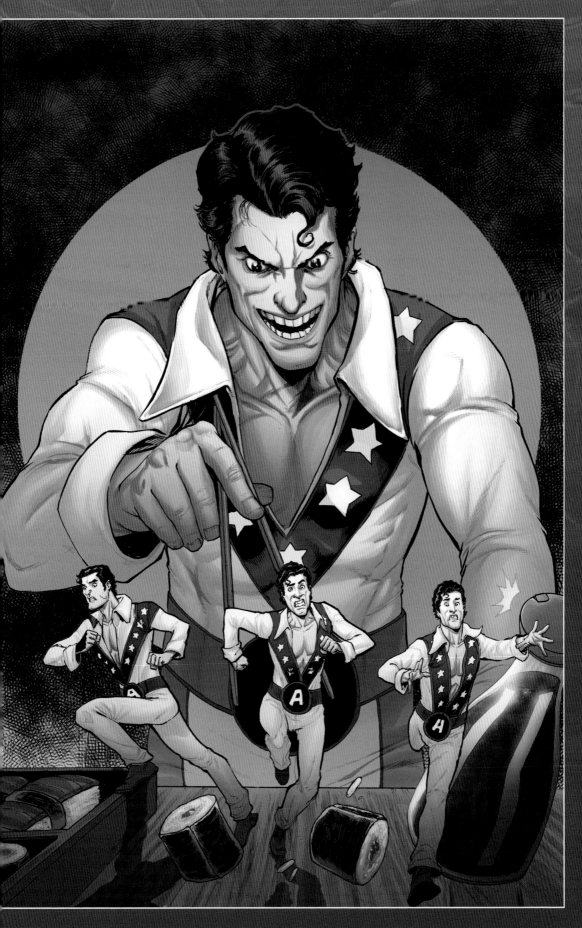

cover to issue #6 by TIM SEELEY, colors by ADRIANO LUCAS

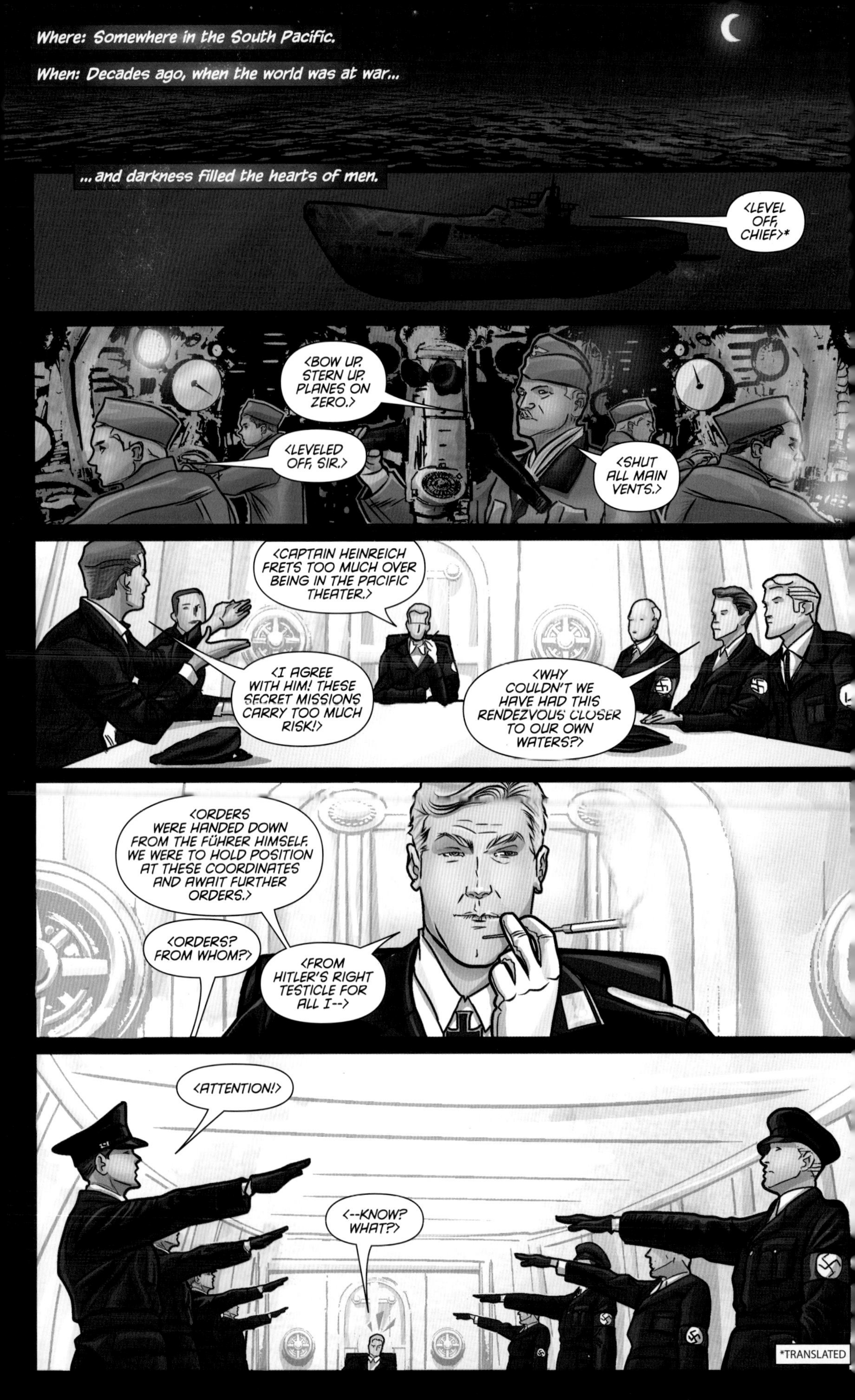
Where: Somewhere in the South Pacific.
When: Decades ago, when the world was at war...
...and darkness filled the hearts of men.
<LEVEL OFF, CHIEF>*
<BOW UP. STERN UP. PLANES ON ZERO.>
<LEVELED OFF, SIR.>
<SHUT ALL MAIN VENTS.>
<CAPTAIN HEINREICH FRETS TOO MUCH OVER BEING IN THE PACIFIC THEATER.>
<I AGREE WITH HIM! THESE SECRET MISSIONS CARRY TOO MUCH RISK!>
<WHY COULDN'T WE HAVE HAD THIS RENDEZVOUS CLOSER TO OUR OWN WATERS?>
<ORDERS WERE HANDED DOWN FROM THE FÜHRER HIMSELF. WE WERE TO HOLD POSITION AT THESE COORDINATES AND AWAIT FURTHER ORDERS.>
<ORDERS? FROM WHOM?>
<FROM HITLER'S RIGHT TESTICLE FOR ALL I-->
<ATTENTION!>
<--KNOW? WHAT?>
*TRANSLATED

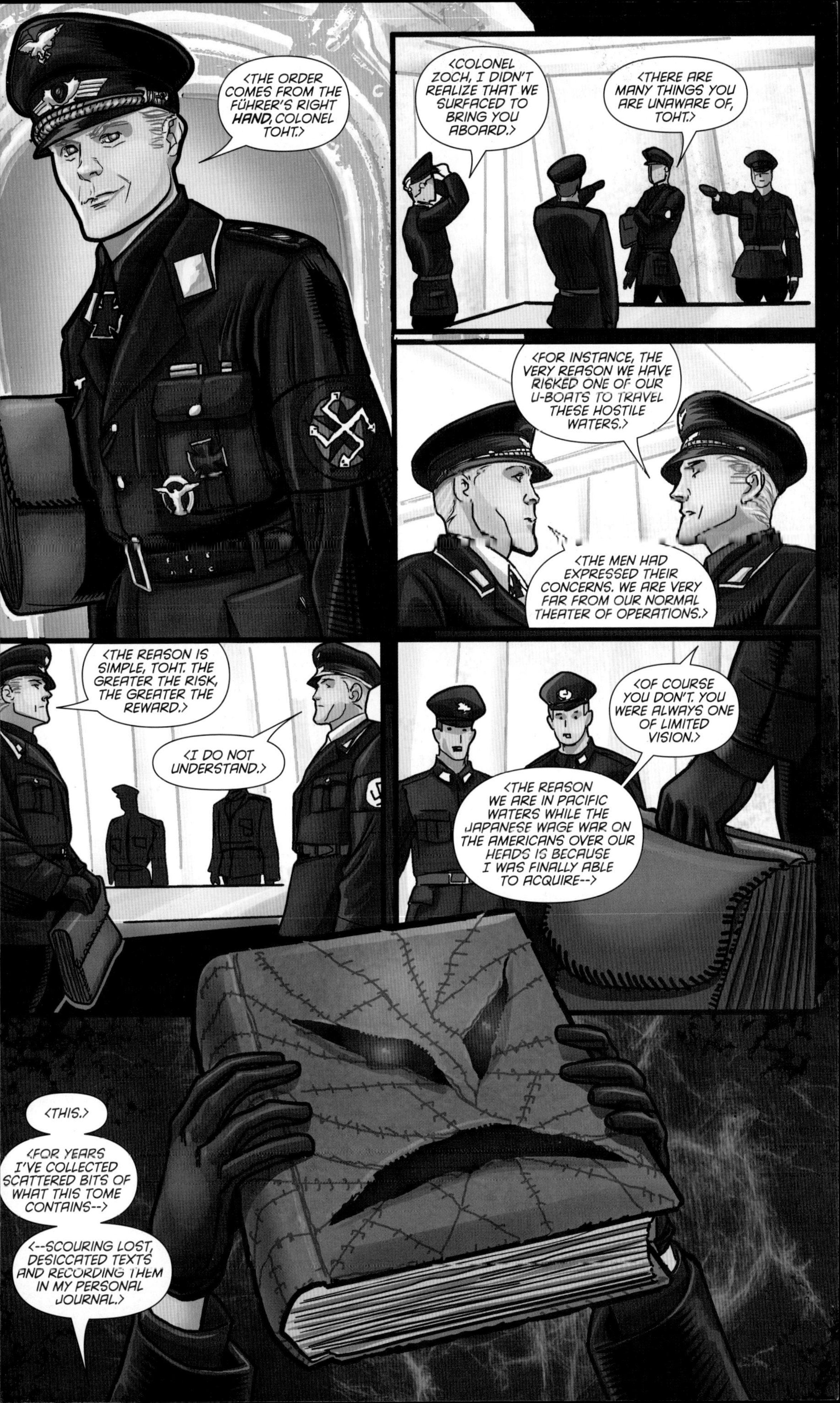
<THE ORDER COMES FROM THE FÜHRER'S RIGHT **HAND**, COLONEL TOHT.>
<COLONEL ZOCH, I DIDN'T REALIZE THAT WE SURFACED TO BRING YOU ABOARD.>
<THERE ARE MANY THINGS YOU ARE UNAWARE OF, TOHT.>
<FOR INSTANCE, THE VERY REASON WE HAVE RISKED ONE OF OUR U-BOATS TO TRAVEL THESE HOSTILE WATERS.>
<THE MEN HAD EXPRESSED THEIR CONCERNS. WE ARE VERY FAR FROM OUR NORMAL THEATER OF OPERATIONS.>
<THE REASON IS SIMPLE, TOHT. THE GREATER THE RISK, THE GREATER THE REWARD.>
<I DO NOT UNDERSTAND.>
<OF COURSE YOU DON'T. YOU WERE ALWAYS ONE OF LIMITED VISION.>
<THE REASON WE ARE IN PACIFIC WATERS WHILE THE JAPANESE WAGE WAR ON THE AMERICANS OVER OUR HEADS IS BECAUSE I WAS FINALLY ABLE TO ACQUIRE-->
<THIS.>
<FOR YEARS I'VE COLLECTED SCATTERED BITS OF WHAT THIS TOME CONTAINS-->
<--SCOURING LOST, DESICCATED TEXTS AND RECORDING THEM IN MY PERSONAL JOURNAL.>

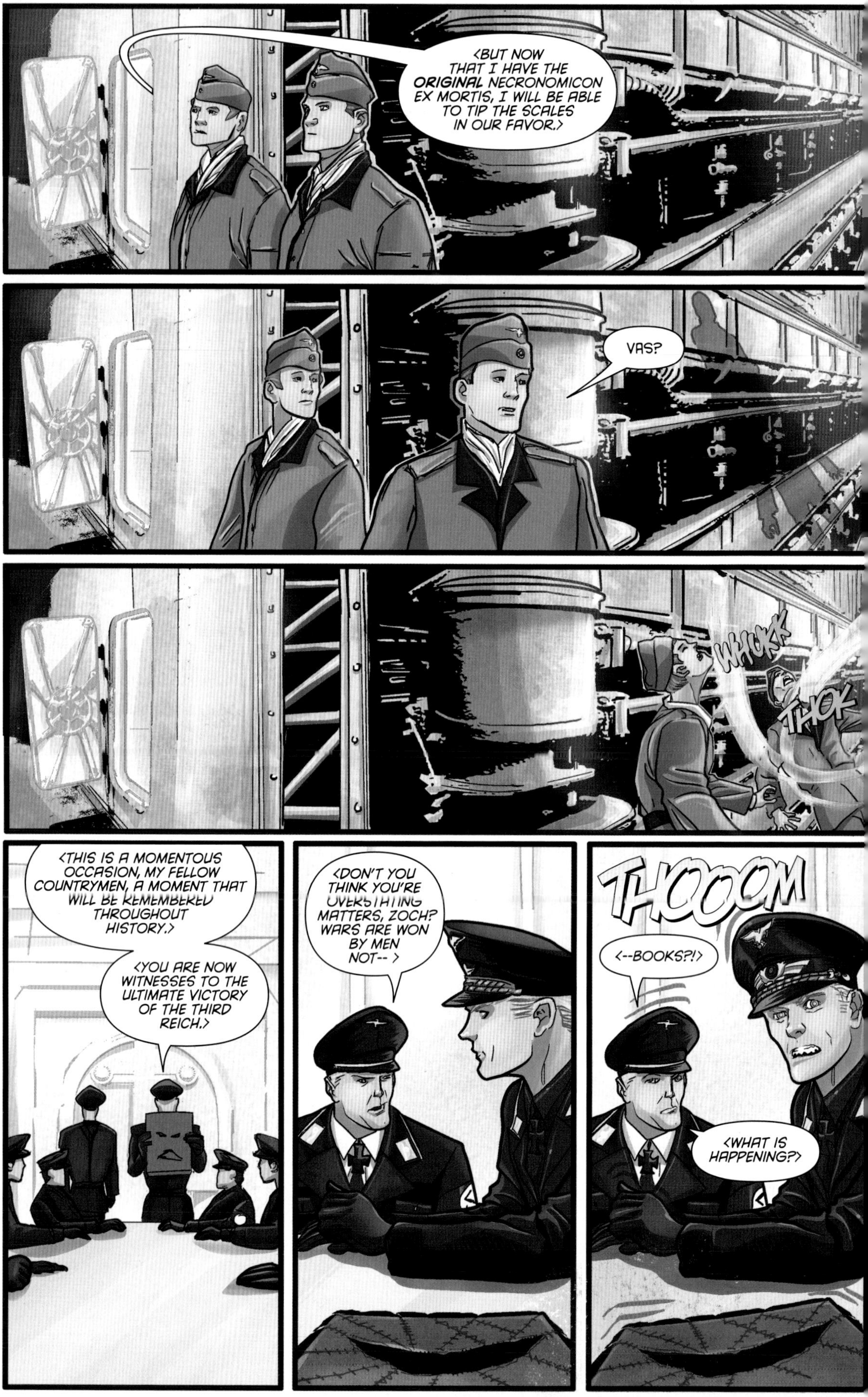

<BUT NOW THAT I HAVE THE ORIGINAL NECRONOMICON EX MORTIS, I WILL BE ABLE TO TIP THE SCALES IN OUR FAVOR.>
VAS?
WHOKK
THOK
<THIS IS A MOMENTOUS OCCASION, MY FELLOW COUNTRYMEN, A MOMENT THAT WILL BE REMEMBERED THROUGHOUT HISTORY.>
<YOU ARE NOW WITNESSES TO THE ULTIMATE VICTORY OF THE THIRD REICH.>
<DON'T YOU THINK YOU'RE OVERSTATING MATTERS, ZOCH? WARS ARE WON BY MEN NOT-- >
THOOOM
<--BOOKS?!>
<WHAT IS HAPPENING?>

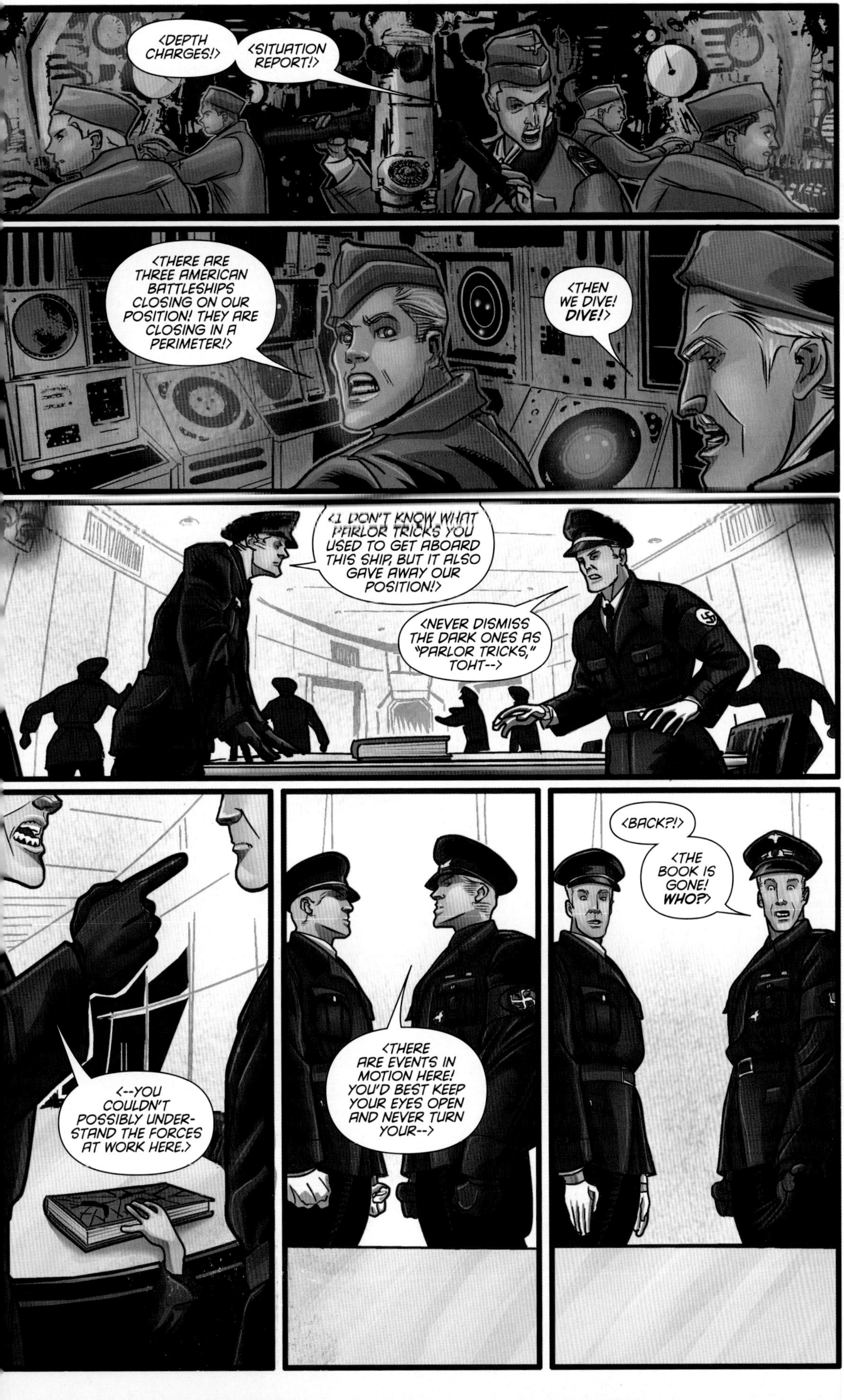
<DEPTH CHARGES!>
<SITUATION REPORT!>
<THERE ARE THREE AMERICAN BATTLESHIPS CLOSING ON OUR POSITION! THEY ARE CLOSING IN A PERIMETER!>
<THEN WE DIVE! **DIVE!**>
<I DON'T KNOW WHAT PARLOR TRICKS YOU USED TO GET ABOARD THIS SHIP, BUT IT ALSO GAVE AWAY OUR POSITION!>
<NEVER DISMISS THE DARK ONES AS "PARLOR TRICKS," TOHT-->
<--YOU COULDN'T POSSIBLY UNDER-STAND THE FORCES AT WORK HERE.>
<THERE ARE EVENTS IN MOTION HERE! YOU'D BEST KEEP YOUR EYES OPEN AND NEVER TURN YOUR-->
<BACK?!>
<THE BOOK IS GONE! **WHO?**>

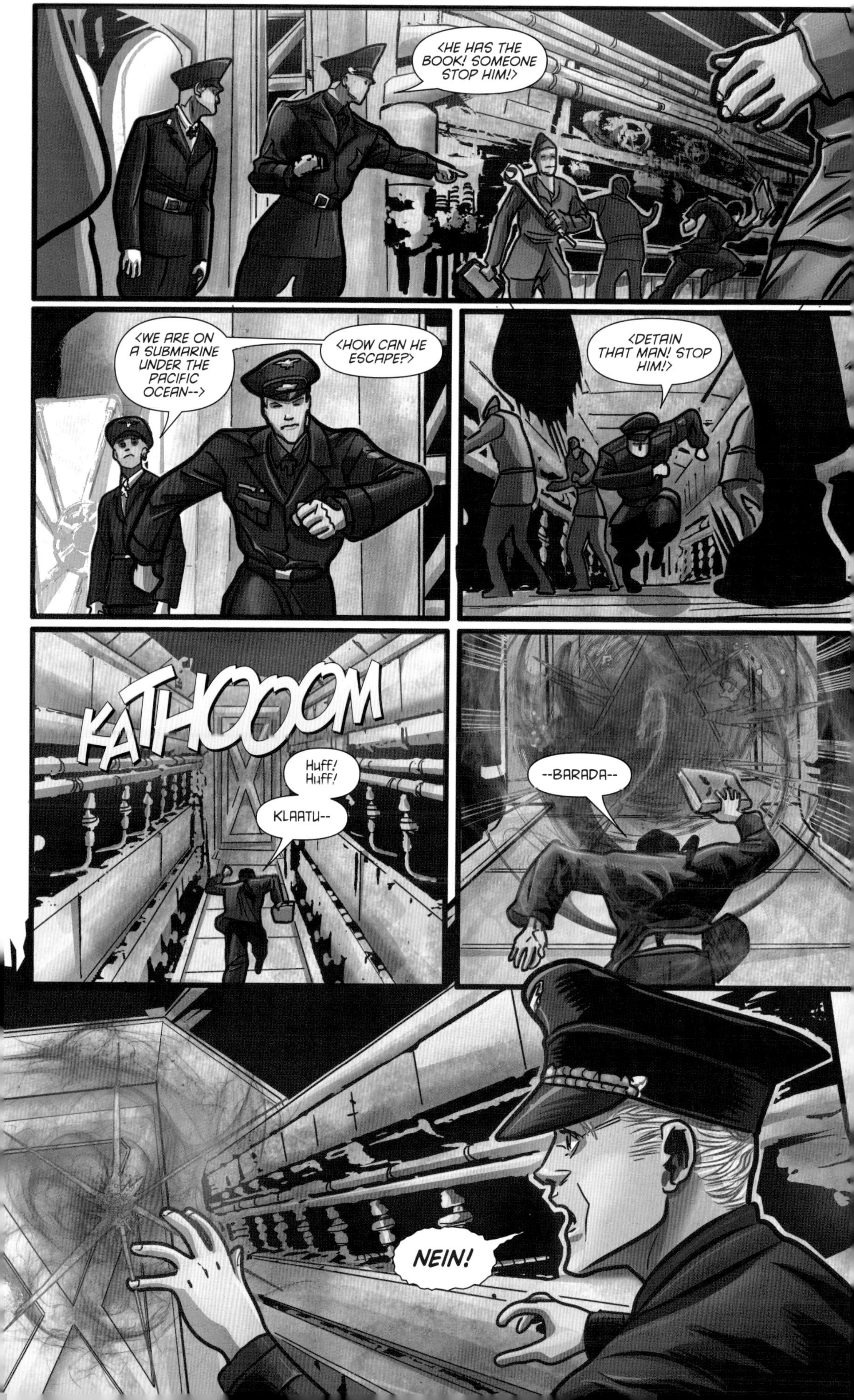
<HE HAS THE BOOK! SOMEONE STOP HIM!>
<WE ARE ON A SUBMARINE UNDER THE PACIFIC OCEAN-->
<HOW CAN HE ESCAPE?>
<DETAIN THAT MAN! STOP HIM!>
KATHOOOM
Huff! Huff!
KLAATU--
--BARADA--
NEIN!

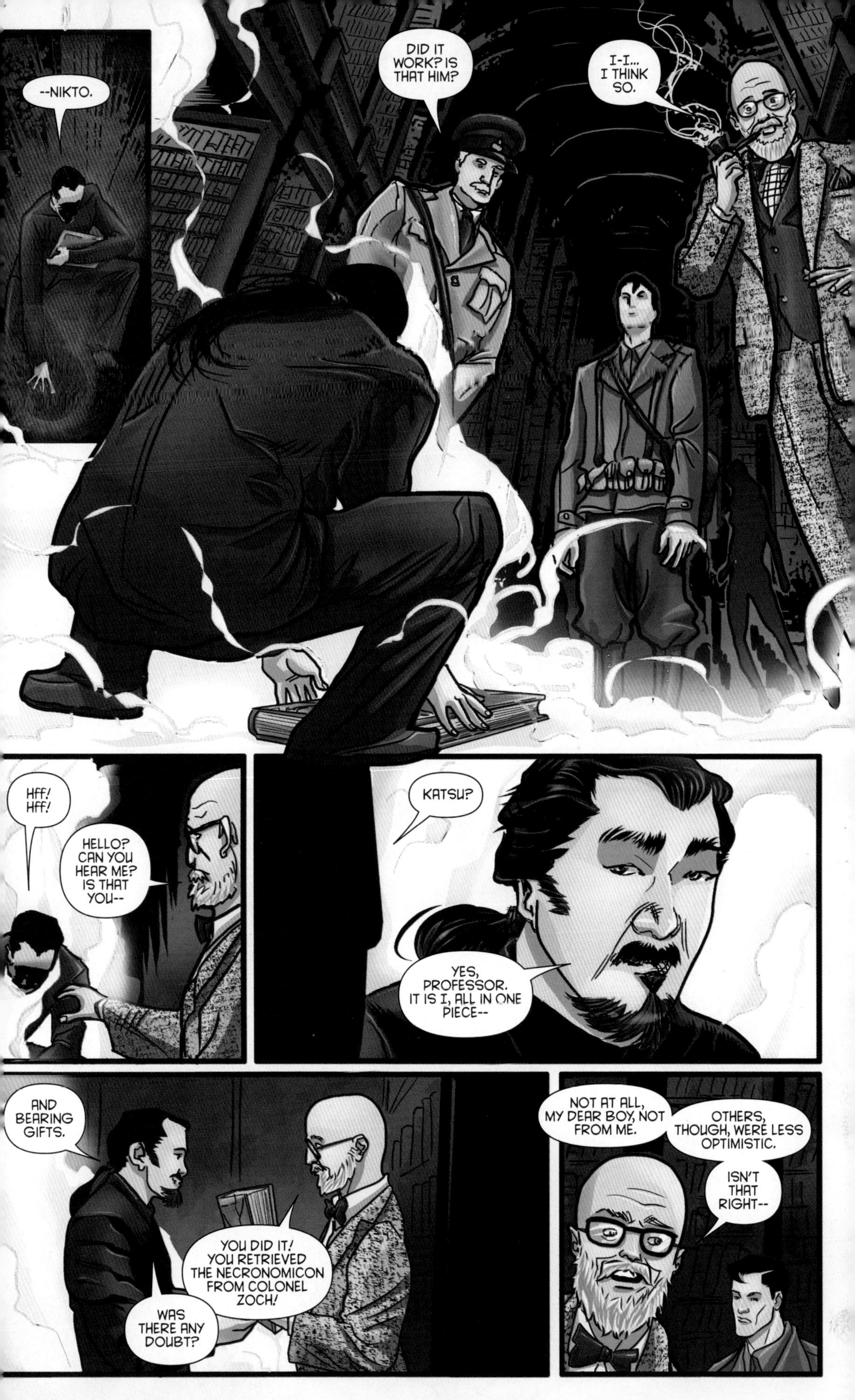
--NIKTO.
DID IT WORK? IS THAT HIM?
I-I... I THINK SO.
HFF! HFF!
HELLO? CAN YOU HEAR ME? IS THAT YOU--
KATSU?
YES, PROFESSOR. IT IS I, ALL IN ONE PIECE--
AND BEARING GIFTS.
YOU DID IT! YOU RETRIEVED THE NECRONOMICON FROM COLONEL ZOCH!
WAS THERE ANY DOUBT?
NOT AT ALL, MY DEAR BOY, NOT FROM ME.
OTHERS, THOUGH, WERE LESS OPTIMISTIC.
ISN'T THAT RIGHT--

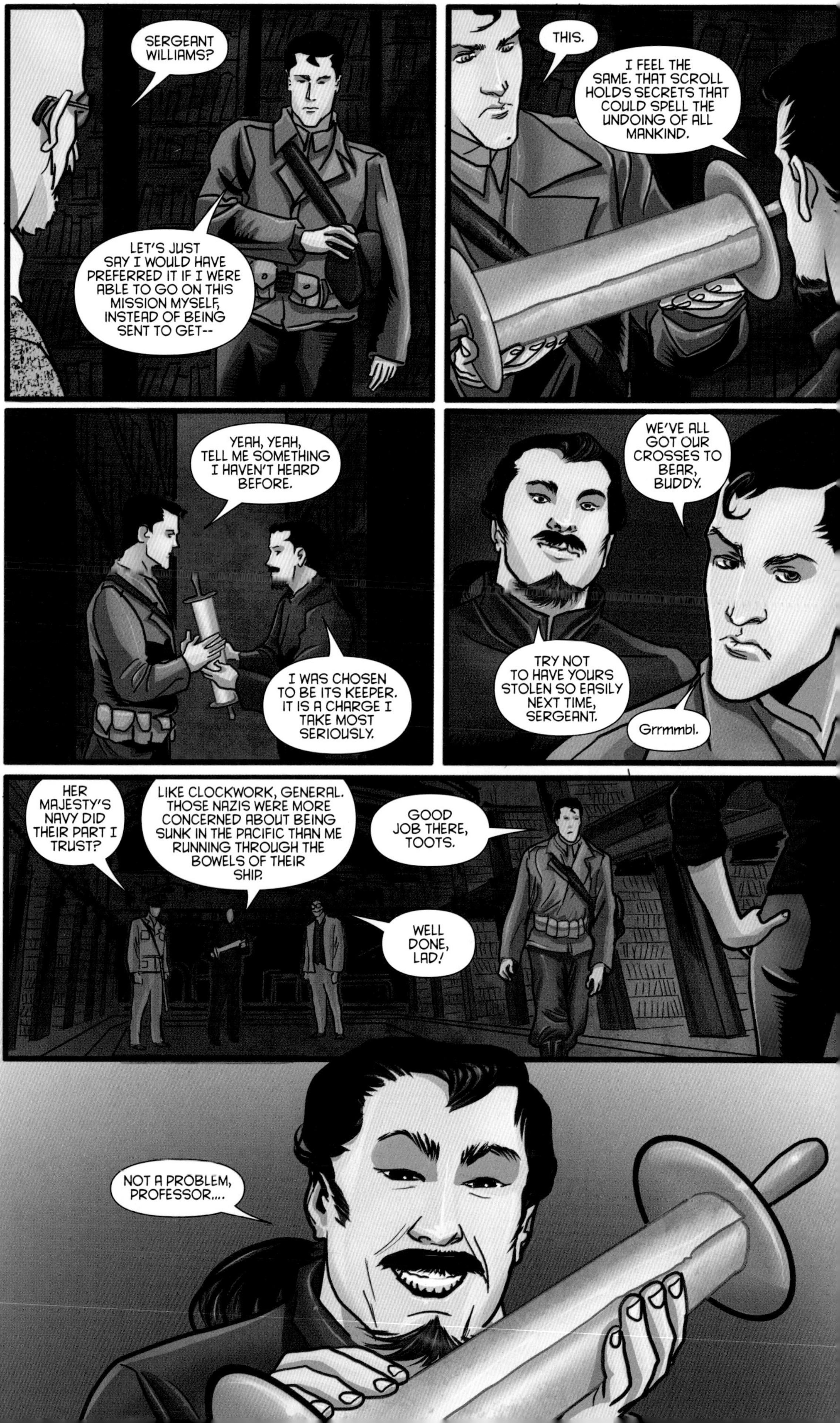
SERGEANT WILLIAMS?
LET'S JUST SAY I WOULD HAVE PREFERRED IT IF I WERE ABLE TO GO ON THIS MISSION MYSELF, INSTEAD OF BEING SENT TO GET--
THIS.
I FEEL THE SAME. THAT SCROLL HOLDS SECRETS THAT COULD SPELL THE UNDOING OF ALL MANKIND.
YEAH, YEAH, TELL ME SOMETHING I HAVEN'T HEARD BEFORE.
I WAS CHOSEN TO BE ITS KEEPER. IT IS A CHARGE I TAKE MOST SERIOUSLY.
WE'VE ALL GOT OUR CROSSES TO BEAR, BUDDY.
TRY NOT TO HAVE YOURS STOLEN SO EASILY NEXT TIME, SERGEANT.
Grrmmbl.
HER MAJESTY'S NAVY DID THEIR PART I TRUST?
LIKE CLOCKWORK, GENERAL. THOSE NAZIS WERE MORE CONCERNED ABOUT BEING SUNK IN THE PACIFIC THAN ME RUNNING THROUGH THE BOWELS OF THEIR SHIP.
GOOD JOB THERE, TOOTS.
WELL DONE, LAD!
NOT A PROBLEM, PROFESSOR....

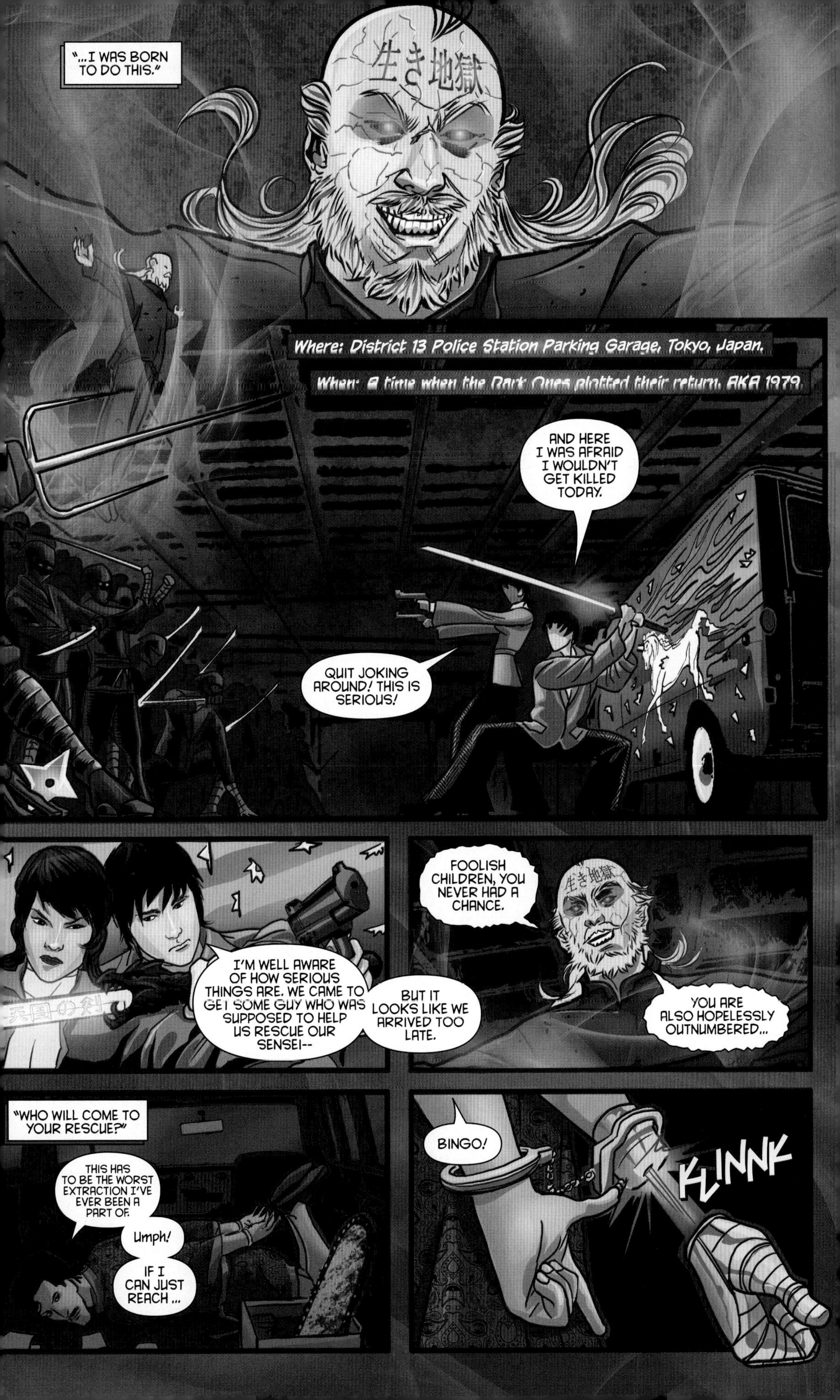
"...I WAS BORN TO DO THIS."
生き地獄
Where: District 13 Police Station Parking Garage, Tokyo, Japan.
When: A time when the Dark Ones plotted their return. AKA 1979.
AND HERE I WAS AFRAID I WOULDN'T GET KILLED TODAY.
QUIT JOKING AROUND! THIS IS SERIOUS!
天国の剣
I'M WELL AWARE OF HOW SERIOUS THINGS ARE. WE CAME TO GET SOME GUY WHO WAS SUPPOSED TO HELP US RESCUE OUR SENSEI--
BUT IT LOOKS LIKE WE ARRIVED TOO LATE.
FOOLISH CHILDREN, YOU NEVER HAD A CHANCE.
YOU ARE ALSO HOPELESSLY OUTNUMBERED...
"WHO WILL COME TO YOUR RESCUE?"
THIS HAS TO BE THE WORST EXTRACTION I'VE EVER BEEN A PART OF.
Umph!
IF I CAN JUST REACH ...
BINGO!
KLINNK

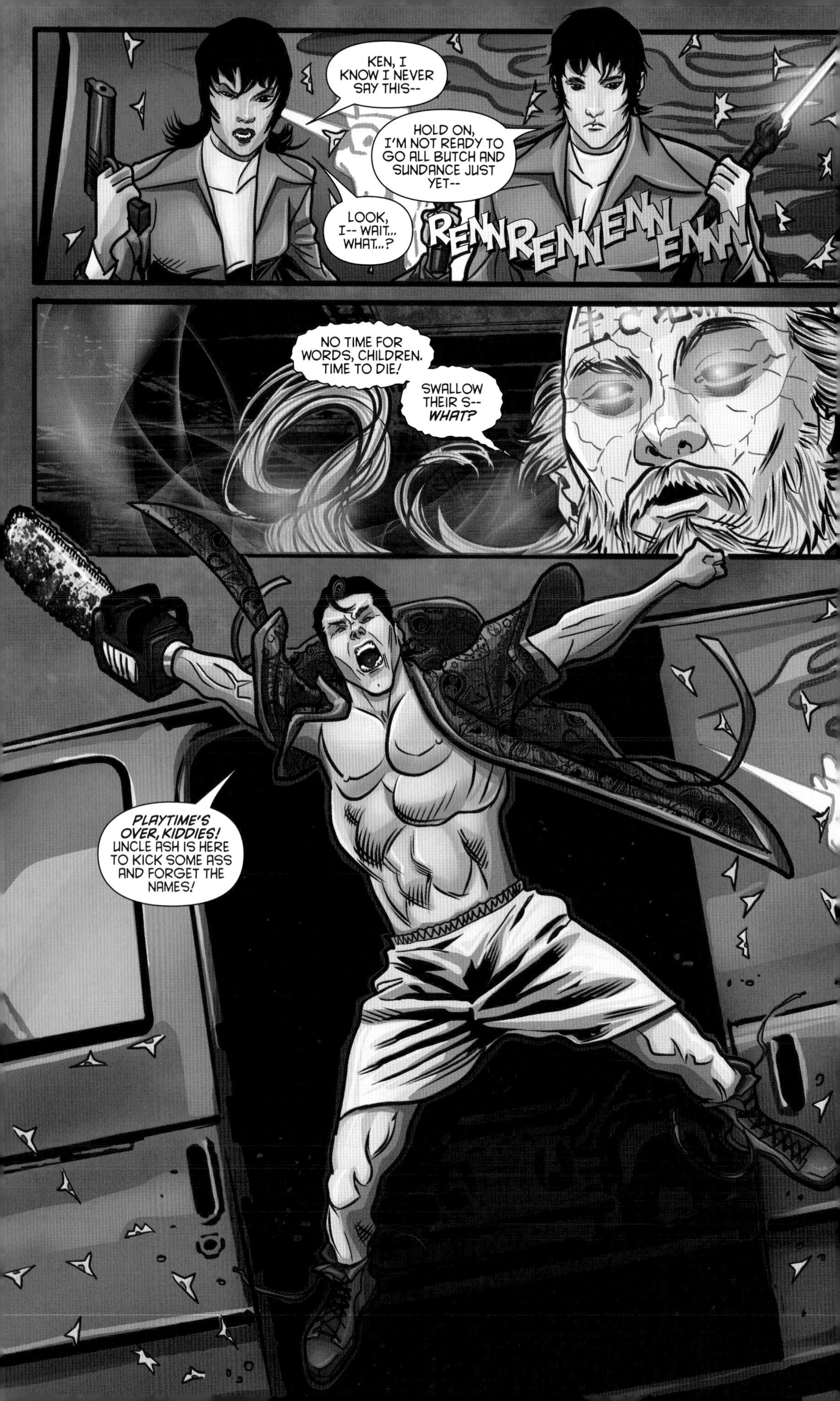
KEN, I KNOW I NEVER SAY THIS--
HOLD ON, I'M NOT READY TO GO ALL BUTCH AND SUNDANCE JUST YET--
LOOK, I-- WAIT... WHAT...?
RENNRENNENNENN ENNN
NO TIME FOR WORDS, CHILDREN. TIME TO DIE!
SWALLOW THEIR S-- *WHAT?*
PLAYTIME'S OVER, KIDDIES! UNCLE ASH IS HERE TO KICK SOME ASS AND FORGET THE NAMES!

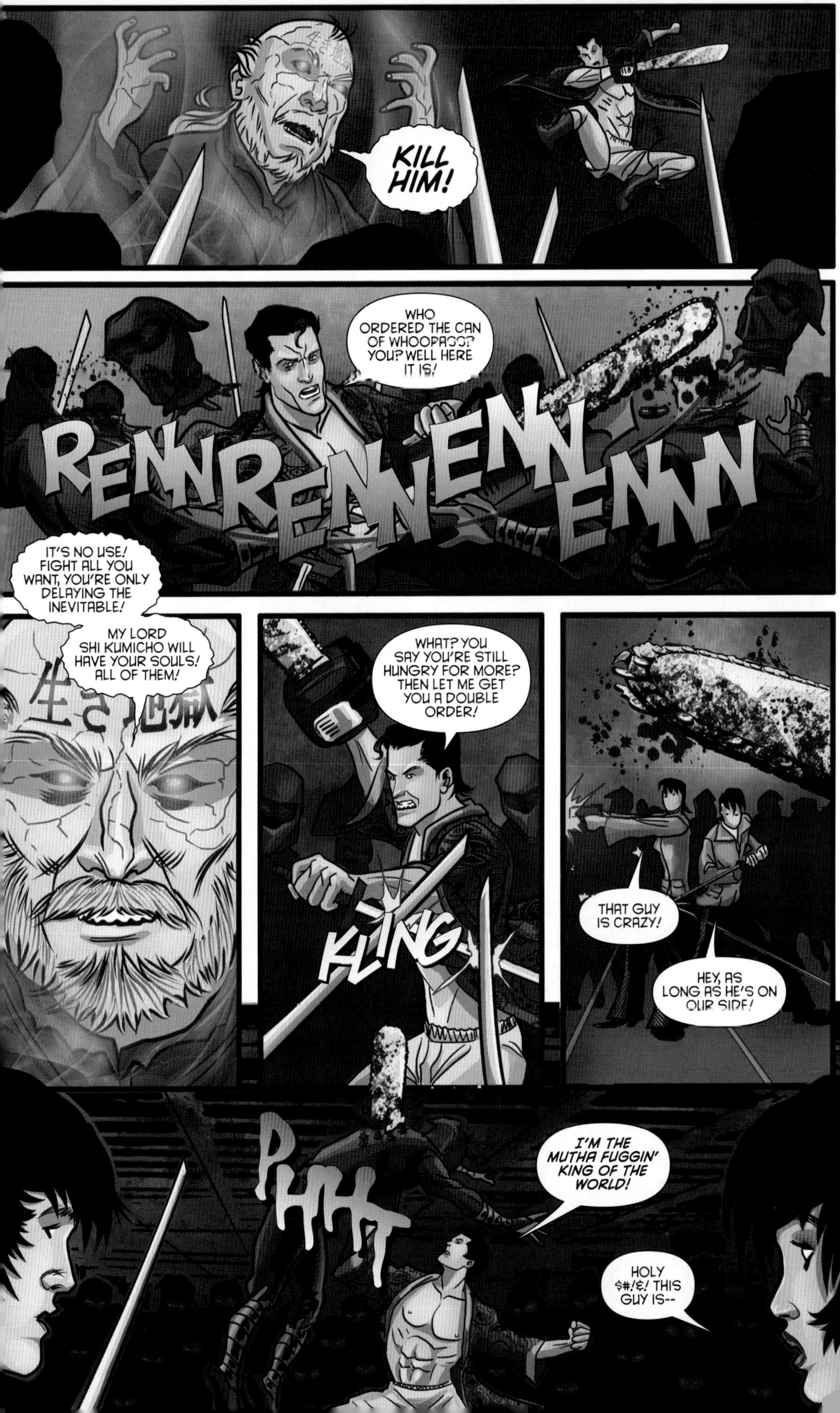
KILL HIM!
WHO ORDERED THE CAN OF WHOOPASS? YOU? WELL HERE IT IS!
RENN RENNENN ENN
IT'S NO USE! FIGHT ALL YOU WANT, YOU'RE ONLY DELAYING THE INEVITABLE!
MY LORD SHI KUMICHO WILL HAVE YOUR SOULS! ALL OF THEM!
WHAT? YOU SAY YOU'RE STILL HUNGRY FOR MORE? THEN LET ME GET YOU A DOUBLE ORDER!
KLING
THAT GUY IS CRAZY!
HEY, AS LONG AS HE'S ON OUR SIDE!
PHHT
I'M THE MUTHA FUGGIN' KING OF THE WORLD!
HOLY $#!&! THIS GUY IS--

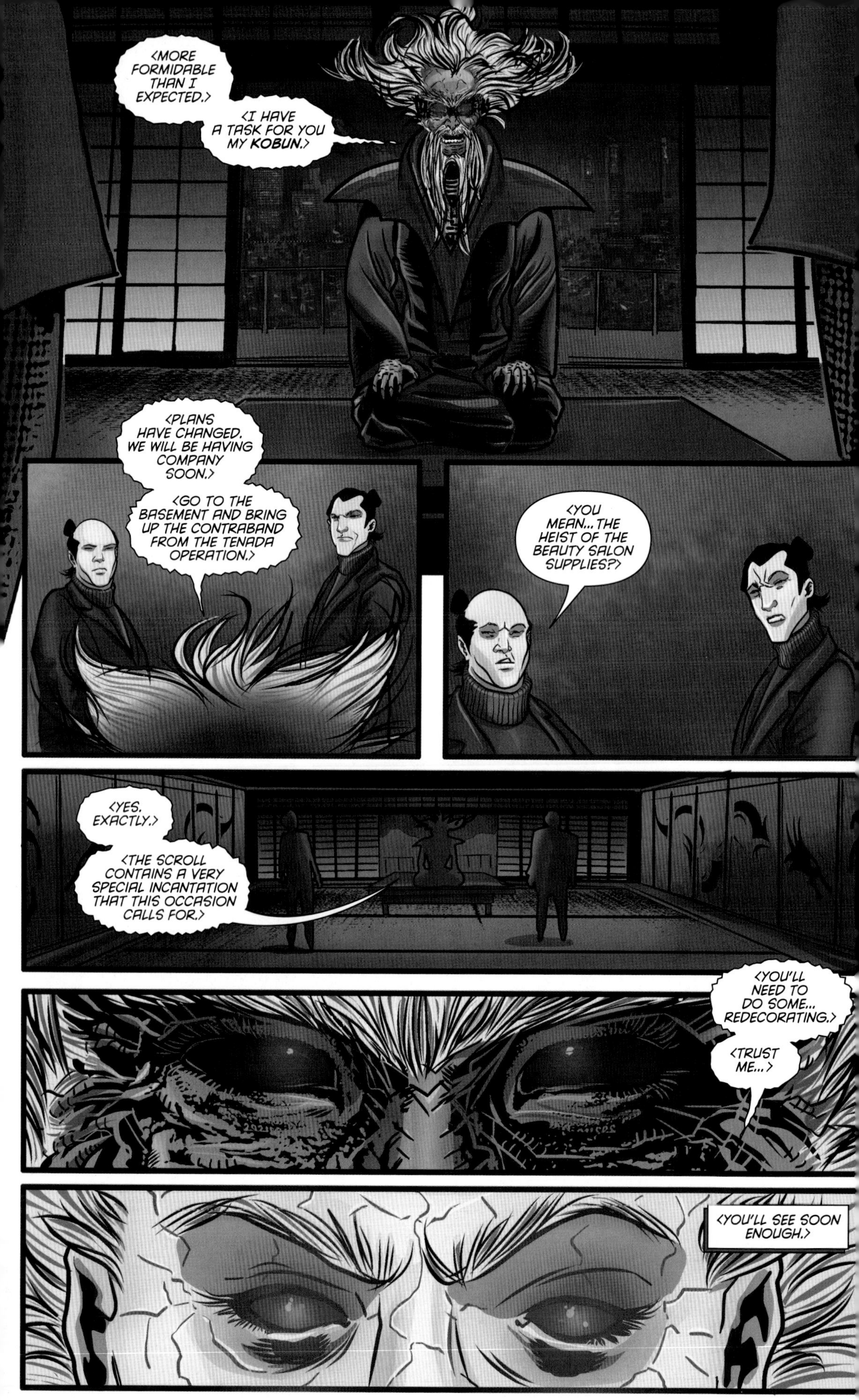
<MORE FORMIDABLE THAN I EXPECTED.>
<I HAVE A TASK FOR YOU MY **KOBUN.**>
<PLANS HAVE CHANGED. WE WILL BE HAVING COMPANY SOON.>
<GO TO THE BASEMENT AND BRING UP THE CONTRABAND FROM THE TENADA OPERATION.>
<YOU MEAN... THE HEIST OF THE BEAUTY SALON SUPPLIES?>
<YES. EXACTLY.>
<THE SCROLL CONTAINS A VERY SPECIAL INCANTATION THAT THIS OCCASION CALLS FOR.>
<YOU'LL NEED TO DO SOME... REDECORATING.>
<TRUST ME...>
<YOU'LL SEE SOON ENOUGH.>

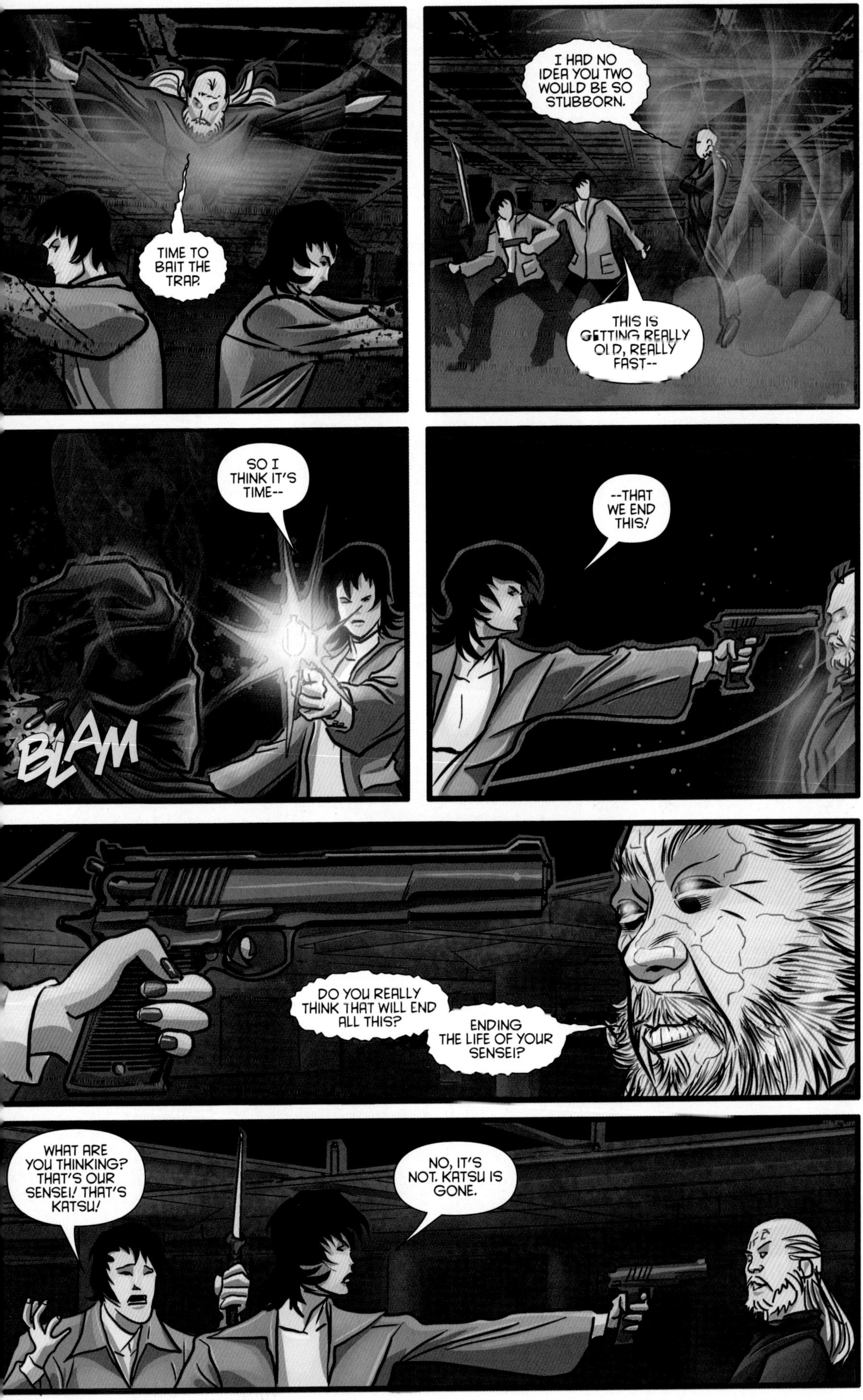
TIME TO BAIT THE TRAP.
I HAD NO IDEA YOU TWO WOULD BE SO STUBBORN.
THIS IS GETTING REALLY OLD, REALLY FAST--
SO I THINK IT'S TIME--
BLAM
--THAT WE END THIS!
DO YOU REALLY THINK THAT WILL END ALL THIS?
ENDING THE LIFE OF YOUR SENSEI?
WHAT ARE YOU THINKING? THAT'S OUR SENSEI! THAT'S KATSU!
NO, IT'S NOT. KATSU IS GONE.

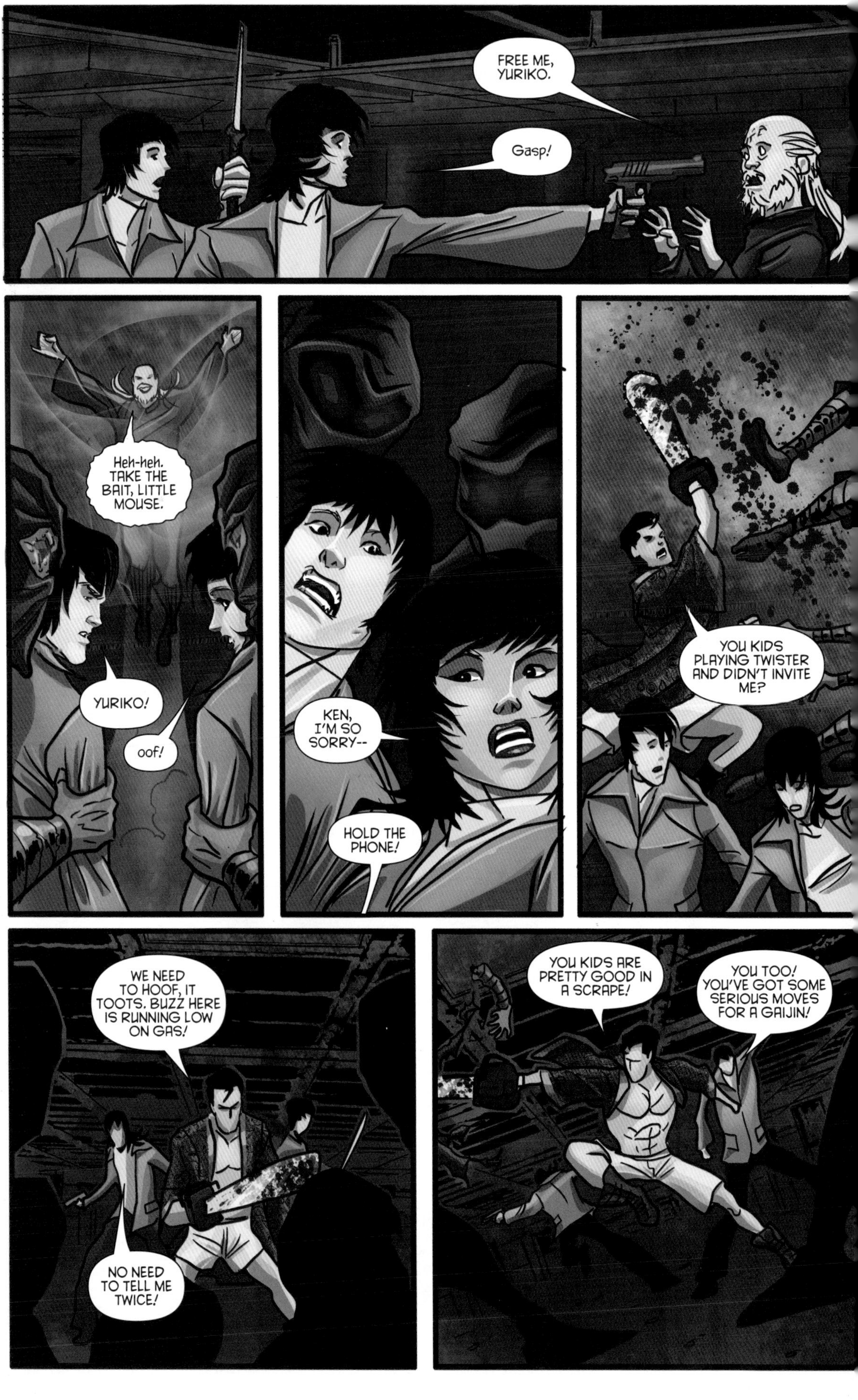
FREE ME, YURIKO.
Gasp!
Heh-heh. TAKE THE BAIT, LITTLE MOUSE.
YURIKO!
oof!
KEN, I'M SO SORRY--
HOLD THE PHONE!
YOU KIDS PLAYING TWISTER AND DIDN'T INVITE ME?
WE NEED TO HOOF, IT TOOTS. BUZZ HERE IS RUNNING LOW ON GAS!
NO NEED TO TELL ME TWICE!
YOU KIDS ARE PRETTY GOOD IN A SCRAPE!
YOU TOO! YOU'VE GOT SOME SERIOUS MOVES FOR A GAIJIN!

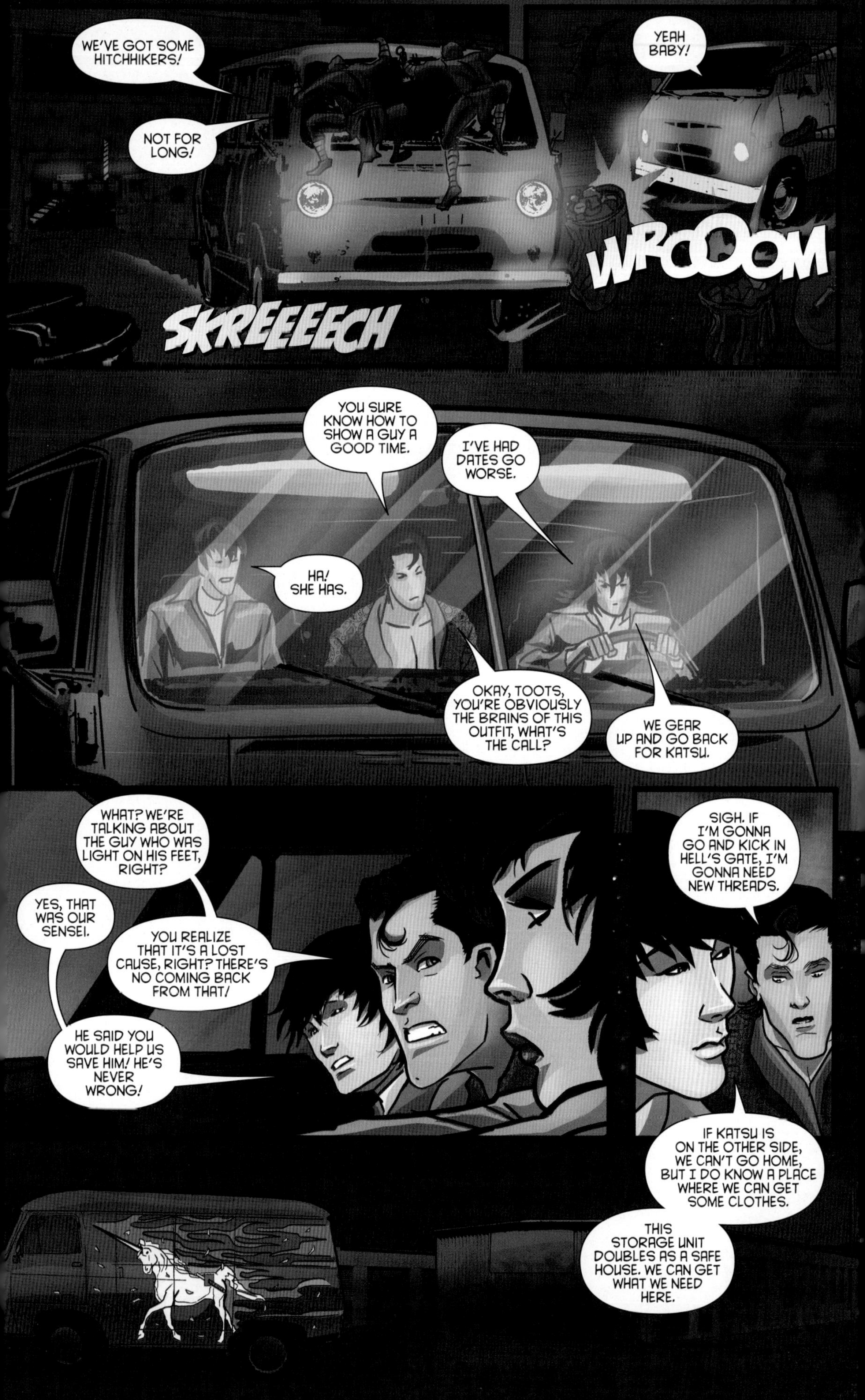
WE'VE GOT SOME HITCHHIKERS!
NOT FOR LONG!
SKREEEECH
YEAH BABY!
WROOOM
YOU SURE KNOW HOW TO SHOW A GUY A GOOD TIME.
I'VE HAD DATES GO WORSE.
HA! SHE HAS.
OKAY, TOOTS, YOU'RE OBVIOUSLY THE BRAINS OF THIS OUTFIT, WHAT'S THE CALL?
WE GEAR UP AND GO BACK FOR KATSU.
WHAT? WE'RE TALKING ABOUT THE GUY WHO WAS LIGHT ON HIS FEET, RIGHT?
YES, THAT WAS OUR SENSEI.
YOU REALIZE THAT IT'S A LOST CAUSE, RIGHT? THERE'S NO COMING BACK FROM THAT!
HE SAID YOU WOULD HELP US SAVE HIM! HE'S NEVER WRONG!
SIGH. IF I'M GONNA GO AND KICK IN HELL'S GATE, I'M GONNA NEED NEW THREADS.
IF KATSU IS ON THE OTHER SIDE, WE CAN'T GO HOME, BUT I DO KNOW A PLACE WHERE WE CAN GET SOME CLOTHES.
THIS STORAGE UNIT DOUBLES AS A SAFE HOUSE. WE CAN GET WHAT WE NEED HERE.

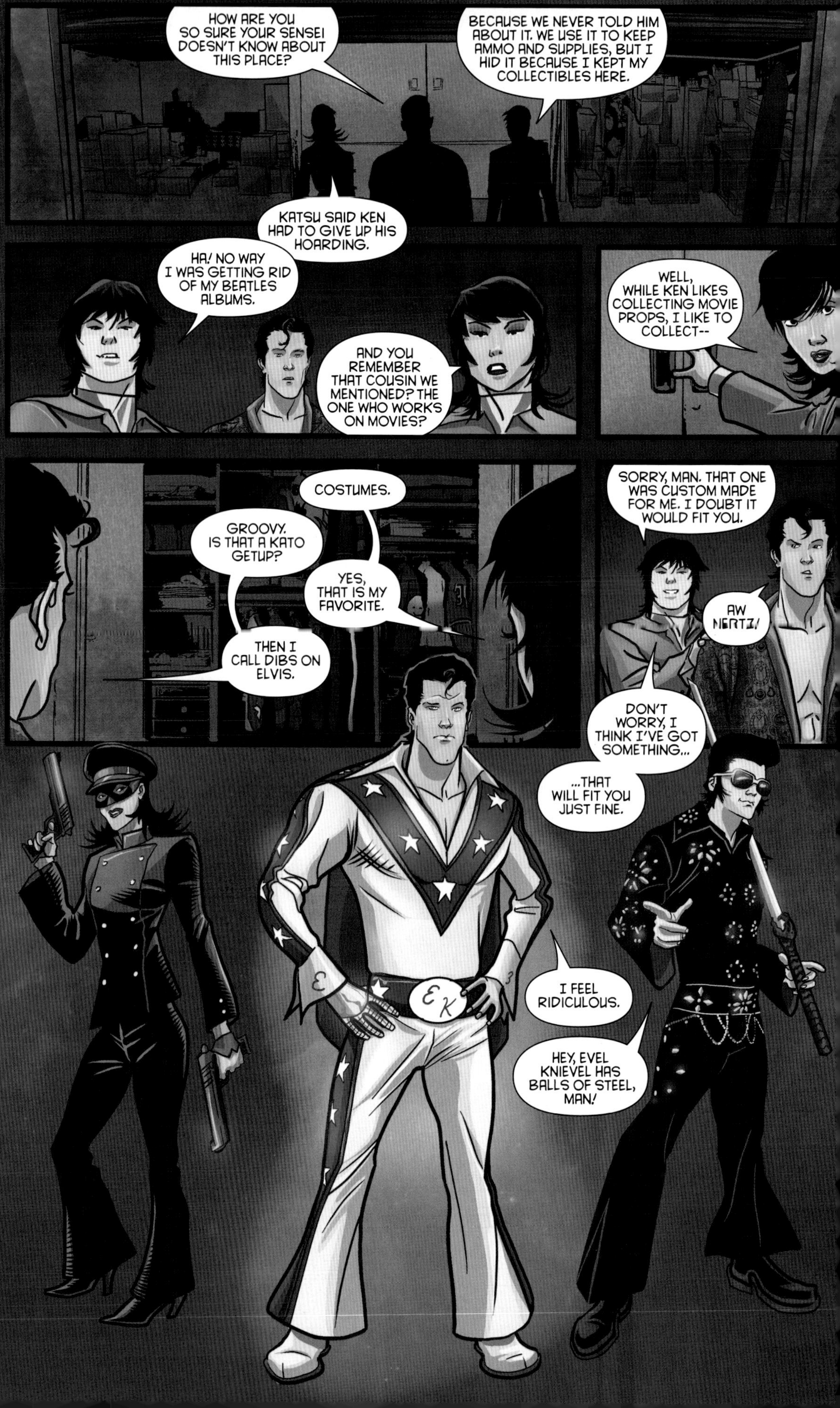
HOW ARE YOU SO SURE YOUR SENSEI DOESN'T KNOW ABOUT THIS PLACE?
BECAUSE WE NEVER TOLD HIM ABOUT IT. WE USE IT TO KEEP AMMO AND SUPPLIES, BUT I HID IT BECAUSE I KEPT MY COLLECTIBLES HERE.
KATSU SAID KEN HAD TO GIVE UP HIS HOARDING.
HA! NO WAY I WAS GETTING RID OF MY BEATLES ALBUMS.
AND YOU REMEMBER THAT COUSIN WE MENTIONED? THE ONE WHO WORKS ON MOVIES?
WELL, WHILE KEN LIKES COLLECTING MOVIE PROPS, I LIKE TO COLLECT--
COSTUMES.
GROOVY. IS THAT A KATO GETUP?
YES, THAT IS MY FAVORITE.
THEN I CALL DIBS ON ELVIS.
SORRY, MAN. THAT ONE WAS CUSTOM MADE FOR ME. I DOUBT IT WOULD FIT YOU.
AW NERTZ!
DON'T WORRY, I THINK I'VE GOT SOMETHING...
...THAT WILL FIT YOU JUST FINE.
I FEEL RIDICULOUS.
HEY, EVEL KNIEVEL HAS BALLS OF STEEL, MAN!

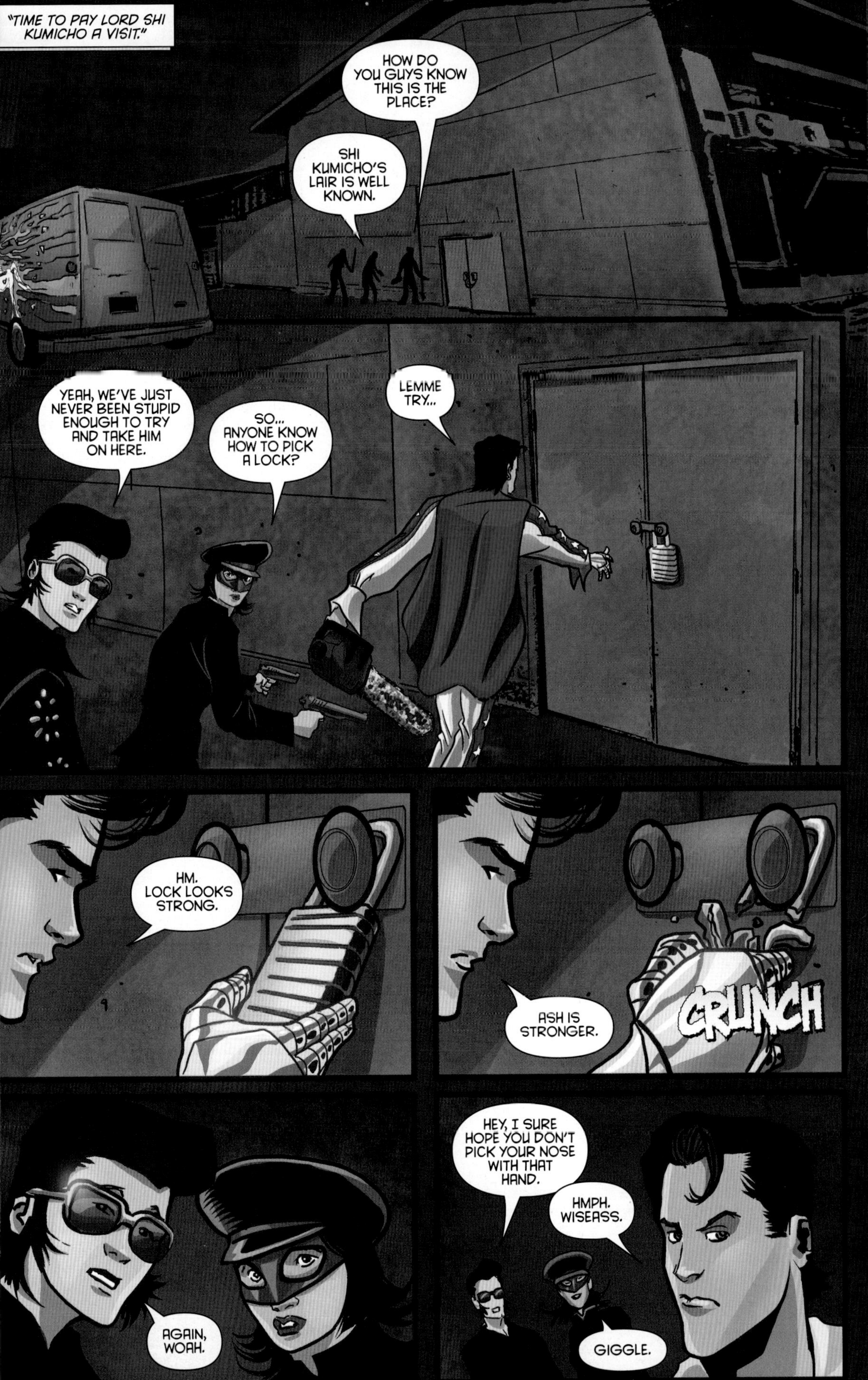
"TIME TO PAY LORD SHI KUMICHO A VISIT."
HOW DO YOU GUYS KNOW THIS IS THE PLACE?
SHI KUMICHO'S LAIR IS WELL KNOWN.
YEAH, WE'VE JUST NEVER BEEN STUPID ENOUGH TO TRY AND TAKE HIM ON HERE.
SO... ANYONE KNOW HOW TO PICK A LOCK?
LEMME TRY...
HM. LOCK LOOKS STRONG.
ASH IS STRONGER.
CRUNCH
AGAIN, WOAH.
HEY, I SURE HOPE YOU DON'T PICK YOUR NOSE WITH THAT HAND.
HMPH. WISEASS.
GIGGLE.

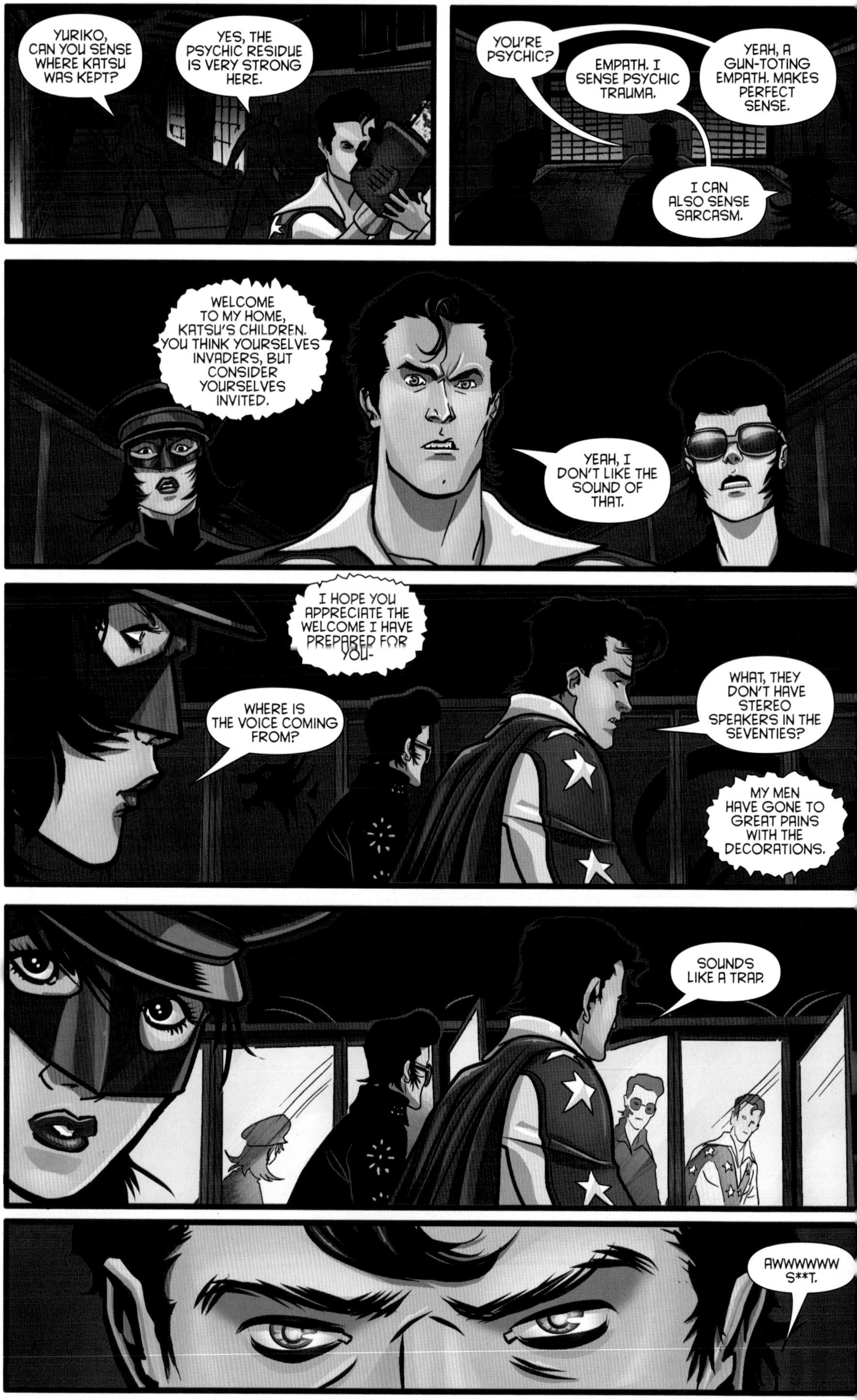
YURIKO, CAN YOU SENSE WHERE KATSU WAS KEPT?
YES, THE PSYCHIC RESIDUE IS VERY STRONG HERE.
YOU'RE PSYCHIC?
EMPATH. I SENSE PSYCHIC TRAUMA.
YEAH, A GUN-TOTING EMPATH. MAKES PERFECT SENSE.
I CAN ALSO SENSE SARCASM.
WELCOME TO MY HOME, KATSU'S CHILDREN. YOU THINK YOURSELVES INVADERS, BUT CONSIDER YOURSELVES INVITED.
YEAH, I DON'T LIKE THE SOUND OF THAT.
I HOPE YOU APPRECIATE THE WELCOME I HAVE PREPARED FOR YOU-
WHERE IS THE VOICE COMING FROM?
WHAT, THEY DON'T HAVE STEREO SPEAKERS IN THE SEVENTIES?
MY MEN HAVE GONE TO GREAT PAINS WITH THE DECORATIONS.
SOUNDS LIKE A TRAP.
AWWWWWW S**T.

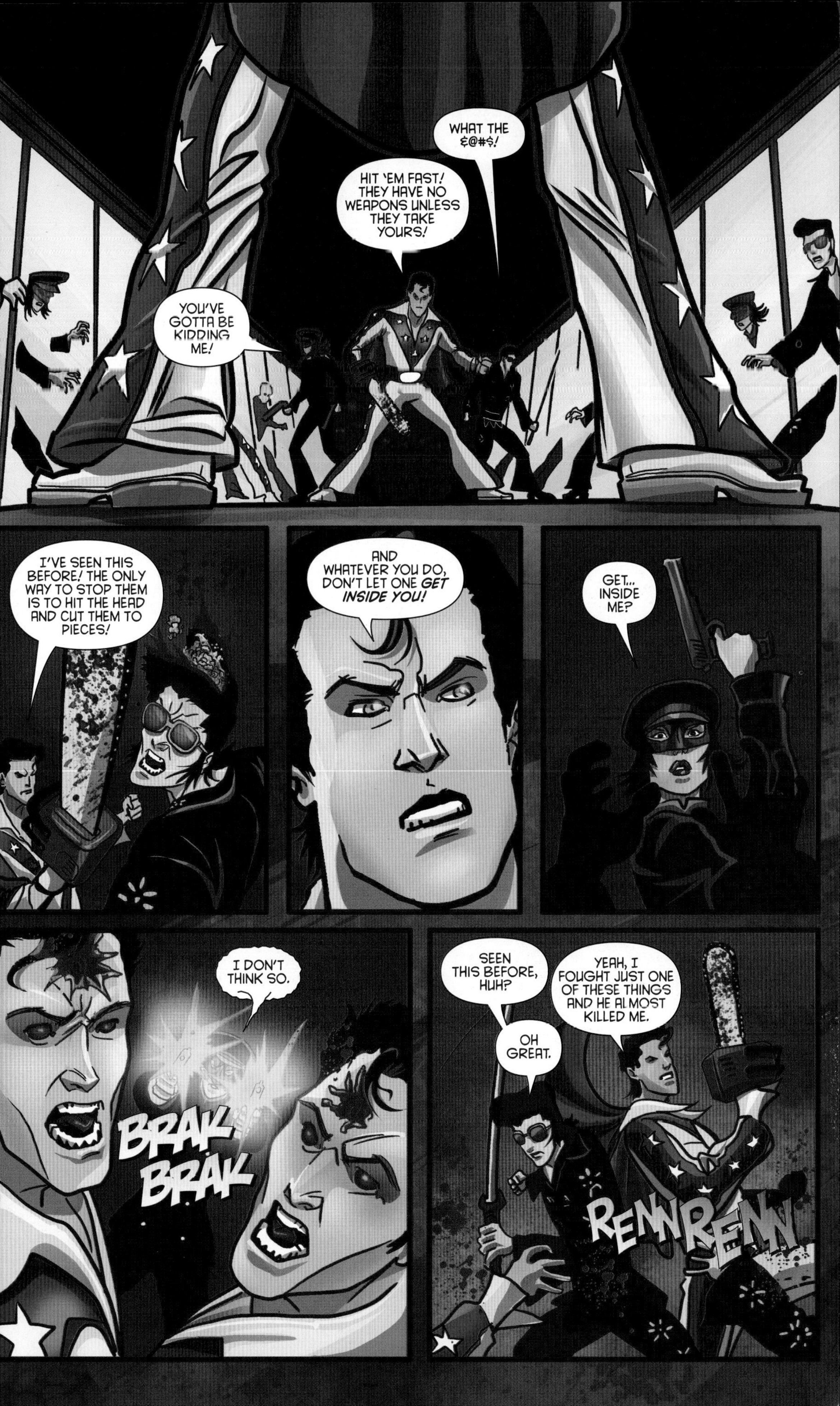
WHAT THE &@#$!
HIT 'EM FAST! THEY HAVE NO WEAPONS UNLESS THEY TAKE YOURS!
YOU'VE GOTTA BE KIDDING ME!
I'VE SEEN THIS BEFORE! THE ONLY WAY TO STOP THEM IS TO HIT THE HEAD AND CUT THEM TO PIECES!
AND WHATEVER YOU DO, DON'T LET ONE *GET INSIDE YOU!*
GET... INSIDE ME?
I DON'T THINK SO.
BRAK BRAK
SEEN THIS BEFORE, HUH?
YEAH, I FOUGHT JUST ONE OF THESE THINGS AND HE ALMOST KILLED ME.
OH GREAT.
RENNRENN

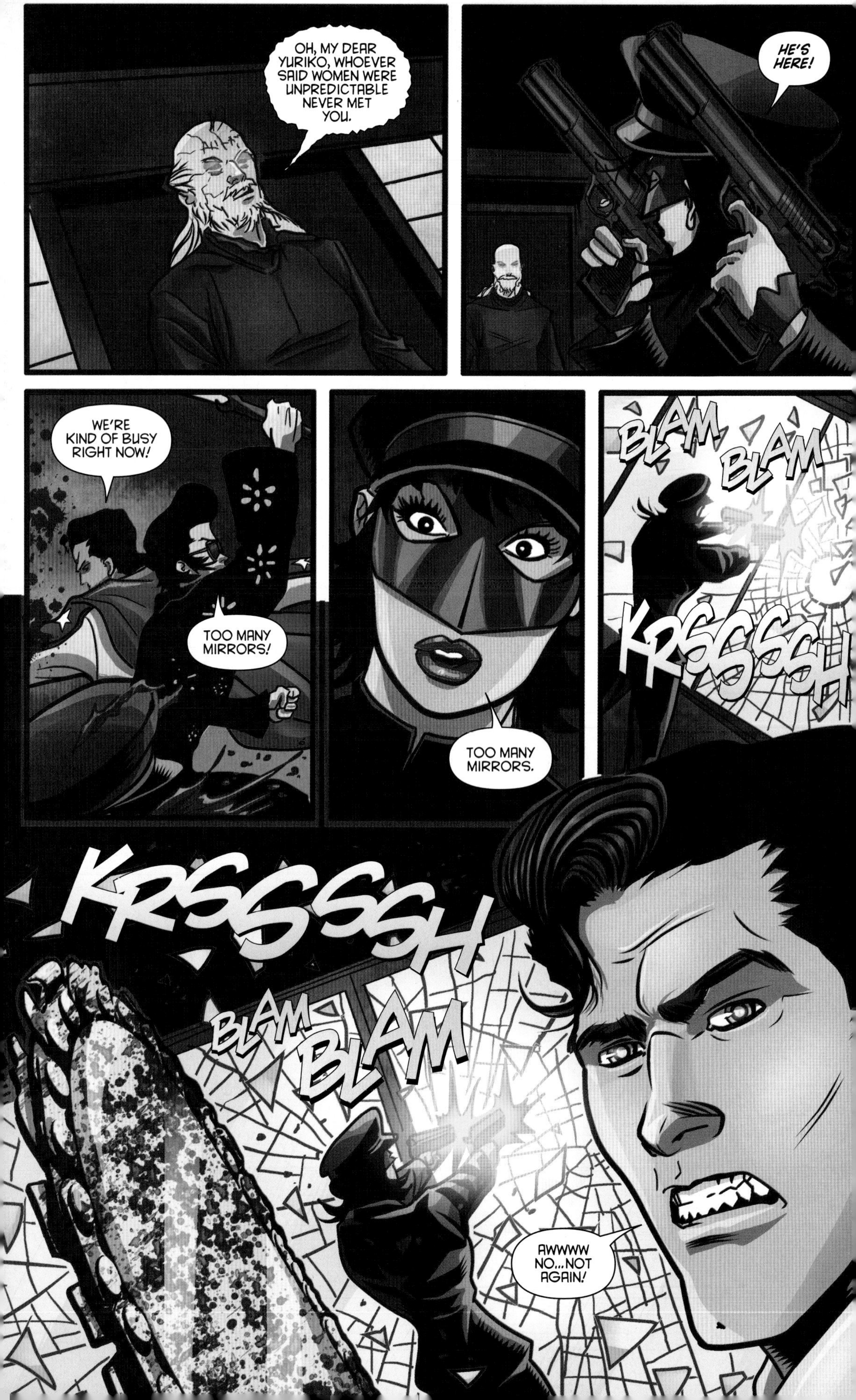
OH, MY DEAR YURIKO, WHOEVER SAID WOMEN WERE UNPREDICTABLE NEVER MET YOU.
HE'S HERE!
WE'RE KIND OF BUSY RIGHT NOW!
TOO MANY MIRRORS!
TOO MANY MIRRORS.
BLAM BLAM
KRSSSSH
KRSSSSH
BLAM BLAM
AWWWW NO...NOT AGAIN!

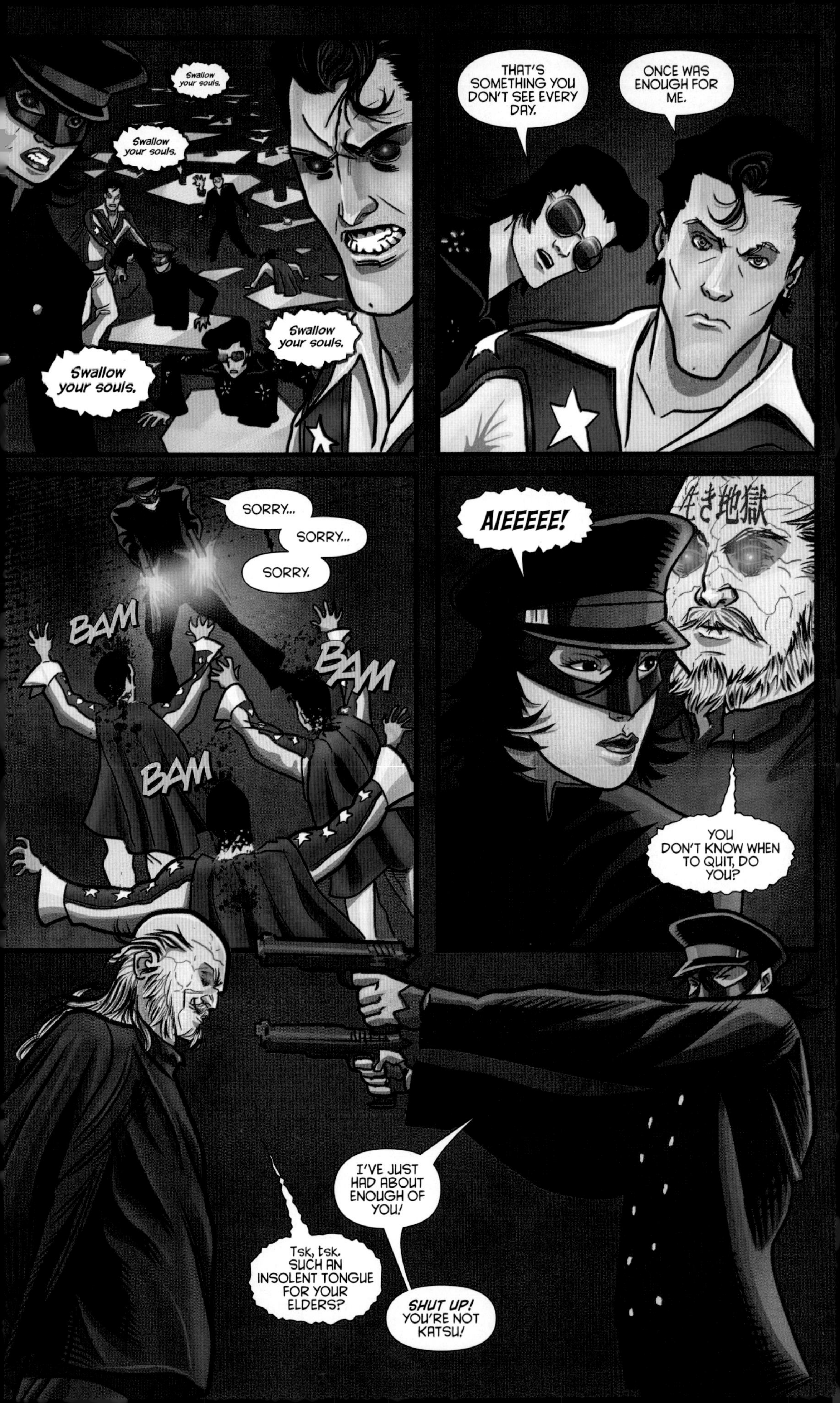
Swallow your souls.
Swallow your souls.
Swallow your souls.
Swallow your souls.
THAT'S SOMETHING YOU DON'T SEE EVERY DAY.
ONCE WAS ENOUGH FOR ME.
SORRY...
SORRY...
SORRY.
BAM
BAM
BAM
AIEEEEE!
生き地獄
YOU DON'T KNOW WHEN TO QUIT, DO YOU?
I'VE JUST HAD ABOUT ENOUGH OF YOU!
Tsk, tsk. SUCH AN INSOLENT TONGUE FOR YOUR ELDERS?
SHUT UP! YOU'RE NOT KATSU!

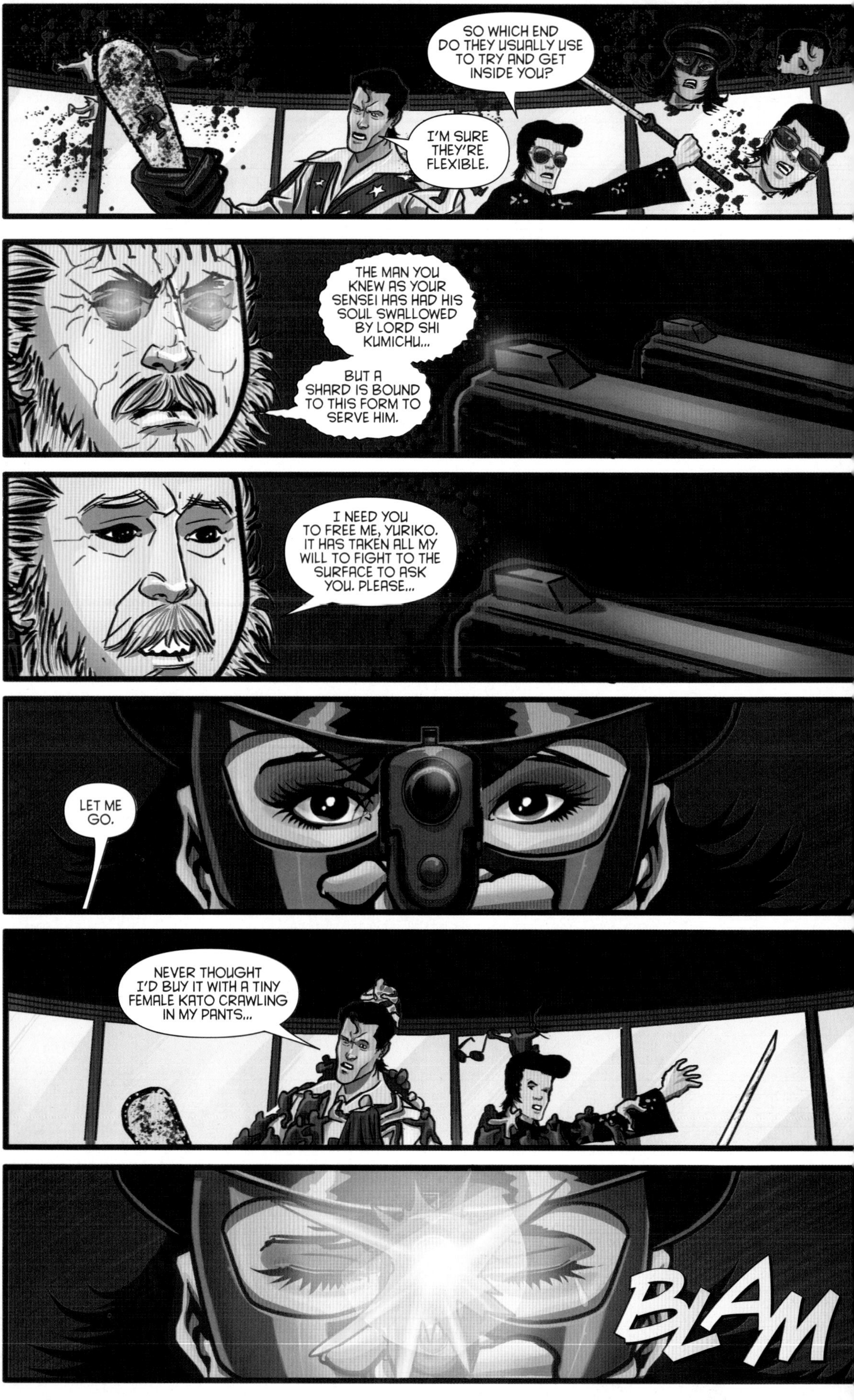
SO WHICH END DO THEY USUALLY USE TO TRY AND GET INSIDE YOU?
I'M SURE THEY'RE FLEXIBLE.
THE MAN YOU KNEW AS YOUR SENSEI HAS HAD HIS SOUL SWALLOWED BY LORD SHI KUMICHU...
BUT A SHARD IS BOUND TO THIS FORM TO SERVE HIM.
I NEED YOU TO FREE ME, YURIKO. IT HAS TAKEN ALL MY WILL TO FIGHT TO THE SURFACE TO ASK YOU. PLEASE...
LET ME GO.
NEVER THOUGHT I'D BUY IT WITH A TINY FEMALE KATO CRAWLING IN MY PANTS...
BLAM

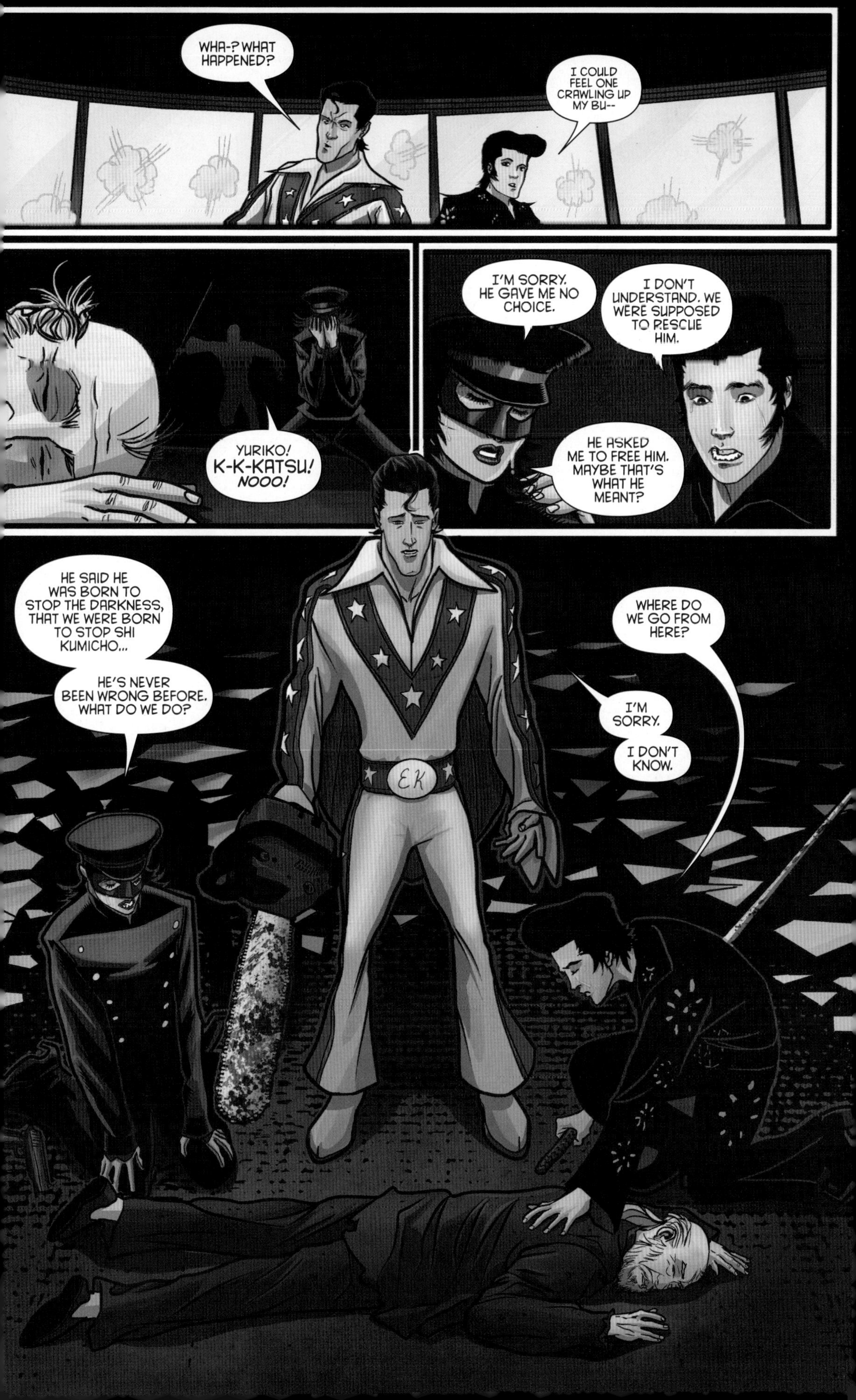
WHA-? WHAT HAPPENED?
I COULD FEEL ONE CRAWLING UP MY BU--
YURIKO! K-K-KATSU! NOOO!
I'M SORRY. HE GAVE ME NO CHOICE.
I DON'T UNDERSTAND. WE WERE SUPPOSED TO RESCUE HIM.
HE ASKED ME TO FREE HIM. MAYBE THAT'S WHAT HE MEANT?
HE SAID HE WAS BORN TO STOP THE DARKNESS, THAT WE WERE BORN TO STOP SHI KUMICHO...
HE'S NEVER BEEN WRONG BEFORE. WHAT DO WE DO?
WHERE DO WE GO FROM HERE?
I'M SORRY.
I DON'T KNOW.
EK

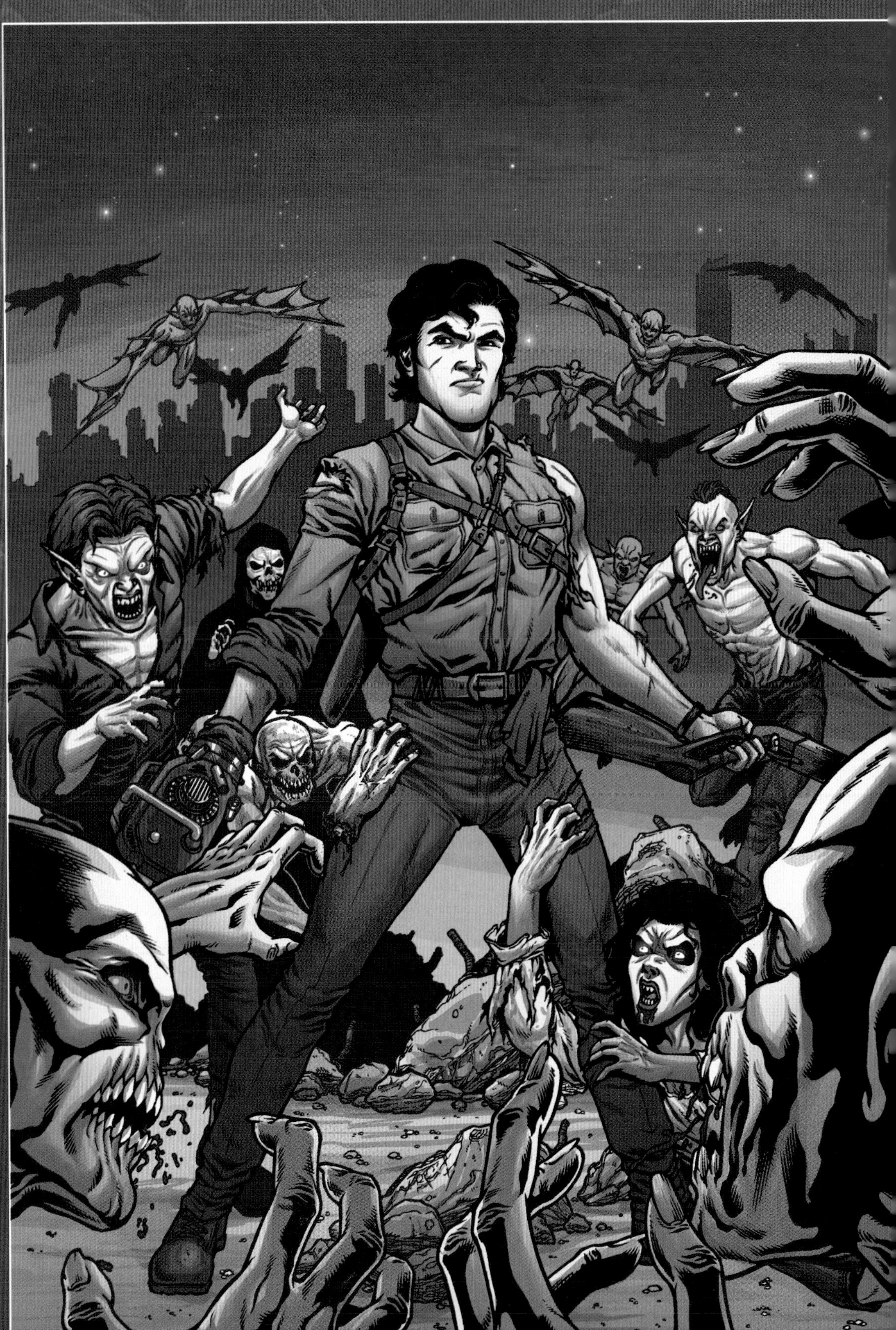

cover to issue #7 by MARCIO FIORITO, colors by ADRIANO LUCAS

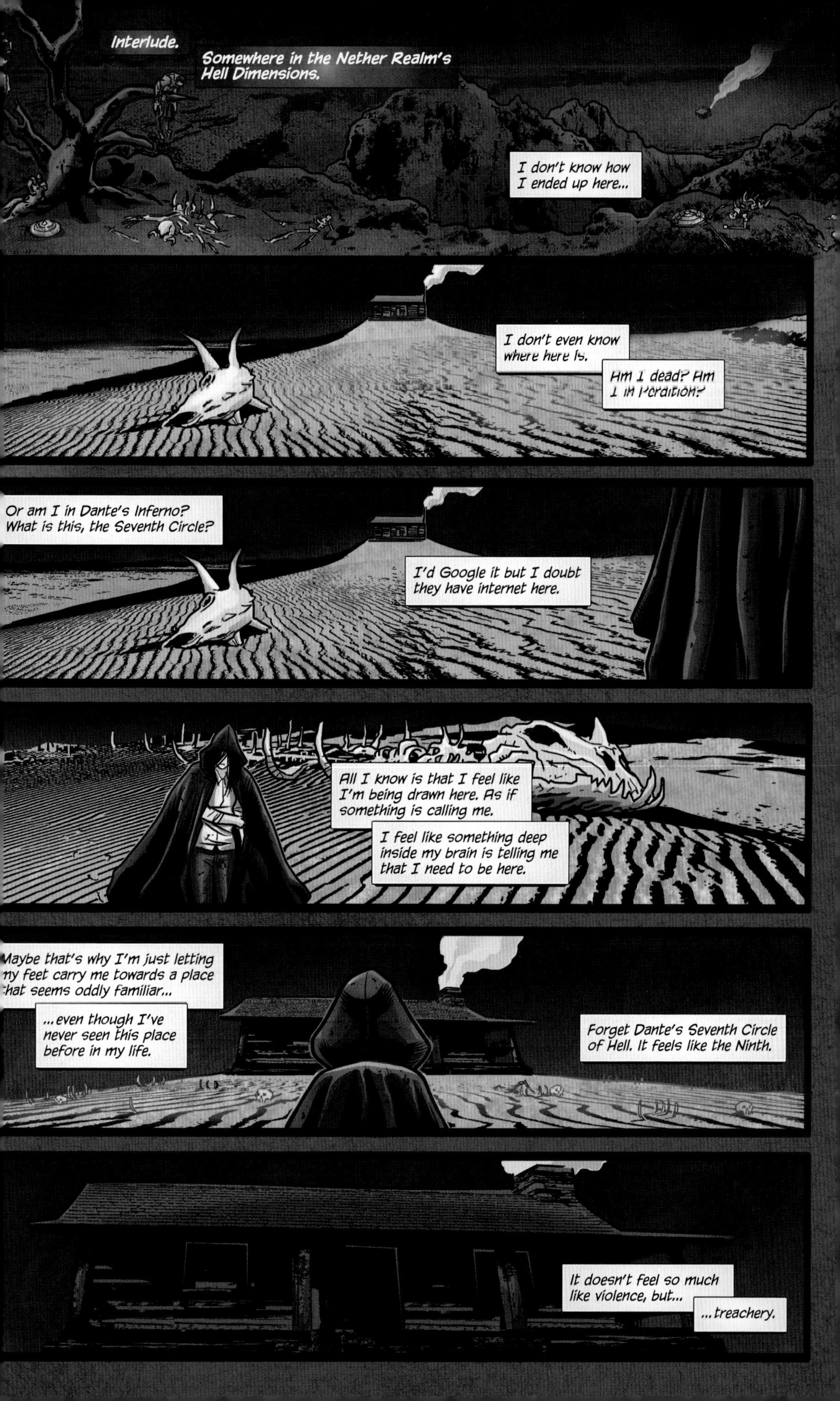
Interlude.
Somewhere in the Nether Realm's Hell Dimensions.
I don't know how I ended up here...
I don't even know where here is.
Am I dead? Am I in Perdition?
Or am I in Dante's Inferno? What is this, the Seventh Circle?
I'd Google it but I doubt they have internet here.
All I know is that I feel like I'm being drawn here. As if something is calling me.
I feel like something deep inside my brain is telling me that I need to be here.
Maybe that's why I'm just letting my feet carry me towards a place that seems oddly familiar...
...even though I've never seen this place before in my life.
Forget Dante's Seventh Circle of Hell. It feels like the Ninth.
It doesn't feel so much like violence, but...
...treachery.

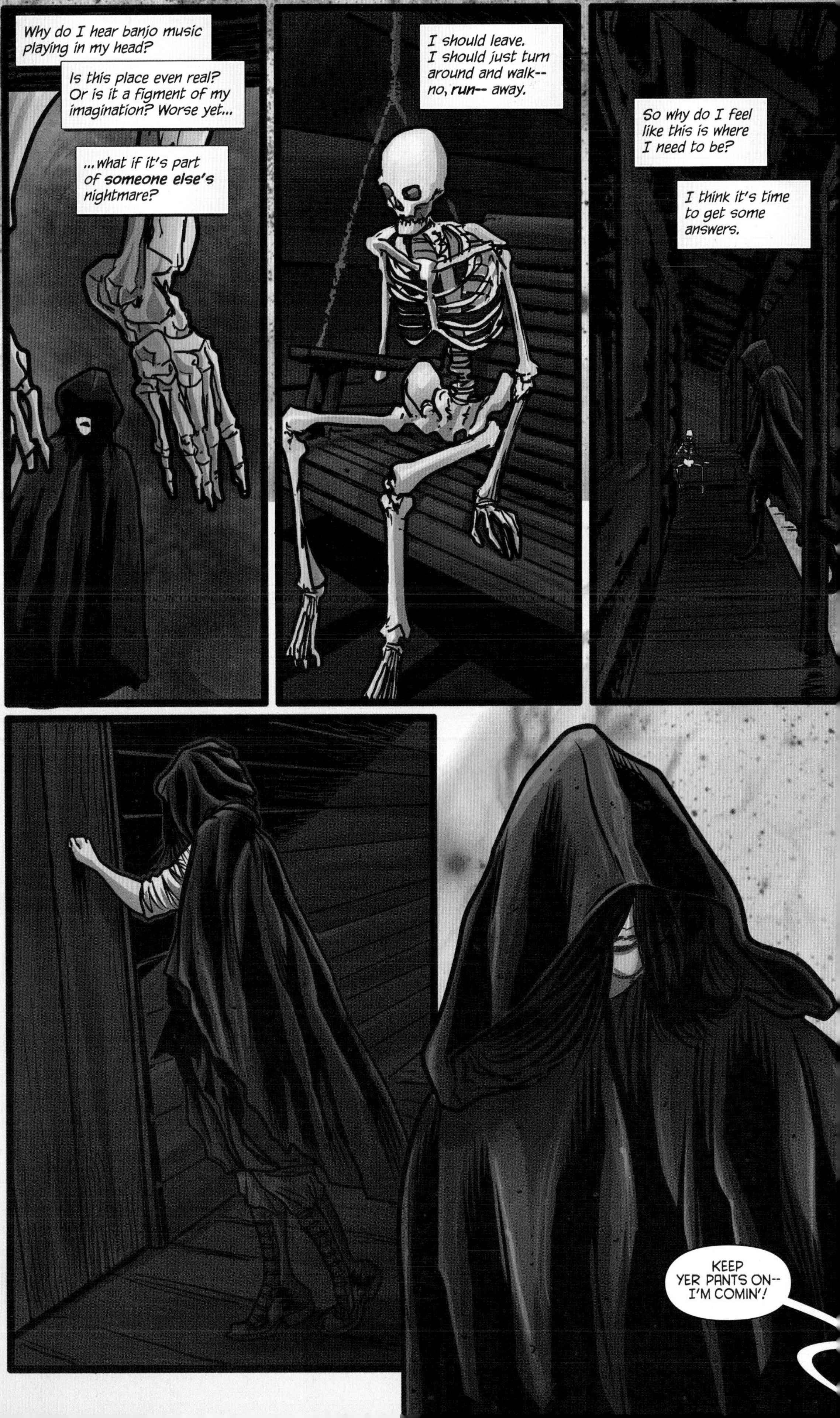
Why do I hear banjo music playing in my head?
Is this place even real? Or is it a figment of my imagination? Worse yet...
...what if it's part of **someone else's** nightmare?
I should leave. I should just turn around and walk-- no, **run**-- away.
So why do I feel like this is where I need to be?
I think it's time to get some answers.
KEEP YER PANTS ON-- I'M COMIN'!

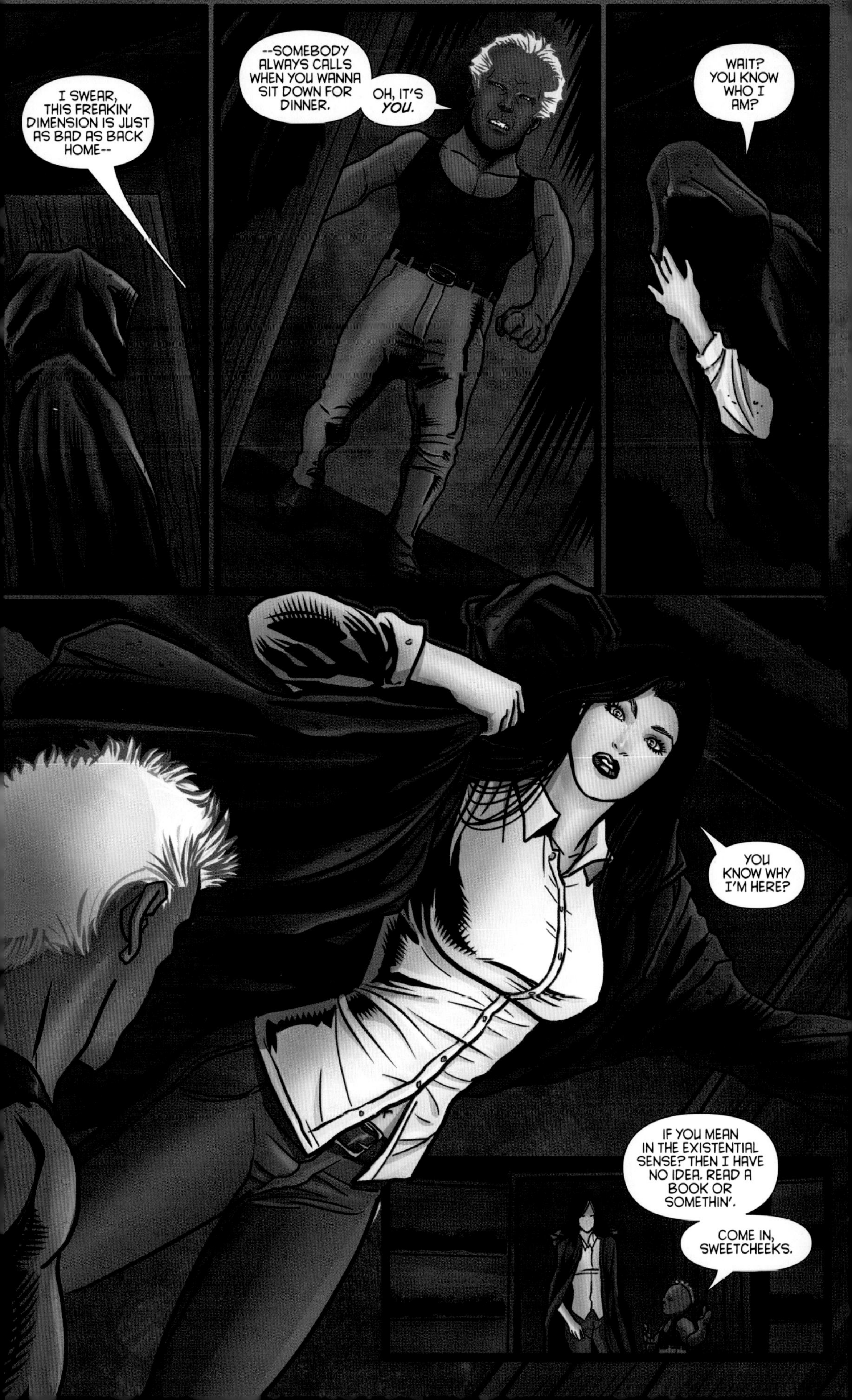
I SWEAR, THIS FREAKIN' DIMENSION IS JUST AS BAD AS BACK HOME--
--SOMEBODY ALWAYS CALLS WHEN YOU WANNA SIT DOWN FOR DINNER.
OH, IT'S *YOU*.
WAIT? YOU KNOW WHO I AM?
YOU KNOW WHY I'M HERE?
IF YOU MEAN IN THE EXISTENTIAL SENSE? THEN I HAVE NO IDEA. READ A BOOK OR SOMETHIN'.
COME IN, SWEETCHEEKS.

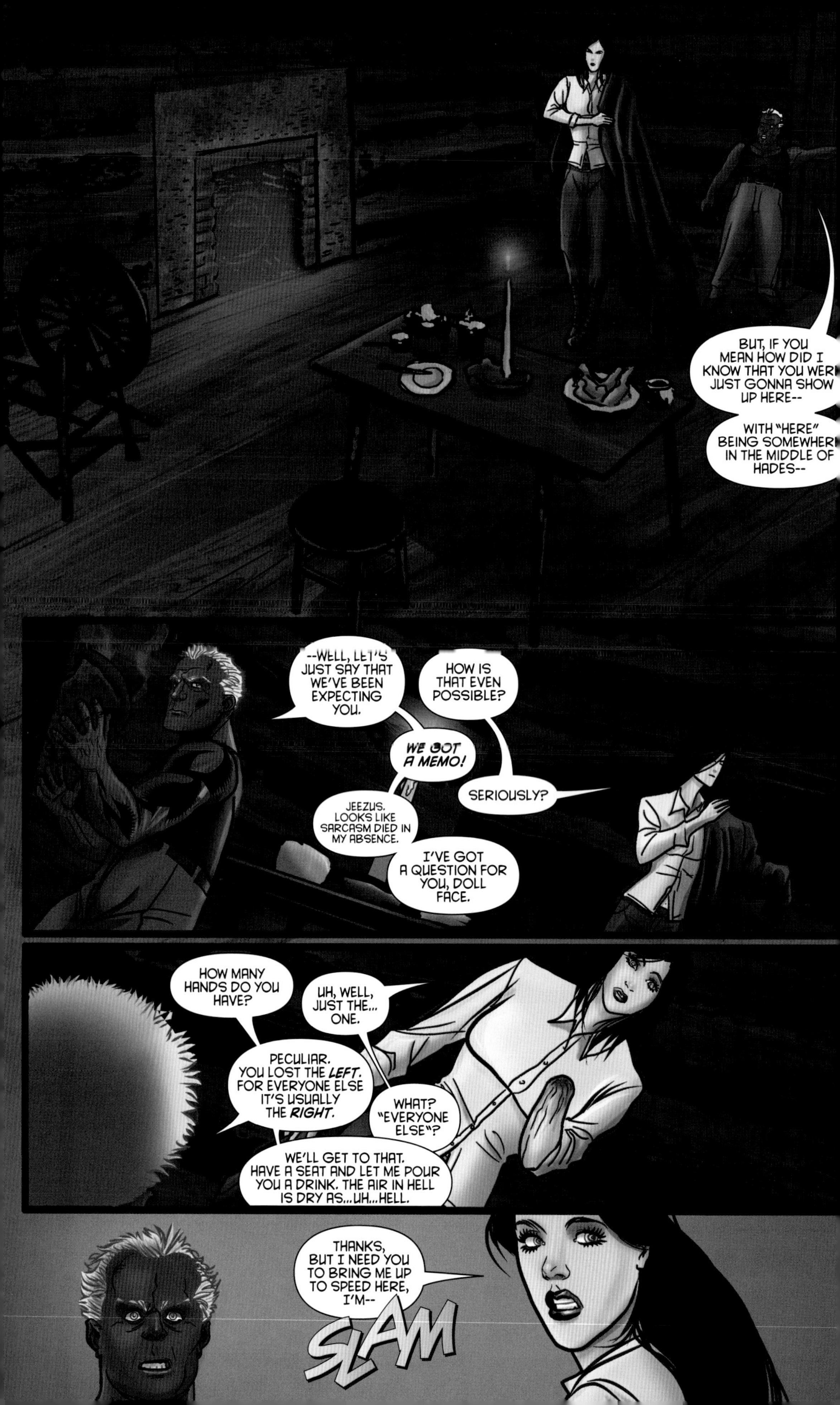
BUT, IF YOU MEAN HOW DID I KNOW THAT YOU WER JUST GONNA SHOW UP HERE--
WITH "HERE" BEING SOMEWHER IN THE MIDDLE OF HADES--
--WELL, LET'S JUST SAY THAT WE'VE BEEN EXPECTING YOU.
HOW IS THAT EVEN POSSIBLE?
WE GOT A MEMO!
SERIOUSLY?
JEEZUS. LOOKS LIKE SARCASM DIED IN MY ABSENCE.
I'VE GOT A QUESTION FOR YOU, DOLL FACE.
HOW MANY HANDS DO YOU HAVE?
UH, WELL, JUST THE... ONE.
PECULIAR. YOU LOST THE LEFT. FOR EVERYONE ELSE IT'S USUALLY THE RIGHT.
WHAT? "EVERYONE ELSE"?
WE'LL GET TO THAT. HAVE A SEAT AND LET ME POUR YOU A DRINK. THE AIR IN HELL IS DRY AS...UH...HELL.
THANKS, BUT I NEED YOU TO BRING ME UP TO SPEED HERE, I'M--
SLAM

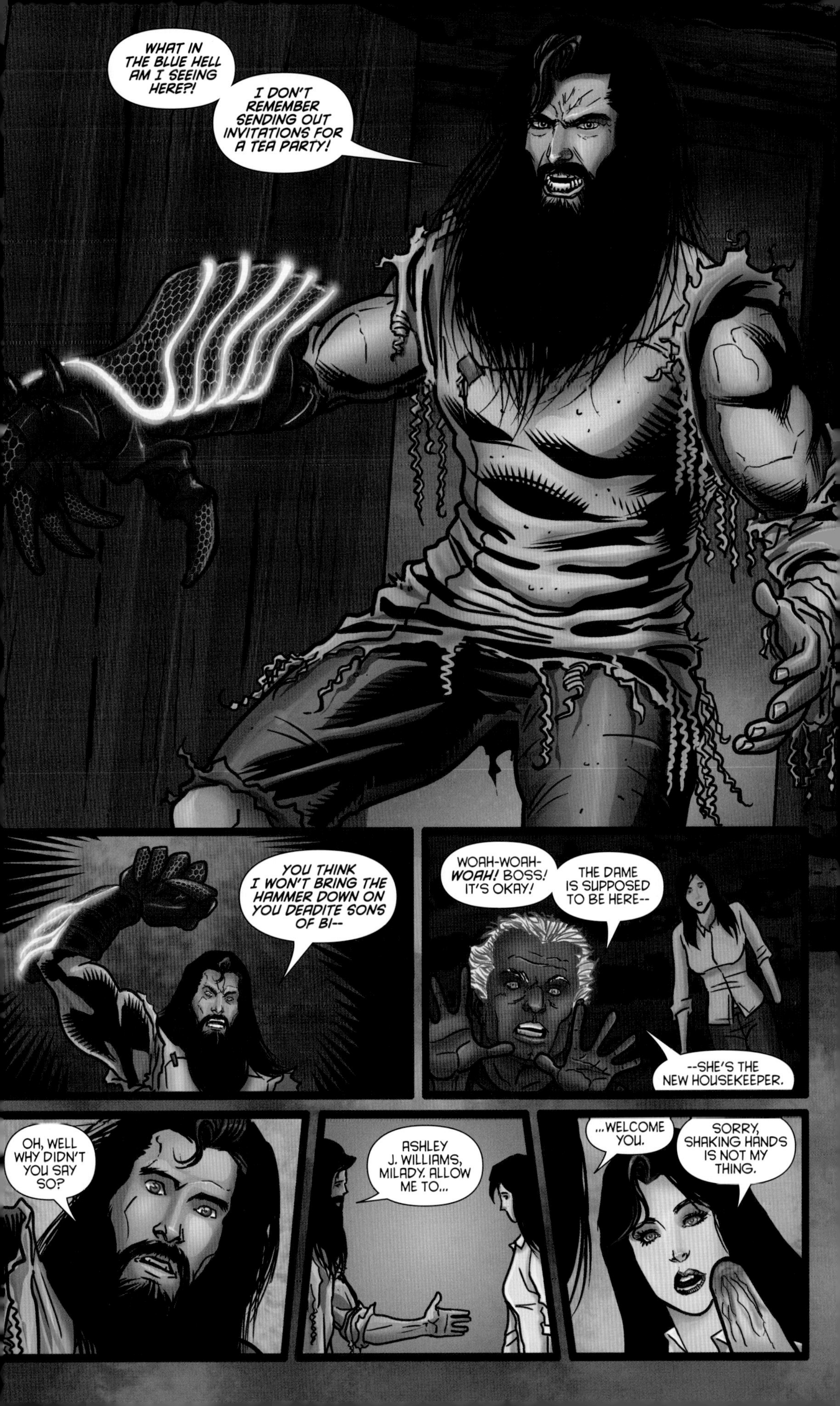
WHAT IN THE BLUE HELL AM I SEEING HERE?!
I DON'T REMEMBER SENDING OUT INVITATIONS FOR A TEA PARTY!
YOU THINK I WON'T BRING THE HAMMER DOWN ON YOU DEADITE SONS OF BI--
WOAH-WOAH-WOAH! BOSS! IT'S OKAY!
THE DAME IS SUPPOSED TO BE HERE--
--SHE'S THE NEW HOUSEKEEPER.
OH, WELL WHY DIDN'T YOU SAY SO?
ASHLEY J. WILLIAMS, MILADY. ALLOW ME TO...
...WELCOME YOU.
SORRY, SHAKING HANDS IS NOT MY THING.

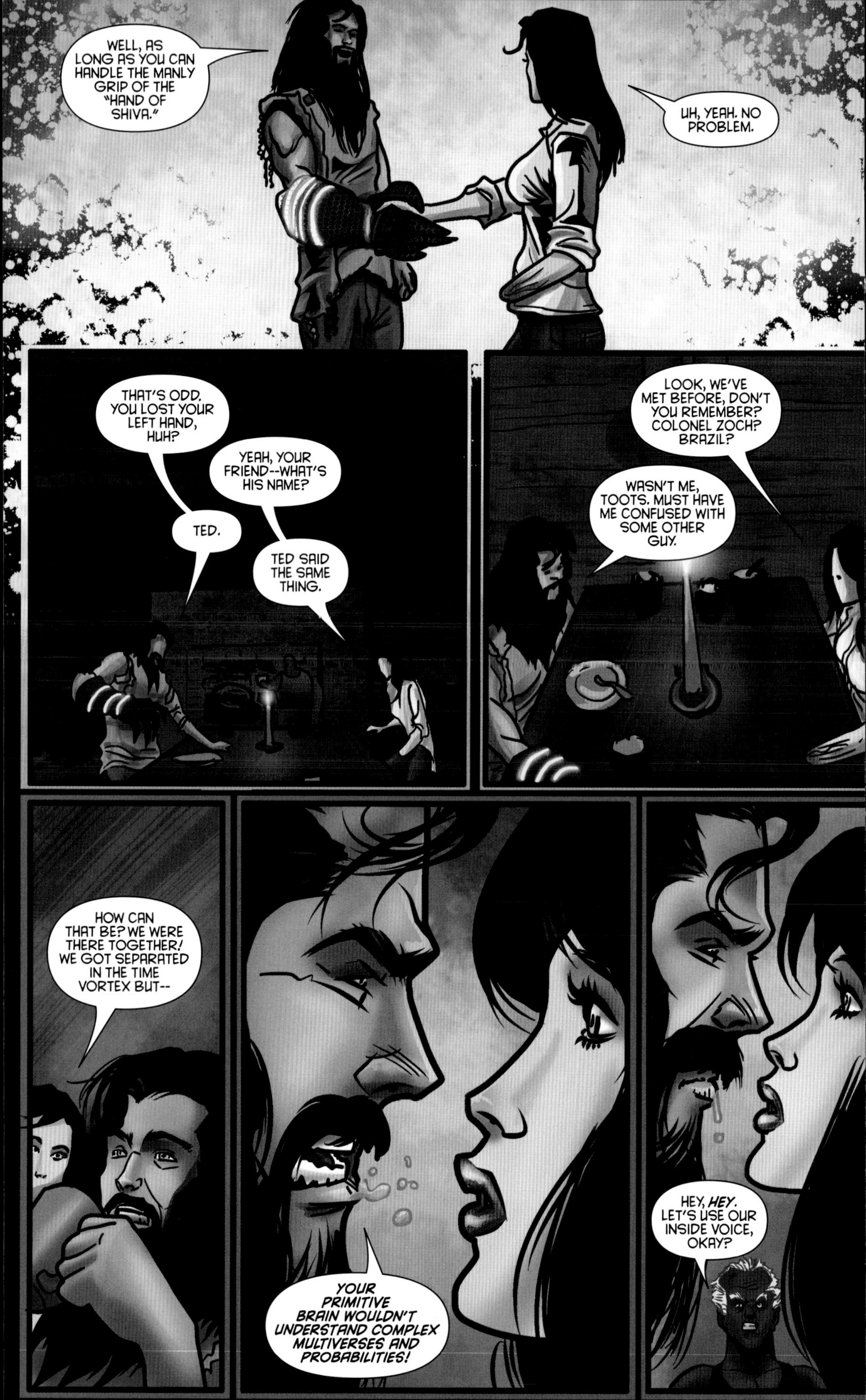

WELL, AS LONG AS YOU CAN HANDLE THE MANLY GRIP OF THE "HAND OF SHIVA."
UH, YEAH. NO PROBLEM.
THAT'S ODD. YOU LOST YOUR LEFT HAND, HUH?
YEAH, YOUR FRIEND--WHAT'S HIS NAME?
TED.
TED SAID THE SAME THING.
LOOK, WE'VE MET BEFORE, DON'T YOU REMEMBER? COLONEL ZOCH? BRAZIL?
WASN'T ME, TOOTS. MUST HAVE ME CONFUSED WITH SOME OTHER GUY.
HOW CAN THAT BE? WE WERE THERE TOGETHER! WE GOT SEPARATED IN THE TIME VORTEX BUT--
YOUR PRIMITIVE BRAIN WOULDN'T UNDERSTAND COMPLEX MULTIVERSES AND PROBABILITIES!
HEY, HEY. LET'S USE OUR INSIDE VOICE, OKAY?

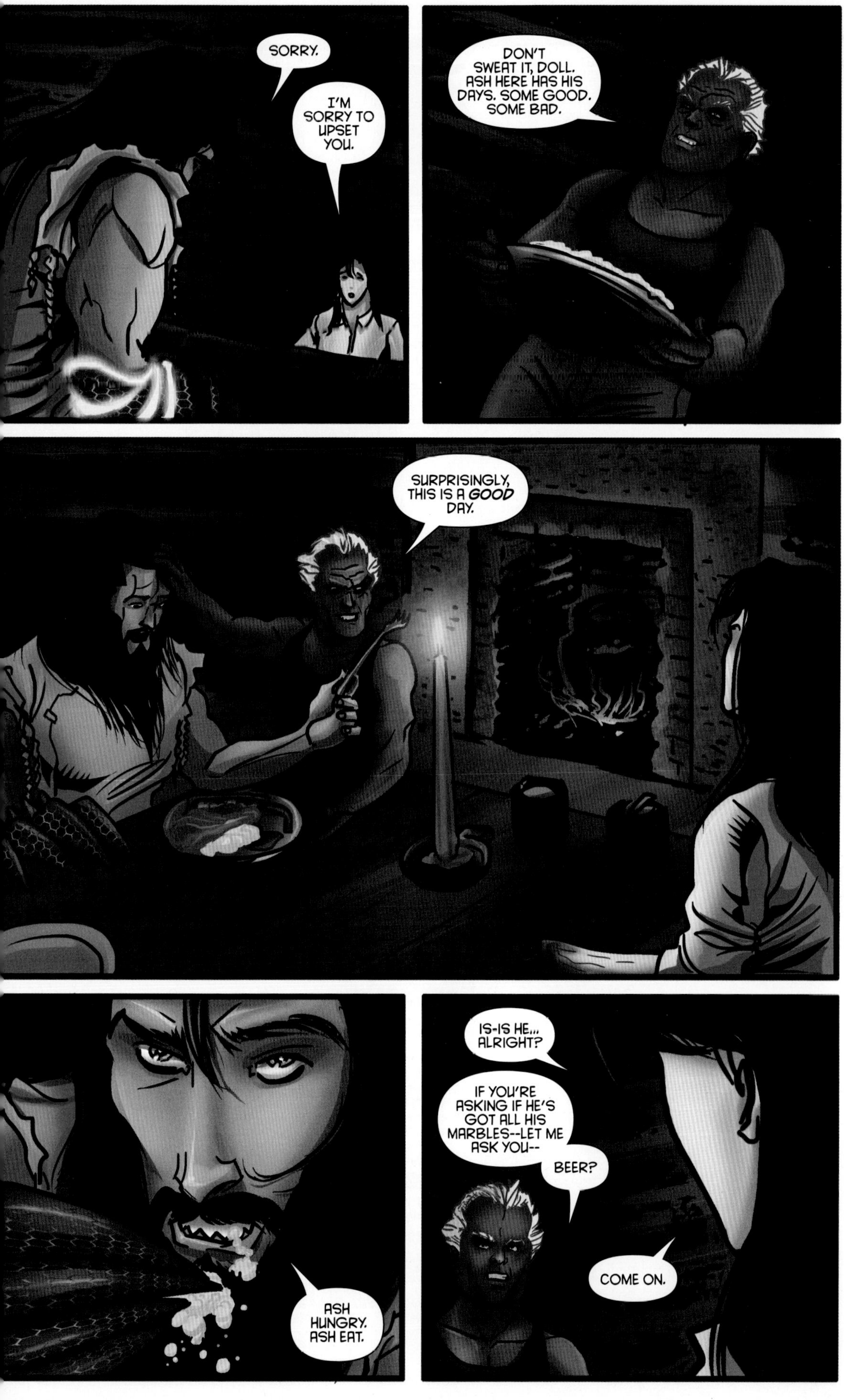
SORRY.
I'M SORRY TO UPSET YOU.
DON'T SWEAT IT, DOLL. ASH HERE HAS HIS DAYS. SOME GOOD. SOME BAD.
SURPRISINGLY, THIS IS A *GOOD* DAY.
ASH HUNGRY. ASH EAT.
IS-IS HE... ALRIGHT?
IF YOU'RE ASKING IF HE'S GOT ALL HIS MARBLES--LET ME ASK YOU--
BEER?
COME ON.

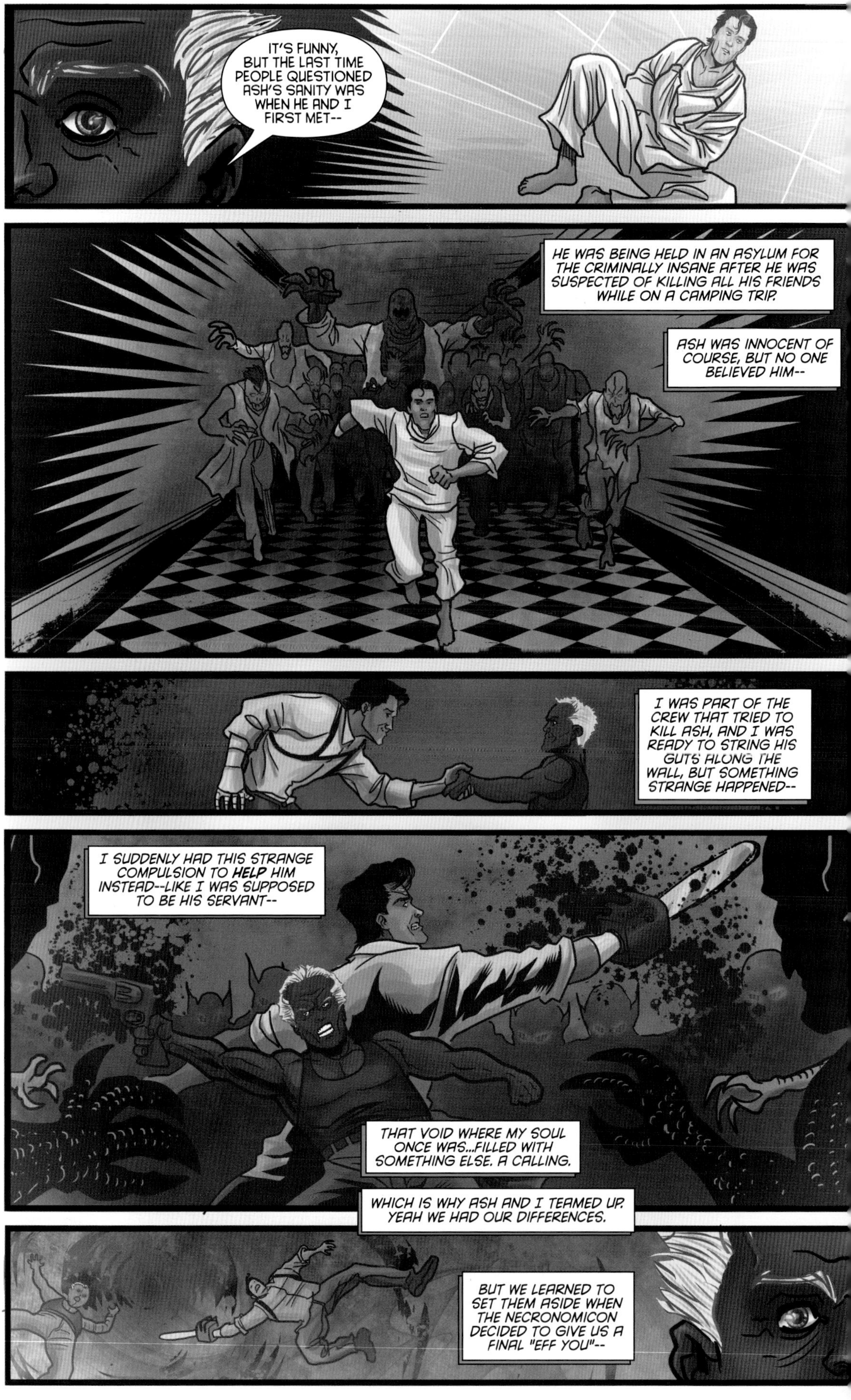
IT'S FUNNY, BUT THE LAST TIME PEOPLE QUESTIONED ASH'S SANITY WAS WHEN HE AND I FIRST MET--
HE WAS BEING HELD IN AN ASYLUM FOR THE CRIMINALLY INSANE AFTER HE WAS SUSPECTED OF KILLING ALL HIS FRIENDS WHILE ON A CAMPING TRIP.
ASH WAS INNOCENT OF COURSE, BUT NO ONE BELIEVED HIM--
I WAS PART OF THE CREW THAT TRIED TO KILL ASH, AND I WAS READY TO STRING HIS GUTS ALONG THE WALL, BUT SOMETHING STRANGE HAPPENED--
I SUDDENLY HAD THIS STRANGE COMPULSION TO HELP HIM INSTEAD--LIKE I WAS SUPPOSED TO BE HIS SERVANT--
THAT VOID WHERE MY SOUL ONCE WAS...FILLED WITH SOMETHING ELSE. A CALLING.
WHICH IS WHY ASH AND I TEAMED UP. YEAH WE HAD OUR DIFFERENCES.
BUT WE LEARNED TO SET THEM ASIDE WHEN THE NECRONOMICON DECIDED TO GIVE US A FINAL "EFF YOU"--

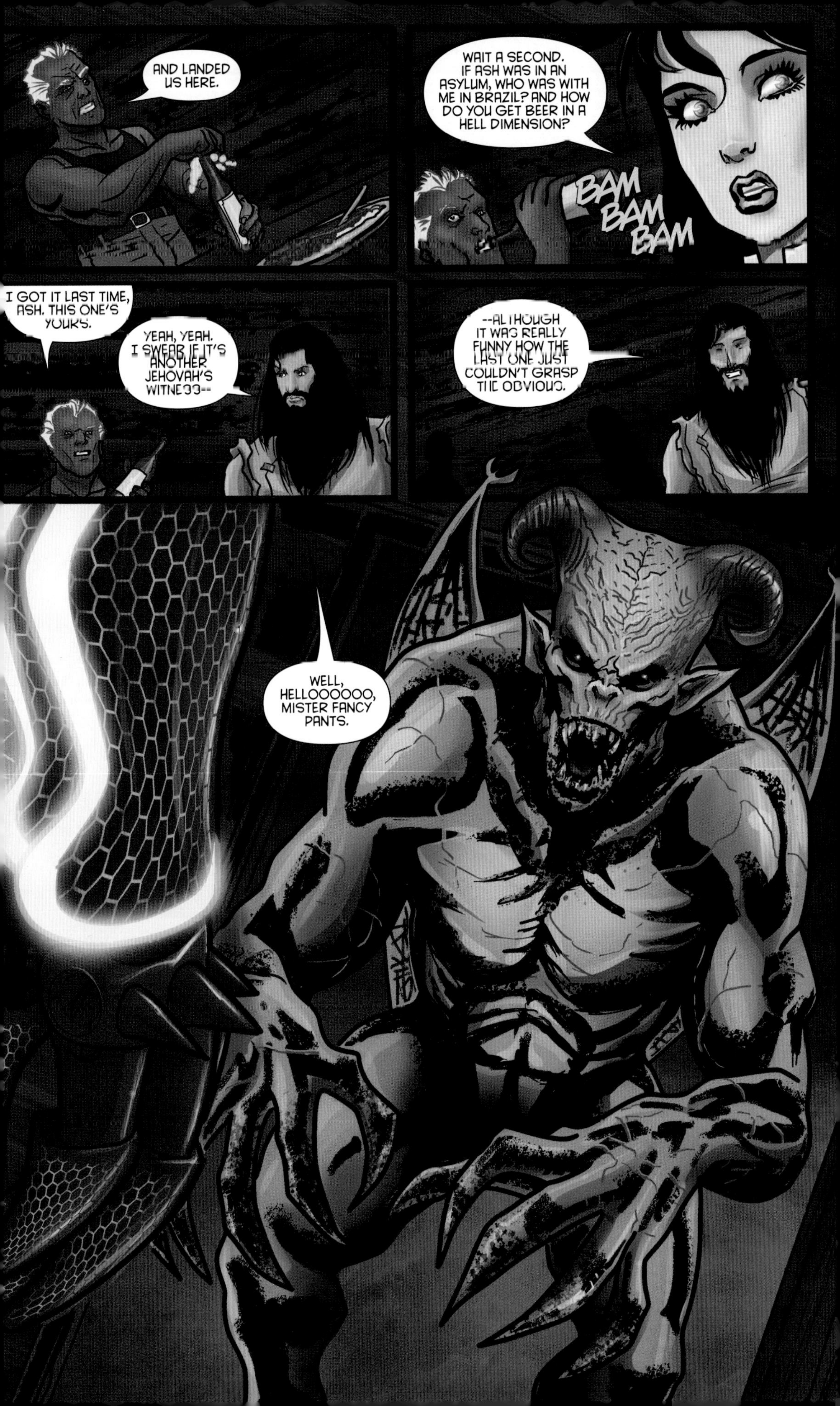
AND LANDED US HERE.
WAIT A SECOND. IF ASH WAS IN AN ASYLUM, WHO WAS WITH ME IN BRAZIL? AND HOW DO YOU GET BEER IN A HELL DIMENSION?
BAM BAM BAM
I GOT IT LAST TIME, ASH. THIS ONE'S YOURS.
YEAH, YEAH. I SWEAR IF IT'S ANOTHER JEHOVAH'S WITNESS--
--ALTHOUGH IT WAS REALLY FUNNY HOW THE LAST ONE JUST COULDN'T GRASP THE OBVIOUS.
WELL, HELLOOOOOO, MISTER FANCY PANTS.

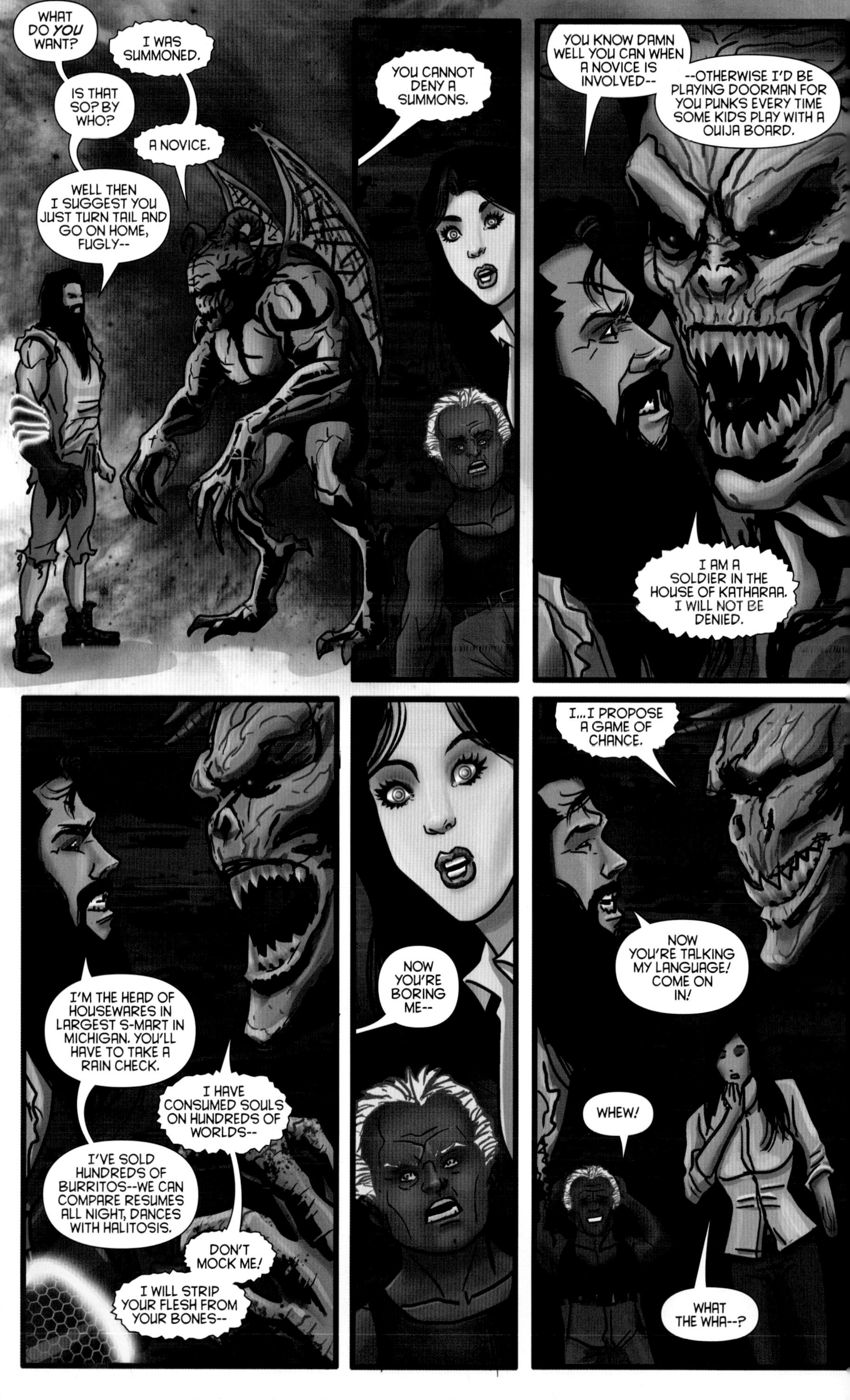
WHAT DO *YOU* WANT?
I WAS SUMMONED.
IS THAT SO? BY WHO?
A NOVICE.
WELL THEN I SUGGEST YOU JUST TURN TAIL AND GO ON HOME, FUGLY--
YOU CANNOT DENY A SUMMONS.
YOU KNOW DAMN WELL YOU CAN WHEN A NOVICE IS INVOLVED--
--OTHERWISE I'D BE PLAYING DOORMAN FOR YOU PUNKS EVERY TIME SOME KIDS PLAY WITH A OUIJA BOARD.
I AM A SOLDIER IN THE HOUSE OF KATHARAA. I WILL NOT BE DENIED.
I'M THE HEAD OF HOUSEWARES IN LARGEST S-MART IN MICHIGAN. YOU'LL HAVE TO TAKE A RAIN CHECK.
I HAVE CONSUMED SOULS ON HUNDREDS OF WORLDS--
I'VE SOLD HUNDREDS OF BURRITOS--WE CAN COMPARE RESUMES ALL NIGHT, DANCES WITH HALITOSIS.
DON'T MOCK ME!
I WILL STRIP YOUR FLESH FROM YOUR BONES--
NOW YOU'RE BORING ME--
I...I PROPOSE A GAME OF CHANCE.
NOW YOU'RE TALKING MY LANGUAGE! COME ON IN!
WHEW!
WHAT THE WHA--?

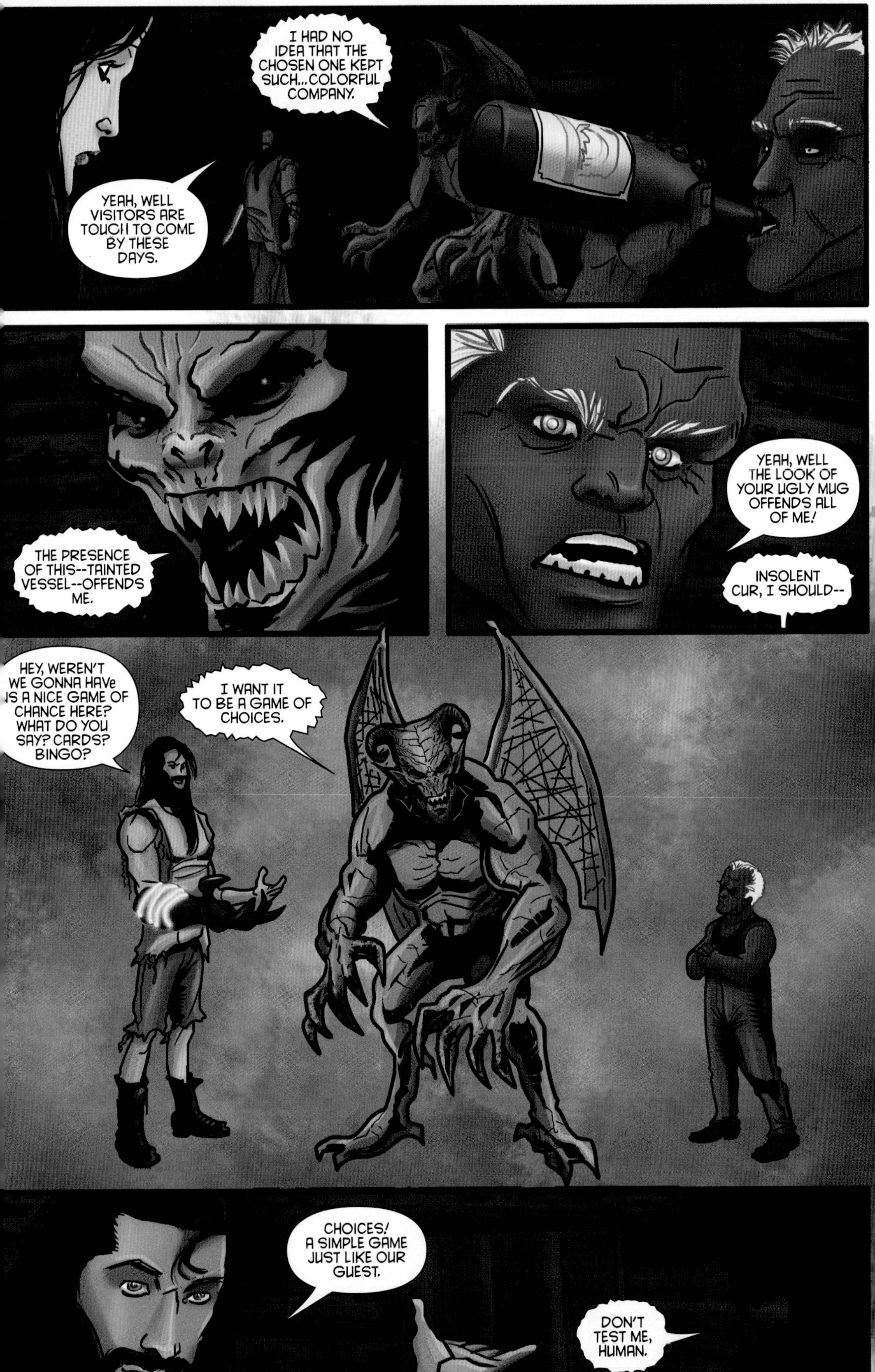
I HAD NO IDEA THAT THE CHOSEN ONE KEPT SUCH...COLORFUL COMPANY.
YEAH, WELL VISITORS ARE TOUGH TO COME BY THESE DAYS.
THE PRESENCE OF THIS--TAINTED VESSEL--OFFENDS ME.
YEAH, WELL THE LOOK OF YOUR UGLY MUG OFFENDS ALL OF ME!
INSOLENT CUR, I SHOULD--
HEY, WEREN'T WE GONNA HAVE US A NICE GAME OF CHANCE HERE? WHAT DO YOU SAY? CARDS? BINGO?
I WANT IT TO BE A GAME OF CHOICES.
CHOICES! A SIMPLE GAME JUST LIKE OUR GUEST.
DON'T TEST ME, HUMAN.

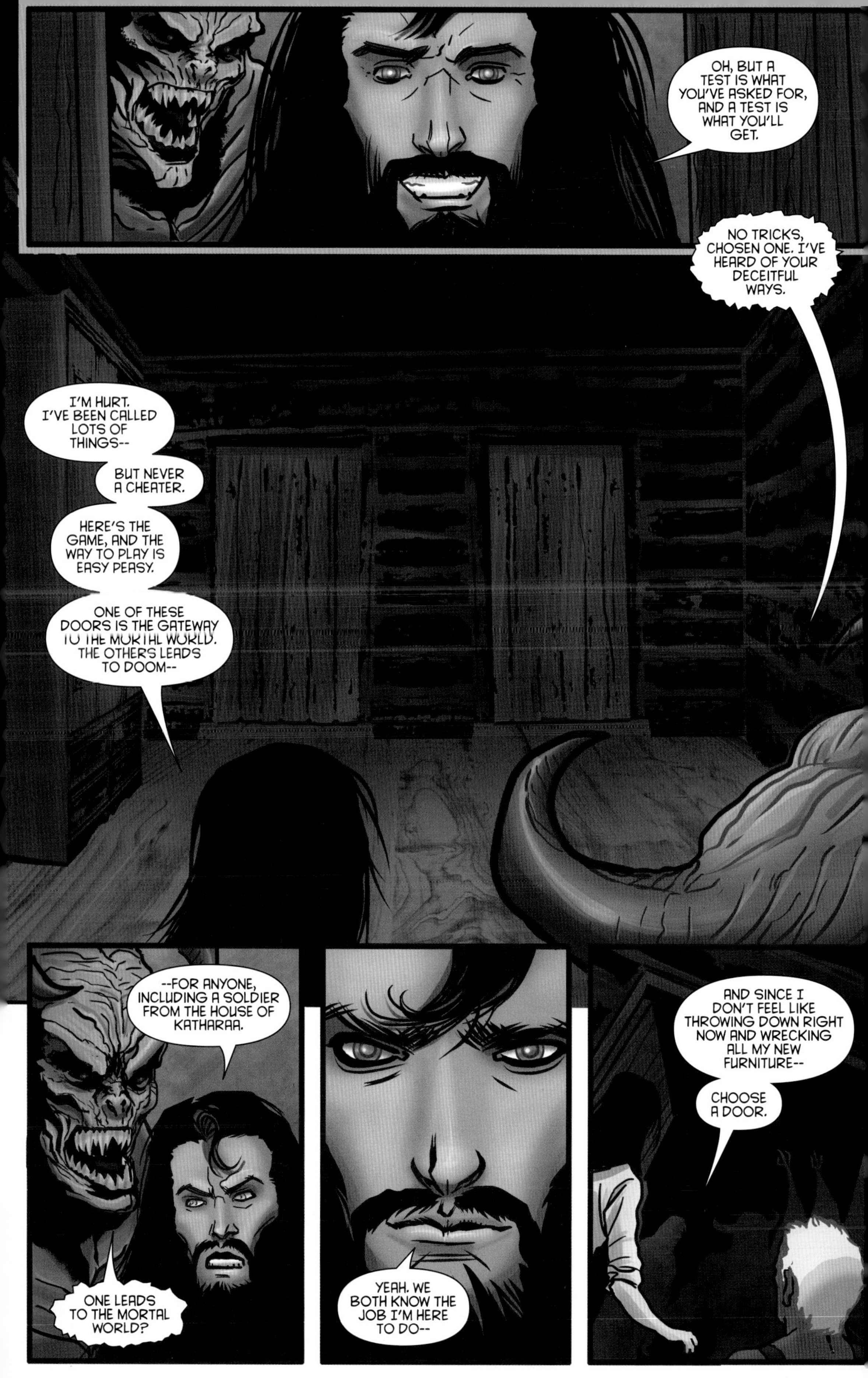
OH, BUT A TEST IS WHAT YOU'VE ASKED FOR, AND A TEST IS WHAT YOU'LL GET.
NO TRICKS, CHOSEN ONE. I'VE HEARD OF YOUR DECEITFUL WAYS.
I'M HURT. I'VE BEEN CALLED LOTS OF THINGS--
BUT NEVER A CHEATER.
HERE'S THE GAME, AND THE WAY TO PLAY IS EASY PEASY.
ONE OF THESE DOORS IS THE GATEWAY TO THE MORTAL WORLD. THE OTHER'S LEADS TO DOOM--
--FOR ANYONE, INCLUDING A SOLDIER FROM THE HOUSE OF KATHARAA.
ONE LEADS TO THE MORTAL WORLD?
YEAH. WE BOTH KNOW THE JOB I'M HERE TO DO--
AND SINCE I DON'T FEEL LIKE THROWING DOWN RIGHT NOW AND WRECKING ALL MY NEW FURNITURE--
CHOOSE A DOOR.

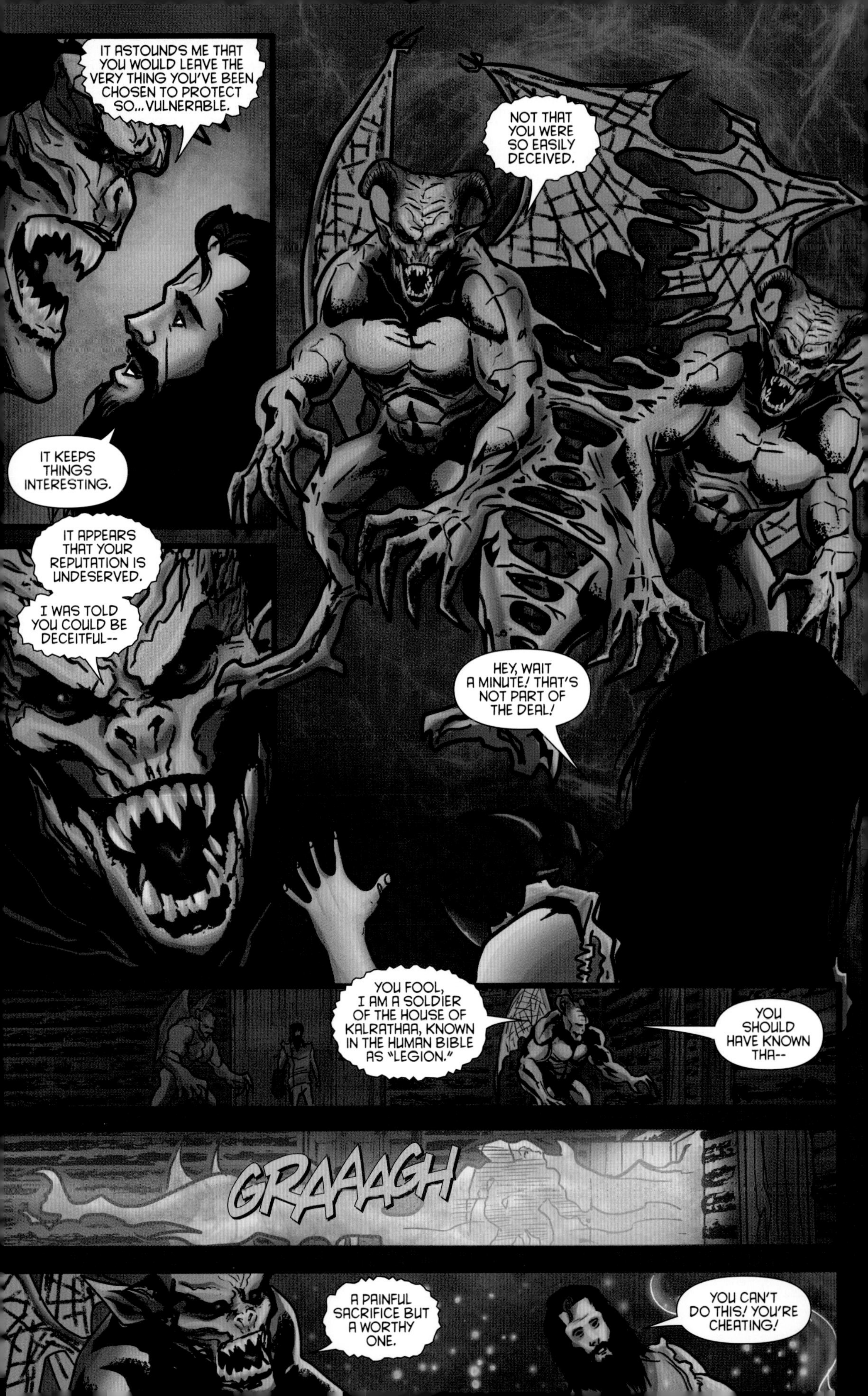
IT ASTOUNDS ME THAT YOU WOULD LEAVE THE VERY THING YOU'VE BEEN CHOSEN TO PROTECT SO...VULNERABLE.
IT KEEPS THINGS INTERESTING.
NOT THAT YOU WERE SO EASILY DECEIVED.
IT APPEARS THAT YOUR REPUTATION IS UNDESERVED.
I WAS TOLD YOU COULD BE DECEITFUL--
HEY, WAIT A MINUTE! THAT'S NOT PART OF THE DEAL!
YOU FOOL, I AM A SOLDIER OF THE HOUSE OF KALRATHAA, KNOWN IN THE HUMAN BIBLE AS "LEGION."
YOU SHOULD HAVE KNOWN THA--
GRAAAGH
A PAINFUL SACRIFICE BUT A WORTHY ONE.
YOU CAN'T DO THIS! YOU'RE CHEATING!

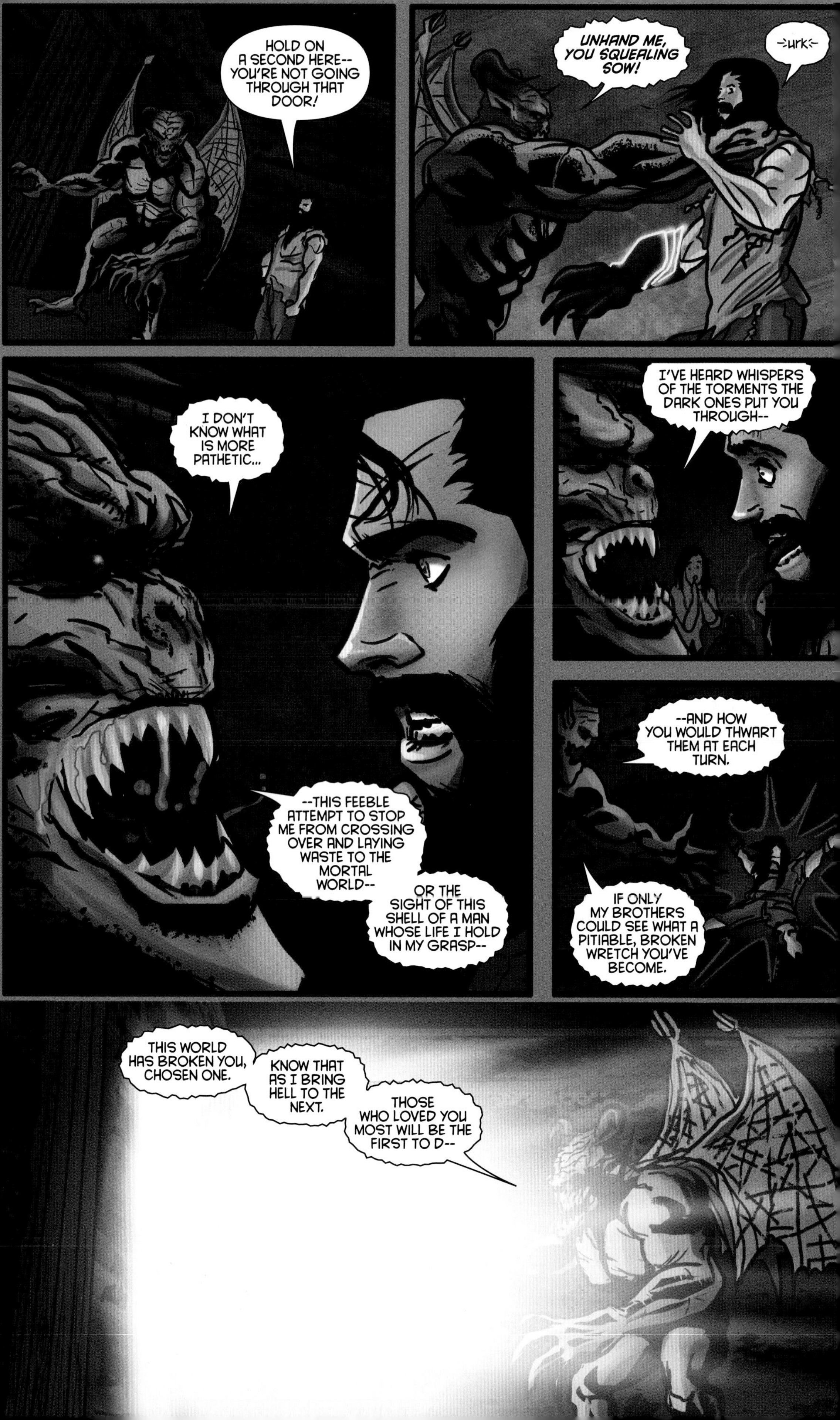
HOLD ON A SECOND HERE-- YOU'RE NOT GOING THROUGH THAT DOOR!
UNHAND ME, YOU SQUEALING SOW!
urk
I DON'T KNOW WHAT IS MORE PATHETIC...
--THIS FEEBLE ATTEMPT TO STOP ME FROM CROSSING OVER AND LAYING WASTE TO THE MORTAL WORLD--
OR THE SIGHT OF THIS SHELL OF A MAN WHOSE LIFE I HOLD IN MY GRASP--
I'VE HEARD WHISPERS OF THE TORMENTS THE DARK ONES PUT YOU THROUGH--
--AND HOW YOU WOULD THWART THEM AT EACH TURN.
IF ONLY MY BROTHERS COULD SEE WHAT A PITIABLE, BROKEN WRETCH YOU'VE BECOME.
THIS WORLD HAS BROKEN YOU, CHOSEN ONE.
KNOW THAT AS I BRING HELL TO THE NEXT.
THOSE WHO LOVED YOU MOST WILL BE THE FIRST TO D--

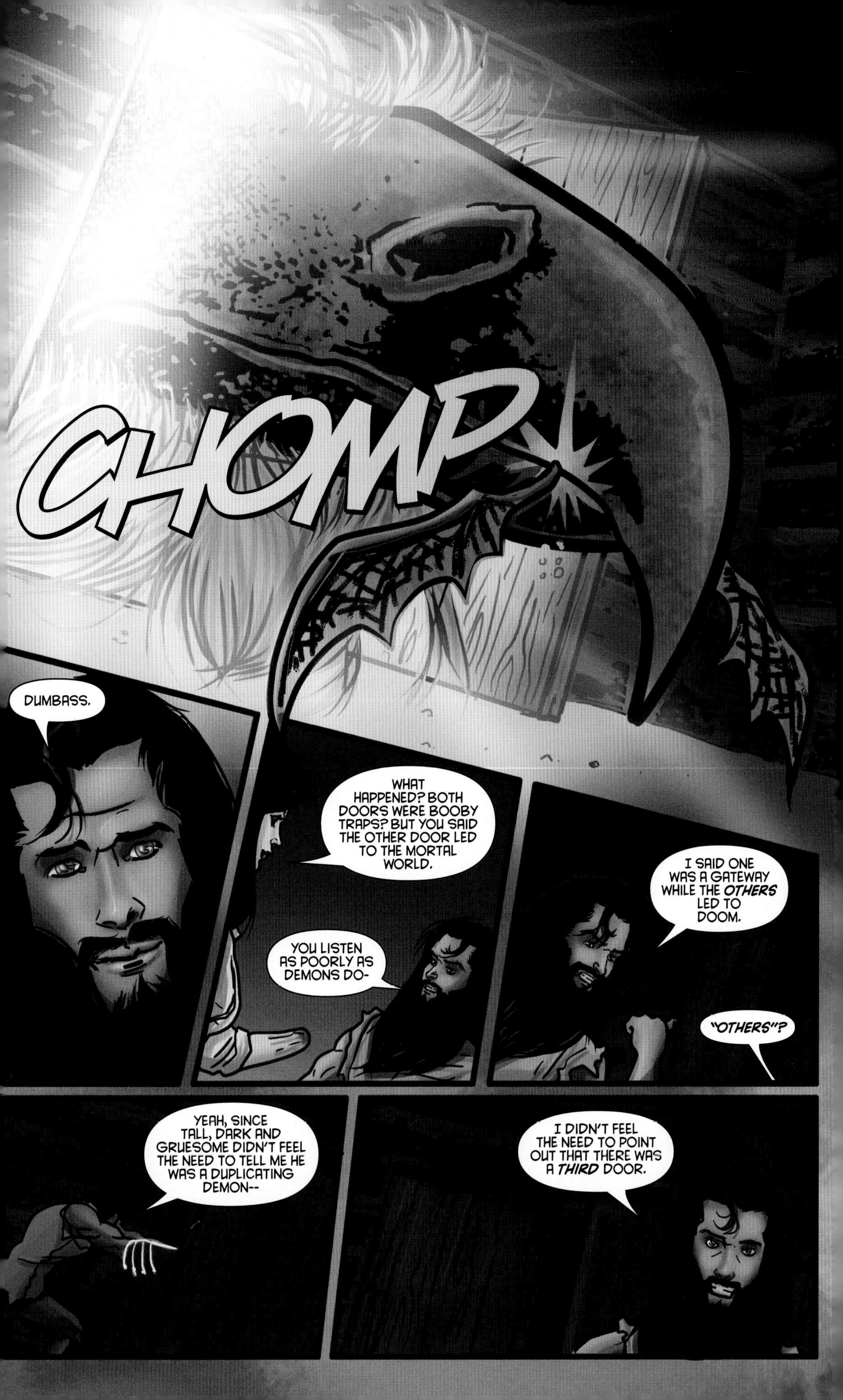
CHOMP
DUMBASS.
WHAT HAPPENED? BOTH DOORS WERE BOOBY TRAPS? BUT YOU SAID THE OTHER DOOR LED TO THE MORTAL WORLD.
YOU LISTEN AS POORLY AS DEMONS DO-
I SAID ONE WAS A GATEWAY WHILE THE *OTHERS* LED TO DOOM.
"*OTHERS*"?
YEAH, SINCE TALL, DARK AND GRUESOME DIDN'T FEEL THE NEED TO TELL ME HE WAS A DUPLICATING DEMON--
I DIDN'T FEEL THE NEED TO POINT OUT THAT THERE WAS A *THIRD* DOOR.

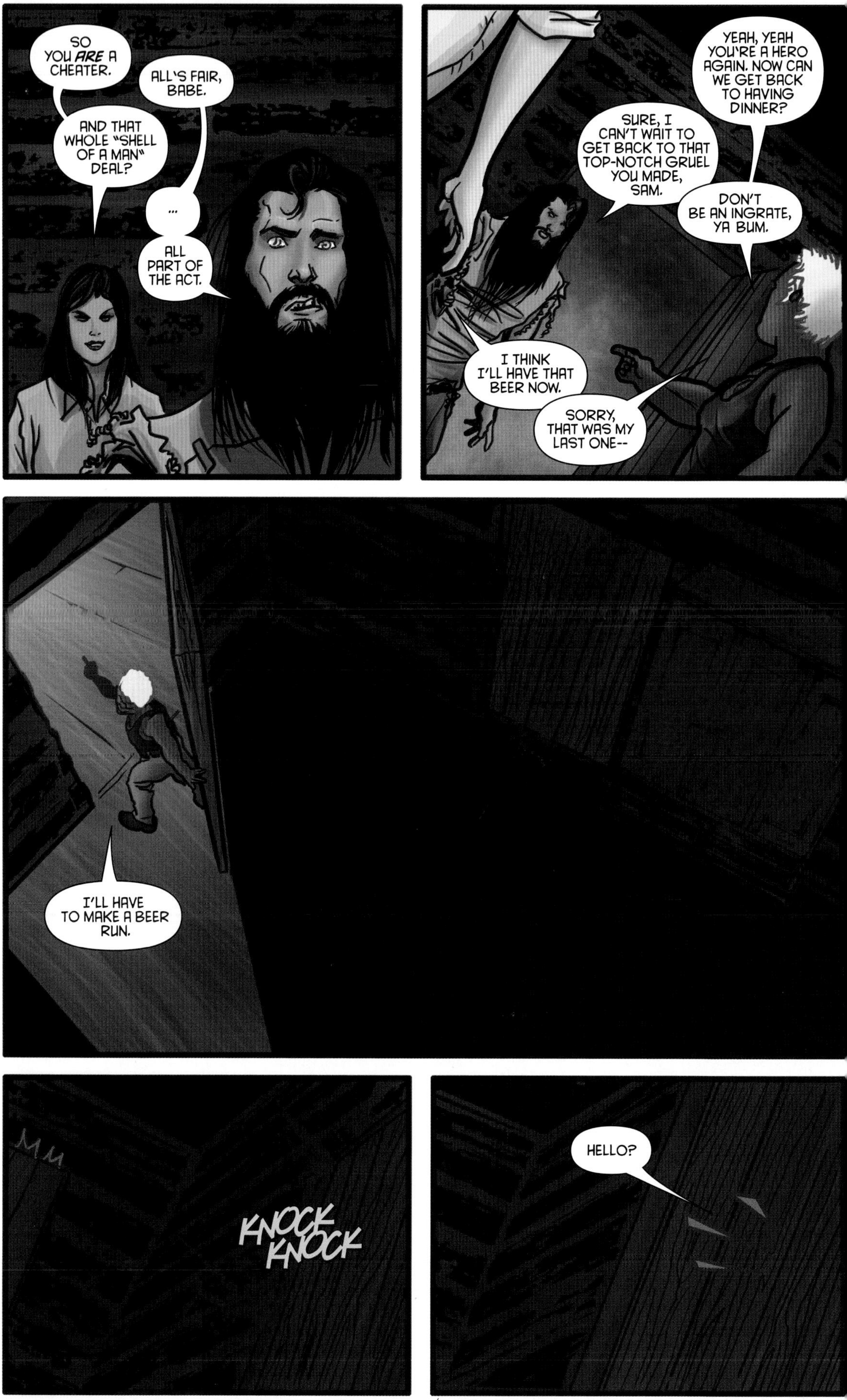
SO YOU *ARE* A CHEATER.
ALL'S FAIR, BABE.
AND THAT WHOLE "SHELL OF A MAN" DEAL?
...
ALL PART OF THE ACT.
YEAH, YEAH YOU'RE A HERO AGAIN. NOW CAN WE GET BACK TO HAVING DINNER?
SURE, I CAN'T WAIT TO GET BACK TO THAT TOP-NOTCH GRUEL YOU MADE, SAM.
DON'T BE AN INGRATE, YA BUM.
I THINK I'LL HAVE THAT BEER NOW.
SORRY, THAT WAS MY LAST ONE--
I'LL HAVE TO MAKE A BEER RUN.
KNOCK KNOCK
HELLO?

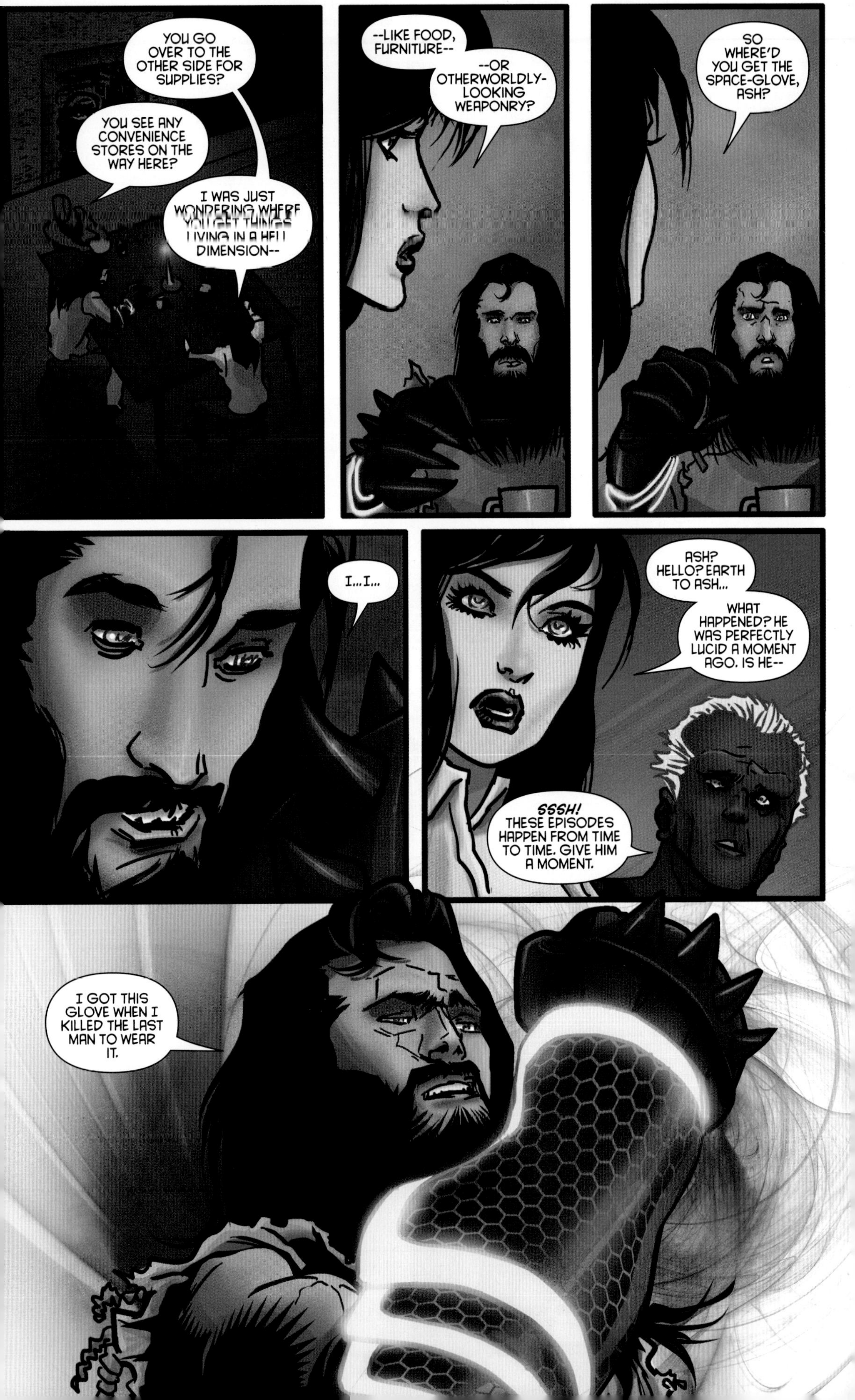
YOU GO OVER TO THE OTHER SIDE FOR SUPPLIES?
YOU SEE ANY CONVENIENCE STORES ON THE WAY HERE?
I WAS JUST WONDERING WHERE YOU GET THINGS LIVING IN A HELL DIMENSION--
--LIKE FOOD, FURNITURE--
--OR OTHERWORLDLY-LOOKING WEAPONRY?
SO WHERE'D YOU GET THE SPACE-GLOVE, ASH?
I...I...
ASH? HELLO? EARTH TO ASH...
WHAT HAPPENED? HE WAS PERFECTLY LUCID A MOMENT AGO. IS HE--
SSSH! THESE EPISODES HAPPEN FROM TIME TO TIME. GIVE HIM A MOMENT.
I GOT THIS GLOVE WHEN I KILLED THE LAST MAN TO WEAR IT.

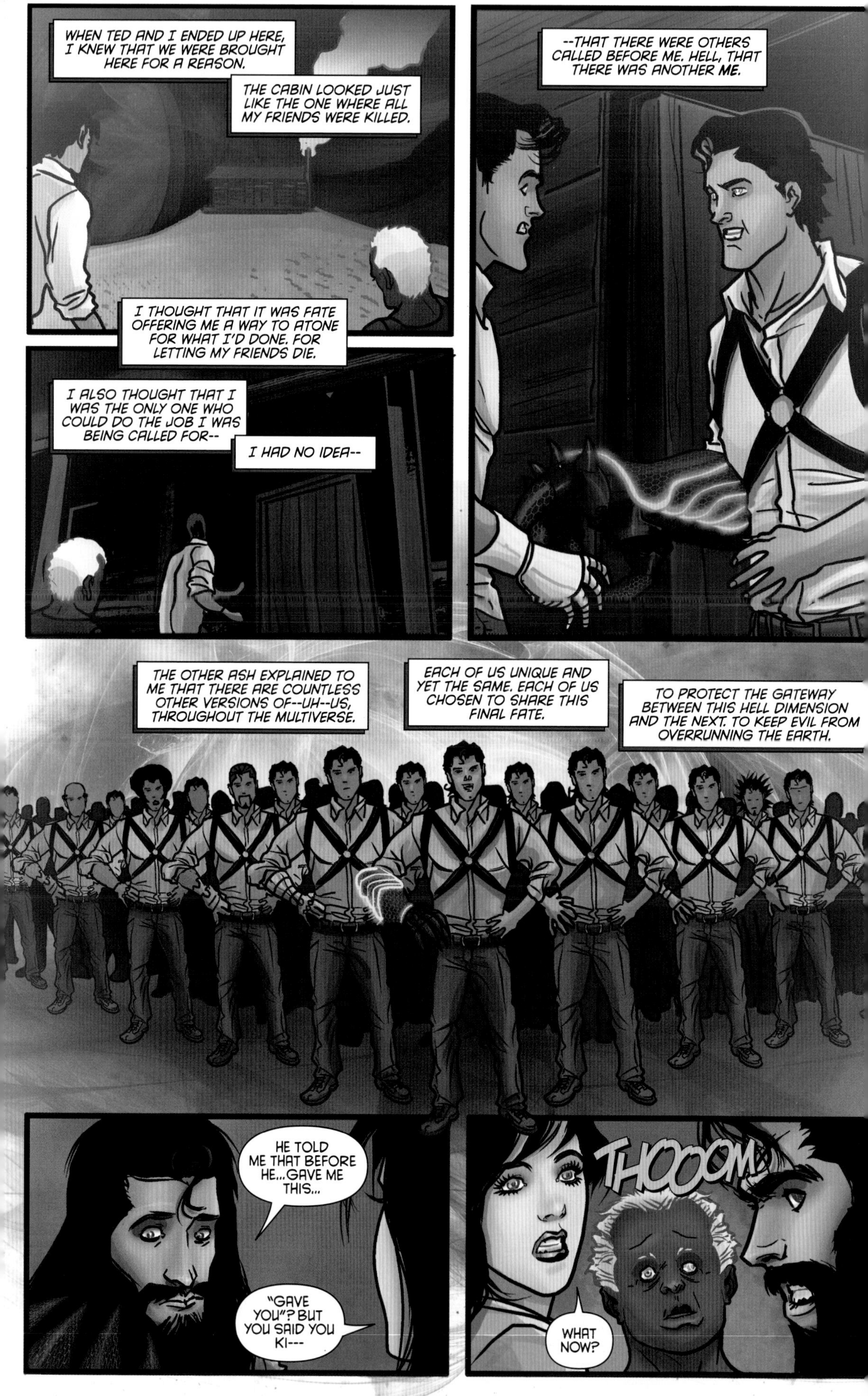
WHEN TED AND I ENDED UP HERE, I KNEW THAT WE WERE BROUGHT HERE FOR A REASON.
THE CABIN LOOKED JUST LIKE THE ONE WHERE ALL MY FRIENDS WERE KILLED.
I THOUGHT THAT IT WAS FATE OFFERING ME A WAY TO ATONE FOR WHAT I'D DONE. FOR LETTING MY FRIENDS DIE.
I ALSO THOUGHT THAT I WAS THE ONLY ONE WHO COULD DO THE JOB I WAS BEING CALLED FOR--
I HAD NO IDEA--
--THAT THERE WERE OTHERS CALLED BEFORE ME. HELL, THAT THERE WAS ANOTHER **ME**.
THE OTHER ASH EXPLAINED TO ME THAT THERE ARE COUNTLESS OTHER VERSIONS OF--UH--US, THROUGHOUT THE MULTIVERSE.
EACH OF US UNIQUE AND YET THE SAME. EACH OF US CHOSEN TO SHARE THIS FINAL FATE.
TO PROTECT THE GATEWAY BETWEEN THIS HELL DIMENSION AND THE NEXT. TO KEEP EVIL FROM OVERRUNNING THE EARTH.
HE TOLD ME THAT BEFORE HE...GAVE ME THIS...
"GAVE YOU"? BUT YOU SAID YOU KI---
THOOOM!
WHAT NOW?

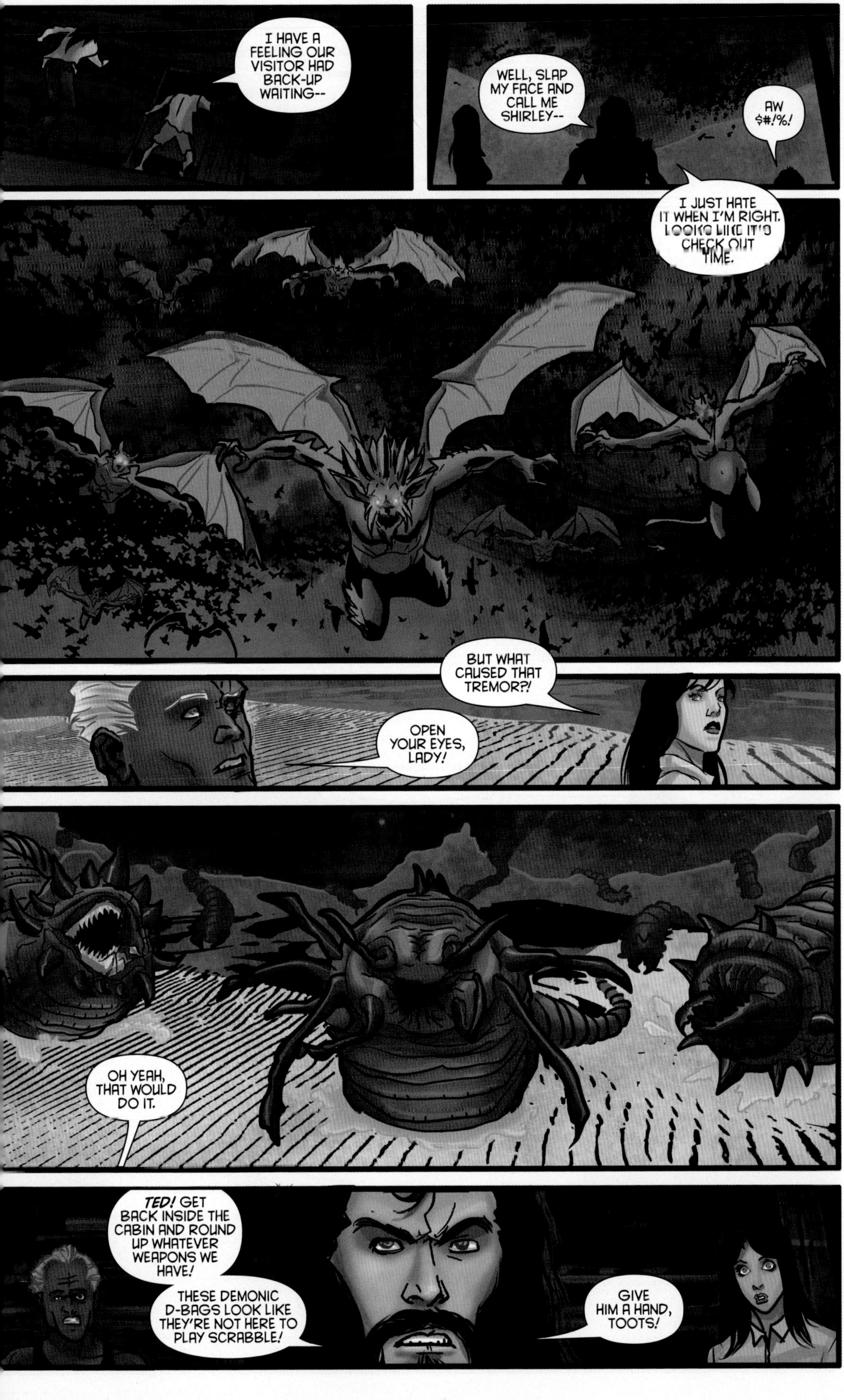
I HAVE A FEELING OUR VISITOR HAD BACK-UP WAITING--
WELL, SLAP MY FACE AND CALL ME SHIRLEY--
AW $#!%!
I JUST HATE IT WHEN I'M RIGHT. LOOKS LIKE IT'S CHECK OUT TIME.
BUT WHAT CAUSED THAT TREMOR?!
OPEN YOUR EYES, LADY!
OH YEAH, THAT WOULD DO IT.
TED! GET BACK INSIDE THE CABIN AND ROUND UP WHATEVER WEAPONS WE HAVE!
THESE DEMONIC D-BAGS LOOK LIKE THEY'RE NOT HERE TO PLAY SCRABBLE!
GIVE HIM A HAND, TOOTS!

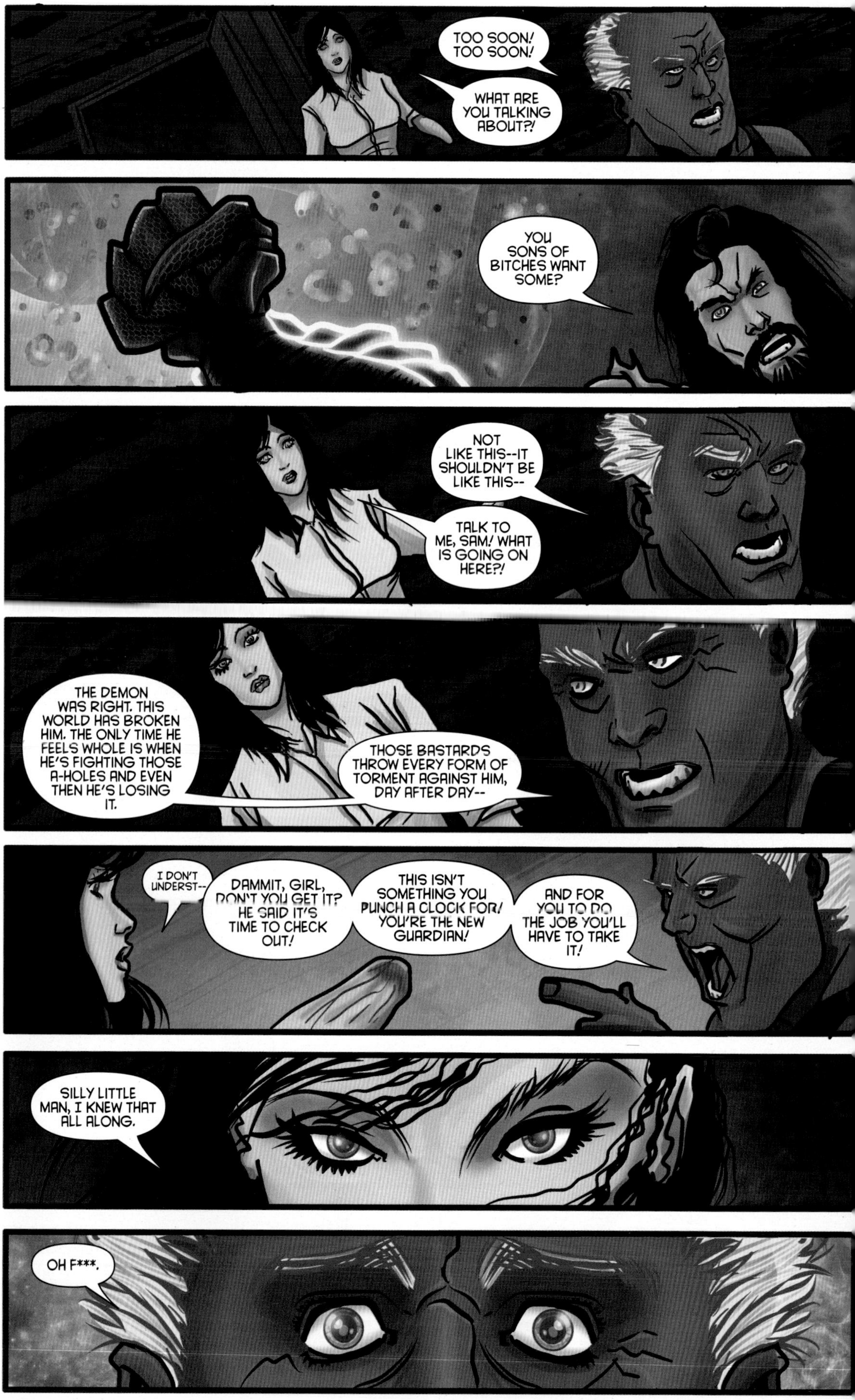
TOO SOON! TOO SOON!
WHAT ARE YOU TALKING ABOUT?!
YOU SONS OF BITCHES WANT SOME?
NOT LIKE THIS--IT SHOULDN'T BE LIKE THIS--
TALK TO ME, SAM! WHAT IS GOING ON HERE?!
THE DEMON WAS RIGHT. THIS WORLD HAS BROKEN HIM. THE ONLY TIME HE FEELS WHOLE IS WHEN HE'S FIGHTING THOSE A-HOLES AND EVEN THEN HE'S LOSING IT.
THOSE BASTARDS THROW EVERY FORM OF TORMENT AGAINST HIM, DAY AFTER DAY--
I DON'T UNDERST--
DAMMIT, GIRL, DON'T YOU GET IT? HE SAID IT'S TIME TO CHECK OUT!
THIS ISN'T SOMETHING YOU PUNCH A CLOCK FOR! YOU'RE THE NEW GUARDIAN!
AND FOR YOU TO DO THE JOB YOU'LL HAVE TO TAKE IT!
SILLY LITTLE MAN, I KNEW THAT ALL ALONG.
OH F***.

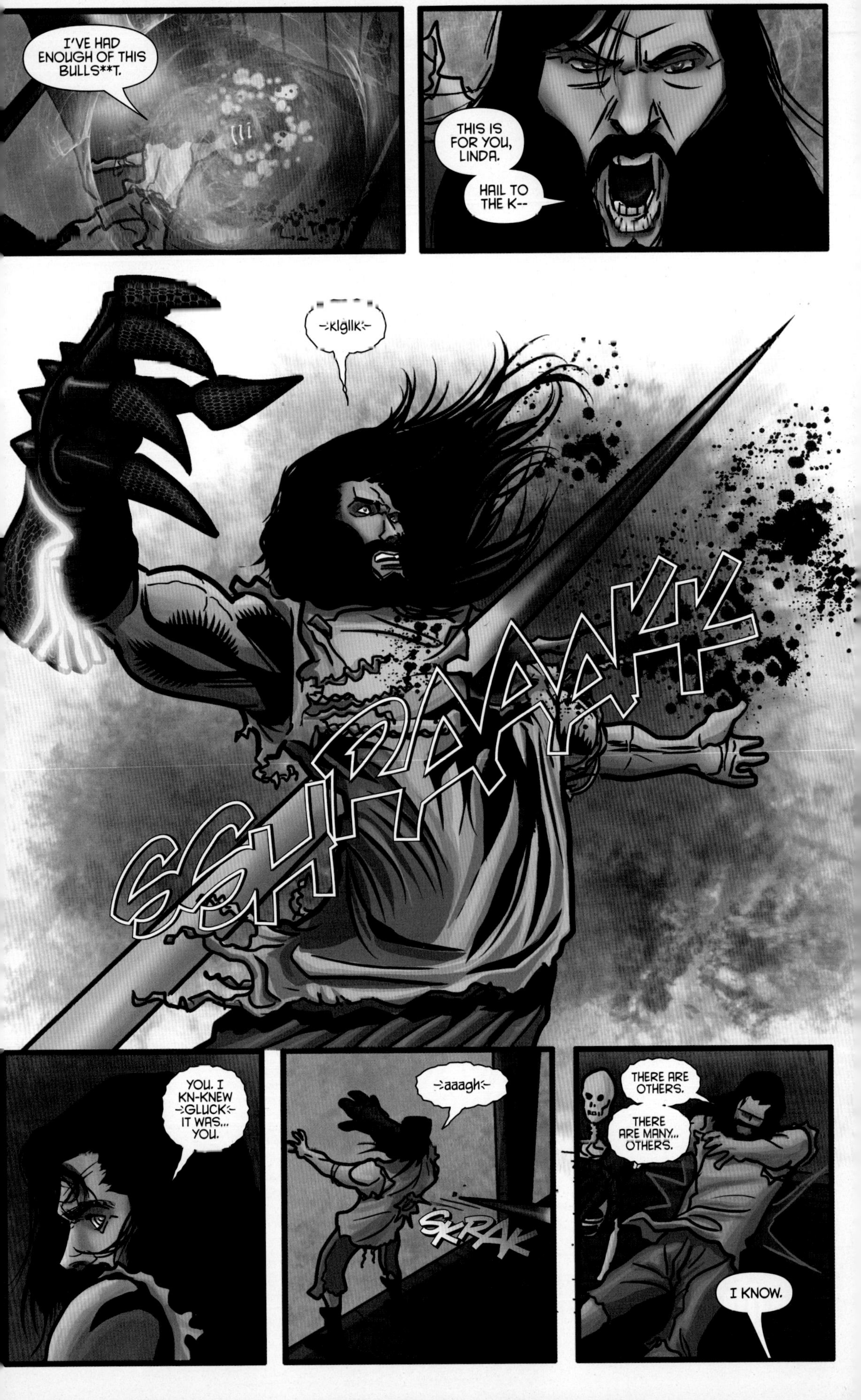
I'VE HAD ENOUGH OF THIS BULLS**T.
THIS IS FOR YOU, LINDA.
HAIL TO THE K--
-klglk-
SCHRAAAK
YOU. I KN-KNEW -GLUCK- IT WAS... YOU.
-aaagh-
SKRAK
THERE ARE OTHERS.
THERE ARE MANY... OTHERS.
I KNOW.

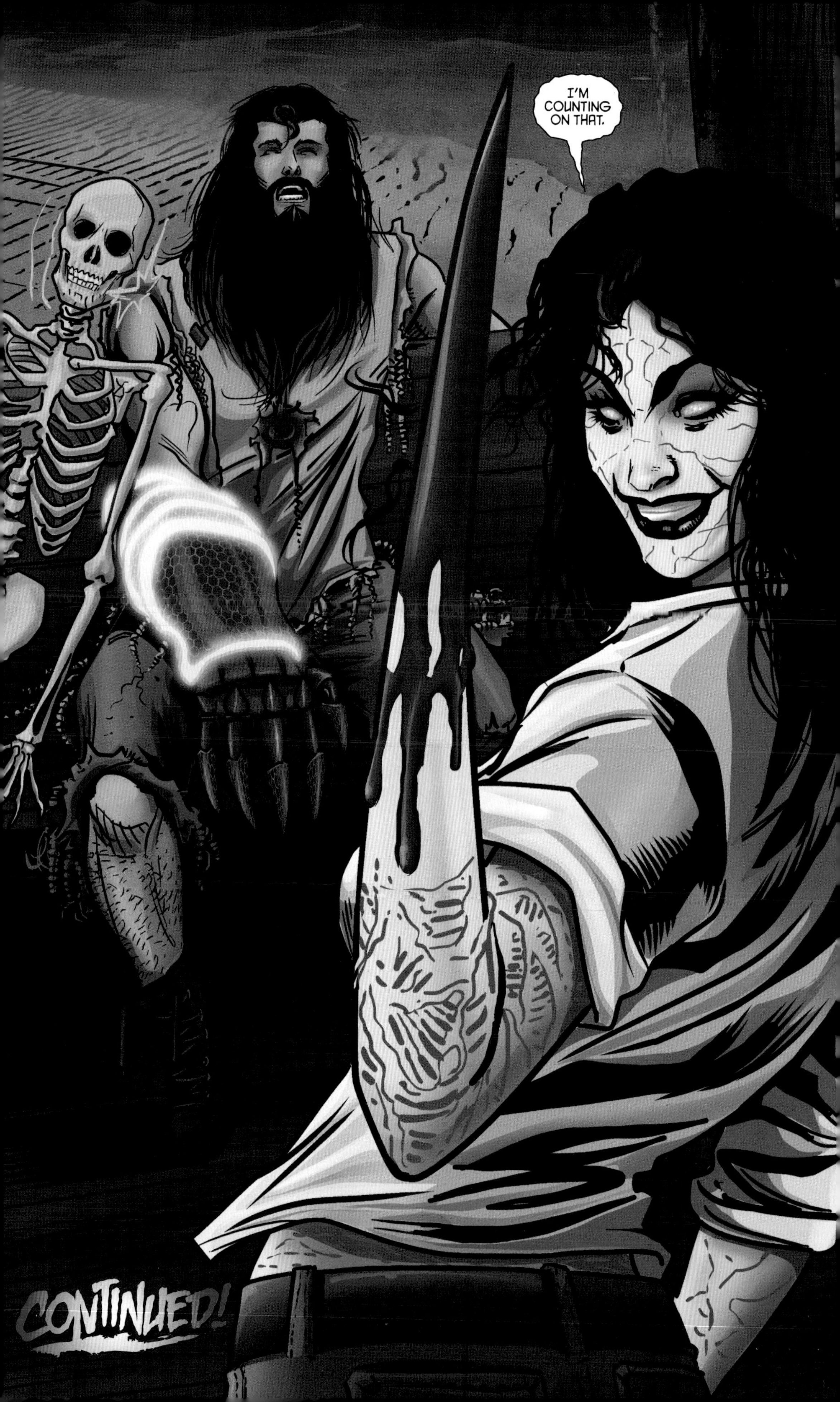
I'M COUNTING ON THAT.
CONTINUED!

WRITER'S COMMENTARY BY ELLIOTT R. SERRANO

Hey, everyone! I'm Elliott Serrano, the writer of the new Army of Darkness series for Dynamite Entertainment. After taking on the book, I asked my bosses at Dynamite if I could write a "commentary track" for each issue so that I could give you a "behind-the-scenes" look at what my process was as I was writing it. So grab your copy of Army of Darkness #1, screw-heads, and let's jump in!

ARMY OF DARKNESS #1
PAGE #1:
When I considered how I wanted to start off the new series, I always had a variation of the opening from the original AoD movie in mind. To me, this would be the best way to "reboot" the story, by starting in a familiar setting. In my script notes, I asked the artist – In this case Marat Mychaels – to emulate the ground level POV shots that were used in the film.

Of course, as the story unfolds, we notice that there are some subtle differences from how the original AoD opened. It's obvious that we're not looking at "our" Ash by the time we get to Panel 4, since he doesn't have boobs. Duh. You'll also notice that our main character here is wearing a uniform shirt that reads "Smart-Stop" and NOT "S-Mart." This little detail is dropped to hint at how unique this person really is in the overall narrative.

Another thing that happened during the scripting process was that I had written a bit more "arguing" between the narrators in the beginning. My editor Joe Rybandt commented that it was difficult to determine who was saying what at the outset and asked that I clean it up a bit.

To tell the truth, I was getting a bit too clever for myself and was putting the "joke" ahead of telling the story, a rookie mistake on my part.

I will say that the colorist did a nice job of lending the dialogue some clarity by assigning different colors to the caption boxes.

PAGE #2
Here's the BIG REVEAL where we unveil our "Lady Ash" (which is what we all called her during the scripting process). Initially, the idea was to try and keep her gender a secret, but in today's instant information age that was pretty much impossible. I'd like to go on record as saying that the idea of having a female protagonist in the AoD series was something we discussed long before talk about Ash being "recast" as a woman in the new Evil Dead movies started circulating. In fact, I'm pretty sure that our creation of "Lady Ash" gave birth to those rumors. If you've been following the news on the Evil Dead "re-imagining," you'd know that they've scrapped the character of Ash altogether. As a fan of the series, I'm not sure how I feel about that.

PAGE #3
Here's where we get into the obligatory "recap" of how "Lady Ash" got into her current predicament. I used the template established by the Bruce Campbell "Ash" in the AoD film, having Ashley summarize her origin as if this were a sequel to a movie from an alternate dimension. The details are changed, with Ashley working at a local convenience store called the "Smart-Stop" and having a tragic encounter with "other worldly evil" and losing a significant other in Brad – just like our Ash lost his girlfriend Linda in "Evil Dead 2."

Another important detail to note is how we've dispensed with the "cabin in the woods" setup and switched it out for a "it came from outer space" scenario. That will play into what's to come later in the story…

PAGE #4
Here's where we learn how the "infection of evil" gets into Ashley. Unlike the one that came from the Necronomicon in the main AoD universe, this one is passed via touch. This is another important detail that will figure into the overall story arc of the new series.

I have a question for you as a reader: Do you think that Ashley was being kind of harsh on losing her boyfriend? When I read that scene, I'm of two minds about it, but that's the way she sounds in my head when I write her. Her aloofness about relationships is something I wanted to get across here. It's not that she doesn't care; it's just the way she deals with loss.

And yeah, we have a bit of a mix-up here with which hand of hers is really 'infected' but we clear it up on the next page…

PAGE #5
Here we have another big reveal, which is when we see what actually happened to Ashley's hand after touching Brad. Gross huh? I love the little bumps that Marat put on her stump. Really gets the idea of an "infection" across.

Also note that up to this point, she doesn't understand what language her captors are speaking. She's in freakin' ANCIENT EGYPT! WHO SPEAKS ENGLISH THERE? I was thinking about adding one of those captions that read "translated from Ancient Egyptian" to the page, but I think most readers are smart enough to know they didn't speak English there and then.

That leads me to dropping another clue as to what effect the powers of the Necronomicon have had on her…

PAGE #6
So at this point you may have been scratching your head and going "WTF?" If so, that means I didn't do a very good job at showing that by saying the words "klaatu barada nikto" Ashley can not only "heal" her hand but also understand other languages.

Keeping up with me so far here?

We then have Ashley encountering one of history's most famous women…

I love the new outfit that Marat created for her, quite sexy…

PAGE #7
Back to recap mode where Ashley explains what happened to her after touching "Deadite Brad." Because she didn't have a chainsaw handy to lop her hand off at the wrist, she had to resort to pure willpower to contain the "infection" to her hand. By virtue of this significant feat, she's able to channel the dark power of the Necronomicon and use it as much as it would use her.

This is another trait that makes our "Lady Ash" unique.

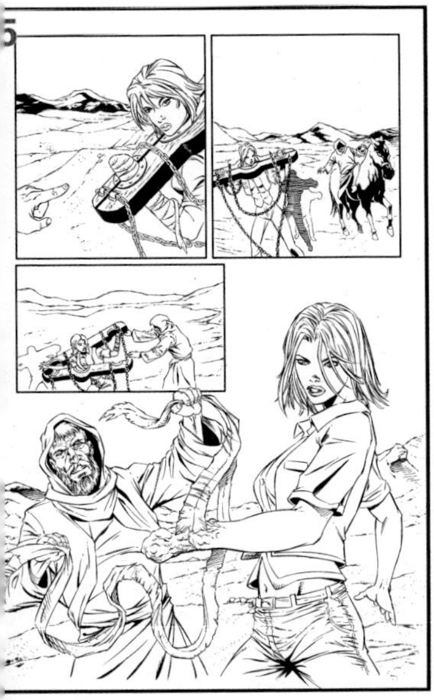
5
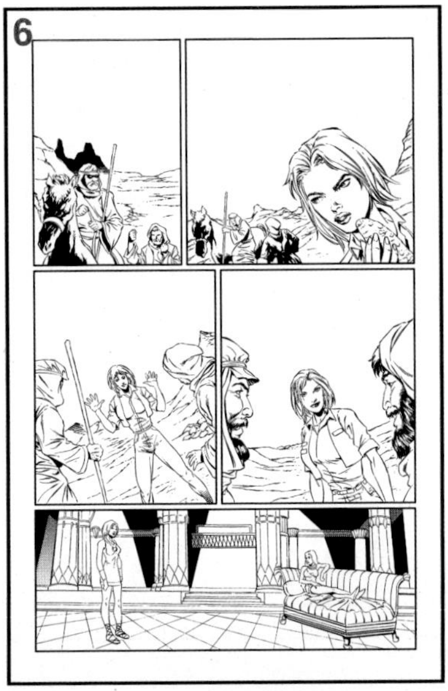
6
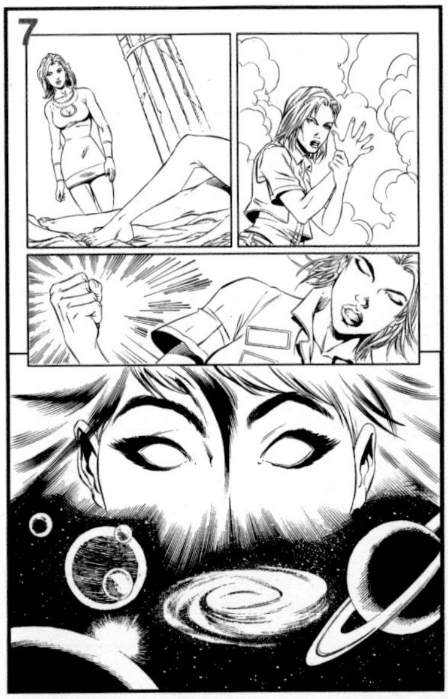
7
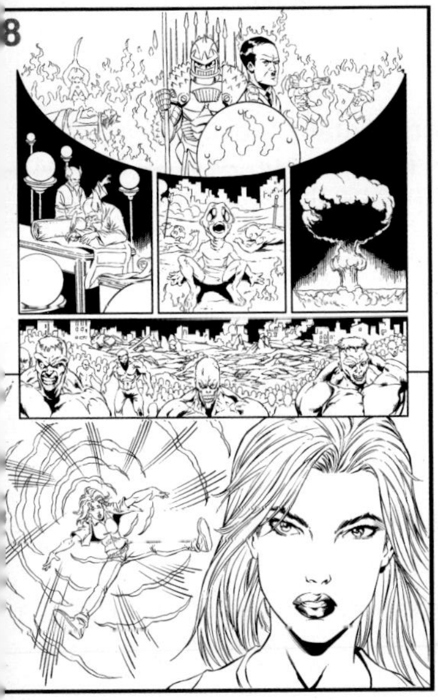
8
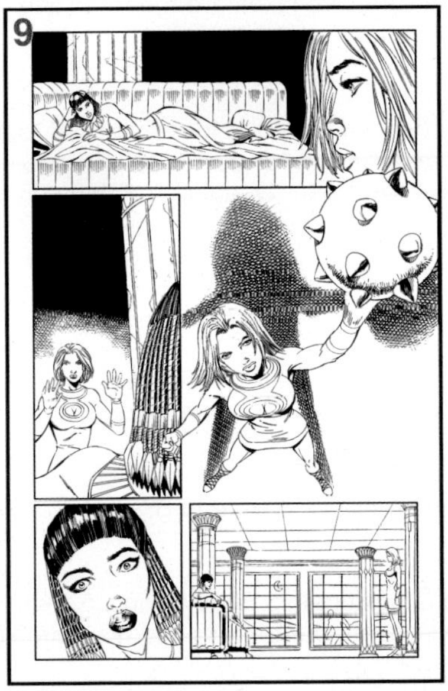
9
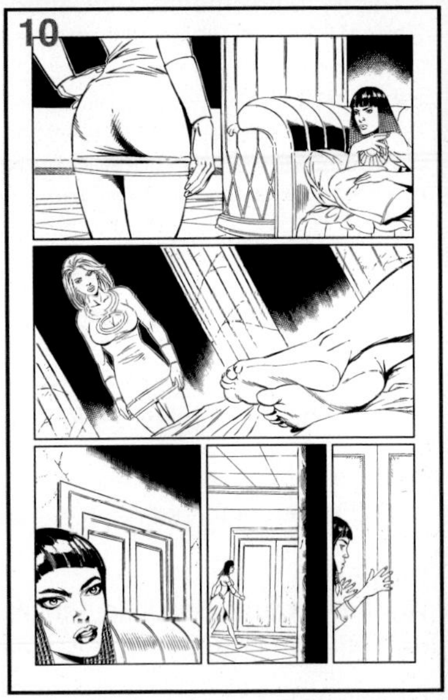
10

PAGE #8
Here's where we get a glimpse of how the evil of the Necronomicon has spread in Ashley's universe. It's no coincidence that in Panel #2 you see those druid-type guys writing on a scroll. The globe is but one of several ways that the evil can be spread.

PAGE #9
Another big reveal! Not only can Ashley make her deformed hand appear like a "normal" hand, but it can also become any sort of weapon she can imagine. I have to give credit for this idea to my former CCW*TV co-host Jose Melendez who was my sounding board for many of my ideas when I first started writing the series.

The ability is really more "Plastic Man" than "Witchblade" but I don't wanna give away too much right now. The how's and why's of her powers will be explored later down the line in the series.

PAGE #10
Now before history buffs start getting on me about what really happened to Antony and Cleopatra, I'll just say that 1) I read several different accounts of how/when they each died and this is a riff on one of those accounts and 2) dramatic license allows me to fudge the facts as well as set up the joke at the end of the page…

I've already had one comic book reviewer tell me they thought the joke was funny, so there was the validation I so desperately sought. (Writers are soooo insecure, ya know?)

 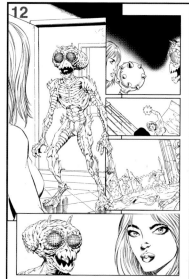 

PAGE #11
I'm sorry, but some classic Saturday Night Live jokes are meant to live forever. I also threw in a line from "A Perfect Murder" which just seems to work in most situations.

PAGE #12
And here is yet another big reveal, when we learn the identity of our "second narrator" from page #1. This character was also proposed by Nick Barrucci who wanted to introduce a "Deadpool" or "Ambush Bug" type of character to the AoD Universe. So I went with "Deadbug". Ashley gives him his name in Panel #3. Get it? GET IT?

It should also be noted that this is not the first time these two characters have met…

PAGE #13
Now things start to really pick up with a reference to "The Simpsons" and then it is recap time for "Deadbug" who reveals his humble beginnings. He was actually a pretty decent fella back in the day…

PAGE #14
…until he made the same mistake that Ashley's boyfriend Brad made. Poor dumb Deadbug.

PAGE #15
Whenever I write Deadbug, I think of a sociopathic Bugs Bunny. So while he may come across as a bit of a buffoon, he's also deadly. And oddly enough, currently taking his marching orders from Ashley…

I wonder why? Hmmmmmm…

PAGE #16
And here we have what appears to be the "Big Bad" of our opening story arc for the new series. For folks who read the Xena/Army of Darkness Vol. 2 crossover that I co-wrote with Brandon Jerwa, this character should look verrrrrrrry familiar.

14
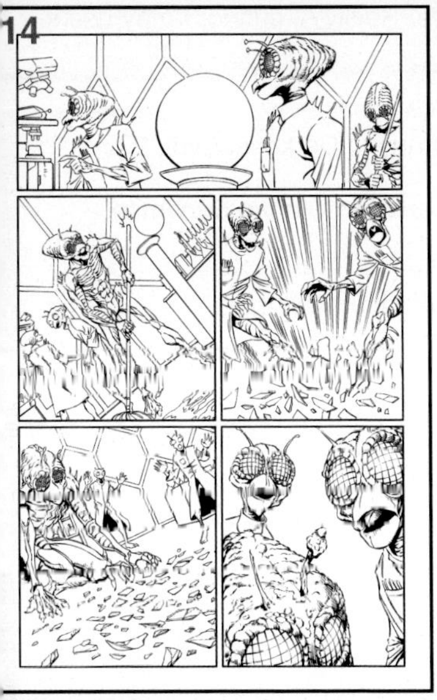

15
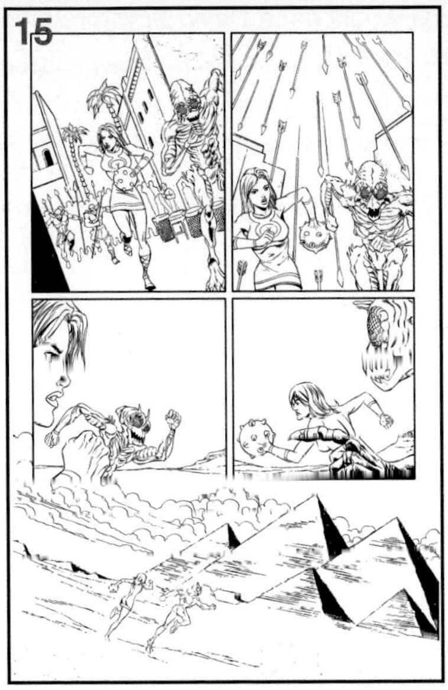

16
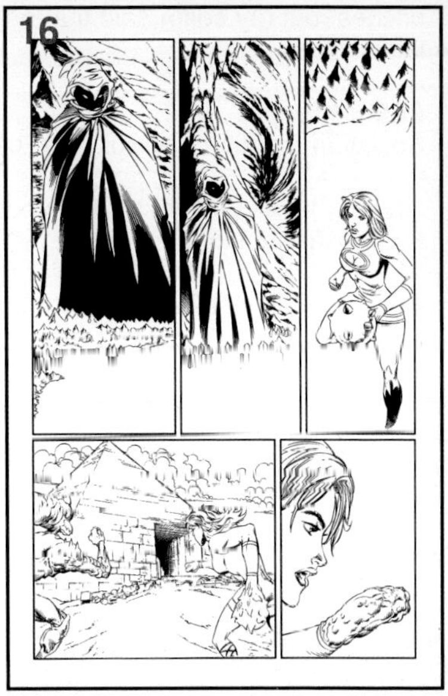

PAGE #17
Now, when I first started plotting out this issue, I had envisioned Ashley tumbling through different time periods, trying to enlist the help of famous historical women, only to have Deadbug kill them in one form or another. Again, it was another case of the "joke" getting ahead of telling the story. So this little quip about Marie Antoinette and her famous "let them eat cake" statement was my way of compromising with myself.

Again, to all the history buffs, I KNOW WHAT ACTUALLY HAPPENED TO MARIE ANTOINETTE! I've actually visited the Royal Court in France and saw where she lived.

So what is this an example of again?

Anyone?

Anyone?

Bueller?

:::points to the back of the room:::

What? What was that?

"Dramatic license"? YES! You get a gold star!

17
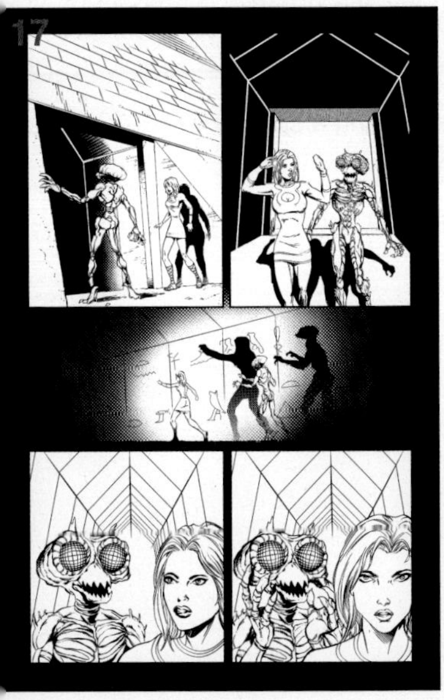

18
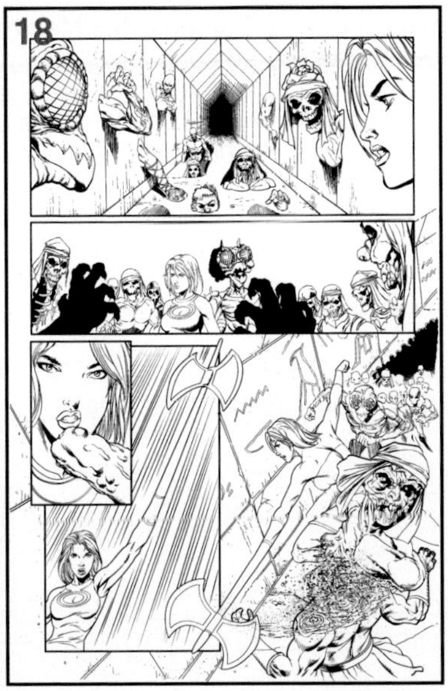

19
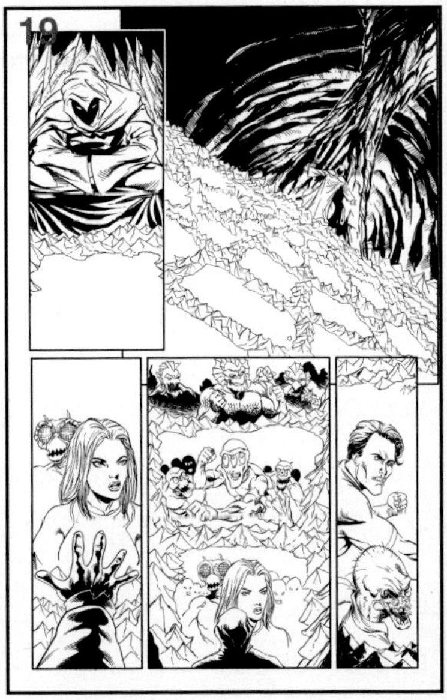

PAGE #18
Time for Ashley to show how kick-ass she can be. I originally had her saying "Welcome to Suffragette City,

bitches" but my editor said that no one would get a David Bowie reference. Really? I dunno, I may use it later.

PAGE #19
So...did I mention that our "Big Bad" looks a lot like the one from "Xena/Army of Darkness" Vol. 2?

I did, right? Did I mention that you can purchase copies of said trade paperback from the Dynamite Entertainment store?

Oh, and while you're at it, pick up a copy of the "Ash Saves Obama" trade paperback too!

PAGE #20
Gee, why is it that these deadites aren't affected by Ashley's control of the "dark power" of the Necronomicon? Is it a case of a writer juggling too many story elements and dropping the ball or setting something up for later on?

I'll let you decide.

(Psst. Hint. It's the latter.)

PAGE #21
Here is where we spell out the "there's more than one Chosen One" idea for the new series. It's an idea that I have teased at in my previous AoD work, specifically in issue #18 of the last volume. The idea of multiple universes was also introduced in the "Army of Darkness VS Marvel Zombies" mini-series too, so it's not like we're trouncing on any previously established continuity.

I will point out that Ashley has been under the impression that she has been living a solitary existence as a "Chosen One" and that this is the first time she's learning that she's not alone.

From this point on, she's going to be devoting herself to finding the original Ash in the hopes that he can answer some questions for her.

That will be a significant theme in the opening story arc.

PAGE #22
Poor Deadbug, just got left behind there. :::cue the sad trombone:::

"You're not just gonna leave him there, are you, Elliott?" you ask.

"Maybe. Maybe not." I reply.

(Psst. Hint. It's the latter.)

END OF ISSUE #1

Hello, everybody! (Imagine Dr. Nick of "The Simpsons" saying that.) Welcome back for another round of writer's commentary for the latest issue of Army of Darkness from Dynamite Entertainment. As the writer of AoD, I was anxious to see what kind of feedback I'd get, and everything I've received so far on last issue has been really positive. I've also been told that readers really enjoy these "behind-the-scenes" features, so I'll just keep writing them as long as you folks keep reading 'em!

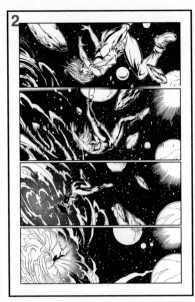
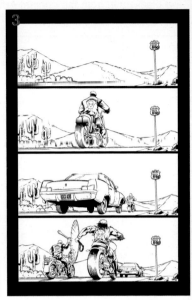

ARMY OF DARKNESS #2
PAGE ONE:
We pick up after last issue, watching as Ashley - the new "Lady Ash" of the series - tumbles through the time stream. While our hero Ash would simply scream his lungs out as he falls through the vortex, Ashley waxes philosophical.

I considered not including Ashley in this issue so that I could get back to the "regular" Ash more quickly, but thought that I'd address where she was right off the bat so as not to leave readers wondering.

And that last panel is a nod to all my geek gal friends who get tired of guys staring at their boobs…

PAGE TWO:
As Ashley - quite literally - fades into the background, she drops a bit of exposition about being a "Chosen One." She also knows - quite instinctively - that her fate is entwined with that of the "original" Chosen One, Ash. As I mentioned in the commentary for AoD #1, she's made it her mission to seek him out.

PAGE THREE:
As we return to the main AoD Universe, we now see what our own Ashley J. Williams has been up to. The bikers are a nod to fellow Chicagoan Matt Kubinski and his "Bikers vs. Zombies" indie comic book "Marauders." (Available at finer comic shops and print on demand! Gotta plug a local guy, so sue me.)

The license plate to the Delta-88 is a play on words - gee, that sure does sound like another comic don't it? -and what I've called my series of comic shop signings promoting the Army of Darkness series.

PAGE FOUR:
BIG MOMENT! And here is the Ash we've known and loved for so long, right in the middle of fighting deadites.

In the script I asked Marat Mychaels to draw the Delta-88 to look as if it had "steel jaws" on the front bumper. One of the things I loved about the original movie was how Ash modified his car into a "Death Mobile." Unfortunately, he drives it for all of five minutes before wrecking it, so I just had to bring it back.

FYI, the Death Mobile will factor into the series overall…

PAGE FIVE:
So this is where we get caught up with what Ash was up to while we were following his female alternate in another dimension.

And I bring back an element from my very first Army of Darkness gig, namely Xena/Army of Darkness 2: What Again? Credit for "Baby boom" go to my Xena/AoD 2 co-writer Brandon Jerwa, though.

PAGE SIX:
Here's where I introduce yet another new element to the series, Ash's detachable hand. Now, when you read this sequence, Ash refers to "hanging out with a fella who was good at inventing things." For folks who've been reading the series throughout each volume, you could assume he was referring to his ally from the League of Light in the previous series. If you'd never read those books, you could presume that it was the blacksmith from the original Army of Darkness film. You know, the guy who helped him build the metal hand in the first place? It works either way.

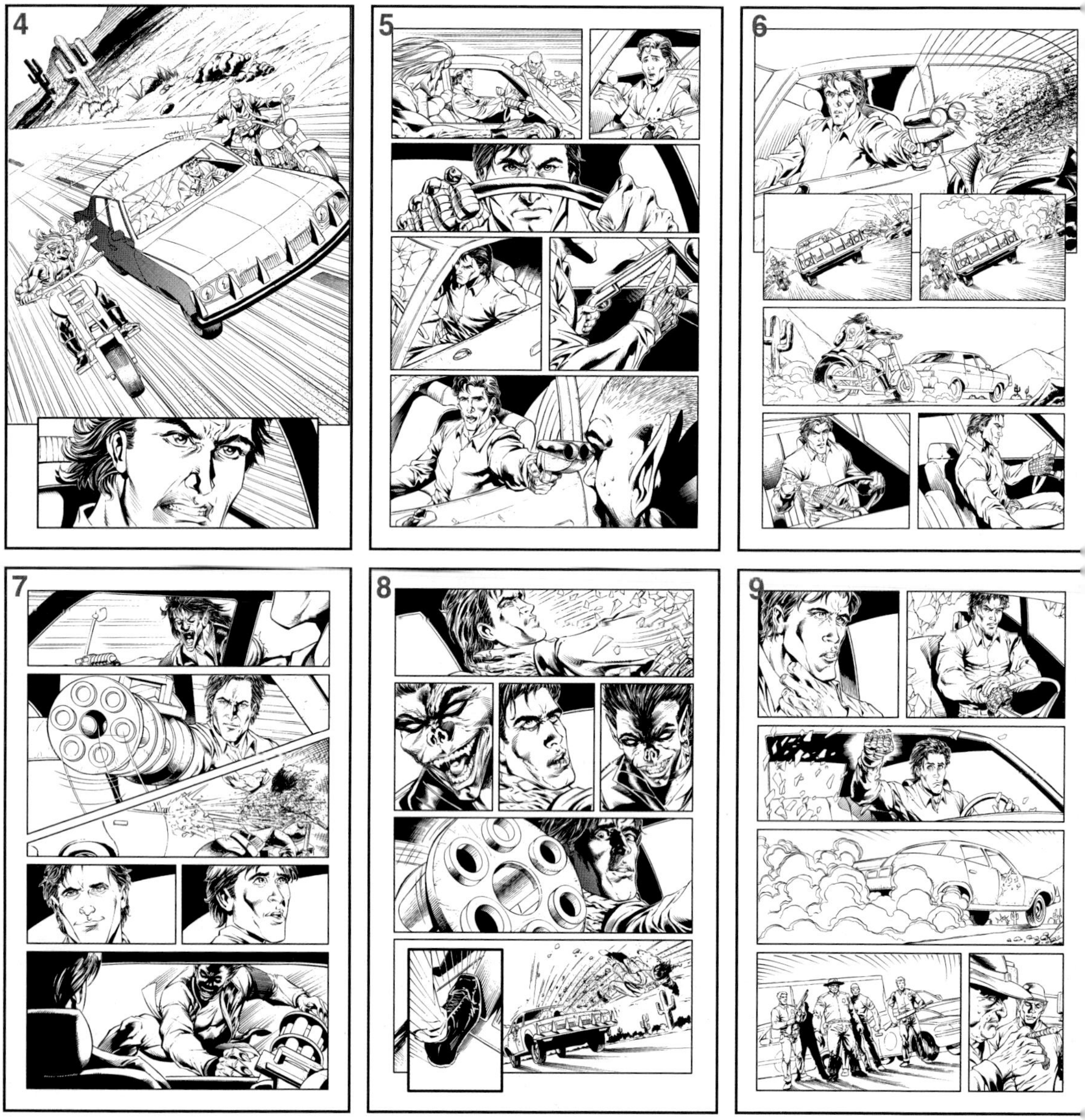

PAGE SEVEN:
We now see how Ash has added new weapons to his arsenal. The mini gatling gun was a weapon that Ash used in one of the Army of Darkness video games. I loved the idea so much, I decided to bring it into the comic.

PAGE EIGHT:
As I wrote this sequence, I tried to fashion the dialogue so that it gave you all you needed to know about the back story without having it sound too much like expository dialogue. I must have re-written these scenes a dozen times.

PAGE NINE:
Now we're getting to the big showdown between Ash and our Big Bad of the issue,"The Sheriff." Another script note I sent to Marat was that The Sheriff should look like a deadite version of "Buford T. Justice," Jackie Gleason's character from "Smokey and the Bandit." I'm pretty sure that's a reference I think only old-school movie geeks like myself are gonna get.

It's funny, I was told to drop the David Bowie reference in the last issue, but got to keep Jackie Gleason in his one. I guess Joe Rybandt is a fan. Now how do I get "The Honeymooners" in here....? Hmmmmmm....

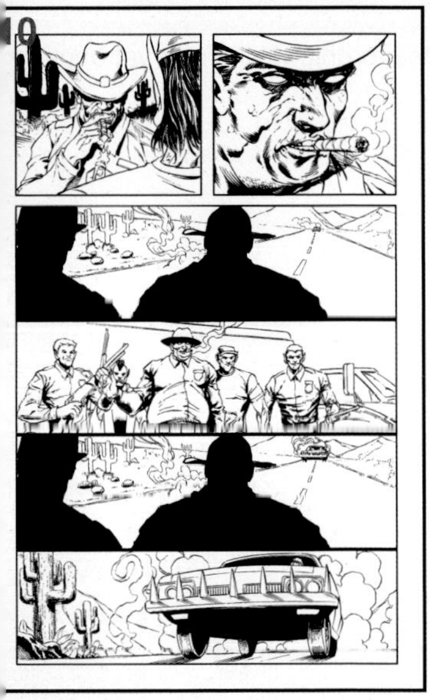

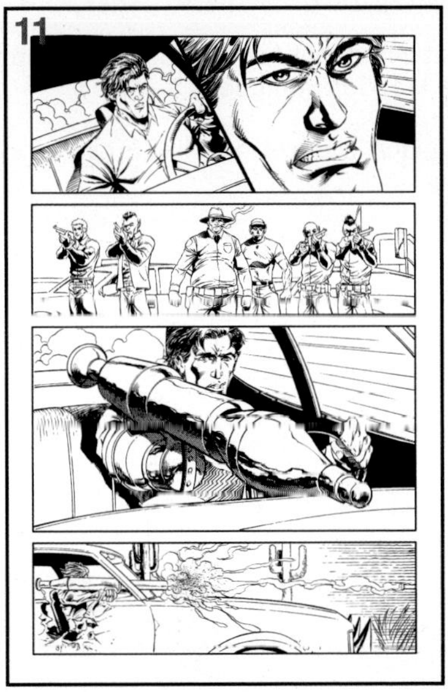

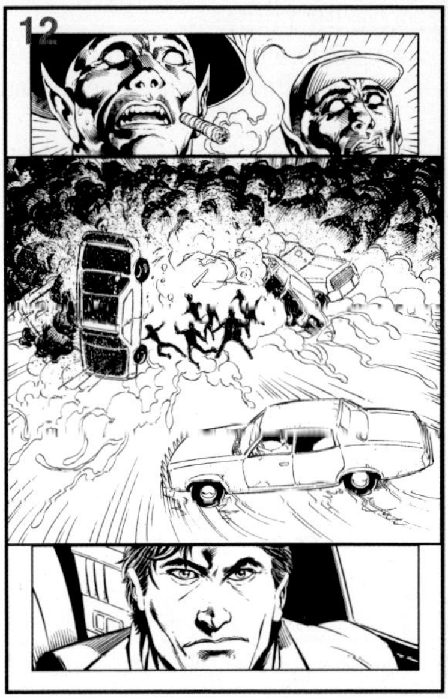

PAGE TEN:
More exposition that I hope doesn't sound like exposition. Ash advertises himself on the web? Hm. I wonder f he also has a Twitter account.

PAGE ELEVEN:
Here is where I try to get into what I feel makes Ash so successful as the "Chosen One." He's willing to do whatever it takes to get the job done. Whether it's to lob off his own hand to keep himself from being possessed by the evil of the Necronomicon, or to strap an experimental rocket launcher on the stump.

PAGE TWELVE:
BIG MOMENT! (Yes, I put that in the script so that Marat knows to make that particular image the largest one on the page.) Here we see The Sheriff get his due, to never be seen again…

Or maybe he'll return....?

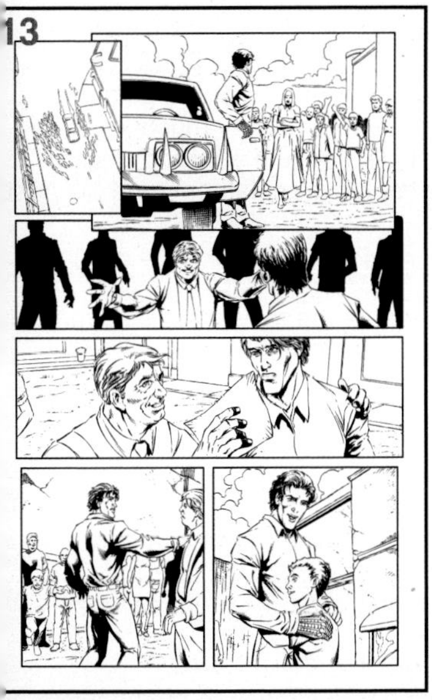

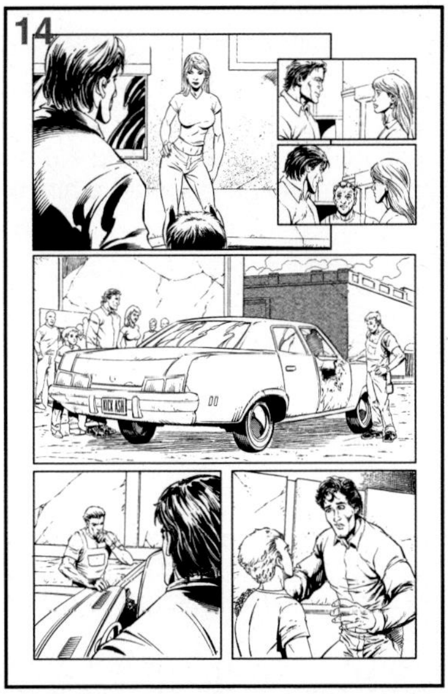

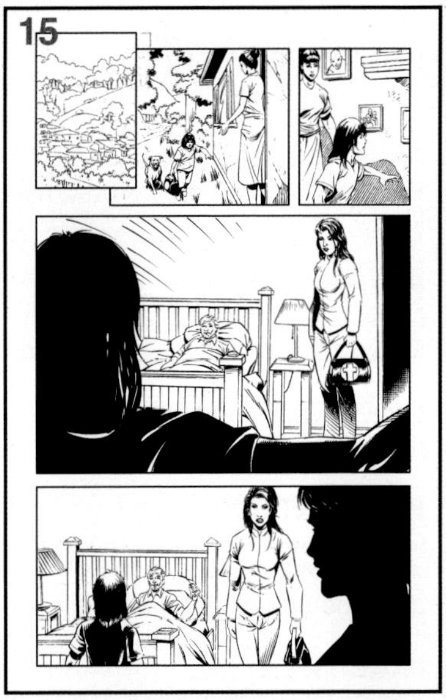

PAGE THIRTEEN:
Now we get to the resolution of this storyline and meet the "cast" of the story for the first (and last) time. I'm playing with the idea that most comic book readers - and movie watchers for that matter - are familiar with all the clichés of the "town in peril." I even considered - oh so briefly - making the town an anachronism of the town that Bruce Campbell visited in "My Name is Bruce." But I didn't wanna piss him off.

PAGE FOURTEEN:
And of course Ash has to have an encounter with a gorgeous gal, much like James Bond does in each of

his adventures. Except this gal is also a single mom. I've never seen 007 hook up with a MILF.

PAGE FIFTEEN:
And just like that we're on to the next threat that Ash will face. I got the idea for this villain from yet another old-school thriller that I enjoyed as a kid. Can you guess the title?

The fact that these event are taking place in Brazil is a HUGE hint as to what the movie was.

Any guesses?

Anyone?

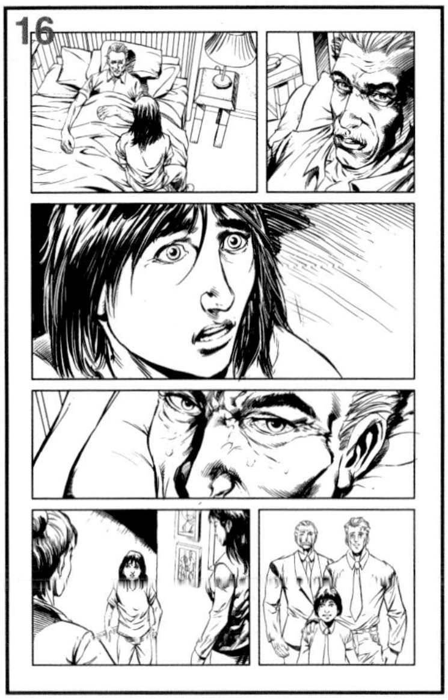
16

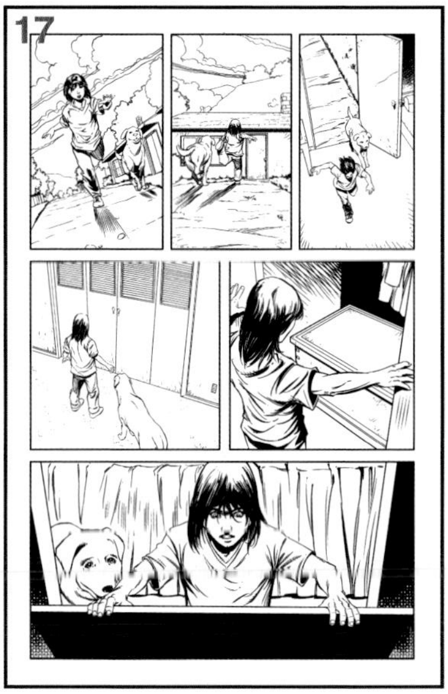
17

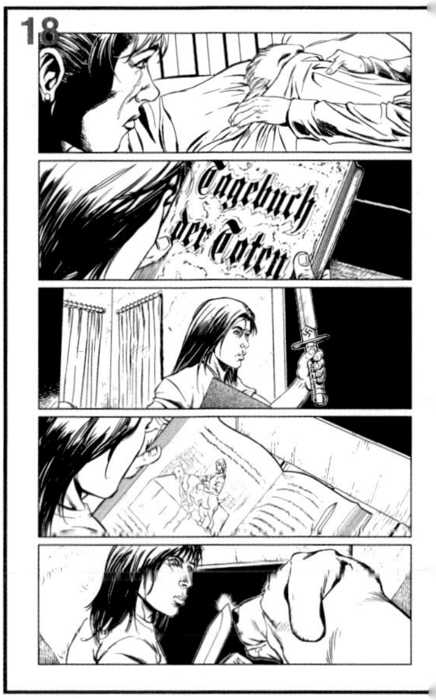
18
Tagebuch der Toten

PAGE SIXTEEN:
What the crap? ANOTHER CHOSEN ONE? How many of them are there?!

Oh, on a storytelling note, the very last panel showing Joaquin with his father and grandfather is there for a symbolic purpose. I'll revisit that in a couple pages.

PAGE SEVENTEEN:
This is where we learn about Joaquin's deep attachment to his grandfather. I wanted to try and give the boy a believable motivation for doing the horrible things that he will be doing in the future. Very much like when Anakin Skywalker couldn't let go of those he loved and turned to the dark side, Joaquin is willing to deal with dark powers to hold onto his grandfather. And here we get a hint of what his grandfather did in his past life…

PAGE EIGHTEEN:
Nazis are all the rage again, huh? By the way, have you figured out the name of the movie that inspired this story yet? FYI, the movie was based on a book by the same name. And also dealt with Nazis.

On a personal note, I am very, very sensitive when it comes to depictions of animal cruelty in media, so it pained me very much to write this scene.

PAGE NINTEEN:
Okay, remember how I said that photo of Joaquin with his family was symbolic? Here we have Ash holding a very similar photo. This sequence illustrates that while Joaquin is unwilling to let go of his family, Ash is quite the opposite. Again, Ash is willing to do whatever it takes to fight evil, no matter the personal cost.

PAGE TWENTY:
And now poor Ashley arrives on the scene, a minute too late. She screams her frustration to the heavens, because yes, she's had this happen to her a couple times before. If I get the chance, we will revisit those times.

PAGE TWENTY-ONE:
Okay, we're about ready to wrap this sucker up and get to the big reveal of our next Big Bad. Have you figured out the name of the story that inspired this character?

You can go on IMDB and look up movie names with the word "Brazil" in them. And no, Terry Gilliam's

"Brazil" would be incorrect.

Go ahead. Give it a look-see.

I'll wait.

::whistles:::

Get it yet?

No?

PAGE TWENTY-TWO:
Well, for those who just need me to tell them, the movie was called…

THE BOYS FROM BRAZIL!

It's a pretty cool flick with a Nazi hunter trying to track down these boys who are clones of Adolf Hitler. At the end of the film, Josef Mengele - played by Gregory Peck - gets mauled by a bunch of Doberman Pinschers. Pretty wicked stuff.

And no, this dude isn't Adolf Hitler. He's Colonel Zoch of Hitler's Occult Squad. And he's gonna bring some baaaaaaaaad stuff down on our boy Ash and Ashley. But that happens next issue.

END OF ISSUE #2

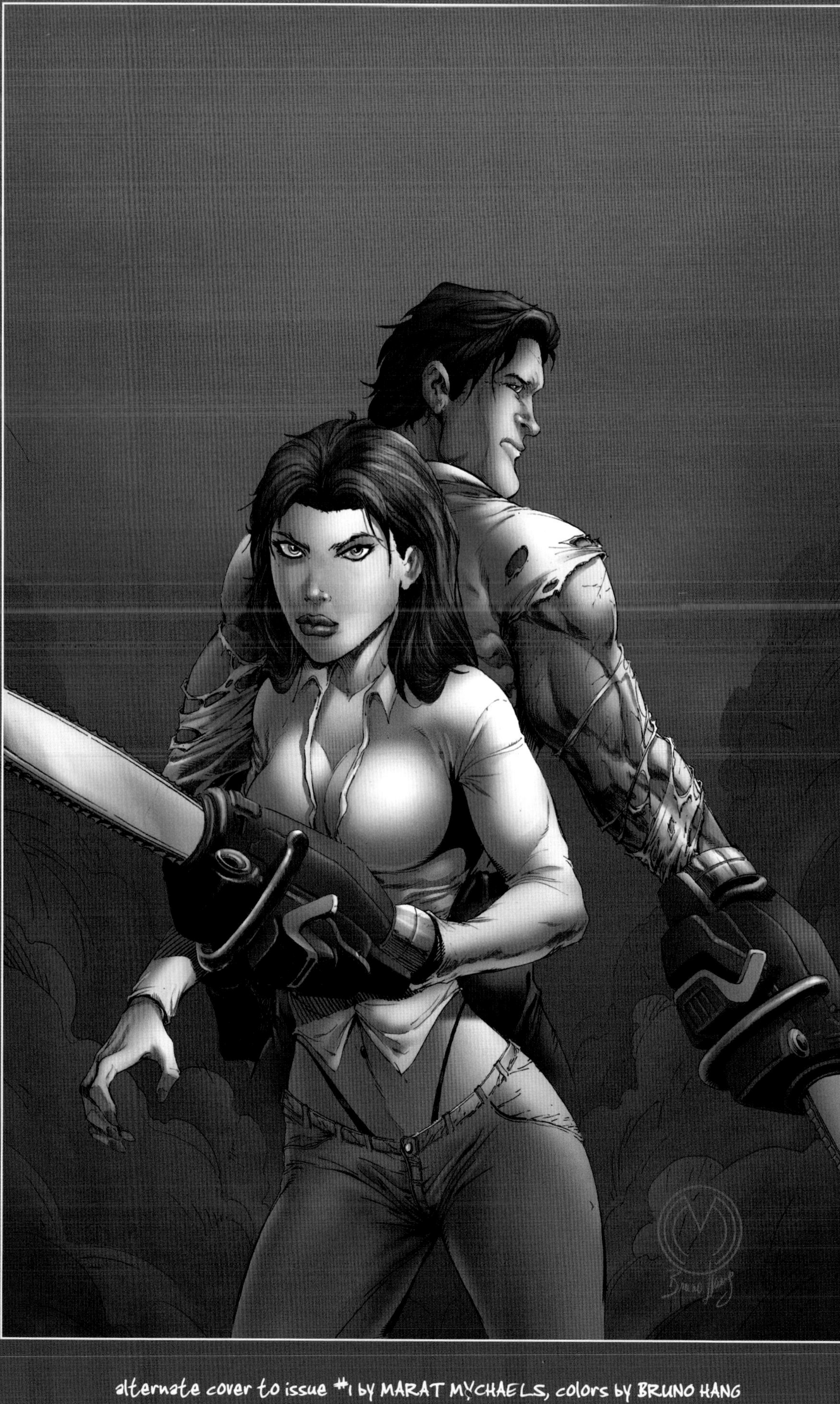

alternate cover to issue #1 by MARAT MYCHAELS, colors by BRUNO HANG

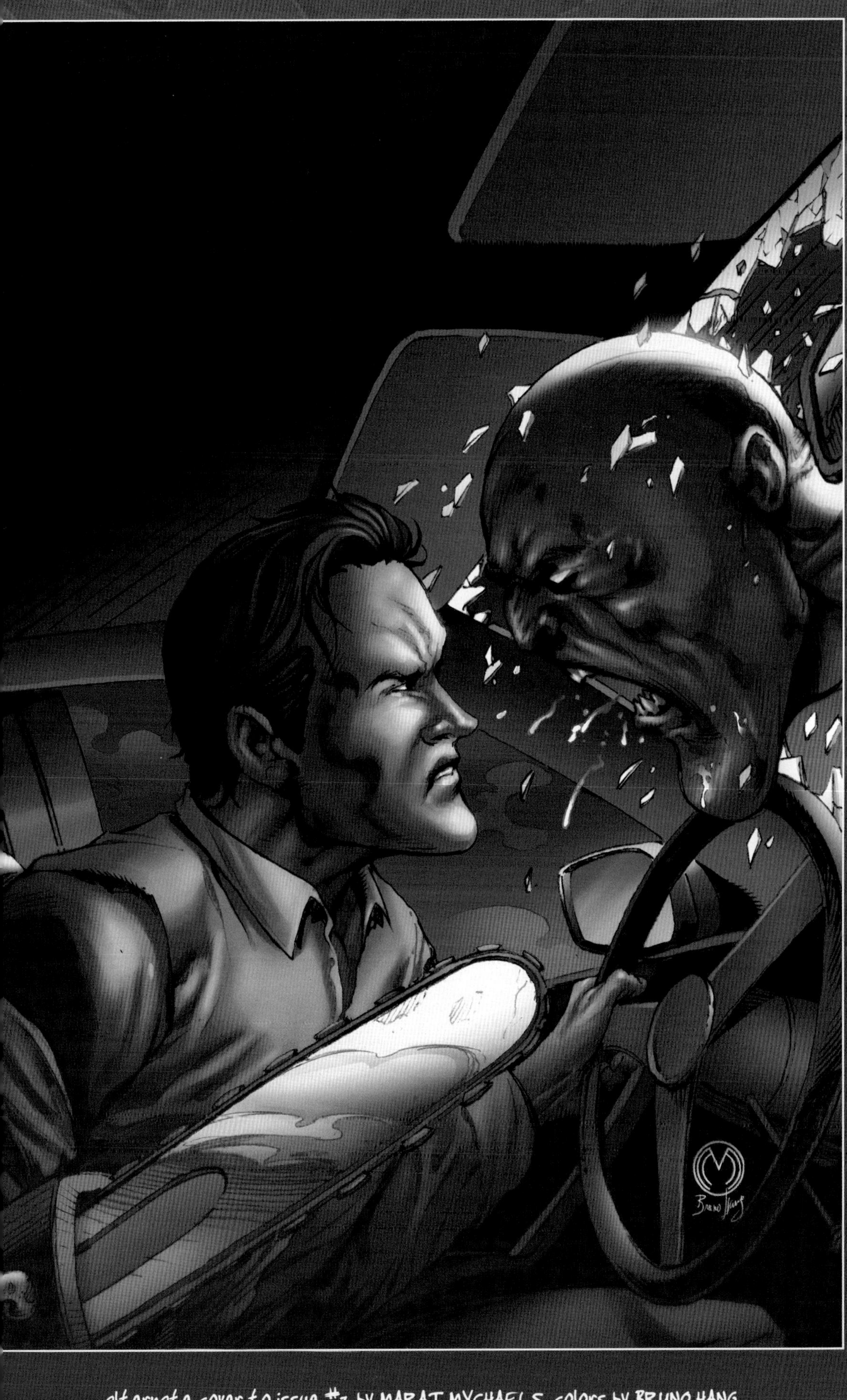

alternate cover to issue #2 by MARAT MYCHAELS, colors by BRUNO HANG

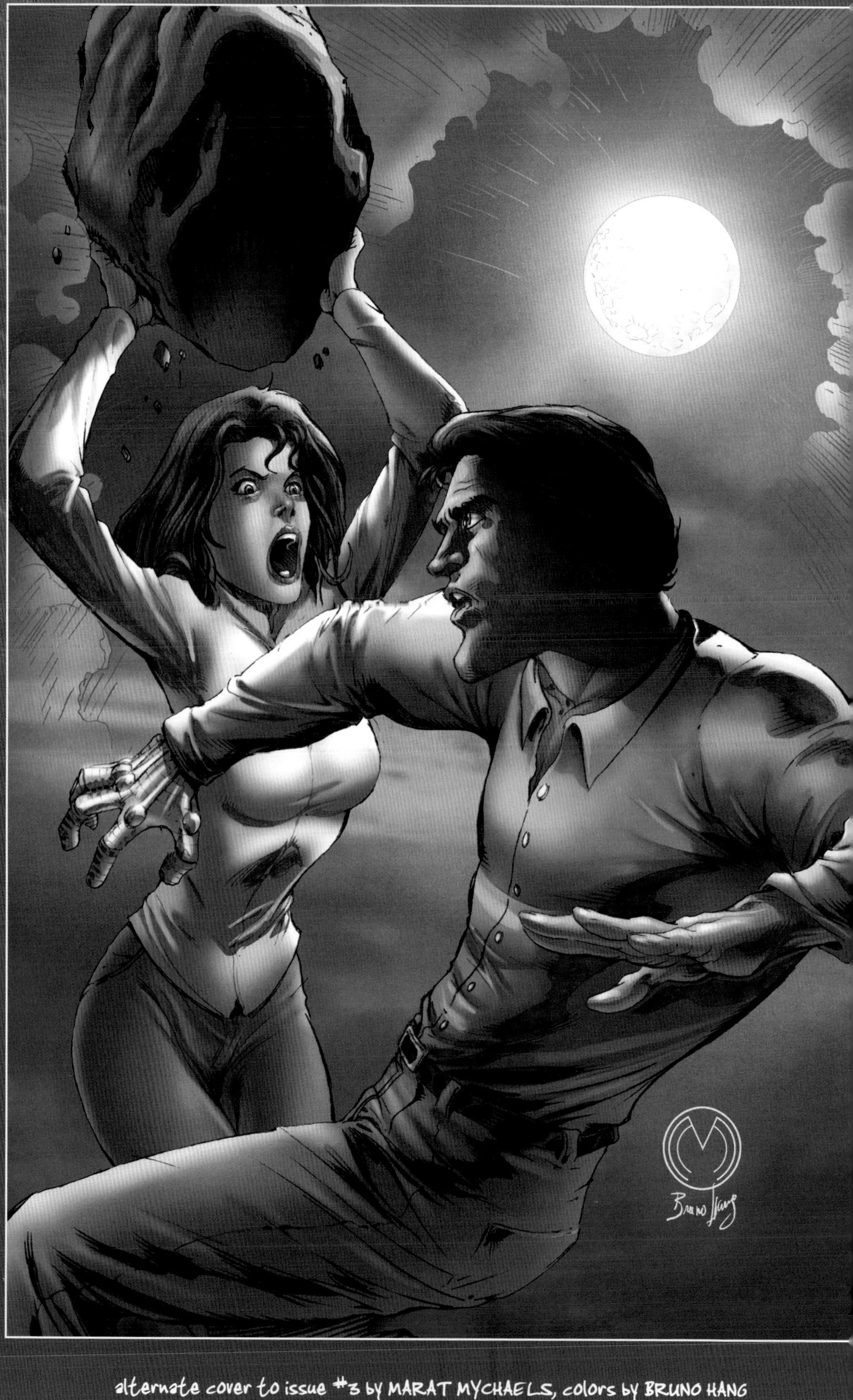

alternate cover to issue #3 by MARAT MYCHAELS, colors by BRUNO HANG

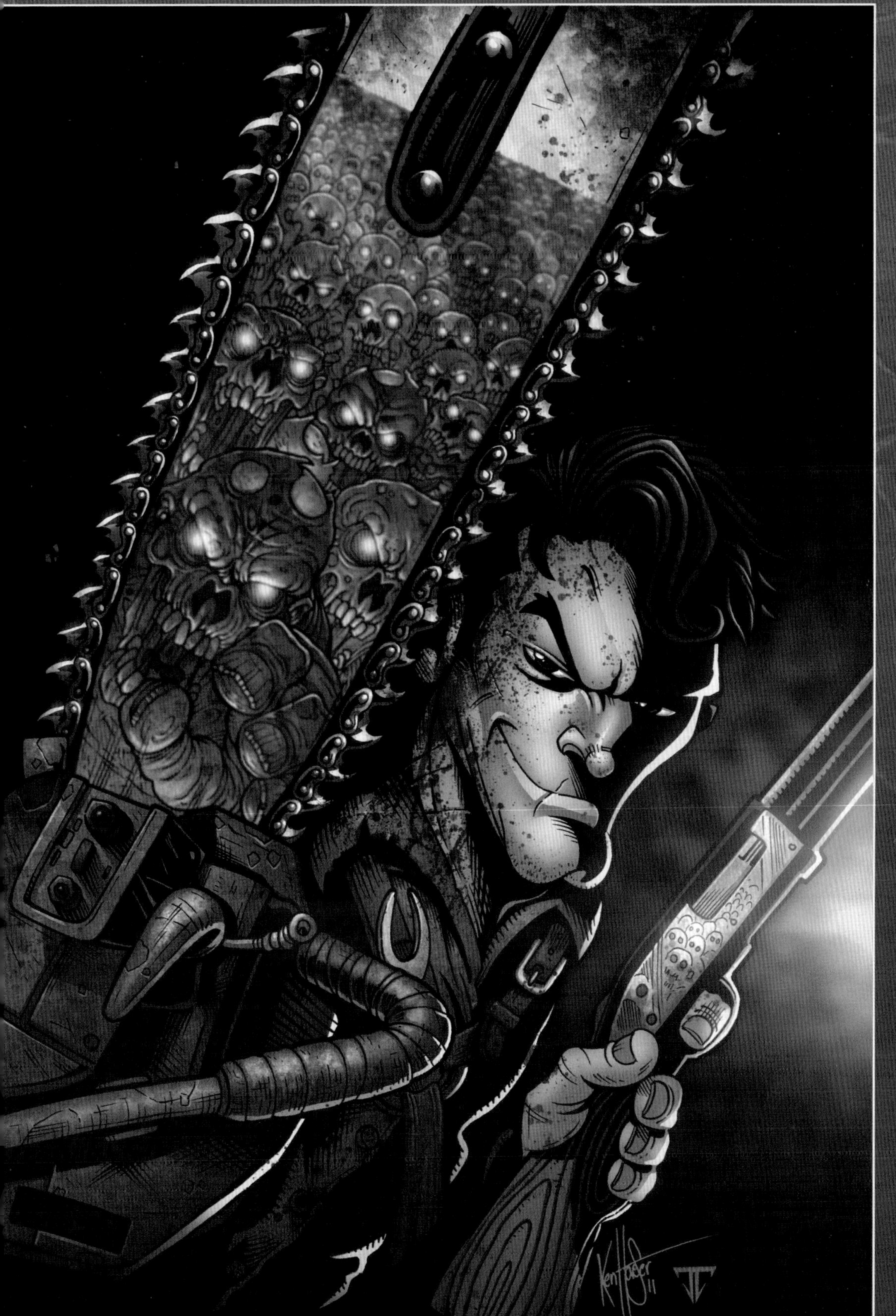

issue #1 pin-up by KEN HAESER, colors by JUAN FERNANDEZ

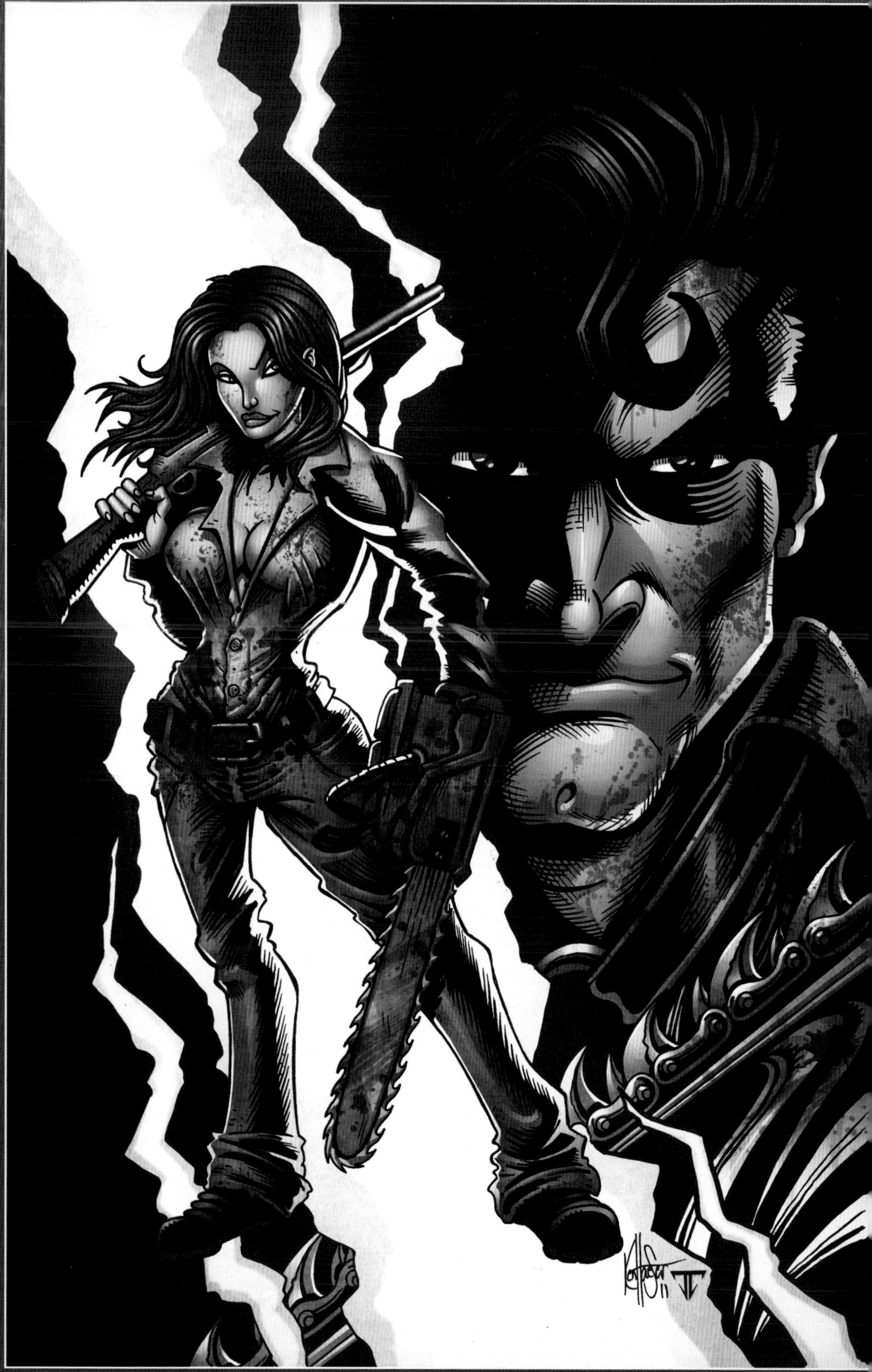

issue #2 pin-up by KEN HAESER, colors by JUAN FERNANDEZ

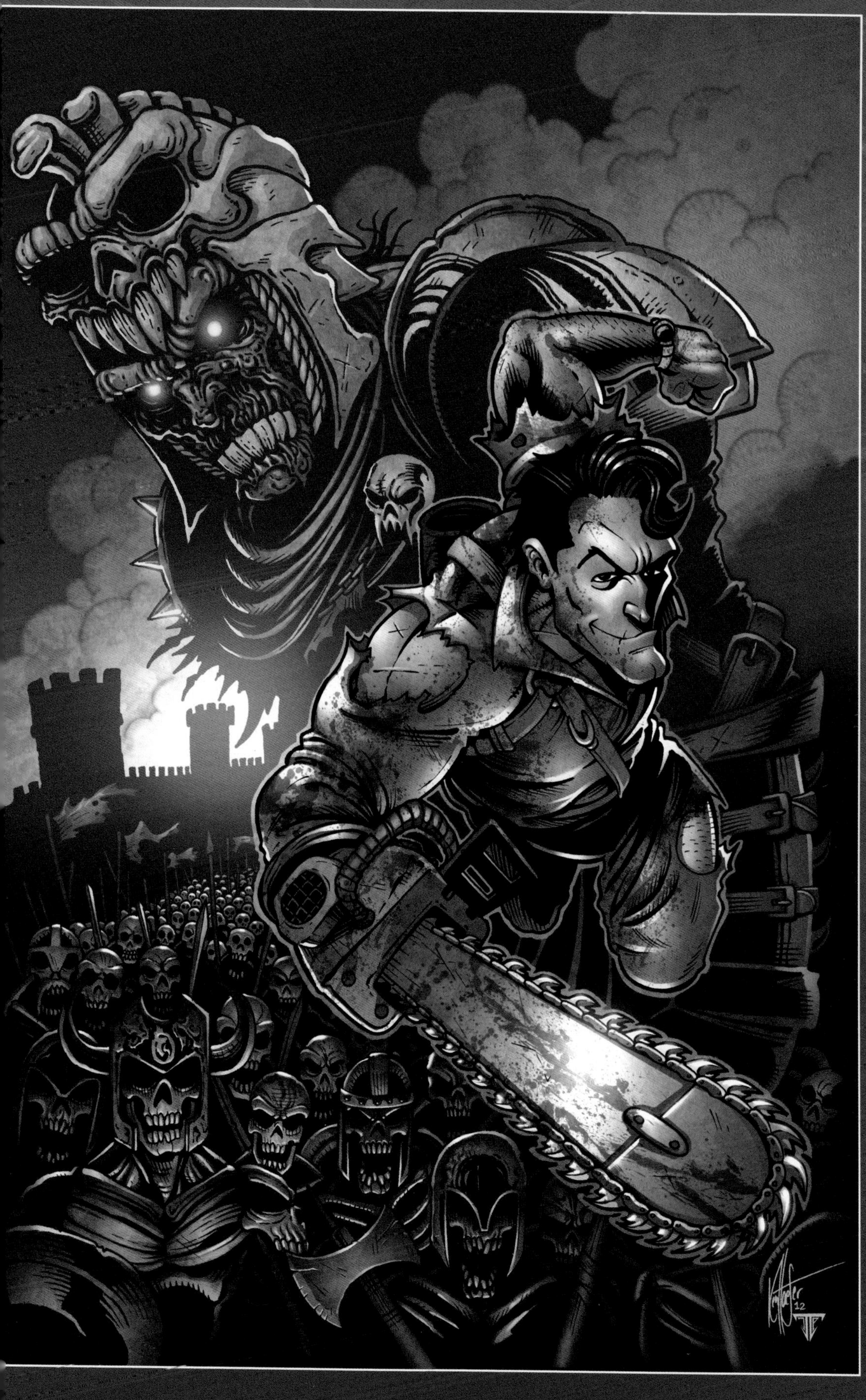

issue #3 pin-up by KEN HAESER, colors by JUAN FERNANDEZ

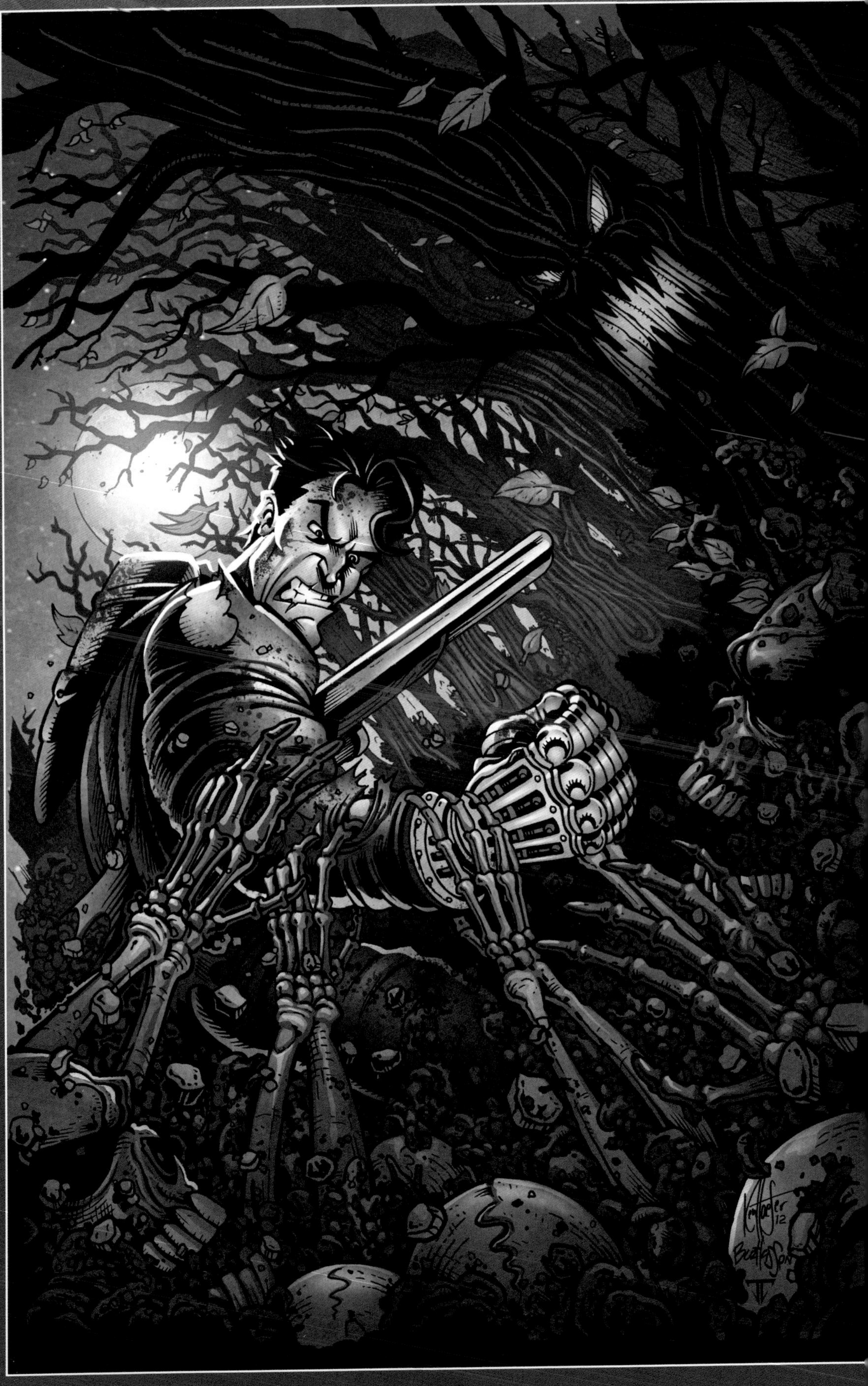

issue #4 pin-up by KEN HAESER, colors by JUAN FERNANDEZ

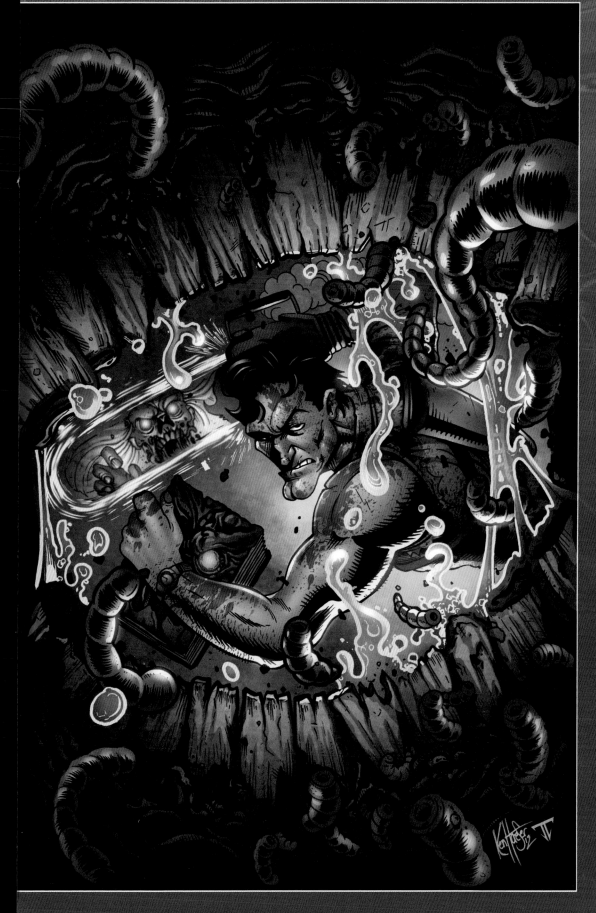

issue #5 pin-up by KEN HAESER, colors by JUAN FERNANDEZ